Redefining Urdu Politics in India

Urdu has been a cradle of literary and cultural diversity.
Since Partition, however, it has steadily declined due to
communal politics, lacunae in policymaking, misconstrued
alignment of Muslims to the language, and plain
indifference. This has resulted in Urdu's systematic
elimination from the secular curriculum, while being
nurtured as a medium of religious instruction in *madrasa*s.
These essays, by seventeen eminent Urdu littérateurs, speak
against such reductionism. They reiterate the need to save
this rich language and its inherent secular character.

The two introductions explore the status of Urdu post-
Partition and try to diagnose the problems that continue to
plague the language. The book's concerns are essentially
fourfold—the need to contextualize Urdu within the ambit
of language politics; an examination of the role of identity
politics and power structures in giving the language
communal overtones; its restoration in the common civic,
educational, and cultural space; and legal concerns and
guarantees with relation to the language.

*'Urdu, a very rich source of modern Indian history until 1947, can
also become a useful medium in the re-shaping of modern Indian
identity relevant today. But for that to happen, we need a new
approach towards the Urdu-speaking community and its
multidimensional progress, beginning with modern and
mainstream education.'*

—**Salman Khurshid**

GW00659714

Redefining Urdu Politics in India

edited by
ATHER FAROUQUI

OXFORD
UNIVERSITY PRESS

OXFORD
UNIVERSITY PRESS

22 Workspace, 2nd Floor, 1/22 Asaf Ali Road, New Delhi 110002, India

Oxford University Press is a department of the University of Oxford.
It furthers the University's objective of excellence in research,
scholarship, and education by publishing worldwide in

Oxford New York

Auckland Cape Town Dar es Salaam Hong Kong Karachi Kuala Lumpur
Madrid Melbourne Mexico City Nairobi New Delhi Shanghai Taipei Toronto

With offices in

Argentina Austria Brazil Chile Czech Republic France Greece Guatemala
Hungary Italy Japan Poland Portugal Singapore South Korea Switzerland
Thailand Turkey Ukraine Vietnam

Oxford is a registered trademark of Oxford University Press
in the UK and in certain other countries

Published in India
by Oxford University Press, New Delhi

ISBN-13: 978-0-19-806846-4
ISBN-10: 0-19-806846-8

Typeset in Lalit in 9.5/12
by Excellent Laser Typesetters, Pitampura, Delhi 110 034
Printed in India by Replika Press Pvt. Ltd.

Published by Oxford University Press
22 Workspace, 2nd Floor, 1/22 Asaf Ali Road, New Delhi 110002, India

For Arjumand
seventeen years of thinking—together and separately

Contents

Preface

In twenty-first century India, all notions of political life are changing due to social compulsions and rapid changes in international polity. Indian socio-political and cultural life is in an advanced phase of transformation, and most of the socio-political issues of the past are irrelevant today. New realities need a fresh orientation to keep up with the times. In its effort to become a part of the global village, India seeks to rid itself of residual colonial influences in order to keep its indigenous cultural heritage intact. It is true that the colonial legacy had a negative impact on Indian identity, and that our cultural past had turned into a complex phenomenon. But it is counter-productive to abuse and blame our past every now and then. It is also ironic that after fifty-eight years of Independence, our academia has not yet succeeded in getting over the colonial mindset to analyse issues related to the emerging realities of India.

Urdu is an issue that has been completely mishandled in free India by politicians across the board, the Muslim élite, and all concerned sections who dealt with the issue either at the social level or as an academic pursuit. Most of them still handle the issue in the same fashion as dealt by the colonial rulers. For a long time the academic discourse regarding Urdu—and other north-Indian languages too—remained the same, that is, oversimplified, colonial and, of course, without depth. In this oversimplified analysis Urdu has always been projected as the language of the Muslim invaders, and later on was deemed responsible for the Partition of India and the formation of Pakistan. In other words, it lost its primary relevance as a language of common Indian civic space. Urdu also suffers from being stereotyped as the mellifluous language of art and literature while

Muslims are often caricatured in Bombay films. In the context of Urdu—and Muslims too—the usage of the word 'culture' is also problematic, as it has increasingly come to denote the world of *qawwali*s, *mushaira*s, and *mujra*s. So, in free India, Urdu has never been recognized as a functional language. This has, of course, saved the government much expenditure.

If one believes the writings of contemporary academia regarding Urdu-speaking Muslims, it would appear that they have nothing to do with contemporary life; they think of themselves as an aristocratic class of erstwhile absentee *zamindars*. All these notions, of course, are far from reality. It is obvious that the government does not want to do anything to help the language flourish, so it has very enthusiastically supported all populist suggestions in the name of literary or cultural promotion through marginal organizations such as Urdu academies, though it was clear that Urdu would not survive until it became an integral part of the school system. This is not possible unless the state apparatus takes a policy decision to include Urdu in the curriculum. After Independence the state did nothing for the inclusion of Urdu in school system of education. It was a convenient situation from the administrative point of view too. Consequently, Urdu remained marginalized and confined as a language of literary expression and did not get its share in the national wealth, nor contribute to social life. In general, the government has never allocated sufficient funds for education and the gross domestic product (GDP) has remained too low to even aspire towards the achievement of the National Literacy Mission's goal. It is not Urdu alone; the fact is that the government has remained indifferent to all the major Indian regional languages as far as their individual progress is concerned. It has not made adequate arrangements for the teaching of regional Indian languages in schools. Had it done so, it would have proved to be an instrument for the multi-dimensional growth of Indian languages and a boost for social transformation.

Instead, the state chose to project English-medium education as a symbol of excellence. In doing so, it evaded the responsibility of making all Indian languages or at least the languages that were included in the Eighth Schedule as part of the education system and to the extent possible, as a medium of instruction as per the constitutional guarantee. That was possible only if the perception of excellence had been associated with Indian languages instead of English. But the fact remains that the state has treated the issue of all Indian languages in the shabbiest manner. It has deliberately avoided making them a part of the education system. Thus these languages have not survived the competition with English education.

Because of communal politics and the fear psychosis of Partition, the Urdu élite has led to the further marginalization of the language. In the backdrop of the Partition, the common Urdu speaker came to be seen as a hostile outsider, and Urdu and Muslim became synonymous with one another. To overcome this phenomenon, many Urdu speakers began to channel all their resources and stamina to preserve Urdu through religious institutions, which they thought would safeguard Urdu. This proved counter-productive and only gave a boost to the *madrasa* phenomenon. Ather Farouqui very aptly feels that one of the consequences of this situation— considerably strengthened after Independence on account of the official neglect of Urdu—has been that the community has been caught up in the morass of backwardness, traditionalism, and narrow communitarian ethos. It has remained peripheral to the modernization the country and the world have witnessed over the years.

It is true that as a part of the Muslim religious community, one of the most backward in economic terms, Urdu-speaking people could not afford to establish their own institutions of modern education as parallel systems of education. So most children within the Urdu-speaking community landed up in madrasas. As per the government nearly half a million full-time madrasas are operating throughout the country with an enrolment of at least 50 million full-time students, to impart religious education. The part-time madrasas, popularly known as *maktabs*, to which students go for necessary religious education only, are not included in this data. The exact number of children attending such maktabs too is not known. But these students attend schools providing modern education.[1] I quote Arjumand Ara on Urdu and madrasas, that perhaps best explains the dichotomy of the phenomenon:

Clearly Urdu as a language is not a synonym of religious education but the lack of Urdu education in secular curriculum through school system, mainly state run schools, has made the madrasas the only shelter and centers of Urdu education because in the madrasas the medium of instruction is Urdu. Only government is responsible for making Urdu the language of Muslims and by corollary confined to madrasas. This situation provided one more window for all those who have ambitions in Muslim politics to use Urdu as a platform by making Urdu education a channel for their personal political gains...

...May I ask the most pertinent question: Why is it that the Muslim community protects and nourishes the madrasas to the extent that even its leaders keep reminding us of the Constitutional provisions that guarantee the smooth functioning in madrasas, but the community is weary of establishing secular educational institutions? I am not in any way suggesting that the State is not indifferent towards Muslim secular education. Of course it should fulfill its Constitutional commitment to guarantee equal educational facilities for each and every citizen. Nor am I saying that Muslims should start parallel education systems in the name of the preservation of Urdu and that by corollary, madrasas should flourish, as is the case today. I am fully aware that being financially the most backward community, Muslims are not in a position to set up their own institutions of secular education as they are investing as a lot to their maximum capacity to make the madrasas run and flourish. The Muslim elite wants only madrasas to flourish for its political interests. We should not forget the most important fact in the backdrop: that madrasas form a parallel system the way they are working in present-day India, blocking the roads of economic growth. But, despite all this, what cannot also be ignored is that Muslims as a community and even their non-Muslim political leadership remain ardently committed by remaining silent to the question of the relevance for the institution of the madrasa; and for this reason madrasas are flourishing with an unprecedented pace. Muslims as a community, and their present leadership—social or political—lacks the penchant for secular education.[2]

The fact is that if the government had sincerely provided school education to children belonging to the Urdu-speaking community, or if the option of government schools had been available to these children in every locality, things would not have been so bad. It is a harsh reality that politics, for a long time, had been trying to put together Muslims and Urdu education as two sides of the same coin. So, trapped by obscurantist Muslim politics, the Muslim intelligentsia has also been urging Muslims to open modern educational institutions voluntarily, without realizing that in a developing economy such as India's, even Hindus cannot survive on the basis of the voluntary sector of education. Also, the institutions of modern education established and run by Muslims generally do not attract non-Muslim students, so the alumni of Muslim institutions grow in an atmosphere where they do not interact with other religious groups, and the result is that they feel like strangers in a common civic space. Basically, private schools that provide excellent modern education are nothing but an élite phenomenon and even in urban India these schools cannot cater to more than one per cent of middle-class children, so they cannot be treated as an ideal option for any section of society in India.

In the contemporary world, most of the communal formulations of the past have no relevance. The polity has its own constraints.

L.K. Advani's latest call to throw away the past formulations of communal politics within the Bharatiya Janata Party (BJP), and his certifying M.A. Jinnah as a secular leader was nothing but an over-simplified approach and the myopic outcome of Rashtriya Swayamsevak Sangh (RSS) training that is not entirely aware of the modern sensibilities of the new social order. The realities of modern polity are an integral part of social transformation, and the process of modernization is urging people to reinterpret history in an appropriate context, and with its correct reading. This would eventually help us in a country where Jinnah has always been reviled as the architect of the bloody Partition of 1947, to redefine our identity—the modern Indian identity. For that, India is making all efforts on the economic front and at the international level.

Urdu, being a very rich source of modern Indian history until 1947, can also become a useful medium to re-shape modern Indian identity relevant today. But for that we need a new approach towards the Urdu-speaking community and its multi-dimensional progress, beginning with modern and mainstream education.

So, one could argue that the idea of India[3] needs reconsideration in one important aspect—the preservation and development of Indian languages. It should not be confined to the communal and narrow idea of monolingualism pushed by a lobby of reactionary north-Indian politicians during the latter part of the nineteenth century. The RSS has also harped on that tune. Its terminology is no different from that of the British who, in pursuit of their policy of divide and rule, gave emphasis to some languages whilst deliberately neglecting others. The emergence of Urdu and Hindi as two different languages and representing the conflicting linguistic identities of north India is sheer nonsense and the handiwork of British policy. After the British, the stance has been supported by the RSS and its ilk. If we do not refer to the colonial or neo-imperial school of thought in linguistics (most of the Indian linguistics experts are trained by either colonial or American discourse and they are often worse than British and Americans as far as their approach towards Indian languages especially Urdu is concerned), Urdu and Hindi are one and the same. They are written in two separate scripts and are understood by any Indian irrespective of the fact whether s/he is a Hindu or a Muslim.

It is worth noting that atavists succeeded in having Article 351 of the Indian Constitution declare 'Hindustani' as a style of Hindi, which was at one stage supposed to be the *national language* of free India and perhaps the only solution to the negative politics played in the name of Urdu and Hindi. Awadhi, Braj, Maithili, Magadhi, and many other languages, despite having independent and rich literary traditions, were also declared as dialects of Hindi. The forcible imposition of political Hindi on any community will lead its protagonists to wilderness and to the opposition of Hindi, which is an unavoidable outcome of the politics done in the name of Hindi nationalism. This would be similar to the one reached in the 1960s— a time when Murli Manohar Joshi of the RSS and Mulayam Singh Yadav as a Lohiate Socialist were sharing the same platform of language chauvinism.[4]

If all Indian languages, whether included in the Eighth Schedule or not, are accorded equal status and importance, this will provide opportunities for all languages to grow as the mother tongues of their speakers by making provisions for their teaching in school curricula. For this, the Eighth Schedule of the Constitution would need to be redrafted to include this spirit and to accommodate all Indian languages.

It is already too late to adopt a progressive policy towards all Indian languages, and for the negation of the colonial mindset in our policy planning. In this regard we should focus on Urdu, which has been claimed by fundamentalists and obscurantists as the language of the Muslim religious community, just as Hindi is assumed to be the language of Hindus alone. Without going into how one can pull Urdu out of the clutches of fundamentalist Muslim leadership, we need to note that even if Urdu is spoken by a section of Muslims, it does not alter the fact that Urdu is a major Indian language sharing a common grammatical structure and cultural lineage with Hindi. The language has to be saved from extinction through teaching it in schools. An opportunity should be provided to any student who wishes to study it. For Urdu mother-tongue speakers too, opportunities for teaching Urdu need to be provided in the education system controlled by the state, and facilities should be made available to speakers of other languages who would like to learn the language.

The RSS cloud over the politics of free India discourages us from speaking about the Hindustani of Mahatma Gandhi. Gandhi's assassination was also, in a sense, the stifling of the language debate. Inevitably, we have mindlessly succumbed to the agenda of a single 'national language'. We now need to seriously reassess the role of all the Indian languages in building an India of the future, if we are sincere about transforming ourselves into a prosperous, plural, and tolerant society. Despite the commercial value and excellence associated with English-medium education, government-school education will continue to be in local languages due to resource constraints, and the majority of our school-going children will go through this system only. Hence, it is imperative that we enrich and empower Indian language-medium schools.

However, one hopes that the 86th Constitutional Amendment,[5] which provides a fundamental right to education up to the age of fourteen, will overhaul the education system and give a fresh lease of life to Indian languages too.

Despite the constitutional affirmation of the status of Urdu as a national language, consistent efforts have been made to drive it out from the social sphere by atavists. After Independence, as a consequence of Partition, Urdu was undermined by the decision that excluded it from the educational curriculum. Much water has since flown down the Yamuna river. Remarkable efforts by Left-wing intellectuals like the late Danial Latifi and Ather Farouqui through Linguistic Minorities Guild at the end of the last century have made a beginning for Urdu's revival as a functional language in the common civic space and through school education. The agenda needs consistent effort through political movement.

As a result of the movement launched by the Linguistic Minorities Guild, people whose mother tongue is Urdu have realized that the revival of Urdu in the secular curriculum is imperative because the isolationist madrasa education has been woefully inadequate for ensuring social and economic growth. In Uttar Pradesh (UP), where at least 20 million Urdu-speaking people reside, there are not even a handful of Urdu-medium primary schools, this despite the constitutional directive (under Article 350-A) for primary education in the mother tongue. More surprising, the north-Indian states, particularly UP, do not have provision for Urdu even as an elective subject in the category of third language, but offer Sanskrit as a *Modern Indian Language,* making it compulsory up to the twelfth standard under the Three Language Formula.

So what is to be done to ensure the option of Urdu-medium education for those who claim Urdu as their language and want to teach it to their children at least up to Class V? A simple formulation is that, in government schools located in Urdu-speaking areas, Urdu should be the medium of education up to Class V. Hindi could be introduced from Class III and English from Class VI so that students can switch easily to Hindi-medium schools at the middle school and also learn English steadily. In north India, Hindi is at present the exclusive medium of education. In UP, Sanskrit is taught from Class III upwards as a Modern Indian Language. English is introduced only from Class VI. From Class VI, a combined course of Hindi and Sanskrit is also taught up to Class XII. In a nutshell, out of 300 marks for languages, 134 go to Sanskrit, sixty-six to Hindi, and 100 to English. Urdu gets nothing! This situation must change for the sake of a multi-lingual and cultural atmosphere that is now badly needed in the changing economic scenario that will have a decisive impact on the socio-political backdrop.

This glaring injustice suffered by Urdu-speaking people has not only posed a threat to the very survival of their language, but the Urdu-speaking community has also begun to equate the survival of Urdu with the well-being of Muslims as a political, cultural, and religious entity. We need to change this mindset. Political will and educational empowerment of people whose mother tongue is Urdu, is needed to revive this language as a functional language and, in turn, for the language to bolster their social empowerment.

In all fairness, our intelligentsia has since Partition been overtly sympathetic towards Urdu, though somewhat ineffectually through their inactivity. Some intellectuals, however, have supported the cause of Urdu through their writings, but most of these writings are mere polemic and paraphrasing of government documents. Needless to say, their arguments were oversimplified and without vision, hence no impact. The only merit that can be granted to the writings regarding Urdu is sincerity towards the language by the intelligentsia; but in academic writings, plain sincerity means nothing. In the social sciences too, focusing on the problems of Urdu as part of the Muslim question, research scholars pay scant attention to it. As a result, we have no academic inputs for policy planning. Government policy concentrates only on Urdu literature and culture—promoting mushairas, fiction, literary criticism, etc. Government assignments for Urdu textbooks are routinely given to Urdu poets, litterateurs, and so-called literary critics. Nobody—including Urdu*walas*—has spoken against this shortsighted treatment meted out to Urdu education. Urdu is either unavailable or else remains a captive of below-mediocre, or rather third-rate obsolete syllabi—thus compelling low-income-group Urdu speakers to put their children through alternative Hindi-medium education where Urdu is unfortunately not available even as an optional subject. In most cases, textbooks are translated into Urdu, increasing the difficulty level and reaching the market late.

While it is deplorable that Urdu-medium school education is not available in north India; in states like Maharashtra where it is provided, the standard of the books is low in comparison to those belonging to other regional languages. Most books in regional languages are translated from English; Urdu books are translated from regional languages, to make matters worse. Serious thought has not been given to re-evaluating these substandard books, which include even those published by the National Council of Education Research and Training (NCERT). The suicidal trend of assigning projects for preparing the syllabi for Urdu-medium students to poets and literary critics was established by the NCERT. Although our academia has promptly reacted against saffronization in the English curriculum, it is sad that it too remains indifferent to the problems of the possibility of communal content in Indian languages, especially Hindi textbooks in north India, where Urdu textbooks are translated from Hindi. In Urdu too, leaving the future of education entirely to poets and writers, such as university-level teachers of literature, is the last nail in the coffin of Urdu literature.[6]

Our aim is threefold: to undertake a realistic re-appraisal of the Urdu language in the formal system of education in contemporary India; to address the issue of representation of Urdu and the community of its speakers; and to explore the possibility of opting for Urdu as a first and compulsory language for Urdu mother-tongue speakers under the Three Language Formula. Urdu has been deprived of its rightful place in the curriculum of secular education and it cannot survive as a functional language unless it is included in the curriculum from the primary to the secondary levels.

Urdu must be offered as an optional subject for students studying in English or in a regional medium. In those parts of north India where Urdu-speaking people are substantial in number and arrangements can be made in accordance with the 86th Amendment, Urdu can be offered as a medium of instruction up to the age of fourteen. Students who get the opportunity to opt for Urdu medium up to Class V can learn it as a first, second, or third language up to the twelfth standard, depending upon the available system and their informed preferences.

As in other dynamic societies, changes are taking place in India too. The 86th Amendment of the Constitution notified on 13 December 2002 gave the Fundamental Right of Education up to the age of fourteen. Children must get this education in their mother tongue— in the case of the Urdu mother-tongue students, in Urdu. We should not oppose English-medium education *per se*. But education in private institutions with English as the medium of instruction is a costly affair, and cannot be a substitute for education in our own languages. Hence, every possible step must be taken to improve the system of education in all Indian languages; this will automatically benefit Urdu and its secular fibre.

NEW DELHI, 2006   SALMAN KHURSHID

Notes

1. For the first time the data was produced in a three-day Seminar between 21–3 March 2003 organized by the Ministry of Human Resource Development through the National Council for Promotion of Urdu Language (NCPUL), an advisory body of the Ministry of Human Resources Development with the purpose of publicizing the data. The data was later published in *Urdu Duniya* (July 2003), a monthly magazine published by the NCPUL itself with editorial comments.

   I was also present in the Seminar when the data was presented as a big achievement and one could do nothing but appreciate the efforts to collect the data, as explained by Dr Halim Khan, then chairman, Madhya Pradesh Madrasa Board. He explained in detail that apart from all the madrasa boards in various states and many other agencies in the Government of India, especially in the Ministry of Home Affairs, did hard to collect the data. For a detailed discussion of the sociology of madrasas please see 'Madrasas and Making of Muslim Identity', by Arjumand Ara, *Economic and Political Weekly*, vol. 39, no. 1, 9 January 2004, pp. 34–8; Bikramjit De, 'Abuse of Urdu', *Economic and Political Weekly*, 27 November–3 December 2004, pp. 5085–8.

   It is a pity that the allocation for the madrasa modernization was only Rs 2 crore in the financial year of 2003, which meant only a few rupees per madrasa. The figures of this ridiculous allocation by the government were also presented in the above said seminar.

2. This quote is from an unpublished letter sent by Arjunand Ara to *Economic and Political Weekly* in October 2004, a copy of which was also sent to the present author. The date, however, cannot be confirmed.

3. See Sunil Khilnani, *The Idea of India*, London: Penguin, 1998.

4. It is significant that Hindi-language chauvinism in north India banks on reactionary Hindutva ideologies, and, over the question of Hindi, even the most liberal Hindus are seen shrinking to the narrow concept of nation and national languages. A news item in a daily newspaper quotes the RSS's Lucknow branch's Kshetra Sanghchalak, Ishwar Chand Gupta's happiness over UP Chief Minister Mulayam Singh's support to the RSS stand on such issues as Hindi and Swadeshi. Talking about the growing proximity between the Samajwadi party of Yadav and the BJP, Gupta said, 'It is a healthy indication that parties that had so far pandered to the whims of minorities are now realizing the importance of Hindutva' (*Indian Express*, New Delhi, 23 December 2003).

5. Initially it was known as the 93rd Constitutional Amendment, which was passed on 28 November 2001. Now the 86th Amendment, notified on 13 December 2002, comes under a new clause—Article 21-A in the Chapter on Fundamental Rights: 'The state shall provide for compulsory education from the age of six to fourteen years, in such manner as the state may be able to decide by law.'

6. For a discussion on irregularities in the production and dissemination of Urdu textbooks, see Chapter 10 of this book (p. 194, n. 2).

Acknowledgements

At the outset I extend my sincere thanks—for which perhaps I do not have appropriate words—to Salman Khurshid for support to the project of revival of Urdu in common civic space, and through school education also. I understand that a project like this has never been a part of his academic life. Most of the articles included in this volume were written for the International Conference on Minority Languages which was organized by the Zakir Husain Study Circle in 2002. The Conference was attended by a galaxy of eminent academics from across the globe. A unique feature of this Conference was that after each paper an open discussion followed on its theme, especially by those sections of academics and common people who claim Urdu as their mother tongue. This Conference brought the agenda of Urdu education on centre stage for the first time after Independence. The then leader of the Opposition and United Progressive Alliance (UPA) Chairperson, Mrs Sonia Gandhi delivered the historic Valedictory address. The UPA dispensation, after coming to power, implemented Mrs Gandhi's wishes and allocated Rs 800 crore in the financial year of 2005–6 for Urdu education under the scheme of 'Sarva Shiksha Abhiyan', a provision that has become more relevant after the 86th Amendment 2002 of the Indian Constitution. No Indian politician has ever contributed so much for the cause of Urdu, academically or politically, in free India. Needless to say, the Conference was successful only because of Mr Salman Khurshid's singular and exceptional efforts.

I am especially grateful to Ralph Russell. We first met in 1993 and do not always agree, but he is completely free of any sense of superiority and continues to be unfailingly supportive.

ATHER FAROUQUI

Introduction to the Paperback Edition

From the Partition of India in 1947 to 1977, writers who tried their hand at analysing the problems relating to the Urdu language and its education came mostly from the departments of Urdu in various universities. First let me explain what I mean by the term 'Urdu education', which is used very vaguely by the whole Urdu-speaking community in free India, partly for political reasons but mostly because of ideological confusion. For me, 'Urdu education' means education provided by schools which are completely secular and teach Urdu either as an optional language, in the category of the first, second, or third language, or are Urdu-medium schools that provide education from the nursery to senior-secondary level and are affiliated to the secondary and senior-secondary boards in respective states. Clearly, the *madrasa* boards in some states are not included in this discussion. The patronage provided to madrasas is not entirely in the spirit of the Constitution. The Indian Constitution is clear and states in no uncertain terms that state funds cannot be spent for the promotion of any religion.[1] It is, thus, doubly unfortunate that state governments are involved in the promotion of madrasas and the Union Ministry of Human Resources Development is willing to establish a central madrasa board.[2]

Since Urdu and Islam have unfortunately become conterminous in post-Partition India, issues related to Muslims in India fall prey to oversimplification. Also, teachers in Urdu departments of universities and their affiliated colleges are often considered ex-officio scholars and experts on Urdu-related issues. It is incorrect to assume that whosoever bears a Muslim name and is a canonized academic is an expert on Muslim affairs. His credentials as an expert on various problems relating to Urdu cannot, thus, be considered impeccable. Nonetheless, in spite of the fact that these people may not be the best representatives of the Urdu-speaking population, they are often the beneficiaries of grants earmarked for the promotion of the language.

The capabilities of teachers in the Urdu departments are so ambiguous that there is little clarity on what is being referred to as 'Urdu education' and even their own writings on the same topic do not reflect this. Most of these people employed by colleges and university departments of Urdu are not sufficiently equipped for the job, appointed by the government as a gesture to uphold 'secularism'. The practice of appointing them as teachers in higher-education institutions to teach Urdu literature (at the college level in India, a teacher is appointed to teach literature assuming that the students at the graduation and post-graduation levels have capabilities to study the literature) was started at a time when Urdu was being suppressed because its speakers were allegedly held responsible for the Partition of India. Even today, the majority of teachers in the Urdu departments comprise people who have never studied Urdu as a language or its literature before their BA or MA Urdu is the only subject in India which can be opted for at the BA (Honours) level or for MA in Urdu literature without proving that one has ever studied the language or its literature.[3] Further, most institutions and organizations that claim the development and progress of Urdu as their aim are under the firm control of the government. Thus, all exercises, short or long term, in support of Urdu, are primarily aimed at serving the interests of the government.[4]

In fact, Urdu has lost much ground since 1947. In the states of north India, the teaching of Urdu as an optional subject has been discontinued at the primary, secondary, and senior-secondary levels. Despite constitutional provisions, those students whose mother tongue is Urdu, are not provided the opportunity of getting an education in the Urdu medium at the primary level. The same is true for education in junior schools and the senior-secondary level where Urdu does not form a part of the optional subjects in the scheme of learning languages. Instruction in Urdu was and certainly is possible in areas with a substantial Urdu-speaking population, provided the state comes up with appropriate policies, action, and funding.

As a result of the general neglect of the language, a whole generation of people whose mother tongue is Urdu has grown up ignorant of the language and the rich culture which it nourished. Moreover, after Independence, the non-Muslims of north India, who had studied Urdu before Partition, became very hostile to it. The *sharnarthis*, a term used for the Hindu refugees who had migrated from the Pakistan side of Punjab, had experienced such mental torture and trauma that they understandably hated Urdu, despite the fact that they had learnt Urdu in pre-Independence India. So, after Partition, they too started regarding it as the language of the Muslims, whom they aligned with the creation of Pakistan. Some political parties were also able to persuade a majority of the Punjabi migrants settled in the cities of north India to enter Hindi instead of Punjabi as their mother tongue in the census returns immediately after Partition in a bid to promote Hindi as a pan-Hindu and pan-Indian language. The issue of not considering Punjabi as the language by a majority of the population featured prominently among the gooses of the notaries of Khalistan later. The country had to pay a high price for this in the 1980s and had to waste a great deal of energy in resisting the growth of this branch of extremism in the ensuing decade.

The chauvinist forces, which had done much to destroy Urdu in north India by classifying Sanskrit, a great injustice to this language as well, as a 'Modern Indian Language' in the Three Language Formula, suffered a heavy defeat when they tried to repeat the experiment in south India in the name of promoting Hindi. The idea was that if Sanskrit is established as a Modern Indian Language, it would be easier to further the spread of Hindi in south India. But south India was conceptually clear: Sanskrit has a rich heritage and valuable legacy but the promotion of political Hindi (or as it was referred to as 'modern Hindi') in the name of Sanskrit, by those who had exploited the language, was not acceptable. And the efforts of chauvinistic forces to impose Hindi on south India brought into being a united front of speakers across all south-Indian languages. The situation became so serious that Dr Radhakrishnan, the then President of the Indian republic, had to advise the central government to douse the flames. The anti-Hindi sentiment even led to such shameful actions as an attack on the Aurobindo Ashram.

Later, at the suggestion of Prime Minister Lal Bahadur Shastri, the then Information and Broadcasting Minister, Indira Gandhi, had to publicly repeat the promise of her father, the late Jawaharlal Nehru, that Hindi would not be imposed on south India. This pro-Hindi campaign proved to be very costly, with the southern states as well as West Bengal opting out of the Three Language Formula, preferring to give primary status to their respective regional languages and opting for English as the second language. All these states have been strict in following the Two Language Formula even to this day. One can understand the situation from the alliance of the Bharatiya Janata Party (BJP) with J. Jayalalitha's All India Anna Dravida Munnetra Kazhagam (AIADMK) in Tamil Nadu in the general elections of 1998, when she came out publicly against Hindi and forced the BJP to make it clear that Hindi would not be imposed in Tamil Nadu. Furthermore, when Jayalalitha demanded the inclusion of Tamil in the list of official languages of the Union, the immediate and enthusiastic response from the people of Tamil Nadu once again thwarted the dream of exploiting Hindi in the name of making it the *lingua franca* of the country by gaining political leverage.

Today, the Urdu language and its speakers face extremely complex problems and Urdu as a language of culture is in its death throes. The teaching of Urdu literature in university departments is perfunctory and its use in Bollywood films is only due to commercial considerations.

Unfortunately, it is only in religious institutions of Muslims, known as *dini madaris*, that Urdu flourishes. These institutions have revived the teaching of the language as an agenda. Urdu was always the medium of instruction for the majority of the madrasas (the madaris which claim to have Arabic as their medium of instruction, have in actual practice Urdu as an instrument of teaching Arabic). But after the 1990s, religious instruction took a new turn. The astonishing rise of Hindu revivalism around this time had an impact on the religious divide and paved the way for atavistic Muslim forces to exploit Urdu, and now, Urdu has established a monopoly in the literature of religious studies. Hundreds of books, booklets, and posters of a religious nature are being published every day all over the country, all in Urdu. Regrettably, however, Urdu's use in the publications of religious institutions is displacing the traditional culture, which is also referred to as the 'composite culture'. Urdu literature and its poetry have always been anathema to the majority of the *ulema* (Islamic scholars), and the language's powerful educational and cultural tradition did not allow Muslim religious extremism to defeat it. An *aalim*, a scholar, like Ashraf Ali Thanavi (who appears somewhat progressive in religious matters in comparison to his contemporaries) in his famous book *Bahishti Zewar*, a copy of which at one time was found in most Muslim households in north India, listed works of Urdu literature which were, in his opinion, destructive to moral values. But it was only after Independence that Urdu faced a real challenge from the views which scholars like Thanavi espoused.

The situation as it stands today is that unless the trend towards the taking over of Urdu by religious fanatics and fundamentalists is halted, the language's secular traditions and its capacity to bind people across communities and regions will be greatly jeopardized. This should worry everyone concerned with the prospects of Urdu, including the State, whose interests would be better served if Urdu survives and flourishes with its secular tendencies. Of course, the State is an abstract entity and the political forces that aspire to rule the country sometimes exploit language as the trusted instrument of the old doctrine of divide and rule. So the call is for those who are interested in the survival of civil society and the essential, fundamental role of Urdu in this revival. They certainly deserve a helping hand. Revival of Urdu studies through a secular curriculum covering the school system is the only way to save Urdu and its character as a functional language in India. This will pave the way for other Indian languages too to face up to the challenges of new technology, which has been the monopoly of English.

New Delhi, 2010   Ather Farouqui

Notes

1. Article 27 of the Indian Constitution bars the state from funding any religious activity, including religious education, at the public exchequer's expense. It is a known fact, however, that no political party has ever disputed the fact that India is a secular State. The debate would become unnecessarily complex if I embarked on the rhetoric of how a State signifies only a secular state.

2. For a comprehensive discussion on the issue of a Central Madrasa Board, which mainly explains the position of Muslim religious organizations, please see the editorial of *Muslim India*, 'Call to the Community to Oppose Central Madrasa Board and Save Madrasas', vol. XXVI, no. 304, October 2009, pp. 2–4. From within the community also, there is a palpable opposition to a centralizing madrasa board but their logic is different and regressive. They do not even want to change the existing syllabus which is no less than 300 years old. In the present system, madrasa boards are not answerable to the income-tax authorities and they feel that any kind of government

intervention will introduce the imposition of checks and expose their irregularities.

3. In most universities, when a student applies for BA Honours in Urdu or for the BA Pass Course with Urdu as a subject, it is not mandatory that he should have studied Urdu as an optional subject. The same is true for MA Urdu aspirants who are not required to prove that they have studied Urdu language and its literature at any level, let alone for graduation.

4. My argument is that religious education should be left to the communities concerned without government support; in the case of Muslims, to them only, and the State should concentrate only on secular education. With the enforcement of the Right to Education Act (RTE) from April 2010, the government cannot find sufficient resources even for basic education. In the circumstances, any move to convert dini madaris to extended schools or use their infrastructure for the implementation of RTE will add up to just an atavistic effort to divide society further.

Introduction

This book is an attempt to examine all aspects of the problem of Urdu and its survival as a functional language in the common civic space. These aspects have often figured in political discourse and form a continuing feature of the north-Indian political landscape in independent India, and thus a part of contemporary history. Having had a glorious past, Urdu has now virtually become pre-eminently the language of those Indians who profess Islam and features in their nostalgia about the past. Once it shared a common space with other communities, particularly Hindus and Sikhs. But Hindu and Sikh Indians have consciously abandoned it in free India and their children do not learn it any more.

It is possible to have more than one view about the future of Urdu as a functional language in India. My view is that Urdu, the mother tongue of more than 60 million Indians (as per the 2001 census), can and will survive in India as a functional language only if it is taught in the educational curriculum as a Modern Indian Language. (This view has persistently been endorsed by several writers included in this book.) But, in fact, due to the persistent denial of a place in secular education in the so-called Hindi belt of north India, where a majority of the Urdu-speaking people live, Urdu has become largely confined to Muslim minority educational institutions and *madrasa*s which mostly accommodate backward and poor Muslims. Thus it has survived only among the lower strata of the Muslim community. For this association with the Muslim community, Urdu suffered the ire of the Hindu majority after the Partition of the subcontinent. The state took cognizance of the mood of the majority and eliminated it from school education without the slightest compunction.[1] Urdu was not recognized as a language of any state in its homeland—the so-called Hindi belt—during the reorganization of states on a linguistic basis. Ironically, it was the official language of Jammu and Kashmir where nobody claims Urdu to be their mother tongue. Thus, due to denial of state support, or rather the denial of the constitutional rights of the Urdu-speaking community, religious aspects define the horizons of Urdu.

Since it is no longer a profitable proposition to learn Urdu, the Muslim élite of north India have altogether abandoned the language. For fear of being accused of having any allegiance with Pakistan (whose national language is Urdu), they had already severed emotional ties with the language. The expanding Muslim middle class is also abandoning it with every forward step on the path of social mobility. To some extent, therefore, the preservation of Urdu is linked with the economic condition of the backward sections of the Muslim community. The role of the Muslim political leaders associated with secular parties is also ambivalent for political reasons as they dare not question the common perception that Urdu is the language of the separatist forces that created Pakistan.

There is no doubt that Urdu, as the repository of the religious heritage of Muslim Indians, is a significant element in the religious identity of Muslims in the Indian subcontinent. Also, it still remains their *lingua franca*. Because of this, Urdu has survived its state-sponsored throttling and elimination from the state school system. This has also saved Urdu from being denigrated as a 'dead language' or being bracketed with 'formerly dominant languages', to use the term coined by Theodore P. Wright Jr.

The problems of the Urdu language are closely linked with the problems of Muslims because Urdu has come to be associated mainly with Muslims ever since the Hindu revivalist movement of the late nineteenth century. This period saw the demarcation of two separate cultures on a religious basis. The divide further deepened with the Partition of the Indian subcontinent along religious lines. Since Independence, the Muslim community has faced double jeopardy in linguistic terms. Its language—language is critical for sustaining the vitality of a community—has been facing an eclipse. Opportunities for learning Urdu are available only in madrasas. As a consequence, some Muslims have been patronizing madrasas as a means of preserving their language. Second, since the Urdu language is the repository of their religious literature, Muslims fear that with the decline of Urdu their religious heritage might be lost.

I submit that it is also possibly because of the hostility of Hindu revivalists against Urdu and the resultant discrimination against it, particularly in north India, that Urdu has now become largely a medium of religious instruction. The syllabus taught in the madrasas is essentially exclusivist. This can give an impetus to fundamentalist tendencies among the students. In the madrasas, they hardly have any access to modern secular education. Lack of knowledge about things other than the religious isolates them in a plural and multi-religious society like ours. Sometimes they speak an outdated, even fanatical, language. Hardliness exploit this situation to justify their campaign against Muslims.

One of the consequences of this state of affairs—considerably accentuated after Independence because of the official neglect of Urdu—has been that the Muslim community has been sucked into the morass of backwardness, traditionalism, and religiosity. It has remained stagnant and become peripheral to the process of modernization that the country and the world have witnessed over the years.

This situation is unlikely to change unless education in Urdu is integrated with secular education. If Urdu is introduced in main-stream educational institutions, a majority of Muslim parents will send their children to these schools rather than to madrasas. Such a move will create conditions for broadening the outlook of the students and promoting a democratic and secular perspective. In order to counter the backward-looking and narrow outlook of the vast major-ity of Muslim Indians, the government would be well advised to give Urdu its due place in the school curriculum. Such an initiative can well become the most important step towards the promotion of a liberal and modern world view among India's largest minority. This was the *raison d'être* behind requesting distinguished scholars and public figures to contribute to this endeavour by focusing on an evaluation of public policies and the social, educational, and political situation of Urdu; assessing the facilities available for teaching in Urdu; and evolving suitable strategies for introducing Urdu into mainstream secular education, thereby promoting a modern and secular frame of mind among Muslims.

This volume is divided into four sections. The articles of the first, 'Contexualizing Urdu', situate Urdu in the backdrop of contemporary history. Pratap Bhanu Mehta, Barbara Metcalf, Yogendra Singh, and Theodore P. Wright, Jr, have attempted to locate Urdu's present status in the social, historical, and political context. Salman Khurshid's preface dwells upon the ghettoization of Urdu and, as a consequence, its acquiring a religion-based identity. He sees the solution in Urdu's inclusion in the secular education curriculum. He emphasizes that the survival of Urdu is, in fact, essential for the survival of secular values in India.

Pratap Bhanu Mehta's paper is something of an interloper in this volume. Unlike the other articles, it does not delve into the historical and practical difficulties facing Urdu, but raises questions about the place of languages in general, and Urdu in particular. The paper also tries to connect the fate of Urdu to certain issues in political theory.

Barbara Metcalf analyses the historical context of Urdu to underline the particular burden that Partition placed on what had come to be seen as a 'Muslim' language as well as a language whose speakers, after 1947, did not represent a geographically concentrated population. Even so, constitutional guarantees should have assured the teaching of Urdu to those claiming it to be their mother tongue. She suggests three strategies that could enhance the teaching of Urdu and its place in the larger society. First, its instruction could be integrated explicitly with instruction in Hindi, with the Urdu script and vocabulary being made available as an option for all students. Second, instead of labelling Urdu negatively as a Pakistani language, policymakers and writers should simultaneously claim Urdu, whose origins are wholly within the current boundaries of India, and recognize all the advantages of embracing it as a transnational language. Finally, writers and publishers should enlarge the circles of those who know Urdu literature by furthering publication in Nagari, including bilingual publications that would simultaneously provide texts in the Urdu and Nagari scripts. Only such steps will help ensure the language a larger place in Indian society.

Yogendra Singh sees Urdu as a very vital part of the Muslim identity. In his discussion, he raises the issues of identity and legitimacy and Urdu's relationship with the Muslim community in India in terms of policy implication. He feels that the cultural identity of the community has evolved 'in a direction which is more in consonance with norms of a cultural pluralism, liberal democracy, and social and economic modernization.' There are, however, still some pockets of 'segmentary ethnicization' of the community. But these arise because the state's economic and educational policies have either not been 'fairly implemented', or have not been evolved in an 'equitable manner' to deal with Muslim backwardness in our society.

Theodore P. Wright, Jr, places the case of Urdu in the context of formerly dominant languages of the world that survived or perished in the wake of historical and political processes such as group status reversal from conquest or revolution. His attempt to compare the cases of many such languages of ancient and medieval Europe (Norman French) and Asia (Manchu) to the colonial languages of Africa and Latin America, each in its unique circumstances, is both instructive and provocative. His theoretical framework is comparative politics rather than linguistics.

The second section, 'Urdu and Identity Politics', has four articles on different aspects of Muslim religious and cultural identity. Arjumand Ara's exclusive essay analyses the role of madrasas in the making of the Muslim identity. She sees these seminaries as an offshoot of the erstwhile feudal society, which Muslims, because of their educational and economic backwardness, refused to discard when India marched forward to evolve into a modern capitalist democracy. She advocates the provision of a progressive, modern, and alternative education system which can provide a promising future for the younger generations and curb the menace of growing educational backwardness among Muslims.

Amina Yaqin studies the problem of the communalization and disintegration of Urdu in literature. One of the reasons for this state of affairs is the non-availability of Urdu education in secular educational institutions in India. Yaqin studies in this context Anita Desai's *In Custody*, an Indian English novel about Urdu. But, unfortunately, the novel itself projects the Urdu-speaking community in a poor light and runs the risk of becoming something like a caricature of an ageing Urdu poet who is supposed to represent the Indian Urdu-speaking community. The so called 'élite' who write about Urdu seem to regard language as something anachronistic. While Desai's picture is not a realistic representation of the community, our 'élite' seem precisely to be drawing upon such representations of Urdu while forming their views and opinions Bombay films, too, have tended to project only the stereotypes of the Urdu-speaking community. This article helps us understand how this community is seen by other language groups, especially those who are economically and politically more powerful than most of the Urdu-speaking community in India.

Kelly Pemberton and Daniela Bredi ponder over the destiny of Urdu through the questions of language, community, identity, and power.

While maintaining Urdu's continued vitality as a link among various communities in India, Pemberton advocates the reconceptualization of Urdu as a language and as a marker of identity. She contends that this should occur on two fronts and at the level of both state and grassroots institutions: definition, through which some measure of standardization can be achieved, and ideologically, by which the meanings of Urdu could be shifted away from association with a particular community or interest group and expanded to reflect the widespread influence Urdu has upon the literary and cultural landscape of India.

The third section of the book, 'Civic Space, Education, and Urdu', comprises a wide range of issues. I survey the sorry state of Urdu education in major representative states of India.

Syed Shahabuddin deals with the hard reality faced by Urdu in today's socio-political map of India. He surveys the relationship of Muslims with Urdu, Muslim educational institutions, the government's role, the problem of shrinking academic space for Urdu, publication of Urdu books in the context of falling demand, and the role of the Urdu-speaking élite. He tries to offer a solution by addressing all these problems at different levels. His solution demands nothing drastic but only an honest application of the existing constitutional guarantees and government policies at the ground level.

Christina Oesterheld surveys the situation of Urdu education in India in the light of the provisions of the Indian Constitution, the Kripalani Committee Report, and articles and newspaper reports on Urdu education in selected states of the Indian Union, supplemented by her own observations during numerous visits to India between 1983 and 2001. Summing up recommendations which have been put forward by Indian scholars over the last decades, she also suggests possible measures for reviving Urdu as a functional language. She briefly touches upon the questions of Urdu versus English as a medium of instruction and of improving the quality of Urdu education.

Kerrin Gräfin Schwerin puts forth an educationist's view while deliberating on basic education and the Urdu medium in the light of the Wardha Scheme of Education or Nai Talim of 1937, which was drafted under the chairmanship of Dr Zakir Husain, the third President of India. While discussing the role of Urdu as a mother tongue under this scheme, she concludes that 'Urdu which is the lingua franca of Indians and Pakistanis outside India and Pakistan, will not disappear from the language map of the world, because it is valued by people as a literature and a language.'

Hasan Abdullah raises several questions while surveying the present state of Urdu in India. He ponders over the relation of Urdu with different segments of society, growth of different languages, and the place of Urdu, its significance as a modern language, the role of the Urdu-knowing élite and Indian intelligentsia, and the social, economic, and educational background of Urdu-knowing people. He offers useful suggestions for answering the important questions that arise.

J.S. Gandhi's article concerns the diminishing centrality of the Urdu language in our life since the Partition of India in 1947. His is a personal, yet poignant, narrative of his life experiences, which takes us through a wide range of personal recollections and encounters, ending indeed on a sad note that a very potent source of unifying people from across community divides, is being lost sight of. He believes Urdu has fallen victim not only to wrongdoings on policy fronts but also to communalizing and bracketing the issue with a specific community. By way of a corrective, a thorough contemporary re-assessment of the political, social, and intellectual scenario is needed to save this powerful but dying legacy.

The fourth and final section, 'Minority Language and Community—Legal Concerns', is written by legal experts. Fali S. Nariman comments on the education for religious and linguistic minorities within the constitutional and legal framework. He then goes on to suggest ways to improve the relations between majority and minority groups/communities. He warns that 'language must never be confused with religion. Languages, as Dr Samuel Johnson once said, are the pedigree of a nation. Hindi, Urdu, and the languages in the Eighth Schedule are the pedigree of the people of Hindustan.'

Soli J. Sorabjee also talks about the status of minorities, their religion, their educational institutions, their language, and their culture. Citing the example of Albania, he points towards an event where a court verdict commenting on minorities emphasized that 'there would be no true equality between a majority and a minority if the latter were deprived of its own institutions and were consequently compelled to renounce that which constitutes the very essence of its being a minority...that in addition to equality in law there must be equality in fact which may involve the necessity of different treatment in order to attain a result which establishes an equilibrium.'

Yogesh Tyagi's article is a commentary on legal aspects of minorities in India. His focus is on the 'concept of minority languages; the domestic law basis of obligations in respect of minority languages; the international legal framework with regard to minority languages; and an international approach towards the promotion of regional minority languages in general and Urdu in particular.' He recommends establishing a nationwide database on linguistic minorities in order to enhance the effectiveness of efforts to promote and protect minority languages.

Let me now come back to the vital question of the mother tongue. According to the Constitution of India, primary education should be given in the mother tongue (Article 350-A), and, as government policy, the Three Language Formula should be implemented from Class VI onwards. Accordingly, the mother tongue should be taught as a first and compulsory language (even if the medium of instruction is the same). In the north-Indian states, Hindi is the medium of instruction from Classes I to XII. From Class I onwards, Hindi is also taught as the first language. This is a gross violation of the letter and spirit of the Three Language Formula. By this act, Hindi has been imposed on non-Hindi speaking people in place of their mother tongue. Urdu is not included even as a third language in the category of a Modern Indian Language. Instead, Sanskrit is claimed to be a Modern Indian Language and is thus invariably taught in this category. Sanskrit is also taught as a compulsory component of the Hindi syllabus from Classes VI to XII. In a nutshell, in Uttar Pradesh (UP), an Urdu-speaking student has no chance to learn his mother tongue while he compulsorily learns Hindi and Sanskrit.

Against this backdrop, the question of the constitutional rights of Urdu under Article 350-A of the Constitution, including Urdu at the primary level, along with other languages, as a medium of education and at secondary level as the first language for those who claim Urdu to be their mother tongue, is not simply one of the survival of a language. It is a question of the survival of the rights of minorities—including Muslims.

It is an established fact that despite all constitutional guarantees against discrimination, Urdu has been very systematically eliminated from the curriculum of mainstream secular educational institutions. Academically, it is possible to devise a formula to introduce Urdu in school education, but these all fail when it comes to implementation. Hence, I feel that the survival of Urdu is a political question and demands political will and strategy to address it. The government and its educational agencies were, and are, responsible for devising new policies that have systematically neglected Urdu. The reasons are obvious. The Constitution of India defines India as a secular state but the ground reality is that the decision-making people are not always secular. This snag prevents the uniform growth of all peoples, cultures, and languages. Urdu is just one example of victimization.

As a student exploring the dynamics of a language, I do not see, as indeed no one ought to, the role of a living language like Urdu in isolation. The role of Urdu in education should be analysed in the context of the facilities provided by the secondary and senior-secondary examination boards. Of course, the socio-economic perspective of the people who want their children to take Urdu as an optional subject has also to be taken into account.

It would be useful to consider why Urdu is not offered/opted for as a language if a child has to learn three languages under the straightjacket of the state-imposed Three Language Formula. In any case, it seems obvious that in India, learning Urdu would be more beneficial than any European language (except English). Especially in north India, learning Urdu is useful as any other Indian language unless, of course, the student intends to take up a career in a particular region. At an early age, a child does not have enough information to decide on a career. Therefore, to ask her or him to learn a foreign language, such as French, German, or Spanish, or, as the third language, Sanskrit, Assamese, or Malayalam, is to impose an extra burden. The child could decide whether to learn a foreign language, a regional Indian language, or a classical language upon completing school education. Even for English-medium students whose mother tongue is Hindi (or any other Indian language, particularly in the northern belt), Urdu may be a useful option. From Class VI onwards, English being the first language of such schools, Hindi can be taught as the second language and Urdu as the third language. I believe that these questions need a fresh approach with the advent of the new era of Information Technology. This is particularly important at a time when culture and identity are being given great emphasis.

The articles included in this volume are unique in that they do not play to the gallery nor subscribe to any current misconceptions of Urdu. Coordinating with the writers for the last several years has made it possible to collect articles on all possible aspects, including the Urdu–Hindi controversy, the historical background, and the political undercurrent of the past and the present. In a developing society like India, it often happens that many problems need a new approach and all discourses tend to become dated with the march of time. Studies on Urdu belong to this genre as Urdu is facing a unique and unprecedented situation in the history of languages, which nullifies many fondly held and otherwise academically competent theories.

I hope that this volume will help in securing for Urdu—I must repeat—its rightful place as a functional language in the common civic space of our multilingual, multicultural, and multireligious society.

At this juncture, I must first thank all the contributors. I am sure that in writing the articles for this volume all of them have put in tremendous effort. Some of the valued authors have taken nearly two years to write their contributions, and some of them took even longer, simply because no academic writing on this theme was available. Till 1990 there was only one book—a part of which dealt with the language issue in north India, published in 1974—in circulation and that too was written by an American professor who never revised the book.

I hope the present volume will also be of help as a guideline for research synopses in the days to come for scholars who are interested in the theme. If that happens, I shall be a happy man.

My sincere—in the true spirit of the word—thanks to all those with whom I interacted at the Oxford University Press, especially to Manzar Khan, Managing Director, for his interest and exceptional generosity. I extend my gratitude with the help of an Urdu verse—

jo kuchh kahun to tera husn ho gaya mehdood—whatever I could say could not adequately describe your beauty.

New Delhi, 2006

Ather Farouqui

Notes

1. The State has not ensured that Urdu-medium schools in or near localities with a substantive Urdu population are started. This goes against the spirit of the Constitution, especially Article 350-A, which says that the medium for primary education should be the mother tongue. The State has not encouraged the existing government or private schools affiliated to the secondary and senior-secondary boards in the states to make arrangements for teaching Urdu as the first, second, or third language for those who wish to study it. Chapter 10 in this book on the Three Language Formula (pp. 180–4) discusses the barriers imposed by the State itself which make it difficult for students to study Urdu in schools, especially in north-Indian states.

PART I
Contextualizing Urdu

1

Urdu: Between Rights and the Nation

What is the appropriate normative framework for understanding the claims of Urdu and education in Urdu in modern India?[1] In one sense, the answer to this question can be stunningly simple. The demands of morality, as expressed in numerous international conventions, suggests that everyone has the right to use the language of their choice and participate in their chosen social, economic, religious, and cultural life. Every person belonging to a linguistic community ought to have the right to use their language in public and private life, with no unjustified distinction, exclusion, restriction, or preference intended to discourage or endanger the maintenance of a particular language. On this view that the state ought not to, either by direct intervention, or through the indirect effects of its policies, sustain conditions that unfairly disadvantage members of a particular linguistic community. If a society or state creates conditions such that it becomes more difficult for members of some linguistic groups to use their language it violates more rights than would be decent to list.

The normative case for Urdu is, in this view, simple enough. The Indian state's policies towards Urdu violate the rights of Urdu speakers by unfairly disadvantaging them. The Indian states' policy directly contravenes the spirit of the Directive Principles of State Policy. Section 21 of Article 350-A of these Special Directives, inserted by the Constitution Act 1956 states that:

Facilities for instruction in mother tongue at primary stage: It shall be the endeavor of every state and of every local authority within the state to provide adequate facilities for instruction in the mother tongue at the primary stage of education to children belonging to linguistic minority groups; and the President may issue such directions to any state he considers necessary or proper for securing the provision of such facilities.

Although the word 'endeavour' gives the state an escape clause, there is no doubting that Urdu has not been given its due entailed by our constitutional provisions. The normative basis of Urdu's claims is non-discrimination. On this view, the Indian state has denied Urdu the privileges that have been granted to a host of other languages. The relevant states have refused to grant Urdu the official status it deserves. Urdu as a medium of instruction in government schools is almost non-existent, even in areas where Urdu speakers are numerically significant. Effectively this means that Urdu-medium instruction, or even instruction about Urdu, is available only in madrasas. Thus, Urdu-speaking students are burdened with a choice their compatriots do not have to face. They can either remain in the government school system but risk being cut off from their own linguistic heritage, or tenaciously cling on to their linguistic heritage by withdrawing from public institutions. Urdu is also the victim of political geography. Although it is the largest minority language, it receives the least effective state support. All other significant minority languages have the advantage of being geographically concentrated enough to be officially patronized by a state government. Urdu is officially patronized only in Jammu and Kashmir, where only a tiny proportion of Urdu speakers live. The Gujral Committee on the promotion of Urdu had recommended, among other measures, the establishment of Urdu-medium primary schools wherever the population of Urdu speakers exceeds 10 per cent. It had also recommended a modification of the Three Language Formula in north India to compulsorily include Urdu along with English and Hindi. The fact that these minimal measures for ensuring that Urdu is not unfairly disadvantaged have not been introduced suggests that the state has not fulfilled its obligations.

It would be very difficult for any reasoned argument to deny that Urdu has been seriously disadvantaged by the policies of the Indian state. Few scholars would deny that this discrimination is not simply an unintended by-product of otherwise neutral state policies; this discrimination was clearly intended. The claims of Urdu have the weight of justice on their side.

This paper is a bit of an interloper in a volume on Urdu. It does not try to do what many of the other papers have so ably done: give an account of the historical and practical difficulties facing Urdu. Rather, it tries to raise some questions about the place of languages in general, and Urdu in particular, in the modern Indian imagination. It tries to show how a particular alignment of language and identity impedes a proper discussion of language issues. The second half of the paper tries to connect the fate of Urdu to some issues in political theory. Why should a democratic society care about the fate of Urdu?

Although the injustice against Urdu speakers has been palpable, paradoxically, the language of justice and rights, of equality and discrimination, has proved to be relatively powerless in helping advance the claims of Urdu. This is because our discourse on language has been entirely colonized by the question of nationalism. In this discourse, Urdu has become the other of the nation, the language that single-handedly has to bear the burden of Partition. The progressive communalization of Urdu, its identification with a particular religious community, and its disintegration as a language are two sides of the same coin. Urdu's claims as a language are diminished because it has come to be identified with the claims of an ethnicity. Indeed, it is one of the few languages in the world that is treated, not as a language, but as an icon, a marker of an identity that puts the project of nationhood at risk. This reduction of Urdu is poignantly captured in Anita Desai's novel *In Custody*. When a protagonist in the novel requests for leave in order to interview the legendary Urdu poet, Nur Shahjanbadi, he receives this vehement reaction from the head of the department:

I'll get you transferred to your beloved Urdu department. I won't have Muslim toadies in my department; you will ruin my boys with your Muslim ideas, your Urdu language. I'll complain to the Principal. I'll warn the RSS you are a traitor.[2]

This reactionary stance bluntly captures the paranoia and fear that Urdu speakers evoke in a context where language becomes a carrier of a religious identity. But language is, in this construction, also a mark of national loyalty. It is small wonder that Urdu has to single-handedly bear the weight of nationalist anxieties. It is as if when it comes to Urdu, all claims of justice are to be immobilized under the pressure of this fear and anxiety.

It is tempting to dismiss the fear and anxiety that Urdu evokes. Certainly this fear has no basis in fact: the association of religious identity or linguistic affiliation with national loyalty does violence to the allegiances of entire communities. But these fears and anxieties also remain remarkably immune to any rational criticism. We can go on endlessly about how Urdu is not simply the language of Muslims. We can attempt to show historically that the current construction of the divide between Hindi and Urdu is an artificial one. We can rehearse facts to the effect that Urdu speakers are hardly more likely to be disloyal to the nation. And many of the distinguished contributors to this volume have done this with great skill. But such efforts have been of little avail. Any reflection on the question of how to make normative demands on behalf of Urdu—has to labour under the shadow of the fact that we are engaging in a debate on this matter in which it is very unlikely that the requirements of justice, or the demands based on rights, will get much of a hearing. What else can we then appeal to?

Jean-Paul Sartre's great insight into anti-Semitism was that anti-Semitism did not take its bearings from the object of its hate. Indeed, anti-Semitism revealed more about the insecurities and fantasies, infirmities and obsessions of the anti-Semites than anything about the Jews. By analogy, an acute recalcitrance to the claims of Urdu does not have much to do with the predicament of Urdu or Urdu speakers. How do we address those who manifestly or surreptitiously circumvent the rightful claims of Urdu in our curriculum or elsewhere?

Part of the difficulty stems from the peculiar way in which what Robert King called the 'iconic' use of language, has debased any meaningful debate on language pedagogy. Any language, of course, has multiple purposes: it is an instrument of transmitting knowledge, it can be a means of communication, or a depository of cultural memory. More ambitiously a language is a way of bringing a whole world into being. As Charles Taylor[3] put it, language enters into, or makes possible, a whole range of crucially human feelings, activities, and relations. But the crucial point is that language is not simply an instrument that makes these activities possible. It is, rather, that language *constitutes* these activities. It is difficult to make exact sense of the expressions a language enables outside its own horizons.

An iconic use of language refers to language as a symbol to achieve non-linguistic goals. At one level an iconic use of language can be liberating. It allows language to be viewed as an instrument for achieving something else. Language, in this view, is not of intrinsic value, to be revered for the cultural memories and vocabularies it embodies. It is more like a piece of software, instrumental to achieving some function. In many ways, English has become iconic in this sense. Those who use it are not inspired by any elevated sense of what English allows them to create, nor are they necessarily taken in by the life worlds that are associated with the use of language. They see it simply as a means to economic advancement. From this point of view, it does not matter whether the English is Oxford English or Hinglish (Hind strewn with English words), so long as it gets the job done.

But language can become iconic in another sense also. It can become a marker of identity. It is not the intrinsic value of the language, its literary merits, or its grammatical possibilities that inspire its users. It is, rather, its association with an identity. Indeed, adherents are persuaded about the substantive possibilities of the language because they think it is a marker of their identity, not the other way round. For instance, many of those who extol the value of Sanskrit do not have the faintest idea of the language—yet advocacy for the language serves as a way of asserting a particular identity.

In Indian discourse, these iconic uses of language have doubly disadvantaged Urdu. To the extent that the wider population comes to see any particular language as crudely instrumental to some practical purpose, it is likely to be stone deaf to the demands for help in 'preserving' any language. On this view, who really cares what language we speak—Braj or Urdu, Hindi or Hinglish, so long as it is getting the job done. All languages must either adapt to the prac- tical pressures of the market or simply give way. On this view there is no conceptual space to understand what harm might be done, what wrong might be committed in the loss of a language. It is important that one learns *a* language, rather than any *particular* language. So, if it is cheaper and administratively easier to have fewer languages, what's the great harm? So, if the languages of minorities fall by the wayside, what's the harm?

This sort of instrumentalism towards language, in north India in particular, is making arguments based on the importance of languages more difficult to mount. In a culture that is increasingly deaf to the nuances of history, any claims about a language being a repository of civilizational values or a distinct culture seem like so much nostalgia. It is no accident that there is a general debasing of language in the educational curriculum of north India.[4] A point about the general de-emphasis on language skills in our educational curriculum may not seem of much relevance in a volume on Urdu, but I have increasingly come to the view that it is—for at least two reasons. First, if the wider culture within which Urdu is placed cannot rise above a crudely instrumental view of language, it is unlikely to be very moved by the claims of any particular language. If you have a society that quite simply does not *care* about language, what appeals will it receive on behalf of Urdu?

Second, a crudely instrumental view of language has a great impact on the pedagogy of languages in our schools, Urdu included. Although I am not a linguist, I suspect that most of the conflicts that we experience between the demands of Hindi and Sanskrit on the one hand and Urdu on the other, can be mitigated by imaginative designing of language curriculum. It is extraordinary that we can give Sanskrit a place as a modern language under the Three Language Formula. Yet, despite the fact that it is widely taught in Indian schools, competence in the language of those who emerge from the Sanskrit curriculum of these schools is fairly minimal at best. What is it about our pedagogical practices that lead us to spend valuable time on teaching a language with so little effect? On the other hand, might it not be possible to integrate some the teaching of Hindi and Urdu so that, even non-Urdu speakers can become a constituency for the language? Are we doomed to see the competition between languages as a zero-sum game or are there imaginative educational techniques that can help us get us out of this quagmire? The trick is to create an educational curriculum where different communities, at least in north India, know enough to care about each other's languages. This is the only way to build up support in the long run for a minority language. It is not an accident that Nehru, who in equal measure seems to have advocated the cause of Hindi, Urdu, and Sanskrit, was someone who understood what a language is about, apart from its merely instrumental usage.[5]

What I have said about the crude instrumentalization of language may sound unconvincing in an Indian context. After all, is India not the site of fierce debates over language? Is language not a potent axis of political conflict? If language were merely instrumental, how could there be so much blood spilled over it? The answer is that language becomes potent when it becomes iconic in the second sense—when it becomes allied with identity. We can see these iconic uses of language all around us. Arguably, the attempt to fashion a chaste Hindi had little to do with either practicality or literary virtue. Hindi never caught on as a mass language and has remained confined to its custodians in the literary establishment. It was rather an attempt to create a national icon in the name of Hindi, which to this day remains irrelevant to the real world of literary practice and to the world of everyday language use. But it was a conception of Hindi that came to be set up in partial opposition to Urdu. This Hindi was mobilized to sever the link between Hindi and Urdu by displacing Hindustani. What is crucial about this move is not its success, but the way in which it made the question of language inseparable from the question of national identity, as if the very strength of the nation depended on the purity of its language. The creation of modern official Hindi is not the story of a spontaneous evolution of a language. Rather it was a strategy to displace the authority of existing linguistic communities. It is not an accident that the hostility towards Urdu arose concurrently with a hostility towards a precariously syncretistic culture in north India. Hindi and Urdu, by definition had to be in competition, because to accept Urdu would have been to acknowledge the syncretistic or hybrid character of north India.

Threatened with the dominance of Hindi as an icon, other regional vernacular languages could mobilize an iconic power of their own. The iconic alignment of language with ethnicity is politically potent because it ties language to personal identity. Many of the regional languages gained their political momentum from just this identification, most notably Tamil. Most of the linguistic passions unleashed were accommodated in the form of linguistic states. But after Partition, Urdu was over-determined to be unavailable for such an iconic mobilization. For one thing, the association between religious identity and language was something that was imposed from the outside rather than embraced from within. And there was every danger that any assertion on behalf of Urdu would only reinforce this identification. How can one talk of the claims of a language when any such talk was colonized by charges of communalism? The iconic uses of the Urdu language by those set against it—a use that made no reference to its vitality or viability—made it a means of exclusion and exile.

It seems to me that if we are to recover any sanity in discussions on language policy and the proper claims of Urdu, we shall have to avoid both forms of reductionism that the iconic use of language entails. If we take the instrumental view of language we shall end up with the absurd position that the Report on the Official Language

Commission ended up with, namely that 'language is of no intrinsic importance'.[6] With this instrumental attitude to language, it is difficult to contemplate any language being given the right kind of importance.

On the other hand, if we align language with identity too closely we run two risks. On the one hand we run the risk of obscuring what is morally at stake in the decline of a language. What is at stake in the survival of a language is not an identity fetish of any sort, but a way of bringing a world into being, a whole world with its own internal tensions and contradictions, its own mode of conduct and change. On the other hand, the iconic status of Hindi has posed a grave threat to Urdu because the identity of 'official' Hindi, at any rate, depended on its distancing itself from Urdu. The attack on Urdu was not simply communally motivated, it was simultaneously an attack on the idea of a syncretistic and hybrid culture. And this attack was made possible by a particular conception of a national identity where a language like Urdu ran the risk of being associated with national disloyalty. Thus we got the Janus face of the Indian state towards Urdu. At the symbolic level, many government programmes were introduced for the advancement of Urdu, and many institutions that teach Urdu received financial support. But the real basis of sustaining a language in the modern world, its place in public education, was consistently denied to Urdu.

Urdu and a New National Identity

What is the battle for Urdu about? Clearly, at one level it is about the preservation, growth, and perpetuation of an extraordinary language whose immeasurable importance to the cultural life of India cannot be recounted in any easy summary. At another level it is about doing justice to members of a linguistic community who have been the targets of linguistic discrimination. But it is also fundamentally about the kind of nation India wants to be. The denial of Urdu's claims bespeaks of a nation fundamentally insecure, unable to reckon with its own complex diversities. Of course, any nation of India's complexity will have to navigate different tensions: between the imperatives of creating linkages between its diverse peoples on the one hand and maintaining diversity on the other. Language politics has been the site of this unresolved tension. On the one hand, the state has tried to create a single national language, and on the other hand, it has had to bow to the imperatives of linguistic diversity.

In any state, citizenship is not merely about possessing a legal status defined by a set of rights and responsibilities. Citizenship is also, to a certain extent, about feeling at home in the nation. It is the capacity to see the nation as a repository of your own history and culture. The idea of freedom itself is also, as Kymlicka reminded us, tied closely to the availability of cultural options.[7] It is only through a rich and secure cultural structure that individuals can meaningfully exercise the options available to them. Their sense of self-respect comes from, in part, a sense that their culture is respected, that it can find unapologetic public expression. The importance of giving recognition to mother tongues in a democratic state stems from this consideration. It is an assurance that the public sphere is not hostile to who you are as an individual. If your language is not available in the key sites in the public sphere, you are confronted with a world whose contours you are unable to exercise any influence on. You simply feel homeless.

The denial of proper public education to a significant linguistic community such as Urdu speakers is, to this extent, an attack on their sense of citizenship. Nehru grasped this point firmly. For him, patronage of Urdu was crucial to assuring Muslims that India was their home in every possible sense of the word.[8] In the long run, to Nehru, the most significant aspect of the language problem, even more important than the role of Hindi or English, was the future of Urdu, because it was tied to the fate of one of the minorities in India. Nehru also understood the political importance of language. Participation in social and political life cannot require a participant to ignore or repress meaningful cultural or linguistic affiliations. The denial of language rights is a denial of the political agency of a group to negotiate their terms of participation, it is to deny them a basis for active citizenship.

Does India want to be the sort of nation that routinely produces a sense of alienation and powerlessness for a significant group of its citizens? Does it want to be the sort of nation where imagined fears abridge the cultural possibilities of Urdu speakers? Does it want to be the sort of nation where a language as significant as Urdu does not find its proper place in public school education, thus unduly burdening its adherents? Ultimately, your receptivity to the cause of Urdu will, I suspect, turn less on an abstract consideration of rights and discrimination. It is when we look upon the fate of Urdu as a mirror to ourselves, that we may be moved by its claims. For that mirror will reveal a nation not living up to its full cultural possibilities, a nation not endeavouring to ensure that all its citizens feel culturally at home within it. The fate of Urdu ought to become a benchmark of our confidence and pluralism.

The Rights of Urdu

What I have been suggesting is that the fate of Urdu is tied to the kind of nation we want to become. It is for this reason that even non-Urdu speakers have a stake in the fate of Urdu. 'Whose homeland are we?' is a question that can haunt us all. The requirements of morality, citizenship, and prudence alike suggest that Urdu find its rightful place in public education. Reviving Urdu is by no means going to be easy. As the case of the Irish language shows, even immense state patronage can sometimes fail to revive languages; yet many survive even when marginalized by the public spheres. I am not a linguist and this paper has been only a plea to clear some space for a *proper* discussion of the question of Urdu. Any discussion ought to be cognizant of the sociological challenges that face most languages these days. There is no doubt that we need Urdu-medium schools as much as we need Hindi-medium schools. And there is no doubt that Urdu has to be more effectively offered as an option in government schools under the formula recommended by the Gujral Committee. The Three Language Formula—by privileging the Hindi-English-Sanskrit triad—has effectively marginalized Urdu. But what precise form should any modification of the Three Language Formula take? One suggestion advanced by Syed Shahabuddin is to modify the formula along the following lines: in north India, make the mother tongue the first language, with Urdu as the second language for non-Urdu speakers and Hindi for Urdu speakers. English should not be introduced at the primary level at all. This formula strikes me as being unworkable for three reasons.

First, whether we like it or not, English is here to stay and is a means of access to resources. It is ironic that Tamil Nadu and West Bengal, two states that had, under the pressures of linguistic nationalism, postponed the teaching of English till Class V have just reintroduced English at the primary level. The state has to accept and recognize that parents now demand English. Second, from the point of view of politics, we are not that far along that we ought to confidently put up

Urdu in competition with Sanskrit and turn the whole language issue into a zero-sum game. Sanskrit as a third language raises some profound issues—most notably whether teaching a third language has any effect whatsoever on its viability as a language of ordinary use. Third, from the point of view of justice, what is the issue? The issue is that parents should have the option of choosing the medium of instruction for their child, or at least what languages the child might learn. Suppose for a moment, we were the designing language policy in an utopian situation. I suspect that most of us would opt for a free choice model of the kind available in private schools, where the choice of first, second, and third languages is left to the child. The injustice against Urdu is that our educational system does not give Urdu speakers the same *choices* it gives everyone else. A just system would be one that satisfied the more important choices of most parents, not make them hostage to more and more compulsory requirements. In a context where Urdu speakers are not even being given their basic dues, it is a little Pollyannaish to imagine that suddenly Urdu can be made at least a second language for every child in north India.

Given the scarcity of resources, no simple formulaic solution is going to work, and each is going to polarize positions. What we are likely to need are well-thought-out mixed strategies. In certain districts we will need more straightforward Urdu medium schools because there is a population base to support those schools. In other places, the government will have to provide more resources to make sure Urdu is available at least as an *option*, along with other languages. In some cases it might be possible to even substitute a language for a substantive subject (or have the content of a substantive subject taught in the language to advance it). The point is that we need not reproduce the very structure of argument that helped marginalize Urdu in the first place. This was the structure of argument that de-emphasized parental choice in favour of state coercion and allocation of resources. There can be different ways, depending upon the context, of giving parents more choices in the languages their children will be educated in. We have been more caught up in giving our language an iconic status rather than in having an imaginative debate on linguistic pedagogy.

Urdu and the Questions of *Madrasas*

There has been considerable controversy over the place of madrasas in Urdu education. Madrasas, traditional religious schools, have come to be a cause for great concern in contemporary politics. Part of the concern is that madrasas have been accused of fomenting extremism and violence. In the Indian case, this threat has been overly exaggerated as part of a general anti-minority discourse. The involvement of a handful of students in extremist activities was the basis of condemning madrasas as a whole. But the fact is that since Independence, political *jihad*-ism has found it very difficult to get any substantive foothold in Indian politics, even though the spectre of anti-Muslim majoritarianism has often been a palpable threat. There are complex reasons behind this, not the least of which is the fact that democracy tames the radical edges of most religious movements. For all its faults and imperfections, democracy itself is a form of political education. The mere fact that grievances can be expressed, even if they cannot always be addressed; the fact that political competition, at least on some occasions, makes it imperative to address Muslim voters, removes the necessity for the kind of extremism that exists elsewhere. This is not to say that extremists do not exist. But they find it difficult to create political support for themselves. It is not an accident that India had made no significant contribution to the wave of international jihad.

But the question of extremism apart, what should be the place of madrasas in education, particularly Urdu education? Like with language rights, what should be the principles in terms of which one would think about an institution like the madrasa? Answering this question is made difficult by the fact that school choice is an endogenous effect. At the moment it seems that a significant number of parents are opting to send their children to these schools. But does this fact actually reveal anything about parental preference? Some have argued that the popularity of madrasas is due to a number of factors that have little to do with madrasas themselves. The lack of availability of secular Urdu education, the sometimes socially unreceptive environment for minorities, the sense of economic despair, the funding opportunities for religious schools, make all the community turn inward. But the popularity of madrasas has little to do with any enduring or necessary features of the Muslim community. It simply happens to be the easy option available. If other, more palatable, institutions that catered to some of the concerns of the Muslim parents were easily available, the madrasas would begin to diminish in popularity. It is for this reason that secular Urdu education schools are vital.

Although the choice for a madrasa education is driven by complex considerations, there is the vital question: what attitude should the state take towards them? As a matter of principle, there is a simple answer. The state ought to provide freedom of association under which communities are free to set up schools as they wish. So long as these schools are not seeking any state aid or even recognition, and in the absence of any compelling evidence that they are not preaching hate, these schools should be free to flourish. But, if any institution demands state aid or state recognition, then the state has a responsibility to ensure that the basic education provided in these institutions equips the child with an ability to navigate the modern world and understand the basic requirements of democratic citizenship. These considerations are still compatible with a wide variety of educational choices.

But the state has a fiduciary responsibility to ensure that any institution to which it provides a significant amount of material aid, or any institution that it certifies, conforms to some minimal requirements of a modern education. It is duty-bound to ensure that students from particular communities do not suffer any particular disadvantage due to unavailability of schools in their primary language. These principles should apply to minority as well as majority institutions. State aid: state standards kick in; no state aid: greater leverage and freedom. This principle will cut away the debilitating politics that surrounds the competition for state aid, and do away with the invidious distinction between majority institutions and minority institutions that has come to mark our politics. There is some reason to believe that even minority institutions will be more secure if protection of their rights were premised on some argument on freedom of association (a right available to all citizens) rather than on their being a minority.

In India, matters are complicated because the state not only subsidizes a number of religious schools, it actively grants them recognition as well. So long as the grounds for recognition are that students of these schools, like children of all other schools, have the ability to pass state-mandated tests there is no particular problem. But it is difficult to justify granting state aid to schools whose curricular requirement does not equip the student to pass modern accreditation examinations.

There are two considerations that might militate against this claim. The first is that given that religious schools are a reality, denying them aid will not ensure that children have other choices. It will only ensure that religious schools suffer a worse fate. This consideration is important in the short term. The state ought not to leave an education system it has supported, high and dry. But it does not follow that the state should not endeavour to give incentives to schools to move towards a modern education. If parents still want a traditional education, they should bear the costs. The second argument is that religious schools are often the choice of poor parents. By not subsidizing them, the state is in fact discriminating against the choices of those who can ill afford to send their children as well. Again, this is an important consideration, but is not decisive. All it points to is the need for having other forms of education cheaply available to poorer families so that they can have a genuine choice. It is possible to justify minimal interference in the affairs of religious schools; it is impossible to justify giving them state support, or accrediting them, if they do not fulfil some minimal requirements.

To the best of my understanding, the problem or the issue related to madrasas is basically that neither the Muslim intelligentsia nor the educated sections among Muslims has tried to analyse the problem objectively. Debate on this matter is too caught up in the fog of passion. It is understandable that non-Muslim and secular Muslim intelligentsia keep themselves away from the issue because of political sensitivities. It would indeed be very presumptuous of them to legislate on the preferences of other communities. But even educated Muslims are quite ambivalent about tackling the madrasa issue in a plural society like India. They have wholeheartedly supported the idea that madrasas should exist, and financially supported them to the maximum extent possible. But there is some evidence that the intelligentsia that supports the madrasas rarely send their own children to them. The few Muslims who can afford a secular education—no matter what the standard might be, or if it happened to be a third-rate government school—prefer sending their child to a madrasa. Not only do the madrasas provide free education, but they also provide food and lodging without charge. Besides, all teaching material in madrasas, small or big, is also supplied free. The madrasas, therefore, are the best option for those who cannot afford to feed their children at home. Free meals and other basic needs of livelihood for a child is a boon for poor parents.

It is true that the overall pathetic economic conditions in India and the allocation of considerably lower percentage of gross domestic product (GDP) for education does not allow the government to address the problem of Muslim education in general, let alone give it priority or due emphasis. This situation gave a boost to the madrasas. If data sources are authentic, half a million madrasas exist in India, where 50 million full-time students are enrolled (although some sources suggest this figure is an overestimation).[9] This, definitely, is a matter of some concern.

The question is, how is this concern going to be properly framed and addressed without using specious arguments or apocalyptic scenarios. My own sense is that the spectre of militancy invoked by the Hindu right exists, but the population speaks against the arguments of the Hindu right. Despite the existence of madrasas, India has not produced any dominant strains of jihadi Islam (though it must be said that secular schools can often produce militant Hinduism as well). We have to balance the discourse around madrasas for a proper discussion to be possible. The Bharatiya Janata Party (BJP) government had very laughably allocated Rs 20 million for madrasa modernization—a drop in the bucket, given the needs of 50 million students.

The real question is whether students are opting for madrasas because they have few other choices. The pertinent question is not militancy but justice. There are two issues of justice involved here. One is giving students choices. The second is the responsibility of the state in ensuring that the students who do go to these schools are minimally equipped to navigate the demands of the modern world.

Urdu is mainly studied by madrasa alumni who do not have adequate knowledge of Urdu literature—as they did not learn Urdu as a language in school—let alone have any grasp over the essence and ethos of literature. Their religious background also plays a role in their not coming to terms with the nuances and richness of Urdu literature. In fact, despite having studied at the university level, they remain unfamiliar with the secular ethos that this beautiful language and its literature contain and convey. Urdu literature has not gone down well with the *ulema* and they consider most Urdu literature as *kufr*. Ralph Russell has discussed this aspect in detail with reference to Ashraf Ali Thanavi, a liberal *aalim*. Thanavi, in his famous book *Bahishti Zewar*, has presented a long list of literary books that he considered as *kufr*. Of course, Urdu has survived due to religious educational institutions in free India. But at the same time, as we argued, it has also come to be regarded as a negative part of Muslim identity and sensibility. Its claims are rendered suspect.

What is going to be the fate of Urdu among the secularly educated Muslims? Have they also, ironically, now confined Urdu to the status of a madrasa language, something that cannot be detached from its religious and social moorings? The tragedy is that Urdu is no longer a market language, and is now shunned by the middle and even lower-middle classes. Like other élite groups, the Muslim élite might also prefer to send their children to English or regional language-medium schools for secular education, As a result, they were not keen to have Urdu schools. The poor, who could not afford a school education for their children, were obviously never in a position to advocate Urdu schools. For a long time now, the Urdu intelligentsia has been demanding facilities for teaching Urdu as an optional subject, but mainly in government schools and not in schools the élite send their own children to. It is of course the fundamental right of every child but, under the circumstances, there is no scope for teaching Urdu unless the issue is taken up in the backdrop of the Muslims' social conditions and is discussed rigorously, leaving aside populist perceptions devised by politicians and the intelligentsia. The Muslim intelligentsia— or for that matter, even the non-Muslim one—will have to take a stand on madrasas and discuss the issue with all its complexities.

Finally, the core issue begs an answer. The question is: if the Muslim community can run half a million madrasas by generating its own resources and not at all willing to accept any kind of grant from the government, what stops it from running the regular educational institutions of secular education? Why do the Muslims themselves run such a huge network of religious education while for secular education they expect everything from the government? To ask this question is not to suggest that they do not have the right to do so. Everything I have been arguing for should guard against this conclusion. But there is the rather curious fact that patterns of private institutional investment do not seem to be supporting secular institutions as much as they should. This is simply a plea that we need a more comprehensive understanding of the determinants of the choice between religious and secular education than we possess at present. It could simply be that patterns of philanthropy, as in all communities, tend to veer towards religious institutions. Hence more religious schools are being set up. But this may not be an indication of the genuine demands and needs of many members of the Muslim community. In short, we need to unsettle our assumptions about what madrasa education signfies.

Of late, the rapid growth in the number of madrasas has made the issue of Urdu-medium education more relevant. As discussed, under the given circumstances and keeping in view the social structure, teaching of Urdu as an optional subject has little relevance. It is for this reason that there was a substantive argument in favour of Urdu-medium schools. There is no reason to suppose that Urdu-medium schools are necessarily incompatible with equipping children with other important skills, including English. Indeed, it is quite possible to have dual medium schools with certain proportion of subjects being taught in different languages. But for this the government will have to take the lead in opening Urdu-medium schools for Muslim children. In any case, if the government, by any compulsion, implements the 86th Amendment, it will have to open schools in Muslim areas under the Sarva Shiksha Abhiyan or any other scheme. In areas with a large Urdu-speaking population, these schools will have to be Urdu-medium schools. In any case, in Urdu-medium schools, a child will have to learn three languages, including the principal language of the state, English as a foreign language, and his own mother tongue. But providing the option of Urdu-medium schools is imperative under the given circumstances. The madrasa controversy makes giving Urdu its due more, rather than less, imperative, as Ather Farouqui has so well argued.[10]

It is important to be clear about the argument being presented. The fact that the state should have some principled basis for accrediting schools or granting them financial assistance is not an argument for uniformity across all schools. These are merely threshold conditions to ensure that education does what it is supposed to do: empower individuals to make their own choices.

We must acknowledge that questions of pedagogy and their effects are complex. After all, militant radicalism can just as easily sprout among western educated middle-class youth as it can among children who go to madrasas (The London School of Economics has produced a number of jihadis in recent years!). So those political considerations should not be overstated. The state has to balance two principles: its interest in creating modern citizens and empowered students, and its interest in protecting the choices parents make for their children. The only way to balance the two is by insisting that any institution that is given incentives by the state conform to the basic requirements of a modern education. Articulating this principle does not entail being hostile to madrasas; on the contrary, it is a plea to leave them alone. But it is an argument for strengthening the secular system and making it compelling enough so that over time, and without coercion, madrasas seem a less attractive option. This will also be good for the future of Urdu.

By Way of a Conclusion

It is inconceivable that a liberal democracy should not commit itself to a more genuinely participatory cultural space where different languages and identities can find space under common institutions. The matter is quite simple. Every linguistic community should have the right to use their language in public and private life with no unjustified distinction, exclusion, restriction, or preference intended to discourage or endanger the maintenance and development of any language. In practice, these rights will be subject to two kinds of trade-offs. Society will determine what the feasible allocations are to make these rights possible. And this allocation will necessarily limit the extent to which languages can be promoted. But the first requirement of public policy is that, whatever level its allocations are pegged at, they should be non-discriminatory. The structure and design of our schools, and the imposition of language formulas have unduly burdened Urdu speakers. Second, the exercise of language rights will, in practice, be governed by a host of factors, including market imperatives. So some languages will naturally face a difficult time and may mutate or degenerate. But from the point of view of justice, it is important that state policies be so designed that they increase the effective choices of parents, especially with respect to preserving their languages. In the case of Urdu we have ensured that the choices of Urdu-speaking parents are restricted.

How these choices can be enhanced remains a complicated policy question. But the first order of business should be to acknowledge the principle at stake and not let the demands of justice be immobilized by prejudice or imaginary fears. My argument is that India will find a deeper, more enduring and meaningful unity if it recognizes that different cultural and linguistic groups ought to feel at home in it. Granting communities more control over their linguistic choices will not produce balkanization; rather, it will produce public institutions where every section feels a stake by acknowledging their language, which is a crucial aspect of a person's well-being. By effectively banishing Urdu from government schools, we have ensured that it survives only outside the mainstream and not organically linked to the wider currents in society. In doing so, we have only diminished ourselves and our democratic hopes. The defence of Urdu ought not be based on cultural nostalgia or on a misplaced sense of the sanctity of every language. It should rather stem from the requirement of democracy itself, our greatest asset.

Notes

1. I am grateful to Salman Khurshid for throwing up this important challenge; and to Ather Farouqui for tirelessly educating me in these matters. I suspect my position differs from his, but I have learnt from our exchanges.
2. Anita Desai, *In Custody*, London: Penguin, 1985, p. 145.
3. Charles Taylor, *Human Agency and Language*, Cambridge: Cambridge University Press, 1985, chapter 1.
4. The fact that the Central Board of Secondary Education (CBSE) has moved to short-answer questions in its exam, at the expense of basic skills like writing essays, is a testament to the debasing of language. We are increasingly producing students who cannot write an essay in any language.
5. See Robert King's lucid account in *Nehru and the Politics of Language*, Oxford: Oxford University Press, 1998.
6. *Report of the Official Language Commission*, 1956, p. 9.
7. Will Kymlicka, *Liberalism, Community and Culture*, Oxford: Oxford University Press, 1993, p. 175ff.
8. King, *Nehru and the Politics of Language*, p. 164.
9. With reference to the Ministry of Human Resource Development (HRD), Government of India (GoI), Arjumand Ara quotes the estimate that there are 50 million full-time students enrolled in madrasas. Arjumand Ara, 'Madrasas and Making of Muslim Identity in India', *Economic and Political Weekly*, vol. 39, no. 1, 9 January 2004. This surely is an absurd estimate perhaps because it was propagated by the HRD Ministry during the BJP regime through the National Council for Promotion of Urdu Language (NCPUL). Given the size of the Muslim population in India according to government data itself, the figures seem absurd, but is symptomatic of the extent to which we do not have credible data in this area. The Home Ministry also cites this data. See Bikramjit De, 'Abuse of Urdu', *Economic and Political Weekly*, vol. 39, no. 48, 27 November 2004.

    It is very unfortunate that every step taken by the NCPUL, an advisory body of the HRD Ministry, GoI, in the last seven years has proved to be either a mere fraud or manipulation during the National Democratic Alliance (NDA) rule when the HRD Ministry was headed by Murli Manohar Joshi. Despite all differences with the BJP, no one can believe that any government can wish to turn its organizations into fraudulent ones. The NCPUL is now also under public security for unbelievable corruption. Urdu-speaking people got a bad name for no fault of theirs when the council's Director was booked for corruption by the Central Bureau of Investigation (CBI) and the news telecast on 24-hour TV channels. For details of the NCPUL's misdoings, see 'The Great Urdu Fraud', *Milli Gazette*, New Delhi, vol. 6, no. 9, May 2005, pp. 1–15, 16–31, and a detailed report entitled 'Vulnerability of the Invincible', *Milli Gazette*, vol. 6, no. 21, 1–15 November 2005, pp. 16–17.

10.   See Ather Farouqui, 'Urdu Education in India', *Economic and Political Weekly*, vol. XXXVII, no. 2, 12 January 2002.

2

Language, Legitimation, and the Identity Status of Urdu and Muslims

YOGENDRA SINGH

Language forms a vital part of a people's identity. The significance of identity in the self-perception of the well-being of a community has increased manifold as societies have passed from tradition to modernity, and are now entering the pathway of post-modernity. Such factors as cultural self-consciousness and sense of identity was always strong in traditional times. Yet, it may be recognized that its intensity and pitch could not but be self-limiting in character due to the rudimentary nature of communication and production technologies. As a result, community identities had a segmentary character that could easily contain tensions of identity-consciousness generated endogenously or through external contacts. The static equilibrium that traditional societies had achieved due to the stable nature of technologies, and consequently of the production systems, also enmeshed languages. Besides, inherited occupations, limited space for migration in search of employment or vocation, and limited means of communication delimited the volatility of identities, whether linguistic or cultural.

The revolutionary advancement in the technologies of communication and production that modern societies have achieved and that are rapidly becoming more acute have enabled them to face post-modernity, and radically alter the traditional equilibrium. Today, as languages are becoming increasingly competitive, they can be differentiated on social and cultural levels. They serve as instruments of integration within the structure of the economic polity and urge for mobility and restructuring within societies. It is at this stage of encounter and challenges that linguistic endowments of a community are exposed to challenges of legitimization.

Language and Legitimation

Identities continually seek legitimation, and linguistic identity is no exception to the rule. However, identities, as they enter into the sphere of legitimation, acquire a more complex and overlapping form in which factors generally not contingent upon language, issues such as social and economic inequalities, social and cultural opportunities, and access to power or its iniquitous denial become more relevant. In this process, the traditional conception of language as a value-neutral phenomenon, implied in most theories of linguistic-structuralism or semiotics, tend increasingly to lose meaning. In this reckoning 'language forms a kind of wealth, which all can make use of at once without any diminution of stores and which thus admits a complete community of enjoyment; for all freely participating in the general treasure, unconsciously aid in its preservation' as postulated by August Comte on the issue of legitimation and power on an illusory assumption of linguistic communism. The fact that languages continually undergo processes of appropriation in the exercise of strategies of access to power, whether symbolic or cultural or politico-economic by classes, institutions, and individuals, is simply ruled out in this analytical domain.

Languages as cultural endowment enter the arena of legitimation through their instrumental linkages with institutions such as the state, market classes, and emergent cultural values or ideologies. The state invariably intervenes through social mechanisms of play of power to designate a language as 'official', which legitimizes its entry into the category of 'legitimate language' as suggested by Pierre Bourdieu. Its role as a teaching medium, and its entry into the school system, colleges, and universities marks its legitimation by the state through political process. The state also legislates, creates, and supports institutions that it recognizes as legitimate. The process through which languages are legitimated by the state for its patronage and recognition is a complex one because all those mechanisms through which this is achieved are indeed not political. The role of cultural and social mobilization of consciousness, the rise of new pressure groups, classes, or movements, and the ability of some sections to appropriate the influence generated by people's linguistic mobilization all enter into the process of legitimation by the state. It also ushers in a movement within the structure of a language influencing its phonology, morphology, or syntactical character. We find examples of this in state-sponsored codification of official lexicons, dictionaries, and other modes of codification of languages.

The market is yet another powerful institution that deeply influences the legitimation process of a language. The term 'market' can be interpreted in a narrow rational–economic sense, or in its much broader sense of general instrumental phenomena of social and cultural allocation of resources of people within the laws of supply and demand or acceptance and rejection. In exceptional cases where the state also fully controls the market, its role in the legitimation process of language may indeed be limited. Such situations being a rarity, it is reasonable to surmise that the market has, for centuries, served as an open-ended instrumentality of perpetrating changes in the structure of language, its role in society, and its legitimate appropriation for uses in varying contexts—economic, social, political, and cultural. The elements of literary creativity, such as style and form, despite enjoying a degree of autonomy over the market (which can always be debated) are yet subjected to forces of the market in substantial measure. The contemporary processes of globalization of the media and economy, however, keep introducing ever-new factors in which market forces dominate or influence linguistic legitimization, its identity, and role in the speech community.

Globalization leads to the unification of market institutions. It imparts its own pressures on the linguistic behaviour of the people from the local, regional, and national to the international levels of operation. It thus not only contributes to symbolic domination of emergent language forms through complex mechanisms of linguistic agglutination and the pecking order, but also activates awareness among languages placed lower in order of symbolic domination—such as languages of minorities, local groups, and of specific sub-cultures—to move towards intense celebration of their identities.

It is at this stage that the social–structural factors begin to impinge deeply upon the processes of legitimation of language in a society or in the global context. Pierre Bourdieu aptly describes this process:

All symbolic domination presupposes, on the part of those who submit to it, a form of complicity which is neither passive submission to external constraint nor a free adherence to values. The recognition of the legitimacy of the official language has nothing in common with an explicitly professed, deliberate and revocable belief, or with an intentional act of accepting a 'norm'. It inscribed, in a practical state, in dispositions which are impalpably inculcated, through a long and a slow process of acquisition, by the sanctions of the linguistic market, and which are, therefore adjusted, without any cynical calculation or consciously expressed constraints, to the chances of material and symbolic profit which the laws of price formation characteristic of a given market objectively offer to the holders of a given linguistic capital.[1]

It would be simplistic to assume that the symbolic domination of one or a set of languages is directly a result of market-governed instrumental rationality. This process is indeed a complex one, and results from people's orchestration of pre-existing linguistic orientations (which Bourdieu calls *habitués*) in stages over a period of time. The market-governed impulses towards linguistic adaptation are variously rationalized, depending upon the social and cultural background of the members of a specific speech community. In this context, the role of the élite and middle classes carries a great deal of significance. It is common knowledge that members of these classes, while professing strong commitment and loyalty to the language of their own speech community for reasons of political or ideological support, deviate markedly from its norm when they send their own children to educational institutions where the medium is a language of symbolic domination—Hindi or English for the Urdu-speaking community. Such duplicity is a rather universal feature of the élite and middle classes in almost all speech communities. It links the issues related to linguistic ideology with the structure of social stratification and classes in a speech community.

A community's response or self-consciousness about the future of its linguistic heritage cannot, however, be understood fully with only the help of a market-oriented paradigm or rationality. The significance of such factors as history and culture; the state of collective memories improvised and continually reinforced by myths, legends, and folklore; the state of internal/social differentiation within the speech/community; the ability to negotiate successfully between the general and specific linguistic ideologies; and finally, a community's overall perception of its future are important to comprehend the process and issues in totality. It is mainly due to the inter-play of these complex sets of factors that language becomes linked with problems of identity, on the one hand, and with the process of legitimization, on the other.

The Muslim Community: Its Identity and Urdu

The discussion of such analytical categories as state, market, social stratification, culture and ideology, identity and legitimation is intended to help the relationships between the Urdu language and the processes of identity and legitimation that have been constantly in operation within the Muslim community in India since Independence. These analytical categories offer a framework through which a relatively objective comprehension of the issues involved can be obtained. This theoretic approach can render it possible to have a more systemic and long-term appraisal of the problem; it could also lend a certain degree of practicality in understanding the parameters needed for formulating a suitable policy for the development of the Urdu language and Muslim community.

Language constitutes the most vital element in the making of the identity of any community, not to speak of the Muslims in India alone. Its orientation and depth, as also its sharpness, is governed by a set of other conditions. These include: historicity of the situation in which Muslims are placed in India after Partition; their socio-economic situation and their perception of the opportunity profile for themselves and their children in the context of their feelings of relative deprivation (in comparison with other communities); the role of their leadership and its structure and function; and the ideological and cultural movements within the community in the process of its historical evolution. All these factors, singly or in unison, influence the self-perception, subjective structure, and identity of Indian Muslims.

The event of Partition came as a serious blow to the Indian Muslims, in terms of both social structure and psychological effects. A larger number of the élite, middle class and entrepreneurial populace migrated to Pakistan, depleting the socio-economic balance of the community. This event also left a stigma for most Muslims living in India in the eyes of the majority community, as if it were they who were responsible for Partition. It also made most Muslims feel guilty at a time when the agenda for national reconstruction and development was being drawn, the Constitution was being adopted, and the planning process set in motion. Even though selectively, the Muslim nationalist leadership played a key role in this process, but the feeling of anxiety and sense of alienation continued among the majority of the Muslim population. During the first decade following Independence,

the Muslim identity in India could be characterized as being invo-
luted and repressed.

It was during this period that the Muslim leadership was co-opted
to help formulate a language policy. Institutional devices/appara-
tuses were created to promote Urdu both as a literary heritage and
as an element in the educational and administrative processes in
India. Probably because of the peculiar identity crisis from which
the Muslims and their leadership suffered, and consequent self-
consciousness, their response to formulate and follow up a vigorous
policy for promotion of Urdu remained weak. The debate among
some Muslim intellectuals on whether Urdu should shed its Arabic–
Persian script exemplifies this crisis of identity.

The quality and structure of Indian Muslim identity, however,
evolved in a more equilibrated form with much self-assurance in
the following decades. Several factors contributed to the process:
Muslims began to regain their self-confidence due to their increasing
significance in the democratic and electoral politics of the country;
they moved away in significant measure from the mode of co-optation
by the state to self-help, and created voluntary organizations
for promotion of their language and culture. This effort has been
particularly more pronounced in the western and southern parts of
India, but as much in the more backward northern states. Muslims
also took to establishing and reviving their entrepreneurial ventures
in trade, small and medium-scale enterprises commensurate with
their traditional vocations, and made noticeable progress in the
educational fields, particularly in south India.

Finally, the community also surmised that the division of Pakistan
and the emergence of Bangladesh was largely due to mismanagement of the Bengali linguistic and cultural identity, on the one hand,
and seemingly the failure of the two-nation theory based on religion,
on the other, which also contributed to the enrichment of Indian
Muslim identity. The deprivation suffered by the Urdu-speaking
Mohajirs in Pakistan and Bangladesh may also have given impetus
to this process.

These elements of history in the evolving of Muslim identity are
largely influenced by the social structure of the community in India.
Sociological studies have amply established that social and cultural
inequalities resulting from birth-ascribed, caste-like institutions among
the Indian Muslims prevail almost in the same manner as among the
majority non-Muslim population. The rules of pollution and purity

and cultural segregation, however, do not prevail among the Muslim communities, and the general social interaction is more egalitarian. Nevertheless, a large number of communities suffer caste-like social, economic, educational, and physical deprivation. This has been established by reports of the states and the Mandal Commission.

A peculiar feature of the Muslim community in India, which also affects their linguistic identity, is the absence of a specific regional or geographic identity, except in limited cases at the district level. According to a Peoples of India (POI) survey, there are 4635 communities in India, of which 584 are Muslim. With the exception of Arunachal Pradesh and Mizoram (where no Muslim community has been reported), all the states have Muslim communities ranging from one each in the states and the union territories of Goa, Nagar Haveli, and Sikkim, to a maximum of 87 communities in Gujarat. Among the states that have more than 30 communities are: Gujarat (87), Uttar Pradesh, UP, (70), Jammu and Kashmir (59), Rajasthan (44), Bihar (41), and Delhi (30). This demonstrates the internal social structural differentiation within the Muslim communities in India, and their significant geographical dispersal. It also impinges deeply on the nature of Urdu as the speech community among the Muslims in India, which is largely concentrated in the north, covering about 185 communities, if the numbers of UP, Rajasthan, Bihar, and Delhi are clubbed together. The POI survey also identifies a number of communities by their spoken languages. In all, 325 languages are recorded, and Urdu is spoken by 162 communities. This includes four communities listed as scheduled caste and 158 as 'other communities'. The term 'community' is defined for the purposes of this survey as, 'generally studied in ethnography which is marked by endogamy, occupation and perception'.[2]

Sociologically, the term community as used in the survey is inclusive of caste-like features, and since it includes many other social formations that are not isomorphic with caste, the term 'community' has been preferred. According to Singh:

The first problem concerned the definition of this type of community in an all-India framework. It required a level of conceptualisation that could subsume caste, non-caste structure, the minorities, and those who stood outside the *varna-jati* framework. First, jati is an all-India word for caste; there is also the word *kulam* or *samudaya*. While caste or caste-like structures are shared by a large number of communities, there are a few communities which both ideologically and in practice deny following caste norms. Caste has weakened to some extent in recent years in term of its adherence to hereditary occupations and norms of purity and pollution. It has also acquired new strength in a political sense as a constituency and as a vote bank. In fact it is acquiring the characteristic of a community as it sheds some of its traditional features. Therefore, the word community or samudaya (as it is called in some states like Kerala) could be a more appropriate concept for an all-India reference than caste with its various local names.[3]

As is evident from the above definitional clarification of the term 'community', the linkage between community and caste-like social organization, identified primarily through hereditary occupations (even though its present-day number may have renounced that occupation), is the predominant phenomenon. It closely affiliates, with some exceptions, the large majority of communities in India with caste-like features. It is quite arguable to infer that Muslims in India, segmented as they are through 584 communities, share equally with the rest of the population in India marks of social differentiation and status hierarchy based on occupational and endogamous exclusiveness. The imprint of this feature on ideology and identity can indeed be remarkable. The POI survey also notes that nomenclature of communities follows secular categories and only 'about three per cent derived their name from religious affiliation, such as adidharmi, ahmadiya, aradhyulu...' It should not, however, make one oblivious of the significance of religious and cultural factors in the emerging identity of Muslim communities in India.

This highlights the importance of social stratification and inequalities among the Muslims in India—internally, in relation to other communities in their midst, and the reality and perception of their economic and social inequalities in comparison with the majority community. Partition depleted the Muslim community of a major segment of the middle classes, élite, professionals, and enterprising population, and left the community impoverished in economic and social terms. However, the past five decades since Independence have restored the Muslim community in India to a level of social, cultural, and economic development. No doubt, its character remains uneven or regionalized, but there is some evidence to suggest that Muslims have made a mark in areas of trade, commerce, and small-scale industries that were in most cases commensurate with their traditional vocation. In the northern states, though, social mobility among the Muslims has taken place in very small measure; only a small middle class has emerged amidst a mass of the backward Muslim population. Recent studies suggest that a new emotional and political cleavage is emerging between the Muslim élite and Muslim *dalits* and backwards in many north-Indian states. There is a growing disenchantment among the Muslim masses who remain poor and backward and who feel that the élite, whether Muslim or non-Muslim, use them only as vote-banks without supporting them in concrete terms for social and economic advancement. The movement for affirmative action by the government in their favour is gaining wider support.

A similar feeling of relative deprivation prevails among the Muslim middle classes as well. Their representation in government jobs, professional positions, and in assemblies and Parliament remains disproportionate to their population. Rafiq Zakaria has in a study brought out such anomalies in telling terms. Muslims form 12 per cent of the population of India. In the general elections to the twelfth Lok Sabha, twenty states including Maharashtra, Punjab, Orissa, Rajasthan, and Tamil Nadu did not elect even a single Muslim. Nor was there any member from any union territory (except Lakshadweep, which is entirely Muslim). The Muslims' 12 per cent of the population should have given them over 60 seats: only 28 Muslims were returned to the 12th Lok Sabha.

Muslim employment in government services and public-sector enterprises presents an even more dismal picture: engineers 2 per cent, doctors 2.5 per cent, Indian Administrative Service (IAS) 2.86 per cent, ITOs 3.01 per cent, class I officers 3.3 per cent, and bank employees 2.18 per cent. Muslim representation in private enterprises is 4.08 per cent, marginally higher than in government-controlled organizations.[4] There is no doubt a complex set of factors that may explain the causes of this level of under-representation. It is also true that a similar sense of relative deprivation prevails among the backward-class Hindus too, and their movement to implement the constitutional provision for affirmative action was accepted by the Mandal Commission. There is a strong case for addressing this problem educationally and socially. The degree of significance, however, that this relative deprivation carries among the Muslim middle classes influences the structure and orientation of their very identity.

The resurgence of movements to strengthen cultural and religious identities, or to constitute Muslim identity on the basis of their cultural and religious exclusiveness, is a product of this perception and reality of social and economic deprivation. The Urdu language has, over the years, assumed a significant space in the structure of

Muslim identity in India. It no longer remains confined to an élite subculture of literary and courtly style. Its aristocratic antecedents have given way to a degree of homogenization, not of its style but its linguistic uses and its institutional foci that pervade among Muslims in almost all parts of India as part of their local cultural tradition. Over the decades since Independence, the class barriers and distinctive stylization in the uses of the Urdu language among Muslims have given way to a perception among them that language articulates their religio-cultural and civilizational identity. Its market orientation has, in this process, weakened along with its administrative patronage. The issue of cultural identity has thus appropriated the maximum space of legitimacy with regard to the Urdu language. This should engage our attention and analysis, as we seek to enlarge this space of legitimization through market, administration, and inter-cultural discourse.

An important consequence of all these changes in the identity-related dimension of Urdu is the weakening of its traditional accept-ability across religious distinctions and cultural divides. Traditionally, it had a wider cosmopolitan appeal among many non-Muslim communities in northern India and the Deccan. No doubt, it was not entirely due to Urdu's literary and cultural excellence or beauty. It was also because of the strong patronage and marketability that the language enjoyed in administration, education, and job opportunities controlled by the state and the feudal nobility. A major change that seems to have taken place in the community's response to Urdu after Independence is that it is now increasingly being confined to cultural, social, and religious uses by the Muslim community. An obvious reason for this constriction in the scope of the linguistic appeal was its systemic alienation from the mainstream processes of education, administration, and market mechanisms evolved after Independence. Besides, the absence of strong and well networked alternate institutional foci or systems among the Indian Muslims for the promotion of Urdu and its modernization, both pedagogically and horizontally, across the country on a voluntary basis has also led to its increasing shrinkage. This factor is invariably linked with the socio-economic backwardness of the large masses of the Muslims in India and shortcomings in their systemic political empowerment. These factors together add on to the emerging linguistic Muslim identity in contemporary India—a volatile structure that is complex and multi-layered.

Educational Backwardness of Muslims

Literature on the sociology of development has adequately illustrated a close, causal relationship between the level of literacy and education, and the overall development of a community. In this parameter, with the exception of a few southern states, India as a whole lags way behind other Asian countries. Even though the gross literacy level has moved up, about half of the Indian population is illiterate and illiteracy is abysmally low (in some north-Indian states as low as 90 per cent) among females. In this scenario of our failure after more than fifty years of Independence, a study of the educational levels of Muslims in India conducted by several scholars have confirmed this phenomenon.[5]

This educational backwardness of Muslims goes together with their economic deprivation and the development policies of the state and central governments have not succeeded in removal of this so far. Studies conducted by the Planning Commission, National Sample Survey, National Council of Applied Economic Research, the Minorities Commission, and Minority Panel Reports consistently confirm this situation. Muslims exist at the neglected end of the spectrum of communities of India in the social, economic, and political fields and in the process of empowerment. Their political representation in assemblies and Parliament, as noted, has been declining in spite of the fact that 'there are 14 districts in India with a Muslim majority and 114 districts where the Muslim population is 15 per cent and above.'[6]

This disproportionate political representation may be due to the electoral process, the nature of unbalanced political mobilization, alliances, or an electoral practice that calls for reform, but the significant outcome of this perception of weakening political empowerment nonetheless deeply influences the sense of Muslim identity. Community identity being a complex and composite phenomenon, the perception built by the Muslim community on the basis of the Urdu language and its present condition of neglect and decline are bound to constitute an organic and vital element in the formation of the Muslims' collective identity.

The State of Urdu Language and Policy

Historical facts and the social psychology following Partition deeply influenced state policy in India after Independence. The Urdu language issue was viewed by political actors and the non-minority at large from an emotive and communal perspective. One could easily discern the shadow of these elements in constitutional and state response in delineating state policy. A major element in the new situation also emanated from the democratic process itself, which had to reconcile a new policy orientation toward Urdu quite iniquitous in comparison with the status that the language enjoyed before Independence or during the British regime. It was marginalized in the affairs of state and administration; in the education system, as a factor influencing curricula or as medium of teaching and research, Urdu was trapped in the Three Language Formula that never quite took off. In terms of actual and credible policy implementation, despite the policy having a positive direction, it turned out to be a sham. Urdu was accorded 'official' status as a language by states without integrating it with the vital institutions of education, educational processes, and administration.

Institutions, panels, commissions, academies, and the National Council for Promotion of Urdu Language (the erstwhile Urdu Promotion Bureau) were created to promote the cause of Urdu but did not succeed. Instead, state-sponsored institutions, academies, and the National Council for Promotion of Urdu Language created a perception among the large masses of the Muslim population in India as being strategies to play self-serving computational politics within the leadership structure of the Muslim community. These neither made a meaningful impact nor enjoyed legitimacy or credibility among the Urdu-speaking community, which was increasingly localized in the Muslim community.

Salman Khurshid aptly articulates this phenomenon:

The fact is that the government has pursued such policies as have resulted in cultivating a whole breed of pro-establishment Urdu people. Most of these people are those who did not get a chance to make it big in life and are keenly looking for a chance to enter the establishment canon. All of them are totally indifferent to the questions of the survival of Urdu. None is ready to touch the nerve of the problem out of a fear that it might incur the wrath of the government. It is ironical that these pro-establishment Urduwalas themselves have become instrumental in executing the detrimental policies against Urdu. As a result, Urdu is facing threat not only from the bureaucracy but from the Urduwalas who comprise mainly university teachers and those whose primary concern is inter- and intra-university politics of language and public-relations only. They are least concerned with the demands of their profession.[7]

The crisis confronting Urdu, to which Salman Khurshid draws attention, is an outcome of the failure of the state to implement the language policy at the primary and secondary levels of education, which could ensure that the Urdu-speaking community in India had a sizeable student population that could join colleges and universities to pursue higher-level studies of either the Urdu language and literature or other disciplines with proficiency in this language as the medium of instruction or examination. Without this back-up from students graduating through high school or the secondary level to pursue higher studies of and through the Urdu language, Urdu departments in colleges and universities have waived the requirement of having learned Urdu as a subject for admission to obtain a degree in Urdu. Many analysts of this problem have felt that this policy had two negative consequences for the growth of Urdu: First, de-linking of qualification in Urdu as a prerequisite for higher studies took away the pressure from the state to effectively implement the policy of teaching Urdu at the primary and secondary levels; second, it produced undergraduates and graduates with degrees in the Urdu language who, in most cases, were below standard. This substandard population of Urdu graduates has in course of time perpetuated a vicious cycle of deteriorating standards of Urdu in India.

We have indicated some of the socio-historical situations that rendered the prospects of Urdu rather uncertain. Given these factors, the choice that Muslim intellectuals in colleges and universities had to make was indeed critical and without any alternative solution in sight. The process of mobilization of consciousness with self-assurance in ideological and cultural terms had not yet been realized. It must be understood that, following Partition, the major institutional anchorage on which the stability of Urdu language was based had been fractured, if it had not totally disappeared. This included the support of the state, which delimited the market prospect of the language. Coinciding with the crisis of ideology and culture, on the one hand, and the self-defensive or guilty response of the élite and middle classes, on the other, Indian Muslims encountered a complex and uncertain situation.

Growth of the Urdu Language Since Independence

One could not possibly evaluate the growth of Urdu in India either substantively or normatively without defining the term 'growth'. As outlined in the conceptual enunciation of this problem, a language can achieve a high-growth trajectory if it enjoys institutional support from the authorities (governments, public bodies), is well integrated with the market forces, which implies production and circulation of communication and intellectual products of high quality, and generates skills in productive resource generation through rational human resource development, is supported by not only the speaking community but also élite and middle classes, and has been able to orchestrate all these forces into a coherent cultural and ideological policy. It is these factors that together define the boundaries of influence a language enjoys as it reaches the credible level of legitimation and inculcates such confidence among people in a world where languages—local, national, and cosmopolitan—are fiercely competing today for 'symbolic domination'.

Unfortunately, a systematic study of languages in India—Urdu being no exception—has not been done using these analytical parameters. However, it is still possible to arrive at some conclusions with regard to trends of development of Urdu in the country since Independence. In substantive terms, a survey of four representative states—Bihar, Andhra Pradesh, Maharashtra, and West Bengal—carried out by Ather Farouqui allows a picture of trends in the education of Urdu in the light of policies, particularly the 'Three Language Formula' enunciated in the Resolution on National Policy on Education and modified in 1975 by the Gujral Committee. The impact of these policies on the promotion of the Urdu language has been disappointing, mainly because of loopholes in the policy that allow an escape from teaching Urdu or using it as a medium of instruction wherever possible. The condition of Urdu education is reported to be the most pathetic in UP. There is not a single primary or junior-high school with Urdu as a medium. The only two Urdu-medium high schools in the state are those run by and affiliated to Aligarh Muslim University. During the last decade, there has been a mushrooming of private schools all over the state. This phenomenon has given rise to several complexities in the field of education. About 50 to 60 per cent of these schools are unrecognized. Yet, the middle and lower-middle classes opt to send their children to these schools, even though it is well known that these institutions are merely business centres.[8] These schools teach only up to the fifth standard. UP does offer students a choice of studying Urdu or through the Urdu medium, but under the scheme the desired choice of optional subjects is not available, which discourages students.

Though UP offers the option of appearing for the junior-high school examination with Urdu as the medium, the number of students opting for it is negligible. It was below 500 in 1982, compared to nearly 40,000 in Bihar in the corresponding year. Even Muslim students prefer the Hindi medium as it offers more options for higher studies of their choice and for employment. New schemes introduced for teaching through the Urdu medium introduced by the late Chief Minister H.N. Bahuguna have not made progress due to lack of any motivation and qualification of teachers. Bihar has, comparatively, done better but this may be due to a self-help policy pursued by the Muslim community. Urdu teaching in the state is integrated with propagation of religious values, and hence *dini madaris* have proliferated with considerable support from the lower and lower-middle-class Muslim population. It is believed that the class character of population support for Urdu is qualitatively different in Bihar, compared to UP. Every year in Bihar, writes Farouqui, 60,000 students take junior-high-school and high-school examinations in the Urdu medium'. The Madrasa Education Board, which runs the *madrasa* schools, is recognized by the Bihar government as being equivalent to other recognized boards. There is some effort to introduce science and technology (vocational) education through these schools, but a major problem faced is the non-availability of Urdu textbooks. The absence of rational management norms or standards in the Madrasa Education Board are also held as factors thwarting progress. Formulation of courses of study and their content in these schools is also an area that requires much reinforcement and reform.

In western India, Maharashtra has emerged as most successful in promotion of Urdu education. This is largely due to private and voluntary initiatives through individual businessmen and trusts who run and manage Urdu-medium schools efficiently; teaching is conducted with regularity and merit. It is reported that Bombay city alone has 124 registered Urdu-medium high schools, while there are 230 such institutions throughout Maharashtra. The state has also pursued a co-operative and helpful policy. Middle-class Muslims there also encourage their children to study in Urdu-medium schools because of their high standards and an appreciable degree of motivation. Probably due to the predominance of the business ethos in the region and its mercantile culture, combined with Muslim cultural self-awareness, Urdu-medium teaching is most encouraging in the state. Urdu as an optional subject is available at college and higher-level educational institutions. Several convents also offer facilities for teaching Urdu. Maharashtra perhaps offers a model of how education through voluntary efforts and state co-operation can produce results.

Andhra Pradesh in south India offers another test case of the state of Urdu education. The Deccan has been one of the major centres of Urdu literature over centuries. Hyderabad, along with Delhi and Lucknow, occupied a significant place in promoting and sponsoring literary creativity in Urdu along with its specific contribution to augmenting linguistic style and sophistication. Before Partition, Urdu enjoyed both political patronage and élite support or acclamation. Osmania University in Hyderabad state (before reorganization) employed the Urdu medium for higher education, including engineering and medicine. Following the reorganization of states, Urdu has not fared well in the new Andhra state. 'Urdu is moving fast towards its imminent death in Hyderabad', writes Farouqui. Most Urdu learning is confined to madrasas or schools run on a voluntary basis. The drop-out rate in these schools is high, running up to 40 per cent between Classes I to IX, and touches 43 per cent at the high school level. In terms of class support, even the lower-middle segments in Hyderabad do not usually patronize Urdu-medium schools.

The implication of the trends observed in Urdu education in these four states in the context of future policy for promotion of language and literature, preservation of cultural identities of these communities, and integrating Urdu education with the forces of modernization such as its marketability, contribution to science and technology, and elevation of the level of holistic development of the individual is obvious. The contribution of the state in this process seems to run into serious self-limiting conditions due to a complex set of factors. The counter-pulls of vote-banks in the democratic political structure, the Muslim community's limitations due to geographic spread, and lack of strong mobilization of the community on this issue render the response of the state lukewarm in extending institutional and financial support on the desired scale—hence the centrality of the role of private and voluntary efforts from within the Muslim community to take control of this dimension of developments. The issue of the nature of identity formation, cultural self-consciousness, and social mobility in the class composition of the community in economic and political fields are important sociological elements that define the level of success in this direction.

For its development as a language and literary style and subculture in India, Urdu had linkages with traditional institutions such as the camp, the court, and the *bazaar*. A qualitative change has taken place in all these institutions of traditional support. The camp and the court have been replaced by a modern democratic state which, in its day-to-day functioning, is guided by pressure groups and special interest group politics. After the reorganization of states on linguistic lines soon after Independence, Urdu—not having a territorial viability—was accorded official recognition but lacked consolidated political punch. This factor, together with the fluctuations in the process of identity formation of the Muslim community, gave way to a set of new social and psychological forces that came into play in the subjective and objective evaluation and perception of Urdu by the Muslim community. Some of the crucial objective factors that have contributed to the marginalization of Urdu education and the prospect of its future growth have already been outlined.

With regard to subjective parameters, a study conducted by Ather Farouqui on issues related to various aspects of the future prospects of Urdu in India and reasons for its inadequate pace of development brings out interesting results. Most scholars continue to view the Urdu language and literature as a part of composite Indian culture shared both by Muslims and non-Muslims. They do not associate Urdu exclusively with either Islam or the Muslim community. They are also not prepared to allow autonomy between Urdu and Hindi as they feel these are 'sister' languages and products of Indian historicity of a secular tradition. They blame over-dependence on the government and indifference among Muslims to teach their children through the Urdu medium for the slow momentum in growth of the language. Obviously, most Urdu literati continue to espouse the secularist perspective with regard to the substantive character of the Urdu language and literature. However, the changing ground realities in respect of the pattern of growth of Urdu education is pulling it fast into an exclusionist Islamic domain. The changing social structural forces, both within the Muslim community and outside, may partly explain this process. However, a lukewarm state policy on Urdu education could be held to share major responsibility for de-secularization of Urdu teaching.

In the absence of incorporation of Urdu teaching into the composite structure of teaching institutions, schools, and colleges, it is the madrasas, under the leadership of grassroot Muslim traders, artisans, and peasants belonging to the lower-middle-classes, that have taken the initiative where religion and religious teaching over-arcs the ethos of education. Thus, a strong linkage between religion and education is established; it is not undesirable by itself and, given the ambience generated, it is possible to integrate it within a composite rationale of culture. The evidence available so far from the evaluation of curricula and textbooks being used in the madrasa schools does not support such orientation. Urdu's exclusive identification with the Muslim community has no doubt increased over the past fifty years despite the fact that some intellectuals continue to believe in its secular and composite cultural character. The indifferent manner in which the policies for the promotion of Urdu education have been articulated and implemented by various states, and the response of the Muslim community to save Urdu as their religio-cultural heritage—rather than as an instrument of modernization, particularly through the dini madaris—have today given Urdu education, language, and literature an exclusivist character that is now enmeshed with the Muslim religio-cultural and even political identity. An important dimension of this problem is the linkage between Urdu teaching and education, and the emergent market phenomenon in our country and abroad.

Urdu Education, Communication, and Market

Traditionally, the scope for Urdu-educated graduates remained largely confined to teaching institutions, administration, civic, judicial and revenue positions, and management of the estates of the feudal nobility with a cultural symbiosis with their court. This system, which reached its peak during the medieval period, continued with some changes throughout British rule in India. It was following Independence and Partition of the country that major changes were introduced in the social structure and in the economic and educational policies that placed Urdu education and its market relationship in an entirely new environment fraught with marginalization from most of the earlier institutional linkages. The market for Urdu graduates began to shrink, and its scope was mainly confined to a few available teaching jobs. Much later, job opportunities in the media and in communication have become available, but they depend upon the growth of the Urdu-language press, the publication industry, and the electronic broadcasting media. A meticulous analysis of the interface between Urdu education and the dimensions of its marketability is required for evolving policies that add vigour to the process of economic and social modernization of the Muslim community.

It needs to be noted that, following Independence, the character of all the institutions with which the the Urdu language and education traditionally derived patronage underwent radical changes. The traditional bazaar, which was essentially anchored on the mercantile economy with an artisan mode of production, was pushed into the industrial phase of development, and is now being increasingly overwhelmed by the predominance of the services sector of economy. The nature of the court as it existed in the medieval and colonial period has been now structurally replaced. A few of its earlier features may still survive, even though de-legitimated. The institution of feudalism and its social and cultural bases have been abolished. The nation is going through a rapid, though painful, process of two revolutions—liberal-democratic and industrial-technological. All these developments have caused a legitimization crisis in many aspects of traditional Indian cultural and social institutions. Most of these are now undergoing rapid adaptive changes to cope with the evolving realities. Language and education are no exception to this process.

In any future planning for the growth of Urdu education, significance of linkages with the market and economy would need to be kept in mind. Globalization of the economy and technology, with enormous backing from the communication and media revolution, creates a unique situation in which the cultural and market space that any language should aim at capturing or integrating with becomes truly international. The pace of migration between societies accelerates, creating a rich cultural and linguistic diaspora of communities and religious sects on a global scale. The magnitude of the service sector overwhelms the production process in an economy in which telecommunication, journalism, media and production, and dissemination of symbols and messages dominate the occupational profile. Trade, banking, insurance, transportation, management, and production of skills begin to play a crucial role in the process of production of commodities. This makes for a significant and qualitative difference in the structure and function of capitalism and industrialism. Skilled and educationally sensitive labour becomes essential to any job performance, even at the lower levels of the occupational hierarchy. With the quick turnover in technological innovations and shifting grounds of the capital-investment relationship, which a global economy pre-ordains, continual upgradation of skills becomes necessary. The occupational profile of an individual ceases to have a lifetime tenure; redundancies of jobs may become endemic and learning of new skills essential.

Education and information tend to have a determining role in defining the market situation for individuals in this scheme of events. This neo-capitalist and post-industrial economy not only globalizes and homogenizes cultures and consumption patterns, but also creates enclaves of local cultures and subcultures globally through expansion of the ethnic and linguistic diaspora and intensification of communication-culture linkages through new information technologies of telephony and the Internet. Thus, even a minority and local linguistic group gets market viability, particularly in the domains of culture, journalism and communication, and commerce. Urdu is no exception to this process.

This new phase of economic development not only alters the market situation for a language externally (outside the country), but also within one's own society. The crucial factors that govern the viability of a language for the internal market are modernization of language training and its orientation, and cultural cohesiveness of the language community and its degree of economic and social development. These factors, together or individually, influence the market prospect of a language. For instance, the literacy level of the community has a direct impact upon the growth of communication through the media via a specific language. The role of the press, radio, television, and other modes of communication in the promotion of culture and skills through the Urdu language has been reduced in India not only because of the faulty policies of the state or corporations, but also because of relatively lower levels of literacy and education of members of the Muslim community.

The condition of the Urdu press and television has not been commensurate with the general expectations of the Muslim community. The number of registered Urdu newspapers/periodicals bears no relationship with those that are actually published or are in viable circulation. According to the Ministry of Information and Broadcasting's figures for 1992, there were 347 registered newspapers/periodicals of which only about fifty were reaching public hands. Studies show that a steep decline took place soon after Partition; only a marginal improvement was discerned in the 1980s when some dailies were freshly launched and a few that had ceased publication were revived.

Compared to newspapers, weekly Urdu publications command a wider readership and have a respectable circulation. The Muslim readership does not effectively patronize the Urdu press, particularly members belonging to the upper-middle segment of the population. In some parts of the country, particularly in south India, the Muslim community runs its own publications in the regional medium although the reach of the Urdu press may have increased. The state-controlled media, such as radio and television, have slots for Urdu programmes, but radio has, in this respect, given a better account of itself than television.

The tolerance for programmes telecast in Urdu, as the communal violence in Karnataka in 1994 following the telecast of a Urdu news bulletin suggests, is indeed poor. The problem is compounded by ad hoc programme scheduling. A comprehensive and well-integrated policy needs to be evolved in this regard, in consultation with various opinion leaders of the community.

The significance of a vigorous and objective Urdu press and publication of literature in Urdu lies not only in its value in enlarging the scope of the market for Urdu graduates, but in serving as a reliable and credible channel of communication within the Muslim community for imparting balanced and responsible information about events, socio-economic, and cultural developments that may effect their well-being. Studies have shown that the press not only serves as a channel for information, but also as a mechanism for construction of realities. In certain situations of ideological or cultural conflicts, it has been amply verified in case of events relating to communal violence that several segments of the Indian press, particularly the vernacular, has been found to suffer from prejudices and biases in reporting events and interpreting them through lead articles and editorials. The national (English medium) press has given a better account of itself in this regard. However, to suggest that it does not ideologically construct realities with regard to events and opinion would be simplistic.

In a plural, and democratic society such as ours, there are bound to exist ideological differences, contradictions of interests, and social, economic, and cultural prejudices. The press has an enormous responsibility and challenge to serve not only as a medium of communication of events, point of view, policies, and decisions in a balanced and responsible manner, but it also serves as a vehicle of articulation of cultural symbols and aspirations that are deeply embedded in the structure of a people's identity. The press, therefore, occupies a major facet of empowerment and legitimization of the identity of the Muslims in India. It has to evolve an active and integrated institutional set-up not only to promote Urdu education, but also to act as a reliable and responsible mediating instrument through the power of communication and information that it naturally enjoys. This is particularly relevant since, on a wider scale, there exists a feeling among the Muslim community that the press in general has not fully empathized with their social, economic, political, and cultural concerns.

As has been witnessed in the case of Urdu education, with regard to the Urdu press, it has been found that regions where the entrepreneurial level of educated Muslims is higher, there is a relatively greater initiative to launch and support the Urdu press. This happens even though the percentage of the population knowing Urdu may not be large. The sense of cultural identity is, however, strong. In a study, Ather Farouqui has reported: 'The state of Urdu journalism is far more favourable in those linguistic regions of India where Muslims are proud of their identity and are actively sharing the region's cultural ethos. In all such regions the percentage of the population that knows Urdu is much smaller than that in north India. Even in those regions where Urdu is not the mother tongue of Muslims, the status of Urdu is much better than in north India, and the attitude of Muslims towards Urdu is pragmatic not emotional.[9] It may be added, however, that the relative advancement of Muslims in the southern and western regions of India in economic and educational fields has given them innate social and cultural strength to articulate their identity in a self-assured manner. Studies have consistently shown a positive correlation between levels of economic and educational development of a community and its cultural and socio-political self-awareness.

Legitimation and Symbolic Domination

A major loss to the Urdu language over the past fifty-plus years has been the decline in its role as a language of symbolic domination. As reviewed earlier, the spread and acceptability of this language to the Muslim community, and also the increasing perception that Urdu is essentially a linguistic and cultural heritage of the Muslims in India following its alienation from the composite cultural stream, has enhanced its significance as an element of its dominant culture. The paradox of the contemporary situation with regard to the place of Urdu in the cultural space of the Muslim community is that while it has gained more space in the sphere of cultural domination within the community, it has lost its significance as a cultural element of symbolic domination. Cultural domination in the sociological sense implies predominance of the impulse in a certain community for accepting the cultural legitimacy of the cultural trait concerned, such as, in this case, language. The notion of symbolic domination, on the other hand, means the degree of prestige that the same cultural trait enjoys within the community or outside. The major changes that came about in the policy of the state toward the Urdu language, affecting consequently or even in a general sense its market value, and the apathy of the upper- and- middle-class Muslims towards the Urdu language and appropriation of the language merely as a medium of religious communication, have reduced both its utilitarian and ideological space.

What is now needed is restoration of the lost symbolic domination of the language. This would require radical restructuring of the policies for its future growth, as also an attitudinal orientation of the members of the Muslim community toward both the instrumental and cultural significance of this language for themselves, and for the nation as a whole. It may be added, however, that contradiction between the roles of cultural versus symbolic aspects of domination for the language may also apply to other Indian languages, including Hindi. For these languages, which enjoy considerable patronage from the state and articulate a higher degree of cultural domination in the social space, there is a painful realization of their increasing loss of symbolic domination. This is due to their precarious linkages with a market that is in the process of economic globalization and revolutionary structural changes in the economy. Regional languages are coming under increasing pressure of deeper and enhanced interaction with other languages and cosmopolitan languages, such as English. This happens due to growth in the volume and scope of communication, greater inter-cultural and inter-regional and international interaction, and a higher incidence of migration between regions and outside the country. This has resulted in a high degree of increase in bilingualism in the country on the one hand, and on the other, a greater tendency toward creolization of languages in India due to uninhibited assimilation of vocabularies of other regional or even cosmopolitan languages. The pressure from the market, which is constantly extending its scope and significance, is such that each Indian language would have to reorient their policy of self-growth.

This applies in particular to Urdu, which suffers from a double handicap: first, from a crisis of legitimacy and increased loss of symbolic domination which, compared to other regional languages, has made it a victim, in larger measure; and secondly, the indifference of the state authorities and administration in augmenting the process of its growth. Analysis so far clearly suggested that, for promotion of the Urdu language and its education, a systematic policy needs to be evolved that is sensitive to all factors responsible for its present state of alienation. It should take into account the factors responsible for the continual failure of state policies for promotion of Urdu. It needs to evaluate the measures for increasing its marketability and its techno-economic and managerial utility. It must evolve policies to draw the interest of the Muslim élite and middle classes to enhance the quality and extent of their support for the language.

In this context, the Muslim leadership would be required to exercise a large measure of autonomy and adopt a policy of self-help by enlarging their participation in a democratic movement for the promotion of Urdu education in relation to their community as well as the state. In a democratic polity, the extent to which the rights of a community are sympathetically addressed by the state depends upon the extent of community mobilization and consolidation of its voice of demand and protest.

It appears that, due to the vacillation and indifference of the élite and middle classes among the Muslim community (with the exception of some regions), the leadership role in the action programme and promotion of Urdu education has been taken over by the lower middle and lower classes. Their efforts have no doubt served the cause of Urdu education. But due to their narrow ideological perspective, mainly defined by the demand for preservation of religious and traditional values, such as in the madrasa paradigm of education, the possibility of its linkages with the modernization process becomes self-limiting. There is a need for an integrative effort by the Muslim community as a whole, incorporating all its various configurations of class and leadership, to evolve a new paradigm for definition of the place of Urdu education that could help in enlargement of its scope of legitimization, and ultimately symbolic domination. Such an effort would involve not only recomposition of policy and structure of social responsibilities, but also reorientation of ideology and the scope of cultural domination that the Urdu language and literature have to impress upon the community.

Ethnicization of the Muslim Community and Urdu Education

This analysis is derived mainly from application of two significant sociological categories—community and ethnicity—to explain the contemporary social processes not only in India, but the world over. What is remarkable about this process is that communities are being increasingly ethnicized. In other words, a composition web of social and cultural relationships that communities traditionally nurtured across religious differentiation is now fast being replaced by segmentary religious and cultural self-consciousness. It takes the form of ethnicity or an ethnic movement when this process is politicized. The ethnicization process evolves primarily from politicization of cultural and existential self-images of a community. This is followed by revival or recreation of myths, legends, and images in order to orchestrate perceptions and orientations. Both the Muslim and Hindu communities in India have been going through this process extensively. The root of communal politics in India is entrenched in such a soil.

However, the ethnicization of the Muslim community, which has been recently accelerated but has had a long history of cultural movement, remains open-ended. It is the result of heterogeneity of local and regional, social and cultural traditions which the Muslims in India continue to acclaim in common with most other non-Muslim communities. The legitimization of a composite culture for India continues to remain valid for reasons of Indian historicity and plurality of its cultures, and social formation with many inter-civilizational traditions that may be defined as Indian heritage and tradition. No doubt, many influential leaders and parties, both among the Hindus and Muslims, wish to culturally segmentalize ethnicity. But the contemporary social reality of inter-cultural tradition of communities in India across the religious divide do not warrant regimented isolation or a closed agenda of ethnicization. The POI survey, using the measure of 776 cultural traits (trait being 'treated as cultural value, which is unique'), records that the correlation of traits between 'the Hindus and Muslims which is very high indeed.' It says that 'communities also share traits in terms of good habits, material culture, folklore, etc. There is also an all-pervasive sense of reverence for the sacred and for life...traditions blend with Islam and other organized religions at the folk level. Almost all communities throng the sacred shrines associated with pirs, etc.'[10] This cultural commonality continues to subsist along with distinct orientation of communities on traits specific to religion, power, and domination that now increasingly assume a relatively larger significance. The process of ethnicization particularly draws inspiration from these latter sets of cultural traits of all communities, to which the Muslims of India are no exception.

Ethnicization as a cultural process has a vital role to play in the developmental strategies of the Urdu language in India. To a large extent, Urdu has been a victim of this process. The halting and half-hearted policies of many states, particularly in Uttar Pradesh, bear testimony to this fact. More importantly, when ethnicization takes emotional overtones, or when its agenda is defined by narrow, segmentary articulation of cultural values that seemingly conflict with other cultures, the result is communal conflict. This obstructs a realistic and objective appraisal and formulation of policies. The two processes begin to spin off in a vicious cycle. This has, to a large extent, clouded even the voluntary promotional efforts by the Muslims for the growth of Urdu, for instance through the madrasa paradigm of education. In such matters, appraisal of policy requires objectivity with a sense of empathy.

Can it be concluded that the ethnicization process of the Muslim community (as also of other communities) in India necessarily obstructs the development of Urdu education? The answer is clearly negative. A review of the development of Urdu education in India since Independence indicates that most promotional activities for Urdu education have come from the internal resources of the Muslim communities, coinciding with increasing sensitivity to their cultural and religious identity. It is no doubt also linked with the process of social mobility among the Muslims, such as the rise of an entrepreneurial and mercantile class, surpluses generated from the Muslim diaspora from India, and the overall improvement in their economic condition in general, even though in limited numbers (as in the case of other backward Indian communities). The fact that promotional successes are more viable in the western and peninsular Indian states than in the northern ones is illustrative of the relationship between voluntary effort for a more integrated form of promotion of Urdu education (as distinct from the madrasa pattern) and the level of economic mobility among the Muslim population.

Towards a Paradigm

A recapitulation of the issues raised regarding identity, legitimacy, and their relationship with Urdu education of the Muslim community in India in terms of policy implication emphasize several facts. It is clear that during the fifty-plus years since Independence, the cultural identity of the community has evolved in a direction that is more in consonance with the norms of a cultural pluralism, liberal democracy, and social and economic modernization. There are, however, still some pockets of segmentary ethnicization of the community. These, however, arise more due to a perception, often legitimate, of the state's economic and educational policies either not being fairly implemented, or not being evolved in an equitable manner to deal with Muslim backwardness in Indian society. There seems to be a credible level of association between positive or negative direction and pattern of ethnicization of the Muslims in India, and the level of their social, economic, and educational upliftment.

The reality and perception of the state's lukewarm response to formulating and implementing an effective action plan for promotion of Urdu education, and a Constitutional covenant for the Indian state has led to considerable alienation of the Muslim community. Consequently, the voluntary efforts by the Muslim community itself for the promotion of Urdu education has served as a more sure and effective measure to achieve the goal. Its negative fall-out, however, is that Urdu has increasingly lost its link with the paradigm of a composite culture for India, hugely celebrated and idealized since Independence. It has become isomorphic to an exclusive Muslim cultural reporter. It has robbed the Muslim community of their confidence in the legitimacy of state policies, which profess or idealize such values. Obviously, it sends a message to governments, both at the centre and provincial levels, to recognize this problem not so much as a cause specific to the Muslim community's welfare and development, but of the nation as a whole in its search for a secular, pluralistic, and democratic path to economic and cultural modernization.

For achieving the dual objctives of national integration and promoting their community's individual identily, the Muslim élite and middle classes need to set a credible example for their espousal of the cause of Urdu through active participation in Urdu education for their family members and children. On this issue, one notices a difference in response between the lower- and lower-middle-class Muslims and their upper- and middle-class compeers. The children of lower- and lower-middle-class Muslims go to Urdu-medium or madrasa schools either because better schooling options are not available to them, or because they cannot afford their heavy expenses. Their inability to get access to an education for themselves and their children that could ensure better jobs and social and economic mobility may, under such circumstances, be misconstrued as their support for Urdu education. This aspect of the problem has not been empirically studied and requires such investigation. But the complaint from the Muslim masses about the double standards practised by the élite who send their children to English-medium private schools or convents while professing their commitment to education through the Urdu medium may have its basis in factual evidence. In this matter, Hindi or other regional languages, encounter identical problems in terms of class orientation to linguistic responses to education.

There is a complex cultural basis to this behavioral phenomenon. It is related to the process of what has been termed 'symbolic domination' and 'legitimacy' of a language in the linguistic cohort within a society based on the perceived prestige value of the language, its association with power structure, élite cultural style and form, and finally its market and economic significance. These factors go in totality to shape the index of a language's 'symbolic domination' or legitimacy in a society. In exceptional circumstances, however, when the ethnicization process in a cultural or religious community becomes highly exclusivist, the index of symbolic domination may get dissociated from market and economic impulses and turn totally culturological. There is evidence from the responses of the Muslim community in India, especially in the madrasa form of education of Urdu, of such dissociation. In such cases, the notion of symbolic domination of the Urdu language is appropriated entirely in a religious-cultural form of orientation. And the notion proceeds together with intensification of the processes of ethnicization of the Muslim community. This issue needs to be addressed while formulating policies for Urdu education in the country in which the state and/or community is involved.

The root of this problem cannot be examined in purely culturological terms. The pressures of job opportunities, the economy, and the market govern educational choices in contemporary societies. It has been observed that market determination of educational-linguistic choices increase within societies with lower levels of social and economic development. In economically advanced societies, where the policy of social welfare with wider scope and range for available jobs, the flexibility in choices for education, at least at the higher levels, is greater. This flexibility is very narrow, or not available at all, in developing societies in broad social structural terms. This process narrows down job opportunities not only in the sectors of the economy controlled by the state but also in the private sectors. During the past few decades, there has been some increase in available jobs, particularly in the media and selected service sectors, but its scope is seriously limited for graduates with degrees in the Urdu language. Most young Muslims with such an education have therefore either taken jobs in the informal sectors of the economy like small business or trade, the family occupation in arts and crafts, low-level jobs, cottage industries, or in various other modes of self-employment. In relatively better or higher quality jobs, employment for Muslim youth is closely related to their qualification through the English medium, which the technical, professional, and vocational education systems continue to mandate. Under the circumstances, and also considering the fact that such pressures for modernization of education have befallen not only on Urdu but most other regional languages of India as well, it is essential to evolve a well-considered strategy for Urdu education that establishes viable linkages with the demands of the market, on the one hand, and the cultural and religious aspirations of the Muslim community, on the other. The Muslim community will have to evolve a consensus on this issue because the institutional focus for available media of Urdu education ranges from madrasas to the relatively more integrated forms of school and college education through the Urdu medium.

Learning from the past, it may be anticipated that a community consensus of this kind may not be immediately possible. There are many complex factors at work. However, one can clearly anticipate that its emergence at the pace of economic and socio-political modernization would proceed onwards in the changing context of globalization. It may be necessary during the interim period, therefore, to offer alternate institutional and pedagogic alternatives for the education of the Muslim youth in and through Urdu education that respond to the emergent demands of the market and culture in a viable fashion. Voluntary efforts and institutions, such as the Nobel Laureate Professor Muhammad Abdus Salam Foundation, have a crucial role to perform in this context. Modernization of the syllabi constitutes a very crucial and strategic aspect of the mechanism establishing viable linkages with the market, the state, and the community's socio-cultural aspirations. In this sphere, work needs to be taken up both at the regional and all-India levels. The various state-sponsored or supported institutional apparatuses made available for the promotion of Urdu literature and heritage that constitute a corpus of talent should be involved in such an exercise. It may also be necessary to coordinate such efforts toward modernization of syllabi in co-operation with national and state agencies of educational administration, and with the private corporate sectors/organizations of the economy.

In conclusion, it may be stated that a paradigm for the promotion and progress of Urdu education in India has to take into consideration the social, cultural, economic, and political aspirations of the Muslim community. These factors, which largely govern the demand side of the community response, would have to be integrated with the social and institutional processes of legitimization, identity, and concerns of symbolic domination. These processes, however, do not operate in isolation. On the contrary, the institutions and social processes that deeply influence or even govern them arise from orientations of the state, the market, the élite, and the middle classes within the Muslim community. Perhaps the manner in which the Muslim community defines or strategically places itself in respect of its perception of cultural and religious identity in this sphere may not pose as many difficulties as specifically defined. It is the aspiration for cultural identity, when contextualized in terms of religion and politics, that renders the process of consensus building precarious and difficult. In this context, the role of the Muslim leadership, élite, and the Muslim middle classes assumes a great deal more importance.

Notes

1. P. Bourdieu, *Language and Symbolic Power*, Cambridge: Polity Press, 1991, pp. 50–1.
2. K.S. Singh, *'People of India: An Introduction'*, Calcutta: Anthropological Survey of India, 1992, p. 23.
3. Ibid, pp. 23–4.
4. Khushwant Singh, 'With Malice Towards One and All', *Hindustan Times*, 25 April 1998.
5. M. Manzoor Alam, '"Indian Muslims" Challenges of 21st Century', *Academy Journal*, 1–31 May 1998, pp. 10–11. The backwardness is reflected particularly in the low level of literacy. According to the Planning Commission survey of 1987–8, the national literacy rate was approximately 52 per cent, while for Muslims it was 42 per cent. There is a marked disparity between Hindus and Muslims in respect of education. The percentage of Hindus who have completed high school is 7.9, whereas for Muslims it is 4.5. The percentage of Hindus who have studied beyond high school is 3.4, while for Muslims it is 1.2. The percentage of graduates among Hindus is 7.9 whereas for Muslim it is 2.3. The drop-out rate is quite high among Muslims. On an average, about one-thirds of Muslims drop-out before attaining the requisite level. The highest drop-out rate is observed at the middle level. The drop-out level in the 20–4 years age group is as high as 50 per cent. Gender disparity in respect of literacy among Muslims is appalling. The literacy rate of Muslim women is 34 per cent. Only one per cent of Muslim women reaches high school. Haryana has reported total illiteracy for Muslim women. At the all-India level, Muslim women are way behind Hindu women. The attainment of higher education among girls is a rare phenomenon even in the urban areas.
6. Ibid., p. 13. There are 120 parliamentary and 700 assembly constituencies all over the country in which Muslim votes are a decisive factor in elections. Compare it to the 5.19 per cent Muslim representation (28 members) in the 12th Lok Sabha. The highest percentage was 8.5 in 1980 (46 members). In UP, the number of Muslims elected to Lok Sabha has fallen considerably in spite of the fact the Muslims constitute 22 per cent of the state's population.
7. Salman Khurshid, 'A Note on Urdu Education' (mimeographed), 1997.
8. Ather Farouqui, 'Emerging Dilemma of Urdu in India: A Viewpoint', *South Asia*, New Series, vol. XVIII, no. 2, December 1995, p. 101.
   _____, 'Future Prospects of Urdu in India', *Mainstream*, Annual, November 1992.
   _____, 'Urdu Education in India: Four Representative States', *Economic and Political Weekly*, vol. XXIX, no. 14, 2–14 April 1994.
9. Ibid.
10. Singh, 'People of India.'

3

Urdu in India in the Twenty-first Century

BARBARA D. METCALF

Bahut samhjee thee ham is daur kii firqa-parastii koo
Zubaan bhii aaj shaikh-o-barhaman hai ham nahiin samjhee
Agar urduu pe bhii ilzaam hai baahar see aanee kaa
To phir hinduustaan kis kaa vatan hai ham nahiin samjhee
Chaman kaa husn too har rang kee phuuloon see hai Raashid
Koo'ii bhii phuul kyoon nang-i chaman hai ham nahiin samjhee[1]

'I understood a lot about the prejudices of this age/Today languages too are Brahmins and Sheikhs? I don't understand.//If there are charges against Urdu, that it too is an outsider/Then whose homeland is India? I don't understand.// The beauty of the garden comes from flowers of every colour, Raashid/Why is any flower at all a disgrace to the garden? I don't understand.'

This verse from an unpublished *nazm* of one Raashid Banaarsi encapsulates themes that are explicit or implicit in any discussion on the place of Urdu in independent India. One theme, of course, is the charm and beauty of the language, which even this modest stanza illustrates as well as asserts. Few would dispute that Urdu is indeed one of the flowers whose beauty is essential to any linguistic garden. Second, the poem points to the accusation that Urdu is an outsider, not our *'ham vatan.'* This the poet stoutly denies. Related to this is the spoken or unspoken assumption that Urdu is a Muslim language. The poet is prepared to recognize that there is sectarian chauvinism on the part of spokesmen—*shaikhs, brahmans*—for some groups, but expresses himself dumbfounded that a language could be mistaken for such a person! All these points deserve attention, as does one not alluded to in the poem but which is at the centre of any discussion of Urdu held in the spirit of Dr Zakir Husain. That, of course, is the theme of Urdu as a medium of instruction whose only goal should be reaching the maximum number of students, coupled with providing methods and materials to assure the psychological and intellectual success of the children and youth involved.

Urdu in India till 1947

Speaking from a historical and not a literary or linguistic point of view, three key points stand out in the modern history of the Urdu language. First, in the eighteenth century, Urdu emerged as a highly developed language of poetry, above all, in the cities of Delhi and Lucknow.[2] A great deal of historical work in recent years has thoroughly reshaped the view of the eighteenth century, that British historiography, and the nationalist historical writing that evolved from it, invariably presented as a period of 'decline, decay and confusion.'[3] This period did indeed see dissolution of central authority and incursions from Afghans and Persians that were devastating for Delhi and the area crossed by the invaders.

But the view from Delhi was not the whole story. Even as central authority dissipated, regional powers arose that were vital, well administered, and gave rise to new cultural and institutional forms. Part of the stimulus to the cultural vitality of the era in such realms as poetry and art came from the dispersal of those who knew cosmopolitan art and literature. In regional capitals, the hybrids that blossomed as a mixture of cosmopolitan and regional cultures, gave rise to new developments in Rajput, *pahari*, and other regional schools of art; to new traditions of music; and to vibrant poetic expression. The Urdu literature of the eighteenth century should be seen in this context. Although not only a product of the north—it had flourished far earlier in the Deccan—Urdu essentially underwent the same process as other regional languages as Persian forms and conventions were used in such languages as Sindhi, Marathi, and Punjabi. Far from being 'foreign', Urdu represented the enrichment of a local language with the vocabulary and literary forms of Persian. It gradually displaced a language based outside the subcontinent (even though after half a millennium of use Persian was thoroughly part of the governing and intellectual life of the cosmopolitan classes).

A second major stage came in the nineteenth century with the decision of the British government to supersede Persian as the official governing language with English at the highest levels and the vernaculars at the provincial and lower levels. Government patronage, moreover, would be primarily directed at these languages and not at classical languages, among them Persian, Sanskrit, and Arabic. This ushered in a long period in which, for a broad swathe across Bihar, the North Western Provinces, Avadh, and the Punjab, educated élite males typically learned Urdu. In this period, Urdu became a modern prose language, undergoing a transition common to regional languages across the country (and in Europe as well, as particular forms of languages became standardized through novels, newspapers, and other prose writing). Urdu was used for new genres of the new intelligentsia, like journalism and the novel, which typically communicated new values and images of the person and society, and in old genres associated with traditional learning—everything from Quranic translations to medicine. It was the language of élite, 'scribal castes' of all religions. Thus, the early tracts of Hindu revival movements like the Arya Samaj at the end of the nineteenth century were written in Urdu.

Finally, a third critical stage came in the movement to replace Urdu as an official language, above all in the United Provinces, with Hindi. The decision of Lt. Governor McDonnel in 1900 to give Hindi equal status with Urdu was a major landmark. There is no need to rehearse the story, familiar from many colonial contexts, of the emerging religio-ethnic identities, the heartache and the bloodshed, that arose in the decades before Independence. In those years, languages may not have 'had' religions but they did indeed come to be important symbols of religion—religion not in the sense of worship, spiritual guidance, or authority but in the precise sense of symbols of the interests of one group rather than another. A major stream in Hindu nationalist thought pictured Urdu as a strumpet, the handmaid of the old, decadent *nawabi* culture, in contrast to the language of respectable people, Hindi. It was, in short, a convenient symbol that Hindu reformers used as a foil for the values of a portion of the new, modern bourgeois. Ironically, of course, Muslim reformers had exactly the same goal. Hindi, on the other side, was dismissed as a language of country bumpkins.[4]

In any case, the fact that Urdu then became the national language of Pakistan, a country established on the grounds of the religion of the population, made the position of Urdu in its own homeland even more difficult. Christopher Lee, who collected the poem quoted above, concluded from looking at a number of recent Urdu poems that 'Urdu' had come to stand in this poetry as a symbol of Muslims themselves who, along with the language, were prejudicially viewed as 'foreign'. Old stereotypes, especially those associated with the quasi-religious values of nationalism, die hard. Rather than insist on the injustice of the views that have marginalized Urdu, one would do well, perhaps, to not re-fight the tired battle of origins, but to focus on issues relevant to the problems of Urdu in the present day in terms of shared national values. As Prime Minister Jawaharlal Nehru said on the day Independence was gained, 'We are a free and sovereign people today and we have rid ourselves of the burden of the past. We look at the world with clear and friendly eyes and at the future with faith and confidence.'[5] Any historical interpretation that defines some of its citizens as foreign is surely a 'burden of the past' that must be shed.

That Urdu is an official language in Pakistan can be seen as a fact of positive importance for India for the simple reason that both countries could profit from their common interest in the language and their efforts to develop it. Urdu was the mother tongue of no more than 4 per cent of the Pakistani population in 1947, and Bengali resentment at the dominant place of Urdu in the country contributed to the break away of Bangladesh in 1971. Language issues continue to trouble the country today. One distinguished literary figure of Pakistani origin has suggested that the most one can hope for in Pakistan is the development of Urdu as a 'functional' language:

No matter how one tries to squash the initiatives to promote it, [Urdu] will grow, if only because our [Pakistani] national life requires it. So there is no danger of Urdu disappearing. But what kind of Urdu would that be? Not the language that will make the subtleties of the poetry of a Mir and Ghalib accessible or result in a renaissance of Urdu literature. It will be a functional language.[6]

I remember many years ago being told with a straight face in Lahore that there were only two people in the city who spoke Urdu, one from Lucknow and one from Jaunpur (two cities in India)! Nonetheless, Pakistan has achieved remarkable success in making Urdu its *lingua franca* and certainly it would be rational and useful for both countries to share their materials and standardize usage in such fields as science and technology. Moreover, let us look forward to a day when, as in the case of Europe, link languages will be welcome as old enmities give way to regional integration that benefits everyone.

Key Decisions in Relation to Urdu Since 1947

Other chapters in this volume cover issues related to linguistic policy in great detail. I wish to touch only on two background issues. The first concerns not language *per se* but the very vision of the independent state. Nothing was more central to British colonial ideology than arguments and policies that justified their rule on the grounds that India was not a nation but a mosaic of separate peoples, infinitely divided by language, caste, region, and, above all, religion. In a pervasive theme in arguments of colonial legitimacy, British colonialists saw themselves alone as providing the umbrella under which these groups could flourish. Their policies, whether in quotas in the army and schools, in the theory of 'martial races,' or, above all, in the creation of separate systems of personal law, helped create the very divisions they took as natural.

As the nationalist movement evolved, one issue became paramount, namely that free India was to be a liberal state in which each individual was a citizen by reason of his or her individual identity and not as part of some larger collectivity. To this end, no decision was more basic or more important than the abolition of separate electorates. Yet, significant vestiges of the old colonial ordering of society persisted. One grew out of the urgent need felt by the new state to rectify the injustices of the old society toward the erstwhile 'untouchables' and 'tribals' for whom a policy of compensatory discrimination in education and government employment evolved. A second was the continuation of separate personal law. Neither was intended to be permanent nor sanctioned as an enduring principle. The overriding commitment to a society undefined by primordial attachments is enshrined in India's Constitution. Citizens do well, therefore, to make their arguments in public life on the basis not of the needs of any one community but of the public good.

The second key decision concerns language. As the nationalist movement grew from the 1920s on, a central platform of the Congress party became the commitment to governance in mother tongues. The old provinces of British India did not take this as a principle.

Although it was clear that there would have to be a reorganization of the states, entailing not only the incorporation of the princely states but also a redrawing of boundaries that were often too large, it is worth noting that Nehru himself resisted this policy of his own party, preferring the kinds of divisions based primarily on territory common to places like the United States rather than any that would intensify any kind of primordial identity. Language however, unlike religion, is, in India, regarded as a legitimate basis for making claims, and Nehru's concerns were, as a result, overridden.

Given that the Urdu-speaking population in India nowhere constitutes a majority and hence the basis for a geographic unit, attention has been primarily given to encouraging literary production in Urdu and the provision of education in Urdu. Nationalists like Mahatma Gandhi, Dr Zakir Husain, and others concerned with basic education had believed that education was best provided in the national languages—of which Urdu was one—and at initial stages wherever possible in the mother tongue. The post-First-World-War years saw the foundation of Jamia Millia Islamia (1920) as an Urdu-medium institution, by people who had left Aligarh where English was dominant, as well as the foundation of Osmania University (1918), the first vernacular language university in the country. One of its leaders was none other than Syed Ross Masud, grandson of Sir Sayyid Ahmad Khan who had pioneered English-language education for Muslim Indians at the university level almost half a century earlier.

Debate on the issue of linguistic medium is a very lively one in educational circles worldwide. As a land of immigrants, Americans have been relentlessly monolingual. In my own state of California, however, with an ever-growing population of first-language Spanish speakers, although considerable sentiment favours an English-only policy, many people recognize the pedagogic value of teaching little children in their mother tongue both to enhance their self-esteem and confidence as well as facilitate their learning. Some even see that having native Spanish speakers in our population (along with those whose language is Chinese, Vietnamese, Punjabi, etc.), should be seen as a resource for all Californians in encouraging a new generation of citizens who speak more than one language. Those who have had first-hand experience of teaching children of Urdu-language families in Urdu, in places like Bihar, believe that such children deserve more schools and better instruction through the medium of Urdu than is currently available.

What is to be Done?

Concern about the condition of Urdu in India is widespread. Urdu illiteracy has increased without question. In both Delhi and Hyderabad, for example, a few years back, I found that libraries with Urdu holdings might have no librarian able to read the script. There is a shortage of teachers able to teach Urdu adequately. Publication programs in Urdu literature and historical texts have languished. One reason to be concerned is a cultural or aesthetic one—that Urdu is indeed a 'flower' of Indian and world value that should not become, as one contributor to this volume described it, 'an endangered species.' A second reason, whether implicit or explicit, is a conflation of Urdu with the population of Muslim Indians whose problems, to speak generally, include poverty; representation in education, government, and the professions; as well as integration into the larger society. It is important to be clear about the limits of that 'conflation' since diffusion of knowledge of Urdu, however desirable, would not solve these problems and might, if it contributed to enclaving or 'ghettoizing' Muslims, be counter-productive.

I propose three suggestions for further consideration. First, it would seem to me that perhaps too little attention has been given to thinking about the place of Urdu outside the boundaries of India and to recognizing the advantages on all sides of embracing Urdu as a transnational language. In part that language, to be sure, exists only in an oral form, above all in the language of Indian film. My Indo-, Pakistani-, and Fijian-American students, for example, whose families may be in origin Punjabi or Gujarati or Sindhi speakers, all are thrilled when I include a movie like 'Mughal-e-Azam' for class viewing. As I write these words, I turn on the radio for the evening news and find a special interview in progress with Sanjeev and Karuna Loomba, sounding very British to my American ears when they speak, but singing Urdu *ghazals* from their new recording. The booklet with the disc of their romantic songs includes not only the Urdu original but also translations in English, French, and Spanish.[7] At a *mehfil* in Hyderabad I had the pleasure of attending in the early 1990s, a literary figure based in England maintained that the future of Urdu was in the diaspora, as the language became something of a lingua franca among populations that might have been originally speakers of other regional languages. Whether his conviction is being, or will be, borne out as an older generation passes is not clear, but certainly, as the example of the new recording suggests, there may be some forms in which Urdu abroad does flourish. In music and film, the Urdu that is shared is largely oral.

Also important would be, as alluded to above, to interact more actively with Pakistani Urdu production, keeping one's eye wholly on the shared goals of literary encouragement and education, striving to view collaboration 'with clear and friendly eyes,' to return to Nehru's phrase, because the goal of linguistic development is a worthy one.

Secondly, while lovers of Urdu have differed profoundly on the value of publishing Urdu in Devanagari, it would be a way to reach those drawn to Urdu but unfamiliar with the script. To enlarge the circles of those who know Urdu literature, even if they only know it through nagri, can only help the language's larger place. There might, for example, be room for more bi-script publications with facing pages in Nagari and *Nastaliq*. Former prime minister Atal Behari Vajpayee himself has said 'there was a need for close interaction between people speaking Hindi and Urdu for enriching both languages', and such dual-script publications could contribute to this goal.'[8]

The final issue I want to propose for general consideration has to do with the truly unique situation of Urdu in India as a second or minority language. Urdu and Hindi are legally two languages but linguistically one. In common use, they are often indistinguishable. I like to tell the story of checking into a hotel in Agra some years back when the hotelkeeper inquired of me, '*aap nee itni shuddh Hindi kahaan seekhi?*' (Where did you learn such pristine Hindi?) I had just, in fact, spent six months learning Urdu in Lahore.

Is the situation of a child of an Urdu-speaking background in a Hindi-medium school, therefore, parallel to that of, say, a Spanish-speaking child in an English-medium school in the United States? In the latter case, a child may not be able to express the simplest needs or respond for some protracted time to the instruction being provided. The Three Language Formula, and the option for mother tongue instruction, should not be an iron frame so that one fits it precisely or gets no support for a language at all. What would be the implications in this case of adding the Urdu script and vocabulary as a second language at a later point, after the child has acquired basic skills and grammar via nagri, especially if facilities for Urdu instruction in primary classes were deficient? The situation would be quite different in a first-language Marathi or Kannada environment. In Maharashtra in particular ,there appears to be considerable success with elementary education in Urdu, whereas in Karnataka the decline of the Urdu medium seems to be going hand-in-hand with a decline in Muslim literacy.[9]

Overall, the challenges to effective schooling go far beyond the issue of language. The colonial legacy of preferred investment in the higher levels of education remains as do patterns of rigidity and rote learning despite all the good intentions of basic education developed in proposals like the pre-Independence Wardha scheme, mentioned above.[10] In the spirit of Dr Zakir Husain, as well as of Mahatma Gandhi with his absolute conviction that the end can never justify the means, the first priority in issues related to education must be the welfare of the children and neither rigid rules nor 'burdens of the past'.

Notes

1. Quoted in Christopher Lee, '"Hit It with a Stick and It won't Die" Urdu Language, Muslim Identity and Poetry in Varanasi, India', *Annual of Urdu Studies*, vol. 15, no. 1, 2000, pp. 337–8, from 'Abdu'l-Hayy', an unpublished Urdu poem from the personal collection of the author.

2. English speakers must be grateful to Khurshidul Islam, C.M. Naim, Frances Pritchett, Ralph Russell, Annemarie Schimmel, and Carla Petievich in particular for making these early literary achievements known.

3. This is the chapter title from Percival Spear, *A History of India*, Harmondsworth: Penguin, 1965.

4. See Christopher R. King, The *Hindi Movement in Nineteenth Century North India*, Bombay: Oxford University Press, 1996, and Vasudha Dalmia, *The Nationalization of Hindu Traditions: Bharatendu Harischandra and Nineteenth-Century Banaras*, New Delhi: Oxford University Press, 1997.

5. Prime Minister Jawaharlal Nehru, broadcast from New Delhi, 15 August 1947.

6. Professor Muhammad Umar Memon in 'A Question of Literature', *The News*, Karachi, 30 August 2001, *http://www.jang-group.com/thenews/index.html*.

7. Interview on National Public Radio, Weekend 'All Things Considered', 13 January 2001. The disc is 'Inspiration Unfolding,' Times Square Records. See *http://www.insideworldmusic.com/library/blrevs70b.htm*.

8. Quoted in 'Urdu to Get its Rightful Place: PM' in *Islamic Voice*, January 1999.

9. See many issues of the '*Islamic Voice*' for reports of successful Urdu-medium schools in Maharashtra, particularly as an option to (often badly taught) English, *www.islamicvoice.com*. I am grateful to Kelly Pemberton for suggesting this link.

10. See for example a report of schools in Tamil Nadu deploring the failure to invest in early education, 'Cart before the Horse', in contrast to a model of investment in primary education in the mother tongue in Karnataka, 'Shimoga Shows the Way', *Islamic Voice*, November 2000.

4

Strategies for the Survival of Formerly Dominant Languages
(With Special Reference to Urdu)

THEODORE P. WRIGHT JR

The declining status of Urdu in north India since Partition[1] is not unique, for it is only one of a number of languages of formerly dominant 'elites'[2] that have lost their power through the overthrow of multi-ethnic dynastic states and/or the dissolution of colonial regimes. I shall analyse fourteen cases for comparison with Urdu: seven that have declined or died out (Manchu in China, Coptic in Egypt, Gaelic and Latin in the British Isles, Quechua in Peru, Arabic in Spain, and German in Eastern Europe), and seven that have not only survived but flourished and even dominated in post-imperial eras (Anglo-Saxon over Norman French, Spanish and Portuguese over Amerindian languages, Afrikaans in South Africa and French in Canada achieving bilingual status with English, Hebrew over Yiddish and Arabic in Palestine/Israel, and Catalan in Spain). In general, those that have survived or even flourished were brought by large-scale colonization and/or religious conversion and were not just the languages of a conquering military élite. For instance, Urdu is the official language of Pakistan and Kashmir, and the *lingua franca* of the former, where many Arabs, Persians, Afghans, and Turks settled and a majority of the pre-existing population was converted to Islam. This is not the case in north India and Bangladesh where, in the former area, the majority of Hindus failed to be converted to Islam and, in the latter, where a majority accepted Islam but not the Urdu language, which remained an élite medium until 1971.[3]

Clearly, the varying characteristics of these cases affect the outcomes and the lessons to be drawn for the survival of Urdu.

First, let us consider the question of whether the formerly dominant language is itself indigenous or alien. One would think in an age of nationalism that an indigenously-based speech would have a better claim for toleration than a foreign one. Urdu, unlike Manchu, was not the mother tongue of the Turco-Mongol invaders of north India who founded the Delhi sultanate, but grammatically a compromise with Brijbhasha, Hindavi, or Hindustani (proto-Hindi popular dialects), the Indo-European vernacular of the conquered Hindu 'mass subjects' but written in the exogenous Arabo-Persian script and with an infusion of vocabulary from Arabic and Persian.[4] Spoken Urdu and Hindi are, I understand, mutually intelligible even though the written forms are not.[5] Can it be that it is the script rather than vocabulary that has been the real stumbling block to its acceptance?

In this respect, the invader's switch to Urdu resembles the eventual victory of Middle English over the Norman French of William the Conqueror (1066).[6] The Norsemen who had invaded France a century and a half before (AD 911) had quickly accepted French in the course of Christianization in place of their own unwritten Germanic language. Over a much longer period of ruling England (1066–1415) they switched again to their Anglo-Saxon subjects' tongue, but with an infusion of French vocabulary. The usual explanations for this anomaly are: too few Normans, too much intermarriage, and the necessity of the rulers to communicate with their subordinates. It must be remembered that, unlike north India, both rulers and ruled were Catholic Christians.

By contrast, the dominant Arabic rulers' language of Moorish Spain (AD 711–1492) never melded with the Romance tongue of their Christian subjects, nor were the bulk of the latter converted to Islam.[7] Arabic in Spain, although more cultured than the Spanish of the time, did not survive the 'reconquista' and the final loss of Muslim political hegemony with the fall of Granada in 1492. Those Muslims who would not convert were expelled. The enforced conversion of the rest to Christianity and the strict prohibition by the Catholic Inquisition of not only the practice of Islam, but the very speaking of Arabic did not save these 'Moriscos' from expulsion in 1609.[8] A few Arabic words in the Spanish vocabulary are all that remains. Indian Muslims, especially in Hyderabad, are well aware of the dangerous precedent that this loss of 'Andalus' to Islam[9] represents for Urdu.

A surprising contrary case to the victory of the Anglo-Saxon subjects' language in Norman England and of Hindustani-Urdu over Turkish in north India is the failure of the Gaelic revival in Ireland despite all manner of support and subsidy by the Irish government after independence from Great Britain in 1921.[10] Two and a half centuries of severe sanctions against both the Gaelic language and the Roman Catholic Church of the Irish majority by the British Protestant 'ascendancy' so weakened the former, but not the latter, that the Census of 1911 revealed that only a rapidly declining 18 per cent of Irish knew the historic mother tongue, and even fewer were 'monolingual' in it. Colonization by Presbyterian Scots in the north produced an English-speaking Protestant majority there, which led to partition of Ireland at independence in 1921, much like British India a generation later. Gaelic had come to be so much associated in peoples' minds with poverty, illiteracy, and rural backwardness that no amount of effort by the turn-of-the-century Irish nationalist movement among intellectuals could reverse the tide. Here, as in Scotland and Wales, the conquered perforce adopted the language of the conquerors, but not their ethnic identity. Lowland Scotland had long been infiltrated by English, so the union of the two countries in 1707 appeared voluntary.

Coptic, the language of ancient Egypt, was overlain with Greek under Macedonian (323–30 BC) and Roman rule (30 BC–AD 640) but continued to be the language of the masses until the Arab conquest. Thereafter, it was gradually displaced even for the Christian minority by Arabic until it was reduced to a ritual language of the Coptic Christian church, like Latin was in the Catholic church until Vatican II (1962).[11]

An example of the quick decline of a former ruling élite's language is Manchu, the mother tongue of the alien Ching dynasty of the Chinese empire (1644–1912) and its 'bannermen' or garrisons. As soon as the First Chinese Revolution overthrew the empire and turned China into a republic, the élite and privileged Manchu warriors, lacking skills other than military, rapidly descended into poverty (typically rickshaw-pullers) and often 'passed' for Han Chinese with Chinese surnames to escape discrimination.[12] One thinks here of the fate of the Urdu-speaking service class in Hyderabad.[13] The Kuomintang or Nationalist government of China (1927–49) followed an openly assimilationist policy towards its linguistic minorities. Even in Manchuria, their homeland in the northeast of China, the indigenous Manchus were swamped by Han Chinese immigration in the 1920s. The subsequent Japanese attempt to create a puppet 'empire' of Manchukuo (1922–45) under the nominal rule of the last Manchu dynasty child-emperor, Puyi, failed to re-establish the Manchu language. The Communist regime of China, which won control of the mainland including Manchuria by 1950, has had an intermittently more benign stance towards the 7 per cent non-Han minorities in the whole People's Republic, including protection of the languages and cultures of these scattered and peripheral people—somewhat like India's regarding the Scheduled Tribes.[14] This sometimes enforced policy produced, by the 1980s, a sharp increase in the number of declared Manchu speakers as some of the assimilated ones 'emerged from the closet' and declared their Manchu origins. This process is somewhat akin to the strong revival of Native American ethnicity, if not language, in the United States (US) since the 1960s because of Affirmative Action, although the eventual outcome in both cases, from sheer lack of numbers and heavy rates of intermarriage, looks dismal for language survival.[15] The cultural and numerical inferiority of the Manchus to their Chinese subjects doomed their language.

A European example of this principle of military supremacy but cultural inferiority was the inability of German to withstand Latin in the aftermath of the Roman empire. When the German barbarians overran the Roman frontier in the fifth century AD and established tribal kingdoms in former Roman provinces with Latin-speaking populations (the Franks in France, Visigoths in Spain, Lombards in Italy, Anglo-Saxons in Britain), the Germanic languages quickly succumbed to the Latin-origin Romance languages—French, Spanish, and Italian—except in Britain where the basically Celtic population may have been overwhelmed by the invasion and mass settlement of Saxons, Danes, and Norwegians, or pushed back to the 'Celtic Periphery' of the British Isles (Wales, Scotland, and Ireland).[16] Even there, as we have seen, English eventually triumphed. On the continent, but outside the Roman borders, various German dialects were retained. In Eastern Europe, because of the *drang nach osten* (pressure to the East) of Germans and the expansion of the Habsburg and Hohenzollern empires into Slavic lands, German became the élite language until the collapse of those empires after World War I and the expulsion of the German minorities after World War II.[17]

The Scenario after World War II

A second group of cases concerns the fate of the European colonial languages after the breakup of overseas colonial rule following World War II. For people in the European channel of history, there was the ominous precedent of the disappearance of the Greek language from the Greek colonies in the Mediterranean basin.[18] Of the later-day colonial languages, English has fared the best because of the economic hegemony first of Great Britain and then of the US, and the existence of the largely English-settled and therefore English-speaking dominions: Canada, Australia, and New Zealand.[19] In all three, the European settlers rapidly outnumbered the primitive native populations. South Africa portends a more doubtful future for English because of competition with Afrikaans and the dozen or so numerically preponderant Bantu languages.[20] Even in India, where English is the mother tongue of only a tiny residue of Anglo-Indians, Christians, and some Christian-educated élite,[21] it long ago joined Urdu as a lingua franca and replaced it as the medium of international communication for the extremely heterogeneous populations in India and Pakistan.[22]

Latin America, whose Creoles threw off the rule of Spain and Portugal by the 1820s, has retained Spanish (and Portuguese in Brazil) as the official and, increasingly, the actual language of the bulk of the population.[23] Despite some symbolic deference to Amerindian culture in Mexico and Peru, one of the main indicators of 'mestizoization' of the large native populations is their adoption of Spanish.[24]

Clearly, in Latin America a distinctive language is not a requisite of nationality. Even in the US, Spanish speakers who were greatly reduced in numbers in Florida and the southwest after the American annexations of 1819 and 1848 respectively, may now be witnessing a peaceable 'reconquista'[25] through the massive legal and illegal immigration from Mexico, Cuba, and Central America (Puerto Rico, the source of the huge Hispanic immigration to New York since the 1950s, has been a US possession since 1898). The US has seen a sudden shift from a policy of coerced cultural and linguistic assimilation to one of 'multi-culturalism' and bilingual education since 1965,[26] but there is some evidence that despite ease of travel to the homelands and compulsory bilingual education, the second generation of Hispanics ('Latinos'), like the European immigrants in

1880–1920, is shifting to the dominant English for the sake of jobs and careers in mainstream American society.[27]

French has not fared so well as English and Spanish, remaining the official language of a tiny élite in a large number of impoverished former colonies in Africa and Haiti, but rapidly disappearing from Vietnam. The French colonists (*pied noirs*) of Algeria fled or were expelled after a long and bloody war of independence in 1964.[28] The Islamic revival and civil war of the 1970s and 1980s is interpreted by some as a protest against the still dominant 'francophone' native élite.[29] Only in Canada, where there was a substantial population of French-speaking colonists before the British conquest of Canada from France in 1763, has the language enough of a geographically-compact mass base for survival. Soon after, the Quebec Act of 1774 wisely guaranteed the subject French their language, law, and Catholic church. While continuing immigration of British, American, and other non-francophones has reduced the French to a 28 per cent minority of the country's population, the Dominion of Canada has become officially bilingual.[30] Despite this concession by the 'Anglophone' majority, a serious secessionist movement and the Parti Quebeçois developed in the second half of the twentieth century, and has nearly won two referenda on independence.

The Dutch East Indies Company left behind in South Africa, unlike Indonesia, one isolated group of its own settlers, the Afrikaans-speaking Boers. Like the French of Canada and the Muslims of north India, they were subjected by the British (twice, in 1815 and 1902). But in their case they were able—first by emigrating inland from the British Cape Province, and then by retaining a majority of the enfranchized European population of the Union of South Africa (1910)—to win back political control and make Afrikaans, if not the predominant tongue, meaningfully bilingual until the end of apartheid in 1994.[31] Now, Afrikaans is only one of eleven official languages and is losing ground again to English because of the latter's greater utility in international trade. Ironically, the best hope for the survival of Afrikaans lies in the co-called 'Cape Coloured', mulattos and former slaves of the Dutch, whose mother tongue is Afrikaans and whose religion is also Calvinist Christianity. The situation is analogous to that of the non-ashraf descendants of Hindu converts in north India who are now the main reservoir of Urdu speakers and Islamic fundamentalism.[32]

The most recent example of an imperial language being put in jeopardy, at least on its geographical fringes and not overseas like the others, is Russian since the dissolution of the Soviet Union in 1991. The independence of the border republics in the Baltic, Caucasus, and Central Asia, has left large, formerly privileged Russian minorities outside the boundaries of the Russian state.[33] They are protected so far only by the need for their technological/managerial skills and by the continued use of Russian as a second language by the former Communist, now 'nationalist' élites, particularly in Central Asia.[34]

The Lesson for Urdu

After this rather dismal recital of cases, mostly of language decline, what can be learned, relevant for Urdu, from other cases of language survival and recovery?

The distinguished American student of linguistics, Joshua Fishman, in his study, 'Reversing Language Shift: Theoretical and Empirical Foundations of Assistance to Threatened Languages'[35] explicates three 'success stories': Catalan in Spain, French in Canada, and modern Hebrew in Palestine/Israel. None of these are quite comparable to Urdu in north India (if not Pakistan): the first two in that they continued to be spoken by solid blocs of the population that maintained a majority in their respective provinces throughout periods of discrimination by central governments and dominant ethnic élites; the third in that Jews had been expelled from Palestine 1,900 years ago and, even in the last era of rule during the Second Kingdom (161 BC–AD 70) the common language was Aramaic. Hebrew had already become restricted to ritual use,[36] like Arabic, for example, the *azan* or call to prayer, among South Asian Muslims.

The story of how European Jews, motivated by Zionism in reaction to Christian anti-Semitism, resettled in Palestine under late Ottoman rule and then the British Mandate is, of course, treated in celebratory manner by Fishman with almost no reference to the price paid by Palestinian Arabs since 1948. He does deplore the decline of Yiddish, the Germanic mother tongue of the *Ashkenazim*, not only in Eastern Europe because of the holocaust, but also in America and Israel where it has been supplanted by Hebrew, as a second language in the former and as an official language in the latter. Ritual Hebrew required an intense campaign of 'vernacularization' to make it compatible with modern life.

The analogy with Urdu becomes problematic in that the Zionists, as we have seen the Muslim invaders of north India did, abandoned their mother tongue for an indigenous one, but written in a different script. As Hebrew and Arabic are both Semitic languages though somewhat more different perhaps than Urdu and Hindi, in theory it ought to be easier to find common ground between the two pairs of languages than between Yiddish and Arabic and Turco–Mongol and Hindavi respectively, but politics and ideology stand in the way in both cases. The Zionist policy would be as if the *Muhajirin*, on fleeing to Pakistan in 1947, had substituted Arabic for Urdu and imposed it on the indigenous Muslims. As it was, their attempt to impose Urdu on the Muslim Bengalis started the dispute between the two 'wings' of Pakistan, which led to its partition in 1971.[37] As for Urdu in India, what a shame that Gandhi's and Nehru's preference for Hindustani in two scripts as the national language of India lost by only one vote in the Indian Constituent Assembly.[38] Is there any possibility at all that Urduwalas, in alliance with the Dravidian and other non-Hindi language parties, could some day get the Constitution amended to reverse that decision? Short of that fantasy, Fishman's recital of the hebraization of Jews in Palestine before 1948 has important lessons for defenders of Urdu:

1. Revival and vernacularization of Hebrew was accomplished without the aid of the Turkish and then British authorities in Palestine. This underscores the advice of Ralph Russell, the British Urdu teacher, that Urdu must be saved self-reliantly by Urdu speakers out of their own resources.[39] The early Jewish settlers (*aliyah*) in Palestine did not have the huge financial resources that the state of Israel has enjoyed since World War II to hebraize the huge new immigration of Sephardic, Indian, Russian, and Ethiopian Jews.[40]

2. The task of 'reversing language shift' requires a movement of devoted volunteers. How can this be accomplished in north India without bringing down on Muslim heads the charge by the *Hindutva-vadis* that they are 'creating another Pakistan'? Fishman admits that the logical outcome of language revival is demands for autonomy or independence by either emigration or secession.[41] Defenders of Urdu would have to emphasize the Indian nationalist roots of the movement (Gandhi and Nehru) and the benefits to all Indians of linguistic pluralism. Knowledge of the Arabic script could be touted as an advantage for doing business in and with the Arab Middle East, especially the Gulf states.[42]

3. Fishman repeatedly underscores in all the cases he discusses that what he calls RLS (reversing language shift) must be

intergenerational and start with pre-school children and the family. In his conclusion, he offers a seven-(actually nine-) stage programme for reversing language shift,[43] the number of which are relevant depending on the severity of intergenerational dislocation:

(a) 'Reconstructing' (vernacularizing) the language and adult acquisition of it (the former irrelevant to Urdu, but the latter relevant to the script for those educated, if at all, in Devanagari.)

(b) Cultural interaction in the language primarily involving the community-based older generation.

(c) Intergenerational and demographically concentrated home-family-neighbourhood—the basis of mother-tongue transmission.

(d) Schools for literacy acquisition, for the old and for the young, and not in lieu of compulsory education.

(e) Own schools, instead of compulsory education, and substantially under own curricular and staffing control. (This was done by Catholics, at the time a very poor community, in nineteenth-century America and largely taught by nuns.)[44]

(f) Public schools offering some instruction in Urdu, but under non-Muslim curricular and staff control.

(g) Use of Urdu in the local/regional (that is, non-neighbourhood), work sphere. (Practically non-existent in the US for languages other than English, but growing for Quebec for French.)[45]

(h) Use in local/regional mass media and governmental services. (I gather that this was lost by Urdu after 1947, but the riot against an Urdu news broadcast in Bangalore shows there are some Urdu radio programs.)[46]

(i) Education (medium of instruction), and use in the work sphere, mass media, and governmental operations at higher and nationwide levels.' (Existed at Osmania University before 1948, at Jamia Milia Islamia and some colleges, but with a majority of non-Muslim students if government-aided.)

How can this be even started in north India when state schools are teaching through the medium of the dominant ethnicity's language, in this case sanskritized Hindi, and from sometimes communally biased textbooks?[47] The Zionists, both in eastern Europe and then in Palestine, developed their own primary and secondary schools. Indian Muslims have a myriad of *maktabs*, but my understanding is that they teach the Quran by rote in Arabic, not Urdu.[48] Except for the Urdu-medium Anjuman schools in Mumbai, they are said to be of low quality and not meant to prepare students for competing in the mainstream economy.[49] Alternatively, the Jewish practice in the US has been to send their children to the state schools, taught in English, but also to set up their own schools for after-school or weekend instruction, often attached to synagogues to teach Hebrew and counteract Christian bias.[50] These were taught in the early part of the last century in Yiddish, but except for the ultra-orthodox *Hasidim*, increasingly in Hebrew. Some Yiddish has infiltrated the American popular culture through the world of entertainment including cinema, in which Jews are disproportionately represented, as Muslims are in Indian cinema.[51] The *nawabi* culture and music of Lucknow, even if dysfunctional for young Muslims, is Urdu's greatest asset among the non-Muslim majority.[52]

4. The greatest threat to the survival of Urdu, and more broadly to Islamic values and culture, may not be Hindi but English.[53] Here, Urdu-speaking Muslims and Hindi-speaking Hindus have an important common interest. I am not speaking of the exclusion of the English language by *angrezi hatao* campaigns[54] that would isolate Indians from the world market, but about the protection of Indian culture of both kinds from the invasion of pornographic and violent American popular culture via satellite television, cinema, and video.[55]

Notes

1. Paul Brass, 'Urdu and Muslim Grievances in North India: 1947–71', in *Language, Religion and Politics in North India*, Cambridge: Cambridge University Press, 1974, Chapter 4, pp. 182–217; M.N. Venkatachaliah, 'Language and Politics: Status of Urdu in India', *Economic and Political Weekly*, 26 June 1999, pp. 1659–60.

2. Employing 'elite' in the sense of R.A. Schermerhorn's fourfold paradigm by size and power of 'dominant majority' (power and size), 'elite' (power but not size), 'mass subjects' (size but not power), and 'minority' (neither power nor size) in *Comparative Ethnic Relations: A Framework for Theory and Research*, New York: Random House, 1970, p. 13.

3. On the failure to convert all Hindus in Hindustan, perhaps for fear of losing the proceeds of the *jizya*, see Khaliq Ahmad Nizami, *Some Aspects of Religion and Politics in India during the 13th Century*, Bombay: Asia Publishing, 1961, pp. 312–25. On the élite minority character of Urdu in Bengal, see Rounaq Jehan, *Pakistan: Failure in National Integration*, New York: Columbia University Press, 1972, pp. 13, 37.

4. Yusuf Husain, 'The Origin and Growth of the Urdu Language' in *Glimpses of Medieval Indian Culture*, Bombay: Asia Publishing, 1959, Muzaffar Alam reminds us in 'The Pursuit of Persian: Language in Mughal Politics', *Journal of Asian Studies*, vol. 32, no. 2, 1998, pp. 317–49, that Persian displaced

Hindavi as the language of administration and poetry from Akbar to Macaulay.

5. Ather Farouqui, 'Future Prospects of Urdu in India', *Mainstream*, Annual 1992, p. 103. But Omar Khalidi argues that retention of the Urdu script is crucial for preservation of the Indian Muslim religious and cultural heritage by analogy with what happened in Kemalist Turkey and Soviet Central Asia with the switch to Latin and Cyrillic script, respectively, in the 1920s and 1930s. See 'Urdu Language and the Future of Muslim Identity in India, *Journal of the Institute of Muslim Minority Affairs*, vol. VII, no. 2, July 1986, pp. 395–403.

6. N.F. Blake, *A History of the English Language*, New York: New York University Press, 1996.

7. Anwar G. Chejne, *Islam and the West: The Moriscos*, Albany: State University of New York Press, 1983, p. 43.

8. Henry Charles Lea, *The Moriscos of Spain: Their Conversion and Expulsion*, New York: Greenwood, 1968.

9. Akbar S. Ahmed, *Discovering Islam*, London: Routledge & Kegan Paul, 1988, pp. 158–71.

10. W.B. Lockwood, 'Irish Celtic', *Languages of the British Isles Past and Present*, London: Andre Deutsch, 1975, pp. 76–9; Iarfhlaith Watson, 'The Irish Language and Television: National Identity, Preservation, Restoration and Minority Rights', *British Journal of Sociology*, vol. 47, no. 2, June 1996, pp. 255–73.

11. Edward Wakin, *A Lonely Minority: the Modern Story of Egypt's Copts*, New York: Morrow & Co., 1963.

12. Pamela Kyle Crossley, 'The Manchus in the Twentieth Century, *The Manchus*, Oxford: Blackwell, 1997, pp. 189–201; Pamela Kyle Crossley, *Orphan Warriors, Three Manchu Generations and the End of the Qing World*, Princeton: Princeton University Press, 1990, pp. 215–28.

13. Omar Khalidi, 'Muslims in the Tertiary Sector', *Indian Muslims since Independence*, New Delhi: Vikas, 1995, pp. 74–7.

14. June Teufel Dreyer, *China's 40 Millions; Minority, Nationalities, and National Integration in the People's Republic of China*, Cambridge: Harvard University Press, 1976.

15. 'The Current State of Navajo' in Joshua A. Fishman, *Reversing Language Shift*, Clevedon: Multilingual Matters, Ltd., 1991, pp. 188–90.

16. Michael Hechter, *Internal Colonialism: The Celtic Fringe and British National Development 1536–1966*, Berkeley: University of California Press, 1975.

17. Peter Schneider, 'Is Anyone German Here? A Journey into Silesia', *New York Times*, Section VI, 15 April 1990, pp. 28ff.

18. V.L. Menage, 'The Islamization of Anatolia', and Peter Hardy, 'Modern European and Muslim Explanations of Conversion to Islam in South Asia...' in Nehemia Levtzion (ed.), *Conversion to Islam*, New York: Holmes & Meier, 1979, pp. 52–99.

19. Fishman, *Reversing Language Shift*, illustrates the near hopeless task of preserving the languages of dispersed, hunter–gatherer tribes in competition with technologically advanced European settlers in Australia (Chapter 9, 'Prospects for Reversing Language Shift in Australia: Evidence from its

Aboriginal and Immigrant Languages',), and New Zealand (chapter 8, 'Maori: the Native Language of New Zealand').

20. Theodore P. Wright, Jr, and Theodore P. Venter, 'Identity and Rights of Former Ruling Elite Minorities: North Indian Muslims and White Afrikaners of South Africa', Paper delivered at the conference on 'Nationalism, Identity, Minority Rights', Bristol, UK, 16–19 September 1999.

21. R.A. Schermerhorn, 'Anglo-Indians', Ethnic Plurality in India, Tucson, Arizona: University of Arizona, 1978, p. 212, cites only 223,781 Indians in the 1961 census with English as their mother tongue.

22. Paul R. Brass, Ethnicity and Nationalism, Theory and Comparison, New Delhi: Sage, 1991, pp. 120, 307; Jamil Jalibi, 'A Common Culture and a Common Language', Pakistan: the Identity of Culture, Karachi: Royal Book Co., 1984, pp. 174–7.

23. Philip Mason, 'Spanish America', Patterns of Dominance, London: Oxford University Press, 1971, p. 245.

24. Francois Bourricaud, 'Indian, Mestizo and Cholo as Symbols in the Peruvian System of Stratification' in Nathan Glazer and Daniel P. Moynihan (eds), Ethnicity: Theory and Experience, Cambridge: Harvard University Press, 1975, pp. 350–87.

25. James Fallows, 'Immigration; How it's Affecting Us', Atlantic Monthly, November 1983, pp. 45–106; Samuel Huntington, Who are We?, New York: Simon & Schuster, 2004.

26. Diane Ravitch, 'Politicization and the Schools: the Case of Bilingual Education' in Richard C. Monk (ed.), Taking Sides; Clashing Views on Controversial Issues in Race and Ethnicity, Guilford Ct: Dushkin, 1994 (reprinted from 1985), pp. 126–44. Nathan Glazer, an early opponent of Affirmative Discrimination, New York: Basic Books, 1975, admits We Are All Multiculturalists Now, Cambridge: Harvard University Press, 1997.

27. Richard Rodriguez, Hunger of Memory: The Education of Richard Rodriguez, Boston: Godine, 1982.

28. David Gordon, The Passing of French Algeria, London: Oxford University Press, 1966, reports that even after the exodus of the pied-noirs, half of the population were French-speaking.

29. Abdel Hamid Mansouri, 'Algeria between Tradition and Modernity: The Question of Language', Doctoral dissertation, Graduate School of Public Affairs, State University of New York at Albany, 1991.

30. Kenneth McRoberts, 'The Rise of Quebecois Identity', in Jeffrey Ross and Ann Baker Cottrell (eds), The Mobilization of Collective Identity: Comparative Perspectives, Lanham, MD: University Press of America, 1980, pp. 225–55.

31. (1) The official languages of the Republic are Sepedi, Sesotho, Setswana, siSwati, Tshivenda, Xitsonga, Afrikaans, English, isiNdebele, isiXhosa and isiZulu.

(2) Recognizing the historically diminished use and status of the indigenous languages of our people, the state must take practical and positive measures to elevate the status and advance the use of these languages.

(3) The national government and provincial governments may use any particular official language for the purposes of government, taking into account usage, practicality, expense, regional circumstances and the

balance of the needs and preferences of the population...but the national government and each provincial government must use at least two official languages.

(4) ...all official languages must enjoy parity of esteem and must be treated equitably.

(5) A Pan South African Language Board...must promote and create conditions for the development and use of: all official languages, the Khoi, Nama and San languages...and all languages commonly used by communities in South Africa, including...Gujarati, Hindi, Tamil, Telegu, and Urdu; and Arabic, Hebrew, Sanskrit and other languages used for religious purposes in South Africa.

See *Constitution of the Republic of South Africa, 1996*, Chapter 1, Founding Provisions, pp. 6–7. Almost more difficult than language *per se* are demands for alternative symbols such as changes in place names, monuments, flag, and anthem. See also Charles Malan, 'Symbolic Unity: the Role of Cultural Symbols in Nation-building', in Nic Rhoodie, and Ian Liebenberg (eds), *Democratic Nation-Building in South Africa*, Pretoria: HSRC Publishers, 1994, pp. 182–9.

32. Like Urdu in post-Independence India, Afrikaans lacks a majority in any of the provinces of South Africa, but has a 62 per cent majority in the Western Cape, if one includes the Afrikaans-speaking 'Cape Coloured'—Interview with P. Mulder in *Potchefstroom*, November 1998. See also, Milton Esman, 'South Africa: Multiple Cleavages', *Ethnic Politics*, Ithaca: Cornell University Press, 1994, pp. 75–110.

33. Steven Erlanger, 'Baltic Identity: Russians Wonder if They Belong', *New York Times*, 22 November 1992.

34. Anara Tabyshalieva, 'The Challenge of Regional Cooperation in Central Asia', Washington DC: US Institute of Peace, 1999, reports a declining use of Russian as the lingua franca in favour of English, partly because of a change from Cyrillic to Latin script for the Uzbek and Turkish languages of Uzbekistan and Turkmenistan, but Arabic script in Tajikistan, pp. 14–15.

35. Fishman, *Reversing Language Shift*, chapter 10, pp. 287–336.

36. Jack Fellman, *The Revival of a Classical Tongue: Eliezer Ban Yehuda and the Modern Hebrew Language*, The Hague: Mouton, 1973.

37. But the Muhajirin, to Pakistan, were a much smaller proportion of the population in both wings than the overwhelming percentage of Jews who immigrated to Palestine both before and after the establishment of Israel.

38. Kerrin Ditmer in 'The Hindi-Urdu Controversy and the Constituent Assembly', *Indian Journal of Politics*, vol. VI, no. 1, January–June 1972, pp. 13–22, points out that the close vote was on the use of Hindi numerals; Nehru lost the vote for Hindustani in the Congress caucus by 63–32 in 1947.

39. Ralph Russell, 'Urdu in India since Independence', *Economic and Political Weekly*, vol. 34, nos 1–2, 9 January 1999, pp. 44–8.

40. Fishman and Fellman stress the intense ideological commitment of the early Zionists to the revival of Hebrew even at the expense of their own mother tongue, Yiddish.

41. Presumably this would not be the case if it is a majority language, for instance Punjabi in Pakistan or Hindi in 19th century UP, which is being

revived against an alien, colonial language or a lingua franca, in which case, proponents are more likely to aspire to use state power to impose their own language on minorities.

42. However, the bulk of Indian workers in the Gulf states have come from the West Coast: Gujarat and Kerala. Saudi Arabia does prefer fellow Muslims.

43. Fishman, *Reversing Language Shift*, p. 395.

44. Nathan Glazer, and Daniel P. Moynihan, 'The Irish: The Roman Catholic Church', *Beyond the Melting Pot*, Cambridge: the MIT Press, 1963, pp. 234–8, but the medium of instruction in these parochial schools, as in Ireland, was English. But Jewish full-time or one-day-only schools taught and were often taught in Yiddish or Hebrew.

45. The tables have been turned by francophones winning political power, and now it is the anglophones of Quebec who claim their language is discriminated against. See Esman, *Ethnic Politics*, chapter 6: 'Canada–Quebec', pp. 147–75.

46. 'Asghar Ali Engineer on Bangalore Disturbances, October '94', *Muslim India*, no. 145, January 1995, p. 30.

47. Susanne Hoeber Rudolph and Lloyd Rudolph, 'Rethinking Secularism: Genesis and Implication of the Textbook Controversy, 1977–9' in Lloyd Rudolph (ed.), *Cultural Policy in India*, Delhi: Chanakya Publications, 1984, pp. 13–41.

48. Mohammad Akhlaq Ahmad, *Traditional Education among Muslims*, Delhi: B.R. Publishing, 1985; Kuldip Kaur, 'Survey of Madrasas and Maktabs', *Madrasa Education in India*, Chandigarh: Centre for Research in Rural & Industrial Development, 1990, pp. 251–76.

49. Ahmad Rashid Shervani, 'Educational Backwardness of Muslims in India', The *Nation*, 26 December 1992, p. 7, and 'Raising Performance Levels of Students in Selective (Muslim) Schools in India', *Journal of the Institute of Muslim Minority Affairs*, vol. III, no. 2, Winter 1981, pp. 99–103. For a report on Shervani's own exemplary Muslim school, see Marcus Franda, 'Education for Young Muslims: the Crescent School of Old Delhi', *Reports* no. 23, Hanover N.H.: American Universities Field Staff, 1979.

50. Abram Sachar, in *A History of the Jews*, New York: Knopf, 1967, pp. 400–1, regards the Jewish supplemental schools as not very successful in maintaining group identity as most Jewish families sent their children to the public schools which were more secular (non-Christian) than in Europe. Louis Finkelstein, *The Jews: Their History, Customs and Religion*, New York: Harper Row, 1966, finds more to praise in their efforts in higher education, founding *yeshivas* (like Muslim madrasas) for training rabbis and culminating after World War II with the foundation of a prestigious, English-medium institution, Brandeis University, the counterpart of Aligarh Muslim University in India.

51. William Safire, 'On Language; Enough Already! What am I, Chopped Liver?,' *New York Times*, Sunday Magazine section, 25 October 1998; Theodore P. Wright, Jr, 'Muslim Mobility in India through Peripheral Occupations: Sports, Music, Cinema and Smuggling', in Marc Gaborieau and Alice Thorner (eds), *Asie du Sud: Traditions et Changements*, Paris: Editions du Centre National de la Recherche Scientifique, Collection des Colloques Internationaux, 1979, pp. 271–8.

52. '...the enormous success of Bombay-made Hindi–Urdu film...in most of (which) the language used is frankly Urdu but, for commercial and diplomatic reasons of censor certification, it is called Hindi. Thus the concept of "Hindi" has been broadened to include "Urdu".' Khwaja Ahmed Abbas, 'Cinema and National Integration', *Mainstream*, 15 March 1986, pp. 18–21; Akbar S. Ahmed, 'Bombay Films: The Cinema as Metaphor for Indian Society and Politics', *Modern Asian Studies*, vol. 26, no. 2, 1992, pp. 289–320: 'Take the Language of the Films, a Hybrid of Hindi and Urdu. It is the lingua franca of an area the size of a continent...'

53. Fishman, *Reversing Language Shift*, p. 315, on the massive use and attraction of English in Israel to the neglect of Arabic.

54. Selma K. Sonntag, 'The Political Saliency of Language in Bihar and Uttar Pradesh', *Journal of Commonwealth & Comparative Politics*, vol. 34, no. 2, July 1996, pp. 8–12.

55. Theodore P. Wright, Jr, 'Asian Values vs. Post-Modernity: the Media and Human Rights in South Asia', paper delivered at the 14th European Conference on Modern South Asia, Prague, September 1998; Faizan Mustafa, 'Information Superhighway, Cultural Invasion and Muslim Umma', paper delivered at the 26th Annual Convention of the Association of Muslim Social Scientists, Brockport, New York, November 1997.

PART II
Urdu and Identity Politics

5

Madrasas and the
Making of Muslim Identity

ARJUMAND ARA

About 200 students in Basala village, 20 km from Meerut, Uttar Pradesh, hoisted the Pakistani flag atop their madrasa and took out a procession raising pro-Pakistan and pro-Osama bin Laden slogans on Independence Day.[1]

In another news item, the Hindi daily *Nav Bharat Times* reported that the then Human Resource Development Minister M.M. Joshi challenged Vishva Hindu Parishad (VHP) president, Ashok Singhal, and others who doubted the credentials of *madrasa*s as centres of learning and demanded proof of their alleged role as terrorist camps.[2]

There are innumerable reports of madrasa activities, both favourable and hostile, questioning their loyalty to the nation. While the Ministry of Home Affairs favoured scrutiny of their activities, the Ministry of Human Resource Development, on the other hand, praised them as centres of learning that contribute positively to the national objective of spreading literacy and education.

If we look deep into the essence of these apparently conflicting views, we find a common thread binding them, something charac-teristic of the prevailing politico-economic set-up in the country. Representative democracy depends upon the competitive bazaar of lobbies and has to be eclectic enough to provide space to the eloquent élites of all those 'identities'. This ensures that any horizontal unity between the oppressed and exploited across numerous identities is successfully thwarted, and is achieved by satisfying engineered popular needs to be represented and by co-opting leaders to represent them. In this process, different ghettoized homogeneities are pitched against each other by generating stereotypical images. The creation of a ghettoized majority also requires the creation of a ghettoized minority. The Bharatiya Janata Party's (BJP) 'defence' of madrasas ought to be seen in this light; it is in harmony with the Sangh Parivar's agenda of Hinduizing Hindus by minoritizing the minorities.

I will not dwell upon the opposing stands of the former two ministers of the former BJP-led NDA government over the integrity of madrasas, which is as dubious as that government's Kashmir policy (according to which the then Prime Minister talked about giving greater autonomy to Kashmir while his deputy, stuck to the official BJP line of demanding abrogation of Article 370 of the Indian Constitution, which gives special status to the state of Jammu and Kashmir).[3] I would emphasize that madrasas are diverse in their nature and objectives.

Ever since 9/11, the intricate world of madrasas has come under scrutiny to determine the extent to which they are institutions propagating religious extremism and supporting terrorist camps, particularly those in Afghanistan and Pakistan. Within India, according to government statistics, half a million madrasas are active, in which about 50 million students are enrolled. Part-time and evening madrasas are not included in the list.[4] These madrasas are not viewed as centres of terrorism, unlike those in Afghanistan and Pakistan, but a sense of anxiety prevails and many groups demand that they should be 'reformed' or shut down.

In the print media, photographs of madrasa students sitting on narrow benches or squatting on the floor and memorizing passages from the Quran regularly accompany articles or news-items on Muslims. Most writing paints them as backward, religious zealots ready to metamorphose into human bombs. This is not an accurate picture of most of the students, though the general view that madrasas have a narrow outlook and oppose everything modern is not far from wrong. Educated Muslims feel uneasy when they see swarms of young madrasa pupils in *kurta-pyjama*s and sporting small beards and skull caps emerging from a mosque or heading toward the home of a Muslim brother for a charity meal. Reflections of this kind do not provide any guidance for progressive action. We need to be more curious about the workings of these institutions and the students who study there. The questions of foremost importance are: Why do madrasas exist? What is the reality behind them? How is it that these medieval institutions still flourish in an otherwise well-developed world? What are the forces responsible for their relative backwardness and isolation? Have socio-economic and political factors anything to do with the situation? Such questions do haunt many of us, particularly after the emergence of religious zealots out to destroy peace and harmony in several regions of the country. This article is an attempt at understanding the madrasa system and its relevance in the present context.

Evolution of the Madrasa

During the medieval period, Muslims did not follow a single formalized education system. Heads of the *khanqah* (seminaries), *sufis*, *ulema* (scholars), *umara* and *ruasa* (the power élite), and social reformers were in charge of the teaching/learning process. They ran private madrasas—generally free of charge—from their homes and seminaries.[5] Numerous madrasas and *maktab*s were founded by Muslim rulers and the élite in the Sultanate period.[6] Maktabs were an essential feature of mosques and khanqahs, where students were taught to recite the Quran and perform *namaz*. However, the children of the rich and powerful were tutored at home.

Madrasa—the Arabic word means a place where you learn or where you are taught—is a neutral word without an exclusively religious significance. There were never separate institutions for religious and secular education. Along with religion (*tafsir, hadith,* and *fiqh* being different branches of religious teaching), other subjects such as philosophy, prosody, grammar, mathematics, logic, history, and geography were also taught. Students who were inclined towards any specialized subject such as *Tibb-e Unani* (a discipline of alternative medicine) were taught and trained by subject experts in private institutions. Training in the martial arts, chivalry, and statesmanship were formally taught to the gentry—amirs, nawabs, and royalty. This system of education became prevalent with the dominance of Muslims and their culture. Akbar was the first emperor to establish an exclusive department of education through which Hindus and Muslims were taught in the same madrasa, but were given the option of separate syllabi.[7] The Hindu élite was not averse to sending its children to madrasas to receive Islamic education.

It is noteworthy that no thought was given to the education of the common people: The social structure of the time would never have allowed it. The Muslim gentry and their Hindu counterparts—to be precise, the Brahmins—who considered themselves the custodians of learning, were not concerned with the education of commoners. The famous Aligarh Tehrik, the movement launched by Sir Sayyid Ahmad Khan in the late nineteenth century (which culminated in the establishment of Aligarh Muslim University) was a movement for modern education meant only for the Muslim élite. Women and low-caste people were not the concern of these 'enlightened' Muslims. In several of his writings, Sir Syed expressed opposition to the education of Muslim women. He considered modern education for women *naa-mubaarak*, or ominous and harmful, and believed that if the overall situation of men in society improved, that of women would improve automatically. He therefore held that every effort should be directed solely to improving the educational and social status of men.

In a lecture addressed to the women of Punjab, Khan told them that his effort for the education of their boys was the foundation of the education of their girls as well.[8] He reiterated these views in 1891 in the sixth session of the Mohammedan Education Conference held in the Deccan: 'Women cannot progress unless the men progress. Hence we are not much bothered about educating women'.[9] In the same vein, he opposed the Congress demand for holding competitive examinations for covenanted posts in India on the plea that this might lead to the selection of low-caste (or low-class) candidates to the coveted posts, which would cause great resentment among the '*sharif qaums*' or upper castes.[10] These references clearly indicate that the kind of education system the educated Muslim élite was seeking to project was actually aimed at preserving a feudal society.

With this indifferent, almost hostile, attitude of the Muslim upper class toward the education of the weaker sections of society, madrasas emerged as a powerful instrument in the strengthening of the caste system among Muslims. Social stratification among them, which was usually on the basis of occupation of different social groups, became caste specific. It resulted in the emergence of the ulema, *qazi* (judges), *maulvis* (religious teacher and interpreter) and *hakeems* (doctor), all of whom belonged to the élite or upper-caste Muslims and observed a social order similar to that of caste Hindus.[11] Though Muslims do not practice untouchability, the entire Muslim community was divided into two classes—*sharif* and *razil*.[12] There was an unwritten law according to which the razil (low-born)—for example, a weaver, a carpenter, or a barber could never become an *imam* of a mosque or a qazi of a city. This unwritten law is followed even today and a qazi who performs the *nikah* ceremony usually belongs to the upper caste. Thus, the education system among Muslims was not substantially different from that of the *pathshalas* and *gurukuls* of the Hindus, where only Brahmins or *dwijas* (twice-born) were entitled to admission. Both systems were meant exclusively for the upper crust.

However, this education system could not maintain its existence as a watertight compartment. People living on the fringes of dominant cultures tend to feel attracted to it. Social scientists have illustrated through studies of various social groups the tendency toward upward mobility and Sanskritization among the less-developed classes. As in any other society, the common people were attracted towards the dominant culture. In the history of Urdu literature, there were *shairs* or poets who were, by profession, tailors, cooks, barbers, watermen, soldiers, and courtesans, and others—this despite the fact that literature was essentially considered the domain of the educated upper class.[13] Upper-caste non-Muslims and *Kayasthas* were easily accepted as Islamic scholars because they were 'perfect' products of the dominant culture, and one could hardly make any behavioural distinction between the Hindu and the Muslim élite.

Changes with Colonialism

With the advent of the British Raj, society underwent a massive transformation. Education systems were more drastically affected because the British rulers, for their own vested interests, introduced education among the masses. With the introduction of modern/ western education, a sharp controversy regarding the 'new culture' and education came to the fore.[14] Those who refused to change with the times tried to swim against the current. As a result, traditional schools or madrasas emerged as a symbol of resistance to imperial rule. Their resistance and opposition to the British later culminated in their participation in the freedom movement (Deoband Movement, Wahabi Tehrik, Khilafat Movement, etc.). However, another outcome of this resistance to the British was that the madrasas gradually became more specific in their objectives and rigid in their world-view. Their syllabi gradually lost relevance to contemporary society.

On the other hand, western education appealed to those who were interested in joining the new service sector of the Raj. This brought with it the inevitable question of loyalty: Which master should they now follow? Those who abhorred the West chose to cling to their medieval values and traditional system of education. Sir Sayyid Ahmad Khan emerged as an ardent advocate of English/modern education. The natural sciences were, according to him, the key to progress, and the English language the only medium allowing access to these sciences.

Society was undergoing another remarkable change. The common people were also exposed to the blessings of the new education thanks to the new values and ideals of equality and justice for all. As a result of this awakening, uneducated people began aspiring to better standards of living. These aspirations led them to send their wards to madrasas, which they still valued as the highest centres of learning and scholarship. The shift in the value system heralded a great change in the mentality of the common Muslims, whose woes and worries were otherwise not different from those of common Hindus. There began to be an overemphasis on religion and religious identity. Even those with a modern outlook, advocates of scientific knowledge, were in favour of combining religious and secular education.[15]

True to the élitist tradition of dominating all spheres of life, the Muslim élite tightened its hold over both the madrasas and the schools of modern education. While they continued to boss over their brethren who were ulema and teachers, they lost no opportunity of sending their own children to *vilayat*/Britain for higher education. The famous Urdu poet Akbar Allahabadi, whose opposition to western culture had many a time bordered on the irrational, sent his own son to Britain.

The new students coming to the madrasas now belonged to the lower stratum of Muslims, and since because most of them came from semi-literate or illiterate families, they had difficulty in comprehending books written in Arabic and Persian. Most of their time was devoted to learning these languages, which they generally failed to master; thus, the quality of education declined rapidly. This was the time when the Mughal empire was on the decline, and Persian was gradually giving up its position as the language of domination. By then, Urdu was taking its place, but the translation of the syllabi to suit Urdu would take time. The emerging educated class could not comprehend this degeneration and, of course, could do little to reverse its course.

Besides, the dominant Muslim élite, whose stronghold over Muslim society was rapidly diminishing, resorted to various tactics to maintain the status quo. Religion thus became the best option for consolidating their hold, and also to keep them away from the influences of the West that could result in a complete transformation of the social order. From the politico-religious movements of the Wahabis and Deobandis, who struggled to restore the pristine glory of Muslim dominance,[16] to the Aligarh and Khilafat movements, all élite groups used the political unrest and economic worries of the masses to retain their dominance. They naturally stressed the religious identity of the Muslims—this was the one sphere where nobody could question them.

Thus, a system of education was born that was a by-product of a feudal society, and one that should have died away with the introduction of a democratic and liberal social order. Religious and political control was taken up by religious bodies such as the Jama'at-e Islami (founded in 1940), which thoroughly represented and protected the interests of the feudal lords, and blatantly protected the autocratic system in the grab of religion. The hobnobbing of these religious bodies with the *jagirdars* is quite clear from the following statement of Maulana Maududi, the founder of the Jama'at-e Islami, in his book *Rasail-o Masayil*:

The ownership of property is justified according to Islamic *Shariya*. It is not within the power of any government or assembly to confiscate them. Regarding ownership of land and *jagirs* it is clear that there can be no limit put on landed property and *jagirs*. If it concerns other means of production such as mills and factories, the concept of their nationalization is in total contradiction to the basic Islamic point of view.[17]

A Transition to Politics of Religion

A system of education in the form of mushrooming religious madrasas along with the preaching of politico-religious groups played a proactive role in shaping Muslim identity as traditional, fundamentalist, exclusivist, and escapist. Madrasas, in fact, became the most effective tool in the hands of people with vested interests. They chose to teach those tenets of Islam that suited them most—preaching that people should not question the authority of the imams and the ulema and should not apply reason in religious matters. They gave more emphasis to rituals than to duties toward others by promising countless *sawab* (blessings) in the other world for every ritual they performed. Innumerable books were written for the common man, exhorting him to adhere to religion by following the path preached in them. The Tablighi Jama'at took upon itself the task of spreading its message among ignorant Muslims, suggesting *Tablighi Nisab* (syllabus for propagation of Islam) that included books on the virtues of performing the rituals of namaz, *haj*, and *roza* along with books on the virtues of [preaching] that contained many fictitious references. Citing the Quran, they upheld the belief that those with *absolute faith* and *just deeds* would be rewarded on earth (that is, they would dominate and rule). They interpreted *just deeds* as earning with legitimate means, restraint of worldly desires, control over the heart, pleasure in God's message, love of God, pleasure in performing duties towards God (rituals), etc. These books maintained that people endowed with these blessings would be prosperous and successful even in abject poverty.[18]

The Islam of the masses exhorted people to have absolute faith in their fate, to observe *sabr-o qana'at* (patience and contentment) despite abject poverty, with the promise of a better life after death—the indirect message being: do not to try to improve your lot, and accept your fate. Religion indeed became the most powerful weapon for keeping people ignorant and exploited by the privileged. The teachings of other-worldliness and sabr-o qana'at appealed to the poor as they could find solace in the thought of a better life after death. They felt, in their own eyes, some respectability for their poverty-ridden status by believing that God loved them more because of their righteousness in poverty. This gave birth to a new class of deprived *shurafa* (gentry) who felt enormous self-respect. The sufi tradition that had appealed to the common people for centuries and had shaped their psyche, also strengthened this new concept of religion.

When it is said that India has its own brand of Islam, it is often this Islam that is meant—a religion practised by the deprived, poor Muslim, which is in stark contrast with the Islam of the rich of the Arab world. It is this Islam that, rather than motivating people to adapt to new conditions, pushes them to the margins. A marked social and educational degeneration of the Muslims is the direct outcome of this local brand of Islam.

Though we see a direct clash between the new education systems of the British and that of the Muslims, it was the feudal élite who reaped the benefits of both. They succeeded in dominating the common Muslims and adapted to the new conditions as well. Thus, the emergence of this variety of Islam inevitably perpetuated a feudal society.

The feudal élite nurtured the madrasa system exclusively for the poor but kept its reins in their own hands. This ensured that the new mass base, created in the name of religion, could be exploited as a significant source of power and a handy tool in their bid for domination in the emerging democratic societies. They thus needed the institution for their own survival. Deprived Muslims who were made to believe that their most valued treasure, Islam, was in danger, vowed to protect the tradition of madrasas even at the cost of their lives. Even today, madrasas are falsely considered to be the institution that played the greatest role in saving Islam from extinction. Ironically, poor Muslims consider madrasas the protectors of Islam without realizing that many of the ulema and the *maulanas*, who exhort them to protect the system, send their own children to public schools, convents, and even to Europe and America for higher studies. The system shows no sign of change even after over half a century of exposure to democracy. A number of heads of madrasas graduated from the élite St Stephens' College or Delhi Public School, but choose to espouse publicly the Indian brand of Islam for the poor. (Some time ago I happened to meet a former student of St Stephens' who is an office-bearer in a powerful religious organization, the Jamiat-ul Ulama-e Hind. This profession will, of course, provide him with a shortcut to a leadership role or at least to prominence and fortune.) Inter-religious marriages are also not uncommon in the families of ulemas and maulanas; they lead modern lives like any modern Hindu or Muslim, but their stand on the perpetuation of the madrasa system is ample proof of the exploitative nature of the system itself.

Institutionalized as a system of education for the poor Muslim who would otherwise never be able to get an education, madrasas have become the greatest obstruction in the path of progress of the Muslim community. While it is true that the community provides almost all the resources for the students' meals, clothing, and boarding from the *zakat* (a 2.5 per cent religious tax on the assets and annual income of prosperous Muslims), the grip of the self-serving maulvi over the system is relentless. Adherence to the more than 300-year-old *Dars-e Nizami*[19] does little to help the student cope with contemporary challenges of competition and survival. Cumbersome and obsolete books in Arabic, Persian, and Urdu invoke little interest in self-learning.

For students with a poor social and educational background, the study of religion and training for a career in teaching rituals has now become the most common option for earning a livelihood. They easily get petty jobs as *muezzins* and imams in mosques or as *mudarris* (teachers) in small madrasas or maktabs. The system has been static for hundreds of years—and there is little sign of change. Small madrasas crop up every now and again, for they are an easy source of income for the unemployed graduates of madrasas. Islam is a religion that tells its followers to review its *shari'a* as and when time demands it.[20] In India, that religion has become a prisoner in the hands of the clergy and the network of their followers.

A system that should ordinarily have been marginalized in the process of democratization of the nation after Independence remains thriving for various reasons. Apathy and indifference on the part of succeeding governments toward the need to introduce reforms and intervene in the affairs of the Muslims has contributed its bit. The *zamindari/jagirdari* system was abolished and Muslim *zamindars* were defeated despite fierce resistance; the same force was not exercised for introducing modern education among common Muslims. The abolition of zamindari did not bring about any change in a social system dominated by religion and religious institutions. In India's democratic system, the only possible remedy would be provision of an alternative—without making Muslims fearful of losing their Islamic identity. Their culture and identity could be protected through providing education in their own language, which in most cases would be Urdu. But instead of formulating such policies, Muslims have been left to their fate.

The System Today

Against this background, to simply brand madrasas as bigoted, narrow-minded, and rigid institutions is in itself narrow-minded. A knowledge of their structural organization is necessary to understand the intricacies of the present system. For example, the maktab is essentially meant to teach the Arabic script, recitation of the Quran, and performance of namaz, thus initiating a child into the basics and the rituals of the religion. This is done in almost all *mohallah* or neighbourhood mosques. Students attending maktab come from almost all social strata after school for this extra learning.

Madrasas—both residential and non-residential—have become a separate system of education. Established in towns and villages, these madrasas run on zakat and charity, and have become shelters and orphanages for the poor and the destitute. In addition, there are centres of religious learning of the highest order, graduates of which find jobs in smaller madrasas, maktabs, and mosques. It is this vicious circle of dependency that ensures the perpetuation of madrasas, on which the economic prosperity of many people depends. To draw an analogy from industry, the major madrasas or *darul ulooms* could be compared to big factories whose products dominate the market of smaller madrasas. It is for this *product* or small group of ulema that the *system* is perpetuated. Had the ulema aimed at any social change and development, they would have utilized the funds of charity, zakat, and *waqf* for meaningful modern institutions of education. While it is true that the development of a modern nation is bound to be impeded by such backward-looking institutions, they cannot simply be shut down, because the ringmasters would not let it happen. They have their own clout, which no political party can dare ignore.

Another serious problem adding to the quagmire is the fact that the students of madrasas are, in most cases, first-generation learners belonging to the poorest of the poor. They are not educated enough to question the system as they are unaware of any alternative education, and are taught to merely receive instructions and follow them. The concept of learning and understanding is alien to them as the only books they have access to give the version of religion that serves the *mullah*'s ends. With the prohibition of literature, sports, TV, etc., they are not exposed to the diverse aspects of life, and the awareness needed to question a situation is non-existent. There is therefore little resistance from within the community and no sign of change in the general condition of Muslims. They remain an uneducated, backward, and conservative community.

It is this system of education that sometimes results in catastrophe by churning out pupils prone to becoming tools in the hands of vested interests that generally belong to the upper echelons of society. In the Indian context, there are many examples of this exploitative use of religion. A Muslim ideology has been inculcated since the second half of the nineteenth century. Such bodies as the

Deobandis and Jama'at-e-Islami sought to mobilize Muslims under their conservative revivalist banner. K.M. Ashraf points out that, from 1912 to 1914, revivalist-led struggles, for example those started by Ahrar League and the Khilafat movement led by the Ali brothers, have repeatedly failed to achieve their goals. 'By now, because of the cumulated consequences of such collective experience the Muslims of India are...mentally fatigued and distrustful'[21] of the old leaders, and frustration and cynicism is widespread. This frustration and cynicism can make the Muslim youth, beset by the uncertainties of the present, fall easy prey to subversive elements. Youth with madrasa backgrounds are especially prone to brainwashing in the name of religious revivalism, Muslim nationhood, and pan-Islamism, and organized in *jihadi* camps. They are generally poor, and may see a double benefit in subscribing to these views. Their attitude is not very different from that of ordinary unemployed Hindu youth who, for monetary benefit or in the name of religion, became rioters in the slum area of Naroda Patia of Ahmedabad during the communal riots of Gujarat in 2002, or *karsevaks* at Ayodhya.

Once again, the solution to the problem is drastic changes in the conditions that have potential to produce the young jihadi and create a new environment to which they can respond positively.

The Minority Card

The core problem for the Indian Muslim community is that nobody is willing to strike the right chord—to address both educational and economic issues. Political parties seldom give a thought to the basic problem of under-priviledged Muslims. Even when the so-called secular parties accuse the BJP and others like them of being communal, they are themselves playing the card of minority communalism—the ploy of vote-bank politics and appeasement of minorities. Otherwise, why is it that the Congress (which has presented itself as the true well-wisher of the community), despite having ruled the country for almost half a century, never properly addressed the educational problems of this 'pampered' and 'appeased' community? Why is the development curve of Muslim education slower? Why do occasional surveys reveal that the number of Muslims in the service sector is diminishing? Why are the Muslims becoming more and more ghettoized? Why is it that their localities do not have an adequate number of schools? Is this appeasement, or sheer negligence, or well planned discrimination? Backward sections of society need positive discrimination to ensure their upliftment. How many policies and schemes have been introduced to effect the uplift of backward Muslims?

Muslims too are Indians, and have a right to equal development. They need primary schools in their localities; these are the only means of halting the phenomenal growth of madrasas. If the state opens a primary school in the vicinity of every madrasa, the locals will promptly opt for a modern education for their children.

The main responsibility of taking initiatives to mitigate the educational problems of the community lies with the educated, progressive, and responsible youth of the community itself. They need to identify and channelize resources for the establishment of schools, and learn how to pressurize the administration to respond to the needs of the minority. For north-Indian Muslims, these primary schools must be Urdu medium, since most north-Indian Muslims consider Urdu their mother tongue. This will give them the sense of security and adherence to their own culture and religion that they seek in madrasas.

The menace of growing educational backwardness through madrasas can be curbed only by providing a progressive, modern alternative with a promising future for the younger generations. This is the only way to take on fascist elements—be they Hindu or Muslim. The progressive people of the community need to fight the fascist forces and, at the same time, adopt a strategy of avoiding unnecessary confrontation. The time has also come to question the motives of the clergy that thrives upon the madrasa system. A fitting rebuff to them would be establishment of model schools for basic education in all the localities where madrasas exist. Muslims must realize that they do not need feudal madrasas of a feudal system to fulfil their educational needs. Rather they need schools. Introducing half-baked and ill-conceived schemes for the modernization of madrasa education will bear no fruit unless the core of the problem is addressed.

Notes

1. *The Times of India*, New Delhi, 17 August 2002, p. 6.
2. *Nav Bharat Times*, New Delhi, 30 September 2002.
3. From time to time, the BJP has been raking up the issue of special status of Jammu and Kashmir (J&K). (For a recent statement please see BJP for

Article 370 Abrogation, *http://news.outlookindia.com/item.aspx?657964*, accessed on 6 July 2010).

Article 370 of the Indian Constitution, which is of a temporary nature, grants special status to J&K. It specifies that except for Defence, Foreign Affairs, and Finance and Communications (matters specified in the instrument of accession), the Indian Parliament needs the state government's concurrence for applying all other laws. Thus this state's residents lived under a separate set of laws, including those related to citizenship, ownership of property, and Fundamental Rights, as compared to other Indians.

Similar protections for unique status exist in tribal areas of India including those in Himachal Pradesh, Arunachal Pradesh, and Nagaland. However, it is only for the state of J&K that its accession to India is still a matter of dispute between India and Pakistan, still on the agenda of the United Nations Security Council, and where the Government of India vide the 1974 Indira-Sheikh Accord committed itself to keeping the relationship between the Union and the J&K state within the ambit of this article. This accord mentions that, 'The State of Jammu and Kashmir which is a constituent unit of the Union of India, shall, in its relation with the Union, continue to be governed by Article 370 of the Constitution of India.'

Indian citizens from other states and Kashmiri women who marry men from other states can not purchase land or property in J&K (*http://en.wikipedia.org/wiki/Article_370*, accessed on 6 July 2010).

4. A report published in the Urdu daily *Qaumi Awaz*, New Delhi, 22 April 2003, p. 6. The news item was released by United News of India.

5. Syed Manazir Ahsan Raza Gilani, *Hindustan men Musalmanon ka Nizam-e Talim-o Tarbiyat*, 3rd ed., Vol. 1, Delhi: Nadvat-ul Musannifin, Jama Masjid, 1987, p. 35.

6. Qamaruddin, *Hindustan ki Dini Darsgahen*, an All India Survey of Hamdard Education Society, Delhi, 1996, p. 34.

7. Salamatullah, *Hindustan men Musalmanon ki Talim*, New Delhi: Maktaba Jamia Ltd., 1990, p. 31.

8. *Khutbat-e Sir Syed*, Vol. 1, Lahore, 1972, pp. 465–660.

9. Ibid., Vol. 2, p. 224.

10. Appendix, *Aligarh Institute Gazette*, 26 June 1877, p. 104.

11. Ather Farouqui, who is an upper-caste Muslim, told me that in his childhood, he and his friends and relatives, mostly Syeds and Qazis, were forbidden to play or interact with lower-caste Muslims. They also brought out a hand-written magazine at the head of which they used to write these words in Urdu: 'The children of Qazis and Syeds ought not to befriend or play with urchins, children of barbers, butchers, and weavers.'

12. Qamaruddin, *Hindustan ki Dini Darsgahen*, p. 35.

13. Mohammed Hasan, *Dehli men Urdu Shairi ka Tehzibi aur Fikri Pas Manzar*, 2nd ed., New Delhi, 1983, p. 98.

14. Gilani, *Hindustan men Musalmanon ka Nizam-e Talim-o Tarbiyat*, pp. 17–18, 302–3.

15. Salamatullah, *Hindustan men Musalmanon ki Talim*, p. 55.

16. Ibid., p. 38.

17. K.M. Ashraf, *An Overview of Muslim Politics in India*, New Delhi: Manak Publications, 2001, p. 143.
18. Maulana Wahiduddin Khan, *Tablighi Tehrik*, New Delhi: Maktaba Al-Risala, 1994, p. 21.
19. The syllabus devised by Mulla Nizamuddin at Firangi Mahal, Lucknow, during the reign of Aurangzeb.
20. Iqbal has extensively written on the concept of *Ijtihad*, which literally means 'to exert' as 'the principle of movement in the structure of Islam.' Seeking 'the revaluation and re-codification of the Islamic Fiqh', he writes, 'The teaching of the Qur'an that life is a process of progressive creation necessitates that each generation, guided but unhampered by the work of its predecessors, should be permitted to solve its own problems' (see Iqbal, *The Reconstruction of Religious Thought in Islam*, New Delhi: Kitab Bhavan, 2000, pp. 151–78).
21. Ashraf, *An Overview of Muslim Politics in India*, p. 13.

6

The Communalization and Disintegration of Urdu in Anita Desai's *In Custody*

AMINA YAQIN

The question of Urdu in India is an extremely layered one, an issue that needs to be examined historically, politically, and ideologically in order to grasp the various forces that have shaped its current perception as a sectarian language adopted by Indian Muslims, marking their separation from the national collectivity. I shall explore those themes through the lens of literature—specifically, an Indian English novel about Urdu titled *In Custody*, authored by Anita Desai.[1] *In Custody*, shortlisted for the Booker Prize in 1984, can be retrospectively read as a literary narration of the communalization and disintegration of Urdu in post-Partition India. The year in which it was published was coincidentally the same that saw the death of an Urdu literary giant, the master lyricist Faiz Ahmad Faiz, who stirred the hearts of millions with his haunting verse and gave hope to many with his romantic vision of a return to a beloved homeland. Symbolizing hope, his poetry revived the disheartened nationalists with its belief in a destination that had as yet not been realized, a hope that marked even his most dejected poem *Subh-e Azadi: August 1947* (Freedom's Dawn) with its important ideological rejection of the 'pock-marked dawn' of freedom from colonial rule:

> The time for the liberation of heart and mind
> Has not come as yet
> Continue your arduous journey
> This is not your destination[2]

It is ironic that Faiz, with his traditional poetic forms and modern themes, was successful in constructing a new direction for Urdu while Desai, working with a modernist narrative, takes it back toward a sensibility rooted in tradition. Her idea of Urdu is that it is trapped in an aristocratic lineage, a theme that she also touches on in her earlier novel *Clear Light of Day*.[3] Desai's perception of Urdu as an artifact of Old India and its communal heritage are key features of her story. One of the narrative devices she uses is that of cultural memory; this, in connection with the theme of Urdu, is inevitably tied to the memory of separation and Partition.

In Desai's book, when the protagonist Deven, a lecturer in Hindi, applies in person for a week's [study] leave in order to conduct an interview with the legendary Urdu poet Nur Shahjahanabadi, his head of department, Trivedi, meets the request with a virulent, short-tempered, and communally charged reaction: 'I'll get you transferred to your beloved Urdu department. I won't have Muslim toadies in my department, you'll ruin my boys with your Muslim ideas, your Urdu language. I'll complain to the Principal, I'll warn the RSS [Rashtriya Swayamsevak Sangh] you are a traitor' (p. 145). The book constructs a culture of fear and paranoia, mistrust, and hatred where language has become a carrier of religious identity and national loyalty. Trivedi's diatribe, long before the destruction of the Babri Masjid in Ayodhya, has an ominous ring to it. With its evocation of the RSS it can retrospectively be seen to anticipate the current Indian political climate, where his voice returns to haunt us in the Bombay riots, the violent eruptions in Gujarat, and the continuing Kashmir crisis.

Sunil Khilnani in his insightful study entitled *The Idea of India* has argued that Partition is a tangible memory in the subcontinent 'around which the inevitable disappointments of modern politics can gather. [...] Partition is the unspeakable sadness at the heart of the idea of India: a *memento mori* that what made India possible also profoundly diminished the integral value of the idea'.[4] For Khilnani, the idea of India is ultimately a political one because, in his view, the history of India since 1947 is marked by a continuing faith in democratic procedures, and expressed through party politics; Indians have in the past been inspired by the charisma of the Congress party, and more recently by regional, caste-based, and communal political groupings. In this respect, the evolving modern nation is still disrupted by hierarchical stratification and—in the sometimes fraught relationship between Hindus and Muslims—the memories of its ruptured birth.

The question for this essay is, what kind of cultural memory is Desai constructing in her text, and how can this depiction be read in relation to the actual machinations of Indian politics with regard to the language question? As a successful author, writing for an international publishing market, she is invested with a certain fictional power to imaginatively represent an 'authentic' India. While she is not a writer who bombards us with an epic-style nar-ration, purporting to offer 'the great Indian novel', her exploration of individual identities and self-formations work in a subtle and problematic way, creating instead miniatures, and guiding the reader's responses through a combination of omniscience, internal focalization, indirect speech, and symbolic tropes.

Her story of Urdu is presented through the eyes of an urban dweller in Delhi who is caught up in the romance of Urdu as a carrier of a pre-modern cultural memory, rather than tied to it as a mother-tongue or second-language speaker. In an interview with Magda Costa in Spain, Anita Desai responded to the suggestion that *In Custody* is a representation of the decay of Urdu literature as follows:

I was trying to portray the world of Urdu poets. Living in Delhi I was always surrounded by the sound of Urdu poetry. Nobody reads it but one goes to recitations. It was very much the voice of North India. But although there is such a reverence for Urdu poetry, the fact that most Muslims left India to go to Pakistan meant that most schools and universities of Urdu were closed. So that it's a language I don't think is going to survive in India. There are many Muslims and they do write in Urdu; but it has a kind of very artificial existence. People are not going to study Urdu in school and college anymore, so who are going to be their readers? Where is the audience?[5]

Aijaz Ahmad, tracing the history of the Urdu language and litera-ture from 1947 to 1965, describes three aspects in the break-up and redistribution of the Urdu-writing community that changed the perception of Urdu after Partition. One was the migration and re-settlement of religious communities across the newly drawn borders; second was the increased communalization of Urdu as a Muslim language, its implementation as a national language in Pakistan, and decreasing status as a language of 'minority right' and 'Muslim interest' in India; and finally, the Indian Parliament's abandonment of Hindustani in favour of Hindi as the official language. In Ahmad's estimation, the loss of Hindustani as a recognized *lingua franca* was a major event because it had served as a 'living link between Urdu and Hindi, which now became more and more distant from each other, especially in their written forms'.[6]

For Ahmad, the political nation and the cultural community are the two ultimate 'framing realities' that dominate post-Partition Urdu literary production in India and Pakistan. In post-colonial India—specifically Uttar Pradesh (UP) where the mother-tongue Urdu speaker has been marginalized through a lack of representation in the linguistic federation of states—Urdu is indeed perceived as an endangered language by the minority who are literate in it. With the absence of a middle-ground Hindustani, the communal perception of Urdu as a Muslim language has become stronger. This religious separatism saturates the verse of a contemporary Urdu poet Raashid Banaarsi from Varanasi:

> We understood a lot about the prejudices of this age
> Today languages too are Brahmins and Shaikhs?
> We don't understand
> If Urdu too is under blame for being an outsider
> Then whose homeland is India? We don't understand.[7]

Banaarsi, in an interview with Christopher Lee, has also voiced his personal opinion on the state of Urdu, commenting:

they will kill its spirit, meaning the life will be taken out of it. You can write Urdu and call it Hindi or call it anything…Look, you can see how the attempts are being made to crush Urdu, just look at films. In films all the language is Urdu but they're given Hindi certificates.[8]

There are interesting similarities between Desai, Ahmad, and Banaarsi, all speaking of Urdu but in varying tones and differing forms. Desai's personal pessimistic view of Urdu's survival in India is tied to the fact of mass Muslim migration; Ahmad sees migration as a contributory factor to the break-up of the Urdu writing community; and Banaarsi articulates the opinion of Urdu as a migrant's tongue. It is also interesting to note that Banaarsi's passionate dis-illusionment as a mother-tongue Urdu speaker is also shared by Deven, the Hindu custodian of Urdu in Desai's novel. However, in order to grasp the nuances of a fictional rewriting of Urdu in English, we need to historicize both the developments that have affected Urdu in pre- and post-Partition India, and the ideological outlook of Indian writing in English.

Writing in the early 1990s, Aijaz Ahmad was of the opinion that the teaching of English literature has created a body of English-speaking Indians who represent 'the only' overarching national community with a common language, able to imagine themselves across the disparate nation as a *national* literary intelligentsia' with 'a shared body of knowledge, *shared* presumptions and a *shared* knowledge of mutual exchange'.[9] Arguably, both Desai and Ahmad belong to this 'intelligentsia' through the post-colonial secular English connection but, equally, as members of an élite English-speaking middle-class, they are implicated in the power structures of the state and irrevocably tied to the colonial discourse of literary education that endeavoured to create a new class of Indians.[10] The task of this essay is thus not to re-inscribe an authentic myth of origin about Indianness through linguistic associations, but to critically assess the value of Anita Desai's intervention in a communally-charged Hindi–Urdu debate.

Language

The knotty issue of national language has been a topic of scholarly deliberation in historiographical and sociological studies of the Indian nation. Several researchers have drawn attention to the contentious themes of Hindustani, Urdu, and Hindi in nineteenth-and twentieth-century India.[11] Such linguistic differences can be read as marking an important distinction from what Benedict Anderson has theorized as an integrated 'Imagined Community' coming to-gether through a common language with the rise of a homogenizing print capitalism. [12] These studies have revealed a multilingual nation which cannot comfortably assimilate its diverse linguistic groups.

Urdu came to prominence in the middle to late eighteenth century at the same time as the ousting of Persian from the courts by the British and its replacement with the official language of government, English. Generally, in eastern and northern India, Bengali and Urdu remained in use in the lower levels of administration and judiciary, while in the northern state of Punjab, the British imposed English and Urdu 'as the languages of government'.[13] On an informal basis they relied on Hindustani/Urdu as a lingua franca in north India, while recognition was accorded to the vernaculars on 4 September 1837 by a resolution of the Governor-General-in-Council. Urdu was officially recognized in Bihar, the United Provinces, Avadh, and the Punjab, while in the south it was patronized by the Nizams of Hyderabad. While a reformer and early modernizer such as Sir Sayyid Ahmad Khan was deeply influential in instigating linguistic reform and advocating cultural change for his community, his interventions for the cause of Urdu with the colonial government suffered setbacks in Bihar in 1881 and in UP in 1900 under pressure from a rising middle-class Hindu lobby.[14] According to Francis Robinson, the British government's favourable response to the proposed replacement of the Persian script by Devanagari, led by a Hindu deputation in 1900, marked a key moment in the increasing sense of separatism among Indian Muslims.[15]

The historical perspective of Urdu's decline has been directly linked to Hindi's rise by Jyotirindra Das Gupta who charts the national movement alongside language associations in pre-Partition India.[16] He asserts that, after 1882, the Hindi movements pressed for teaching Hindi universally in all primary and secondary schools in north India. It was in the North Western Provinces that the Hindi movement displayed a virulent stance toward Urdu. 'The constant refrain of the public petitions was that Urdu was an alien language. A petition signed by 500 Hindi graduates and undergraduates declared Urdu to be 'an alien and upstart language' while another petition described Urdu as a 'hybrid production...forced upon us by our former rulers'.[17] In Das Gupta's view, 'a large part of the language conflict in UP is influenced by the memories of past conflict transmitted to the Hindu and Muslim communities by the cultural and political leaders'.[18]

In his study, Das Gupta lays an emphasis on the centrality of sociological perspectives in understanding the language shifts from colonial British India to the post-colonial, post-Partition modern nations of India and Pakistan with two 'separate' national histories, languages, and literature. In his view, in a traditional multilingual society, the power of representation came to lie with a small élite whose community consciousness dictated their group loyalty, and in the early nationalist phase in India 'leaders rarely drew a distinction between the categories of common language, national language and official language'.[19]

For David Lelyveld too, sociological perspectives are paramount in examining the organic history of languages such as Hindi and Urdu, rather than an abstract theorizing that focuses on 'who gets to speak, who is allowed to listen, which topics and settings are appropriate to which linguistic codes'.[20] He suggests that in attempting to understand this linguistic code we may come closer toward grasping the unique formula which delicately balances the formation of self-conscious identity against the facts of power, competition, and exploitation. To put his theory to the test, Lelyveld examines Gandhi's role in nurturing an Indian national consciousness through a unified Indian language, which would both reflect the self-identity of Indians and bridge the linguistic diversity of its many regions. He argues:

It would be debatable in 1916 to say that Hindi was Hindu and Urdu was Muslim, but there were certainly grounds and occasion for relating language and religion in this way. It was one of the central projects of Gandhi's life, and a tenet of the Indian National Congress after 1920, that the national language must overarch this distinction, that instead of being Hindi or Urdu, it should be Hindustani.[21]

Historically, the Indian National Congress gave official recognition to Hindustani in its 1934 constitution. Hindustani, suggested by Gandhi as a neutral solution to the thorny Hindi–Urdu controversy, would reflect a unified national consciousness free from religious affiliations. But the stumbling block around which the neutral solution fell apart was that of the script. In Sunil Khilnani's view, after Independence: 'Nehru's initial hope had been for India's regional states to continue as the mixed, multilingual administrative units established by the Raj.'[22] Nehru's government resisted the pressures from the Hindi lobbyists for a centralizing national language, and reached a compromise with the post-Partition Indian Constitution (1950) recommending a fifteen-year usage of English for official purposes, Hindi in the Devanagari script as the 'official' language of the Union, and also extended recognition to other regional languages. But eventually this pluralism had to be altered to accommodate the demand for decentralization and the formation of linguistic states.

The Official Languages Amendment Act of 1963 gave Hindi the hegemonic status of 'official language' and English the secondary role of 'associate' or additional official language.[23] The Official Languages Amendment Bill adopted in 1967 included the acceptance of a historic Three Language Formula that would be implemented in secondary education for language teaching. It recommends: '(a) the regional language and mother tongue when the latter is different from the regional language: (b) Hindi or, in Hindi-speaking areas, another Indian language; and (c) English or any other modern European language'.[24]

With regard to the situation of Urdu in contemporary India, the language controversies of the past have had a detrimental effect on the status of Urdu wherever religious identity has come to inform the ideologically separatist stance of Muslim=Urdu=Pakistan and Hindu=Hindi=India. The Urdu-as-Muslim issue has been particularly volatile in UP, where the recent bone of contention has been the alleged statistical miscounting of mother-tongue Urdu speakers. UP, once the heartland of Urdu's urban élite, is now unable to meet the needs of its mother-tongue speakers. Political intervention on a regional scale was officially led by Dr Zakir Husain and a seven member Urdu-speakers' deputation to the UP education minister (Sampurnanand) in 1952, registering the marginalization of Urdu in the state. In 1954, the grievances were made known at a national level to the president of India and a request was made on 15 February 1954 under Article 347 of the Constitution for the recognition of Urdu as a regional language in UP, Bihar, Punjab, and Delhi. In 1958, Sampurnanand, the chief minister, said in the Legislative Assembly that Urdu could not be recognized as a regional language in UP.

However, these political maneuverings have not resulted in any concrete legislation which aims to resolve the issue. What has happened, according to Ather Farouqui, is that the situation of the mother-tongue Urdu speaker has deteriorated in Uttar Pradesh to such an extent that 'there is not even a single primary or junior-high school of Urdu medium. The only two Urdu-medium schools are run by and affiliated to Aligarh Muslim University'.[25] For Farouqui, the Three Language Formula in UP has thus far failed to serve the needs of mother-tongue speakers of minority languages. He dismisses the formula as a whitewash as far as the Urdu language is concerned. Farouqui is outraged at the whimsical interpretation of the north Indian chief ministers in their implementation of the formula which recognizes Hindi as the only regional language, Sanskrit as the modern language, and English as the foreign language. To him this signifies a sinister political manipulation of the Urdu minority in north India, particularly at the time of census collection, which he argues took for granted that everyone's mother tongue in the area was Hindi.[26]

In Zoya Hasan's estimation, the Hindi–Urdu controversy in UP has an explicit agenda of 'political dominance and equally significant subtexts on the cultural identity of the state and alternative conceptions of political community'.[27] Hasan places the blame squarely on government policy, which has treated Urdu as a minority Muslim affair, breaching the stance on linguistic pluralism and the separation of language and religion. The conflation of language and religion in the Sanskritized official Hindi expansion programme has also created further alienation and division among the already communalized linguistic groups.[28]

More recently, the communalist equation was detected in the field of education—specifically, history textbooks used by secondary schools recommended by the National Council of Educational Research and Training (NCERT), an issue that was highlighted in the English language press both within and outside India. According to Dr R.M. Pal, the NCERT had stepped away from its previously 'scientific humanist' guidelines for textbooks set in 1994 and surrendered its autonomy to the [atavist] government by agreeing to 'delete certain portions from a few textbooks'.[29] He says that subsequently the NCERT was in the process of doing away with the present textbooks to make way for new ones that were in touch with the then government's policy. Thus, the political Hindu nationalist agenda of the BJP had begun to interfere with the work of Indian historians and educationists. This represents a worrying trend in the democratic Indian state, particularly as the past was being reordered through political intervention intent on furthering the communalist divide. There is no doubt that the manipulation of education on religious lines will have an exacerbatory effect on the language conflicts that have been exploited in the construction of a religio-ethnic national identity in India.

Literature

In Custody tells the story of the decline and decay of Urdu in modern India. Deven, the anti-hero of the novel, is a Hindi lecturer devoted to the classical tradition of Urdu poetry, a devotion that stems from his childhood association with the language as a mother-tongue speaker. Born in Lucknow and educated in Delhi, he is a poor widower's son who has found employment as a university lecturer in Lala Ram Lal College in Mirpore. While his career choice of language specialist is not particularly lucrative, it has been directed by a practical consideration of the market economy, which favours Hindi, the language of communication in north India. Urdu fulfils his imagination and Hindi sustains his corporeal needs. 'I am—only

a teacher...and must teach to support my family. But poetry—
Urdu—...I need to serve them to show my appreciation' (p. 43).
Deven feels trapped in the confines of his chosen home, so when the
opportunity of returning to the capital presents itself through the
intervention of his childhood friend, Murad, he takes an uncharac-
teristically risky step by agreeing to his suggestion.

In taking this decision, he is temporarily freed from the constrictions of his
existence in the small town of Mirpore which had come to resemble the meta-
phorically 'impassable desert that lay between him and the capital with its lost
treasures of friendships, entertainments, attractions, and opportunities'. (p. 24).

The northern plain of Mirpore, situated 'more than a thousand
miles from the coast', had been shaped by the presence of Muslim
aristocracy, in this case a long forgotten Nawab, who had fled Delhi
to escape the aftermath of the 1857 Mutiny and built a mosque in
Mirpore as a memorial and in thanks to his Supreme benefactor
for preserving his life. The narrator tells us that the history of the
mosque has been swept away in the dust that saturates the Mirpore
atmosphere, and all that remains of the 'marble and pink sandstone'
is a decaying filth-ridden stone structure overtaken by the debris of
modernity. But the narrator reiterates its continued use as a mosque.
Continuing to map the cultural traditions of Mirpore, she tells us:
'the temples were more numerous but had no history at all. There
was literally not a man in Mirpore who could have told one when
they were built or by whom' (p. 20).

Here it can be argued that Desai's reconstruction of the geography
of Mirpore is interesting and problematic because it links
the Muslim presence in Mirpore to a pre-modern urban aristocracy
and contrasts it with the timelessness of an indigenous Hindu
tradition that is embedded in an infinite antiquity: 'the same kind
of antiquity that the shacks of the poor had, and the stalls of the
traders—they were often wrecked, rebuilt and replaced, but their
essential form remained the same' (p. 20). While it is in no way my
intention to suggest that Anita Desai is articulating a communalist
viewpoint, there is a particular historical and ideological freight
around the usage of Hinduism as timeless and Islam as a latecomer,
which the narrative inevitably duplicates. The miniature portrait of
the town grafted on to the larger narrative of Urdu replicates what,
to borrow a phrase from Edward Said, might be seen as a problematic 'structure of attitude and reference' toward a whole cultural
tradition.[30] The narrator tells us that the Mirpore communities were

mutually observant of the segregated 'Muslim' and 'Hindu' areas. While this separation was mutually respected, the delicate balance between the two communities threatened to spill into bloodshed and violence when the ritual mourning of Mohurrum coincided with the festival of Holi. Despite police patrols, the communities.

clashed...from time to time, knives flashed, batons flailed and blood ran. For a while tension was high, the newspapers—both in Hindi and Urdu—were filled with guarded reports and fulsome editorials on India's secularity while overnight news-sheets appeared with less guarded reports laced with threats and accusations (p. 21).

Here, the reference to the Hindi and Urdu newspapers is highly charged and can be seen to be indicative of the manipulation of ethnic differences in the regional print media. This print culture has the power to stoke the fires of dissension in a tense situation and intensify a separatist stance through divisive linguistic narratives. Deven, who is not explicitly mentioned in the descriptive overview of Mirpore's Hindu–Muslim tensions, is the idealist who is caught between the novel's unbridgeable divide of Hindu–Hindi and Muslim–Urdu.

Desai begins her narrative with an unscheduled meeting between the two childhood friends with contrasting personalities and backgrounds; Deven and Murad, his Muslim friend: 'the spoilt rich boy with money in his pocket for cinema shows and cigarettes' (p. 11). The story symbolically unfolds at the beginning of spring in the month of March, conventionally signifying birth and hope. The encounter between the two friends takes place in the college grounds of Deven's university. Murad who is given the qualities of a changing March wind, 'whirling dust and dry leaves around violently' (p. 10) bringing with it the promise of change, has travelled from Delhi to Mirpore to involve Deven in his latest project and sow the seeds of Deven's fateful journey from Mirpore to Delhi. Murad, in his capacity as editor of a leading Urdu journal *Awaz*, commissions Deven to interview the renowned Delhi poet Nur Shahjahanabadi for a special issue of his journal on poetry.

Deven is torn between the desire to interview his hero and to vent his own creativity as a poet for Murad's 'special issue', but Murad brushes aside Deven's tentative suggestion and, instead, accuses him of betraying his mother tongue by selling out to the professional service of its arch-rival Hindi. This accusation is to haunt Deven throughout the book each time he enters the Urdu arena. Murad feels he is on higher moral ground because, unlike Deven, he has not surrendered to Hindi. For him, his job as an Urdu editor displays his commitment and lifelong struggle toward the continuity of a golden tradition despite the constant worries of diminishing subscriptions, low readership, and escalating costs of production. Murad's outlook of Urdu is marked by a sense of the 'glorious' past, and an intention to recover the lost high cultural tradition that flourished in the pre-modern urban literary landscape before its present relegation to the nameless margins of the city. He wishes to

keep alive the glorious tradition of Urdu literature. If we do not do it at whatever cost, how will it survive in this era of that—vegetarian monster, Hindi?'...'That language of peasants', Murad sneered, picking his teeth with a matchstick. The language that is raised on radishes and potatoes...it flourishes, while Urdu language of the court in days of royalty—now languishes in the back lanes and gutters of the city.' (p. 15).

Urdu has, it seems, plummeted from the central heights of the Qutub Minar in Delhi to the peripheral labyrinthine bazaars of Chandni Chowk. Symbolically, Murad's character is physically disfigured by pockmarks all over his face rather like his beloved Urdu, which no longer has the patronage of emperors and nawabs, and his love for Urdu is tainted by his contempt for Hindi. However, his prejudicial attitude toward Hindi does not seem to extend to a communal rejection of Hindus as he confers the task of Urdu's custody onto Deven. He tells Deven:

Nur will be the star of the issue. The light that blazes in the center and sends its rays to all corners of the world where his verse is known—in Iran, Iraq, Malaysia, Russia, Sweden—do you know, we have sent his name to the Nobel Prize Committee for literature once again?' I want a full feature on Nur—Nur in his old age, the dying Nur before he is gone, like a comet into the dark. I want you to do that feature (p. 17).

Here Desai's reference to a well-known, socially aware poet may be seen as an indirect nod in the direction of Faiz, the revolutionary Progressive poet who was awarded the Lenin Peace Prize in 1962. Faiz excelled in interweaving the classical ornamental style of an aristocratic stylized Urdu rhyme and metre with the modern functionality of social realism. Desai's narrative has a lyrical quality with its use of symbolic tropes, and echoes some of the indefinable nuances of Faiz's verse but, unlike Faiz, she is not sending out a message for social change. Faiz's political agenda radically changed the classical imagery of the lover and the beloved, the literal and metaphorical desert of their separation, and the hopeful symbol of the morning breeze, imbuing them with a new meaning. The nation became the unattainable beloved and Faiz its devotee, the morning breeze was tinged with revolutionary powers of change, while the pain of separation between the beloved nation and its lovesick poet remained as agonizing as ever.[31] For Faiz, the poets were 'the warriors–the riders of dawn' who wrote first against colonialism and then the oppressive post-colonial state giving hope to people where there was none.[32] In the story we are told that Faiz, one of Nur's contemporaries, is in Beirut, a fictional reference true to life that marks Desai's acknowledgement of a living legend (p. 97). Nur's legendary persona borrows the revolutionary traits of Faiz's poetry. For Deven, an Urdu poet living outside his homeland is lost to the 'Urdu cause', which in his view needs most urgent support in India from someone living within India. So, when fate intervenes in the shape of Murad, he decides to take the risk and embark on a symbolic journey from Mirpore to Delhi to re-claim his beloved Urdu.

In Desai's narration, Nur holds the key to Urdu's revival. However, her characterization of Nur is conservative. Nur, contrary to the reader's expectations, is reluctant to part with the old metaphors and lifestyle of an aristocratic lineage, and his lifestyle appears to be untouched by a Progressive outlook. He is obsessed with his pigeons, his body is saturated with an excess of rich foods and alcohol, he lives in a dusty, faded house with his two wives, and entertains extravagantly. His poetic influences are Byron and Shelley. This link between the melancholic Romantic English poets and nostalgic Urdu poetry is also developed as a motif in Desai's characterization of Raja in *Clear Light of Day*. In the days leading up to Partition, when Raja is struck down with tuberculosis, it is said:

His situation was Romantic in the extreme, Bim could see as she sponged his face and helped him…his heavy, limp body as she lifted it as spent and sapped as a bled fish, and the city of Delhi burning down about them. He hoped, like Byron, to go to the rescue of those in peril. Instead, like Byron, he lay ill, dying.[33]

Similarly, Nur too is 'prepared for suffering' and his bodily ailments are a mirror to the sickened state of Urdu. But unlike Raja he is not suffering the flames of Partition, his pain is of a different kind. This pain is absorbed by his alter-ego Deven trapped by the harsh realities of a material world but, unlike Nur and Faiz, his poetic spirit is destined for failure, locked as it is in the 'sufferings of the time'.[34]

In taking on the task of a custodian, Deven must sideline his own creative output in favour of the living poetic legend. But, in fulfilling his duty as custodian, he has to overcome many obstacles, some of which are foreseen and others that are not. His immediate priority is to establish contact with the poet and obtain his consent for an interview. In getting close to the poet he finds himself embroiled in the minutiae of Nur's domestic life, an involvement that ultimately spirals out of his control. Contrary to his expectations, he finds himself at the mercy of the two wives, who appear to have charge over Nur's life. Having had the upper hand in his own domestic life, Deven is often confounded by the differing power structures of Nur's household and unable to cope with the idea of a woman as an equal, leave alone an intellectual. Deven, inadvertently and through a series of coincidences, is asked by Murad to fulfil his task by immortalizing the verse of Nur in an audio recording. Initially, he is dismissive of the idea, seeing it as a belittling gesture to the great poet—reducing his poetry to 'some song for the cinema, or radio' (p. 91). However, Murad criticizes his small-town sensibility and convinces him that the idea of a tape recording of Nur Shahjahanabadi is 'brilliant' even though Deven has never bought or used a radio before. Sarcastically, Murad exclaims, 'This is the age of electronics, haven't you heard? Or hasn't the news traveled to Mirpore yet?' (p. 92). Murad continues to field the forces of change and modernity in Deven's life and Deven, despite suspecting his sincerity, submits to his friend's oratory— only to reflect nearer the end of the novel, when things go disastrously wrong, whether their friendship too is another meaningless symbol of a lost custom.

Deven finds an unexpected ally in the Urdu section at Lala Ram Lal College who assist him in acquiring college funds for purchasing a tape recorder for his assigned project. Deven's poverty as a Hindi lecturer is matched by the diminishing stature of his colleague, the head of the Urdu department, Abid Siddiqui. Siddiqui, another symbolic custodian of Urdu, is described as 'a small man, whose youthful face was prematurely topped with a plume of white hair as if to signify the doomed nature of his discipline' (p. 96). Lala Ram Lal College could afford the luxury of an Urdu section because of 'a very large donation from the descendants of the very Nawab who had fled Delhi in the aftermath of the 1857 mutiny' (p. 96). Like the dying culture he represents, Siddiqui lives in a deteriorating *haveli* that re-emphasizes the decay of Urdu and the peripheral position of Muslims in the modern Indian environment. Desai's references to Siddiqui's lifestyle disturbingly reproduce the colonial constructions of a morally decrepit Muslim aristocracy collapsing from drink, debauchery, and decay. The inevitable death of this self-indulgent aristocratic Muslim culture is symbolized in the destruction of Siddiqui's house, when the 'decaying' haveli is razed to the ground by developers and is lost in the metaphorical swirling dust that absorbs Mirpore.

Siddiqui has knowingly participated in the sale of his house to a Delhi businessman. 'He wants to...build a block of flats with shops on the ground floor, cinema house at the back, offices on top.... And as I need the money—you know my weakness—the offer was too good to refuse' (p. 198). The conclusion is that he, too, has left Urdu behind in favour of industrial modernization. From a different angle, this depiction reinforces the idea that Siddiqui's class can no longer be the custodians of Urdu as they have little power to make themselves heard at the national level. The official situation and status of their language literally makes them outsiders in their own home. Deven has the potential to release the sickened language and its people but he, too, is constantly reminded of his position as an outsider when he is around Nur and his cronies. Nur says:

'He has come to speak for me...through his throat, my words will flow. Listen and tell me if my poetry deserves to live, or if it should give way to—that fodder chewed by peasants, Hindi?'... Nur was inviting him to join the fray, allowing the sublime concept of time to dwindle into the mere politics of language again... He knew he ought not to have stayed, listening to this kind of talk, he a Hindu and a teacher of Hindi. He had always kept away from the political angle of languages (pp. 54–5).

In this instance, Desai overtly connects the theme of language with religion and politics. What the novel ultimately shows us is that a mother-tongue speaker of Urdu, Deven is economically disempowered by his first language, which he studied as a boy in Lucknow, and was taught to him by his father—a teacher, a scholar, and 'lover of Urdu poetry'. It does not stand him in good stead when, after his father's death, his mother decides to move to Delhi. 'I was sent to the nearest school, a Hindi-medium school, sir', says Deven when he first meets Nur Shahjahanabadi. 'I took my degree in Hindi, Sir and now I am temporary lecturer in Lala Ram Lal College at Mirpore. It is my living, sir. You see I am a married man, a family man' (p. 43). For Deven, in post-Independence India, his love for Urdu and his job as a Hindi lecturer are at odds with each other and he finds it increasingly difficult to hold on to both. Nur openly attacks him saying:

Those Congress-wallahs have set up Hindi on top as our ruler. You are its slave. Perhaps a spy even if you don't know it, sent to the universities to destroy whatever remains of Urdu, hunt it out and kill it...It seems you have been sent here to torment me, to show me to what depths Urdu has fallen (pp. 42–3).

Deven remains on the fringes of Urdu culture because he does not come from an élite background and has chosen to teach the language that offers better employment prospects and economic growth than an Urdu education. The unexpected opportunity of interviewing Nur temporarily frees him from his caged existence, but it is a freedom fraught with danger.

This sense of danger communicates itself to the reader during Deven's first bus journey to Delhi and is crystallized in an ominous premonition after his arrival at a teashop near the inter-state bus terminal on Ring Road in Delhi. Finishing his cup of tea:

...he saw a dead fly floating in the dregs of his tea. The gasp he gave was only partly of horror at the teashop owner's filthiness and the wretched standards of hygiene in his shop. Or even from a fear of typhoid and cholera. It was the revelation that all the omens of the day had come together and met at the bottom of the glass he held between his fingers. In it lay the struck dog, the triumphant crows, the dead fly—death, itself, nothing less. Coming together in the separate prisms of the fly's eye, drowned but glittering in the tea, it stared back at him without blinking (p. 29).

This portent is mediated through an omniscient narrator who foregrounds the theme of dying through the symbolic motifs of the dog, the crows, and the fly. It appears that Deven's journey has ended before it has begun because the language he wishes to save is already dead.

It is of course inevitable that the tape recorder which is purchased by Deven with Murad's unreliable help is second-hand, and that he does not know how to operate it and has to rely on Chiku, the boy technician, to help him make the recordings. The tape recorder is a symbol of modernity and functionalism; it therefore fails to record the voice of tradition or pre-modern India. Chiku's ineptitude with a symbol of progress is a metaphor for the continuing inequalities of language and opportunity in India. The failed recordings are symptomatic of the dysfunctionality of Urdu. 'It was a fiasco. There was no other word for it. Disbelievingly, Deven had the first tape removed, the second tried and then the third and the fourth' (p. 173).

It seems that the book does offer an alternative vision through the poetry of Nur's second wife, but this vision is rejected by Deven because he sees her as a snake, an impostor who has stolen her husband's verse. Again, Desai's characterization of Imtiaz Begum is problematic because she is the typecast intellectual yet predatory courtesan/poet who is the chosen companion of the Progressive, pre-modern Muslim poet as his second wife. Yet, the woman who sends her manuscript to Deven for critical perusal is desperately looking for a patron who will give her talent its due recognition and, through his intervention, make her persona acceptable to a middle-class Urdu readership. The tone she takes with Deven is confrontational:

The recording is no secret. Whatever your reason for concealing it from me, Nur Sahib could not conceal it from me. Was I considered incapable of understanding the need to record Nur Sahib's voice for posterity? Was Safiya Begum considered wiser and more capable because of her greater age and her longer years with him? Dear friend, I beg to put it to you that you have insulted my intelligence by your deception...you thought I was a prostitute who dazzled Nur Sahib's eyes with my dance and so inveigled my way out of a house of prostitution into the house of a distinguished poet. [...] Kindly remember that unlike Nur Sahib and unlike your respected self, I am a woman and have had no education but what I have found and seized for myself. [...] When you rose to your feet and left the *mehfil* while I was singing my verse, was it not because you feared I might eclipse the verse of Nur Sahib and other male poets whom you revere? Was it not intolerable to you that a woman should match their gifts and even outstrip them? (p. 195).

Deven's answer to her challenge is to shred her manuscript and reject her plea as a false one. It seems that Urdu cannot sustain the modernity of a female narrative either. She cannot shed her first skin as a performer, and Devan relegates her poetry to the rubbish heap.

The problem in Desai's story is that there are no variants of Urdu—she does not draw upon what, to borrow from Aijaz Ahmad, one might call an Urdu lineage of the present.[35] Her vision of Urdu is in stark contrast to the opinion of the renowned Urdu novelist Intizar Husain, who has argued that the cultural tradition of Urdu lies in its shifting regional locations. According to him, this language cannot be associated with one region and one culture because it is by nature hybrid and adaptable to new regions.[36] Desai's Urdu is destined to wither away in the stultifying heat of summer, unable to sustain the hopeful beginning of spring.[37]

* * *

Desai's central characters Deven, Murad, and Nur are all caught in a nostalgic view of Urdu, wishing to restore it to its former glory. Their cultural memory of a pre-modern past rejects the values of an evolving industrial modern present. Desai's overall novelistic portrayal of Urdu marks an elegiac farewell to a lost tradition. Her symbolism is tinged with the tropes of a communally charged present, unable to break out of the fragmentary Hindu–Hindi and Muslim–Urdu divide despite her staging the debates within the 'secular' Indian-English novel. Despite his many journeys, Urdu's custodian Deven is unable to bridge the metaphorical desert that separates the small regional town of Mirpore and the national capital Delhi, because in the words of one of Nur's cronies: 'Urdu is supposed to have died, in 1947' (p. 56). And Delhi has moved on.

Notes

1. Anita Desai, *In Custody*, London: Penguin, 1985. All subsequent references are taken from this edition and direct quotations cited will give page numbers in the text.

2. Khalid Hasan (ed.), *The Unicorn and the Dancing Girl: Poems of Faiz Ahmad Faiz*, trans. Daud Kamal, London: Independent, 1988, p. 36.

3. Anita Desai, *Clear Light of Day*, London: Penguin, 1980. See Part II, which details Raja's attraction to Urdu poetry, his heroic character, and his admiration for the neighbour and landlord, Hyder Ali, who encourages his interest in Urdu.

4. Sunil Khilnani, *The Idea of India*, London: Penguin, 1998, pp. 200–2.

5. *http://www.umiacs.umd.edu/usevs/sawweb/sawnet/books/desai_ interview.html.*

6. Aijaz Ahmad, *Lineages of the Present: Political Essays*, New Delhi: Tulika, 1996, pp. 201–02.

7. Quoted in Christopher Lee, '"Hit it with a Stick and it won't Die": Urdu Language and Muslim Identity and Poetry in Varanasi, India', *Annual Of Urdu Studies*, vol. 15, no. 1, 2000, pp. 337–51, p. 338.

8. Ibid., p. 339.

9. Aijaz Ahmad, *In Theory: Classes, Nations, Literatures*, London, New York: Verso, 1992, p. 278. See chapter 7 '"Indian Literature": Notes Toward the Definition of a Category', pp. 243–86.

10. See Gauri Viswanathan, *Masks of Conquest: Literary Study and British Rule in India*, London: Faber & Faber, 1989.

11 This is reflected in monographs such as Christopher Shackle and Rupert Snell, *Hindi and Urdu since 1800: A Common Reader*, London: School of Oriental and African Studies, University of London, 1990; Amrit Rai, *A House Divided: The Origin and Development of Hindi-Urdu*, New Delhi: Oxford

University Press, 1991; Paul Brass, *Language, Religion and Politics in North India*, Cambridge: Cambridge University Press, 1974; Christopher King, *One Language, Two Scripts: The Hindi Movement in Nineteenth Century North India*, New Delhi: Oxford University Press, 1994.

12. See Benedict Anderson, *Imagined Communities: Reflections on the Origin and Spread of Nationalism*, rev. ed., London: Verso, 1991, and also Homi K. Bhabha (ed.), *Nation and Narration*, London: Routledge, 1990.

13. Sugata Bose, and Ayesha Jalal, *Modern South Asia: History, Culture, Political Economy*, London: Routledge, 1998, pp. 84–5.

14. Shackle and Snell, *Hindi and Urdu since 1800*, p. 8.

15. Francis Robinson, *Separatism Among Indian Muslims: the Politics of the United Provinces' Muslims 1860–1923*, Cambridge: Cambridge University Press, 1993, pp. 133–74.

16. Jyotirindra Das Gupta, *Language Conflict and National Development: Group Politics and National Language Policy in India*, Berkeley, London: University of California Press, 1970.

17. Ibid., p. 103.

18. Ibid., p. 150. While the Hindi petitions gathered strength, there was only one petition, signed by a small number of people, submitted in favour of Urdu in the North Western Provinces. As this shows, language petitions in the 19th century were becoming communally charged and reflected the divisive forces of language and religion on the communities. The culture of language petitions survived in post-Independent India, and the late Dr Zakir Husain's act of collecting 2.25 million signatures from the Urdu-speaking people in UP supporting a petition asking the President to save Urdu under Article 347 of the Constitution in 1952 proves a case in point. For a critical comment on politicians taking up the Urdu cause in UP see Danial Latifi, 'Urdu in UP', *Nation and the World*, 16 August 1999, pp. 44–6.

19. Das Gupta, *Language Conflict and National Development*, p. 36.

20. David Lelyveld, 'The Fate of Hindustani: Colonial Knowledge and the Project of a National Language' in Carole Breckenridge and Peter van der Veer (eds), *Orientalism and the Postcolonial Predicament: Perspectives on South Asia* Philadelphia: University of Pennsylvania 1993, pp. 189–214, p. 192.

21. Ibid., p. 192.

22. Khilnani, *The Idea of India*, p. 175.

23. King, *One Language, Two Scripts*, pp. 4–7.

24. Das Gupta, *Language Conflict and National Development*, p. 243.

25. Ather Farouqui, 'Urdu education in India: Four Representative States', *Economic and Political Weekly*, vol. XXIX, no. 14, 2 April 1994, p. 782.

26. Ibid., p. 783.

27. Zoya Hasan, *Quest for Power: Oppositional Movements and Post-Congress Politics in Uttar Pradesh*, New Delhi: Oxford University Press, 1998, p. 187.

28. Ibid., pp. 187–8. Also see Christophe Jaffrelot, 'The Sangh Parivar between Sanskritisation and Social Engineering' in Thomas Blom Hansen & Christophe Jaffrelot (eds), *The BJP and the Compulsions of Politics in India*, New Delhi: Oxford University Press, 1998, pp. 22–71.

29. R.M. Pal, 'Objectionable Nonsense', *Mainstream*, 22 December 2001, p. 39.

30. Edward Said borrows and modifies Raymond Williams' phrase 'structure of feeling', as 'structures of attitude and reference', to describe 'the way in which structures of location and geographical reference appear in the cultural languages of literature, history, or ethnography, sometimes allusively and sometimes carefully plotted, across several individual works that are not otherwise connected to one another or to an official ideology of 'empire' (Edward W. Said, *Culture and Imperialism*, London: Chatto & Windus, 1993, p. 61). I consider such structures to be inherent in all hegemonic discourses which address an 'other' from a position of power, as is the case with Urdu in India and the problematic place of Islam in Indian history.

31. Gopi Chand Narang, *Urdu Language and Literature: Critical Perspectives*, New Delhi: Sterling, 1991. See the chapter on Faiz Ahmad Faiz which discusses in detail aspects of tradition and innovation in his poetry.

32. Hasan, *Quest for Power*, p. 74.

33. Desai, *Clear Light of Day*, p. 60.

34. Victor Kiernan (ed. and trans.), *Poems by Faiz*, Lahore: Vanguard Books, 1971, p. 65. This poem marks an important initial stage in Faiz's career as a poet. For a critical reading of Faiz as a Progressive poet, see Carlo Coppola, 'Urdu Poetry: the Progressive Episode', PhD thesis, Chicago: The University of Chicago, 1975. Also see Estelle Dryland, *Faiz Ahmad Faiz 1911–1984: Urdu Poet of Social Realism*, Lahore: Vanguard Books, 1993.

35. Ahmad, *Lineages of the Present*.

36. Intizar Husain, '*Urdu ka tehzibi mizaj*' (Urdu's cultural etiquette), *Annual of Urdu Studies*, vol. 15, no. 2, 2000, pp. 372–6.

37. Interestingly, the novel was adapted as a screenplay for a film nine years later by the Bombay-born director, Ismail Merchant, the successful partner of the internationally acclaimed Merchant–Ivory production group. The script was rewritten in Urdu by Shahrukh Husain in collaboration with Anita Desai. There is a crucial shift of power dynamic in the telling of this tale from an English narration about Urdu to a re-appropriation of the story of Urdu *in* Urdu. Merchant's view about Urdu is completely different to Desai's because he does not think that Urdu can die. The making of the film is a powerful statement of his belief (*http://web.mit.edu/newsoffice/tt/1994/jun15/36722.html*).

7

The Destiny of Urdu in Independent India:
Language and Muslim Identity

DANIELA BREDI

Linguistic and political phenomena are strictly related[1] and, as Paul Brass has skillfully demonstrated,[2] in the case of Indian Muslims this relation has conditioned the destiny of Urdu in Independent India. Muslim nationalists, among whom Dr Zakir Husain had considerable relevance, did their best to avoid the sacrifice of this cherished language at the altar of Indian national identity. Nevertheless, the question is any thing but simple and far from a solution in India today, where an increasingly less tolerant and communalist atmosphere seems to prevail. Urdu, in fact, still has a primary importance for the integration of the largest Indian minority, the Muslims, into mainstream society. It is, therefore, worth going back to its genesis in an effort to highlight the difficult intercourse between Urdu, the Muslim community, and Indian national identity.

In South Asia, there is a great social and linguistic complexity. Indian society is composed of people segmented along ethnic and culturally distinct lines—groups not always living in separate territories, and speaking different languages and dialects not easily submerged by inter-group communication.[3] Moreover, in the course of Indian history, literary styles have always been intimately related to religious membership. Each of the four Vedas, for example, was cultivated by a particular Brahmin subgroup, only whose members had the opportunity to learn it. Religious schisms implied the creation of new literary languages: Pali owes its existence to Buddhist rebellion against Brahmins; Prakrit was the language of the Jains, etc. Literary styles usually differed from colloquial languages, and to learn them one had to spend years studying.

Linguistic compartmentalization appears to have reached its peak in some areas of northern India at the beginning of the modern age. Persian was the language of administration and government documentation, Sanskrit the language of Brahmin rituals, Avadhi the language of mythology and philosophical poetry, and Brajbhasha the language of ballads and lyrics. Urdu was in use in the bazaars and military camps, and traders and certain artisan groups had special codes to keep secret their activity from outsiders. In such linguistic conditions, few people had the ability to deal with every matter of their interest by themselves. Commoners usually knew their own dialect and the language of the bazaar and, even if a few could read and write in a particular style, this did not mean that they could read court documents or religious texts without the help of a specialist. Several languages had groups of specialists, whose linguistic knowledge constituted their means for earning a living.[4]

From the nineteenth century, the earlier specialized literary and commercial languages were substituted with English and the modern vernaculars but, to a certain extent, some compartmentalization has still been left. Hindi and Urdu, as literary languages, differ mainly in the source of their borrowed terms, since one takes cultured words from the Sanskrit lexicon and utilizes the Nagari script, while the other makes use of Persian and Arab words and the Arab script. Pronunciation causes another difference as formal Urdu requires a correct pronunciation of Persian sounds, while Hindi lays stress on the retroflexed and nasalized. In practice, people speaking these languages make themselves distinct by following the rules of pronunciation peculiar to one or the other language. In Hindi–Urdu, therefore, the transition is gradual or fluid. However, knowledge of standard languages in India is still relatively limited in comparison to other parts of the world, as alphabetization is at a quite low level and partially remains a class and caste function. Most people tend to be bilingual: they speak their dialect at home and the standard language outside.

The linguistic situation today is considerably less complex than a few centuries ago, though the language differences are on the whole greater than in most western industrialized societies. Government policy about language should be considered in this linguistic context and put in relation with national identity.

Political development is a combination of several processes, and implies a high level of mobilization of men and means through an institutionalized political order. In this sense, political integration of a nation can be said to be a crucial element in determining the pace and direction of development. Political integration refers to the process of putting together and coordinating different social groups in a common political enterprise.[5] This process of construction and development of a political community involves, among other factors, a tremendous growth of the function of communication in the political order. Since language is the most important medium of communication, it becomes a significative social factor and is a cause of concern for a ruling class willing to promote national integration. Interaction between language and politics acquires a dramatic importance in India as the plurality of languages has become remarkably complicated. After decolonization, the process of substituting an official foreign language—English—with an Indian language that could be acceptable as a national language,[6] made things worse.

The Pre-Independence Dilemma

The linguistic question was anyway raised in pre-Independence times, at the beginning of political mass mobilization. The Hindi–Urdu question, in particular, proved its relevance when, in the course of forging a national identity, Urdu was chosen as a symbol of Indo-Muslim culture and the Muslim League put it forward as the national language of the Muslims. Urdu, however, was not peculiar to the Indian Muslims. Rather, it expressed Mughal culture, intrinsically composite and not exclusively Muslim. Millions of non-Muslims in Kashmir, Punjab, Uttar Pradesh (UP), Bihar, and Bengal adopted Urdu as their language.

The Indian national movement was aware of the need for a national language to take the place of English after Independence, but was not sure that Hindi would be acceptable to all the linguistic groups that took part in it. Most nationalist leaders, anyway, were persuaded that a form of Hindi, variously defined as Hindi-Hindustani or simply Hindustani, could be popularized in the whole subcontinent as a common language that would eventually be accepted as a substitute for English. For this reason, they supported Gandhi's proposal in 1925, when he succeeeded in getting the approval of the Indian National Congress in adopting Hindustani as the language of its proceedings at national level.[7] In order to fully understand the meaning of these and later events, and their political importance, it is necessary to take a step backward and look at the history of the Hindi–Urdu controversy. It is in the course of this history, in fact, that the creation of their difference can be read, from a certain point of view, as an identity-making process.

Authoritative dissenting voices holding that 'Urdu and Hindi are two separate languages and should be described as such'[8] notwith-standing, many others believe that there is a single language that is common in northern India and is variously described as Hindi, Urdu, or Hindustani. Christopher King and Alok Rai maintain that this unitary language, in the course of history and for specific interests, was purposely separated into two through the sanskritization of one of its versions, while increasingly opening the other to Arab–Persian influence. Rai singles out the time when this separation occurred as the late nineteenth century. He does not mean to affirm the existence of a preceding Arcadian harmony between the two main communi-ties of South Asia, but simply to state that, up to that point, language as such was not an issue of community differentiation. British miscon-ceptions and the efforts of the 'Fort William's pedants' had not yet affected the real language which merrily reflected the glorious con-fusion of the north India vernacular, freely getting its borrowings not only from classical sources of Sanskrit and Arabic and Persian, but also from the hybrid offsprings of a whole series of Prakrits and other languages.[9] Up to this point, even if written in both Arab-Persian and Devanagari characters, the language was one. Unfortunately, the British were soon confronted with the problem of deciding which was the language of north India, and choosing one of the two versions. At the beginning Muslims denied that Urdu had a communalist and religious connotation, but Hindus held since 1870 that a language written in Arab-Persian characters could not be termed as their own.[10]

Towards a Modern Language

Two organizations had a pivotal role in shaping modern Hindi: Nagari Pracharini Sabha in Benares, and Hindi Sahitya Sammelan in Allahabad. The first, founded in 1893, centred its activity on spreading Nagari characters. The second was more openly politically oriented. Its first convention in Benares in 1910 was presided over by Madan Mohan Malaviya, and two subjects were prominent on its agenda: education and social benefits deriving from its diffusion; administration language. Administration language, directly related to political power, was due to gain prominence in the following ten years. This, in its turn, was a consequence of British policy in the field of education which, around the middle of the nineteenth century, produced two trends: one favouring adoption of the Nagari alphabet and connected with Sanskrit, and the other giving preference to the Arab–Persian script. To this belonged mainly urban Muslims, professionals, and Kayasthas, while the first was prevalently composed of high-caste Hindus. Arab–Persian script users had a prominent place in colonial administration—in 1879, an ordinance was promulgated requiring knowledge of this alphabet to get access to every public appointment with a monthly salary over ten rupees. Nagari users constituted a class of educated people, whose frustrated ambitions led them to give birth to agitations in favour of Hindi. They got a significative result with the McDonnell ordinance of 1900 recommending the Nagari script. Unluckily for them the governor-general modified the vice-governor's proposal and, in the official text, rather than 'Persian and Nagari script', the wording was 'Hindi and Urdu languages'. This gave rise to a dichotomy that would become a symbol of harsh conflicts.

Up to this point, the conundrum is easy to understand. A new proto-élite, using the Nagari alphabet, seeks a share in power management by asking for the recognition of that script. On the flip side of the coin, the old élite tries to safeguard its privileges. The government in the end cannot do anything but make some concessions, and eliminate the education system's inconsistency with access to administration. The unexpected, yet in some ways predictable, result is that a language born as genuinely secular, not only because it originated from the contact between communities borrowing freely from different languages but also because it was essentially mundane in its origins and scope, becomes a symbol defining a religious community.

This development can occur because the opposing parties, both trying to describe their counterpart as 'the other', in an effort to reinforce and give credibility to their claims, *de facto* generate and crystallize a reserve of immediately available supporters. Each party is thus compelled to keep a distance from the common land in the middle, that is, the common language, and build a symbology and a collective imagination supporting the cultural exclusivism it needs. This differentiation process began to bear first fruits in the 1930s, when the defence of Urdu was put among the claims of the Muslim community, which was far from being homogeneous, but whose leaders would orient its biggest part towards separatism. Many Urdu authors and poets gave a historical destiny to the Indian Muslim nation they meant to build, and projected the Pakistan movement as a crusade for the foundation of an Islamic state. They catalogued the social and cultural difference between Hindus and Muslims, described distinctive Indo-Muslim characters glorifying the past of Islam in India and elsewhere, and took pride in Pan-Islamism. They idolized Jinnah and presented him for mass veneration as the custodian of the community, their great leader, and a symbol of Islam.[11]

Aligarh Muslim University (AMU) was, as Jinnah once said, 'the arsenal of Muslim India', but it became so only by the end of the 1930s, when the All-India Muslim Students' Federation (AIMSF) was born. The AIMSF published a periodical in Urdu and English, circulated pamphlets on the Pakistan concept and regularly invited Muslim League politicians to address student meetings, transforming Sir Syed's citadel into Jinnah's stronghold. Later, many AMU students became Muslim League activists who toured the countryside, talking to villagers about children compelled by the Congress provincial government to sing *Bande Mataram* (a symbol of Hindu nationalism and revival), lamenting Hindi's exaltation to the detriment of Urdu, and deploring Muslims' exclusion from the local administration and civil service.[12]

Urdu newspapers reflected both emotional involvement and differences among intellectual and political trends. Aligarh's *Urdu-e Moalla*, Lahore's *Zamindar*, Calcutta's *Al-Hilal*, and Delhi's *Hamdard* are milestones in the history of Urdu journalism. After having reached a zenith during the Khilafat movement, they went on to feed intellectual and political debate and created a Muslim public opinion. They presented several opinions and mirrored a spectrum from Abu'l Kalam Azad's 'composite nationalism' (*Al-Hilal*) to Zafar Ali Khan's separatism (*Zamindar*).[13]

The great traumatic events of Independence and Partition in 1947 found Urdu practically identified with the Muslim community. Muslim separatists accepted, made it their own, and upheld this identification, and utilized it as a means of mobilization in the

Pakistan movement. 'Composite nationalism' supporters in the Congress, however, generally denied it.[14] At the time, in India as well as in Pakistan, the claim for a national language was basically a nationalist aspiration, coloured with the simple belief that usually characterizes nationalist politics in the pre-Independence period. Relative lack of evaluation of the complexity that goes with the national language question in a multilingual society, can be detected in the speeches and writings of leaders in pre-Independence India.[15] At that stage, leaders rarely make a distinction between the categories of common language, national language, and official language, and incline to use them indifferently. After independence, anyway, the need for greater precision arises, and the language of administration and communication between rulers and the ruled has to be termed as the official language, the language generally understood in the whole of the state territory should be called the common language, and the natural idiom of the majority linguistic community for which the members of this group have a primordial affection should be referred to as the national language. Once this distinction is made, it is possible that in a political society the official language does not coincide with the common language, and more than one language could be recognized as the national one, even though not all of them had the status of official languages.

An Official vs. Common Language

Indian leaders, confronted with language issues requiring specific official responses, began by talking of an official, not of a common language. This clearly amounted to recognizing the fact that, in a multilingual country, the only rational way of tackling the problem was an attempt to establish an official language in the hope that it would be widely accepted, rather than finding a single national language that everybody could understand and utilize.

In independent India, with the complex linguistic conditions and the labelling of Urdu as the language of the Muslim community, even if not condoned by more secular people, Urdu's destiny looked uncertain and darker because it was not the language of any territorially distinct area.

As far as language is concerned, the Indian Constitution recognizes fifteen languages,[16] but of these fifteen Hindi is the only one with the status of an official language. Hindi, in any case, is spoken by only 30 per cent of the population. For this reason, there has been a strong reaction against this move, especially in south and east India. But Hindi could rely upon government political will to impose it, besides a network of voluntary organizations, originally born as literary societies, which systematically promoted it.

The strongest centres of these associations are in Uttar Pradesh, where the Hindi élite's operative centres are located. Many members of these associations identify the promotion of Hindi with its sanskritization—meaning the elimination of foreign influences, that is, the influence of the Urdu lexicon and style. As an Urdu scholar has aptly said, 'Urdu is being constantly termed as only an off-shoot or variety of Hindi, a foreign language, a language of the Muslims, an instrument of communal hatred and an enemy of Indian unity. All these contrary things are said in the same breath to suppress it'.[17] Not by chance, in fact, some important members of the Hindi movement happen to be supporters of Hindu fundamentalist organizations as well. This is one of the reasons why the rivalry between Hindi and Urdu has a trend to coincide with the Hindu–Muslim conflict in this politically crucial state.

From the nineteenth century, north India in general and UP in particular have been the centre of Hindu cultural and political revival opposing Muslim influence, while also being the centre of major Muslim institutions and the base of the most significative leaders of Muslim nationalism. Hindu and Muslim literary associations have deep memories of this political rivalry and contribute to crystallize Hindu–Muslim differences. This poses a serious problem for Muslim integration in mainstream society, which gets even more difficult for the continuous process of eliminating mutual language influences and having constant recourse to classical sources—Sanskrit for Hindi, and Persian for Urdu. This process of classicalization has, as a result, created an increasing gap between the spoken language and the literary language, and between élite communication and mass understanding.[18]

Some national leaders—Gandhi, Nehru, and Azad included—made attempts at correcting this process, promoting the idea that Hindi was the same as Hindustani, by which they meant a mixture of the Urdu and Hindi commonly understood in north India. Nehru, who personally appreciated Urdu poetry and prose and was a friend and admirer of such authors and poets as Anand Narain Mulla, Sajjad Zaheer, Josh Malihabadi, Firaq Gorakhpuri, and Faiz Ahmed Faiz, was a supporter of Hindustani. In this, he followed Gandhi's example when he tried to throw water on the fire of the Urdu–Hindi controversy and do away with this major obstacle in the integration of Muslims. Nehru refused to understand why, once Hindi's position as the official language was established and Urdu could not be its rival, the Hindi movement's zealots were so keen on suppressing the language of Mir and Ghalib.[19] He put the question in these terms to Tandon, Pant, Govind Das, Sampurnanand, Kamalapathi Tripathi, Ravi Shankar, and K.M. Munshi, who represented Hindu nationalism within the Congress and were against every trace of a Muslim heritage, Hindustani included. They regarded Hindustani as Urdu in disguise, an essentially Muslim language identified with the Pakistan movement.[20]

Muslim leaders did not contest Hindi's position as India's official language, but wanted Urdu to be recognized as a second regional language in the areas where it was generally spoken by Muslims as well as by Hindus. Uncompromising Hindu nationalists, such as the members of the Hindi Sahitya Sammelan in UP, would not concede even this, and opposed Nehru's proposal for an enlargement of the national language concept to include Urdu and its script.[21]

Thus, Hindi and not Hindustani was recognized as India's official language. The UP Board of High School and Intermediate Education decreed that, 1953 onward, high school examinations would be written in Nagari only. In 1954, the Congress Working Committee recommended that Hindi should be compulsory in schools and universities. In the meanwhile, active and aggressive campaigns against Urdu, as if it were a dangerous foe, were initiated and spread in towns. The UP and Bihar governments stopped giving funds to Urdu-medium schools and deprived the younger generation of the opportunity to study and learn in this language.

Nehru deplored this trend in the Congress-ruled states, for he knew that this clear injustice towards Urdu speakers endangered national integration. But he was also resigned to being unable to take any action without an agreement with his fellow party members.[22]

Among the Muslim members of the Indian National Congress, Zakir Husain, an exponent of great relevance for the more secular-minded intellectuals accepting composite nationalism and a moving spirit of Jamia Millia Islamia since its establishment in 1920, tried his best to defend Urdu up to the point that political considerations allowed him. He became alienated from the Muslim League and the

Muslim consensus in the late 1930, when, as president of the Wardha
Committee on Education set up by the Congress, he brought out a
report that most Muslims saw as too inclined towards an educational
policy oriented in favour of Hindu revivalism. A staunch nationalist,
he identified himself completely with the hopes and aspirations of
an united India and extended his full support to the plan of action
for freeing India from colonial shackles. All his thoughts rotated on
the axis of national integration; he opposed partition of the country.
At the height of communal frenzy, he brought Jinnah and Nehru on
the same platform in November 1946 and warned them: 'This fire is
burning in a noble land... For God's sake, sit together and extinguish
this fire of hatred. This is not the time to ask who is responsible for
it and what is its cause. The fire is raging. Please extinguish it... For
God's sake do not allow the foundations of a civilized life in this
country destroyed'.[23]

On nationalist and secular positions, he expressed the necessity
for integration of Muslims in independent India, but did not give up
the defence of the right of the Muslim minority to develop its own
cultural heritage. Husain emphatically denied that any culture could
be superior to another, and refused to promote an indistinct uniformity. He was for giving due recognition to every culture, and supported the concept of tolerance that allows everybody to exist. Husain
thought that from variety and difference could, and should, develop
a composite culture and an open society, able to accomodate every
religion, caste, class, language, mentality, and lifestyle, provided
they contributed to the general social welfare. As far as Muslims
were concerned, his opinion was: 'Indian Muslims love their country
as much as any of their compatriots... but they would not accept the
complete loss of their cultural identity. They would like to be good
Muslims as well as good Indians'.[24]

The Muslim Vision

Zakir Husain's work in defence and for the promotion of Urdu in
independent India has to be seen as a part of his vision of an open and
multicultural society, within which Muslims had to be integrated. As
president of the Anjuman Taraqqi-i Urdu (Hind) from 1948 to 1956,
while he was vice-chancellor of AMU—not appointed by the government with the aim to 'normalize' this forge of dissent, but unanimously elected by the University Court in the hope that AMU, like

Jamia Millia Islamia, might work for Muslim integration—he acted as an interpreter of the Muslim feelings of anxiety and need for reassurance, and promoted a signature campaign in 1952 for the recognition of Urdu as the second official language of UP under Article 347 of the Indian Constitution. Article 347 (Special provision relating to language spoken by a section of the population of a State) provides: 'On a demand being made in that behalf the President may, if he is satisfied that a substantial proportion of the population of a State desire the use of any language spoken by them to be recognized by that State, direct that such language shall also be officially recognized throughout that State or any part thereof for such purpose as he may specify'. His signature campaign support-ing a petition asking the president to save Urdu under this article of the Constitution had enormous success. A delegation met the president of India and urged his intervention. Zakir Saheb himself led a delegation to Dr Rajendra Prasad on 15 February 1954, but nothing came of it—probably because subsequent census reports were manipulated by mistaking the mother tongue of Urdu speakers as Hindi.[25]

As AMU's vice-chancellor, Husain took all possible initiatives to convey the message that AMU had changed, that it was integrating itself fairly well with the mainstream, and that it had something distinct to offer to Indian culture. But his action was not universally well accepted, and there were those who spread rumours that Zakir Husain was an intruder, and that he had been planted by the government for the *shuddhi* of AMU. Thus, when the time came to approve the amendment of the AMU Act, the community was needlessly agitated that the university would lose its minority character. The Urdu press excited Muslim passion on two issues: that religious instruction would no longer be compulsory in the university, and that the membership of the University Court would be thrown open to non-Muslims. The Urdu press did not realize that, in opposing the amendment, they were reinforcing the majority's suspicions about AMU's loyalties, and jeopardizing Maulana Azad and Zakir Saheb's efforts to keep AMU's character in its main purpose of offering higher education to Muslim boys, and of becoming an agent of social change in the community.

Unable to resort to polemics, Zakir Husain offered his resignation and, in September 1956 it was accepted. After having been a member of the Indian delegation to United Nations Educational, Scientific and Cultural Organization (UNESCO)—a task that suited his vocation of teacher and educationist—he became governor of Bihar on 6 July 1957. His duty implied that he had to act as the cultural ambassador of New Delhi, and he started using more Hindi words in his speeches, which annoyed the Urdu press. He only wanted a vocabulary that could be understood by all but, like the politics of the country which divided the land, the language, too, was dividing the people into two camps.

Zakir Husain's stand on Urdu was made clear on 27 November 1959, while speaking at the Urdu Research Institute. He said:

I feel that this language is prophetic of the blossoming of the new life which we Indians desire for our country in the era of its freedom...the longing to build out of distinctive and diverse elements a common culture, as the Ganges and the Jamuna together make one mighty stream...Urdu is not the language of the community or of a religion, it was not imposed by any government, or created artificially with a particular motive. It is the language of the people, of the common people...It is the language of the *faqirs* and saints, who were desperately anxious to communicate the love which overflowed their hearts to the common people...Urdu is, therefore, the language of affection and love, the language of tolerance, of an intercourse animated with goodwill...As Urdu is not a language confined to a particular region and those who speak and understand it are found all over the country, it should be foremost among the means of forging national unity...To regard a language in which we find the whole literature of the Arya Samaj, a language which the Christians have utilized to the full for their religious purposes as a Muslim language and thereby cultivate narrow mindedness is neither honest nor wise...[26]

Unfortunately, this way of thinking went against the Hindu and Muslim revivalists' positions. The protection of Urdu had become a political issue after Partition. The Hindi–Urdu question, in spite of its essentially economic nature, as it was connected with jobs in the Hindi belt, had become a cultural–religious issue around which the community's policies were built. Urdu, as a powerful symbol of Muslim identity, was the target of the Hindu nationalist and revivalist movements' attacks, and Urdu speakers of north India, mainly educated urban Muslims of *ashraf* groups,[27] considered this as proof of the aim to destroy their cultural identity. The refusal of Urdu, in fact, indicated a denial of the Muslim contribution to Indian culture and the will to make it exclusively Hindu.[28]

A Language Run Aground

Urdu's growth and enormous creative potential were suppressed after Independence. It ceased to be utilized in administration—with the exception of some districts in UP and Bihar—in courts and police districts, and survived painfully thanks to government-funded academies. The authorities, in fact, worried by the increasing gap between the two linguistic groups that were once practically one and the same, adopted a dual policy. Aiming to pacify those lower middle-class sections whose means of survival consisted in the diffusion of Urdu culture, they created public-funded institutions, a system of scholarships and grants for publishing their literary work, and released financial aid.

On the other hand, and this has much more importance, Urdu has almost ceased to be a medium of education; it is hardly a mass medium of communication, and it has been confined to the private sphere of life and to that very limited part of the public sphere that has to do with literary production. In an essentially urban and petit-bourgeois environment, where the role of the family as a builder of social agents and cultural operators is rapidly decreasing, and school and place of work are determining factors, a literary production so largely based on the family's linguistic culture is bound to sclerotize and become increasingly marginal.

The fundamental problem is not a question of figures, because the number of people declaring Urdu as their mother tongue is increasing. Urdu speakers—who happen to be Muslims at 99.9 per cent—are mainly illiterate, and those who have access to education are deprived of their right to get primary education in their mother tongue. This is the basic reason for the widespread ignorance of Urdu literature and culture among the younger generations, which arouses fears of a kind of cultural genocide making true the most dreaded equation integration=homologation. In Hindi-speaking states, the Three Language Formula, the aim of which should be to enable a child, at the primary level, to get familiar with other important and necessary languages along with the national language, worked in a perverse way. The chief ministers decided to place Sanskrit in the column of modern languages, practically throwing out Urdu from the Indian education system. Parents who want their children educated in their mother tongue have the only alternative of sending them to religious schools. Not all Muslim schools and colleges at any level, even in the states with a high level of Urdu-speaking concentration, offer instruction through the medium of Urdu.[29]

Minority educational institutions established by the Muslim community under Article 30 of the Constitution, from what can be gathered from the reports of the Bharat Seva Trust, New Delhi, are mostly of an abysmal standard, particularly in UP and Bihar.[30] The stilted Urdu taught by religious seminaries have become the official standard of the language, wiping out the immemorial Urdu tradition that constitutes the priceless wealth of composite Indian cultural heritage. The 'new' Urdu thus created alienated non-Muslim speakers and simultaneously strengthened the [atavistic] non-Muslims. The new generations of the 'official' Urdu intelligentsia is now composed of these conditioned Urdu scholars, whose cultural background veer them dangerously to pro-fundamentalist Islam.[31]

Uninspiring Educational Standards

Urdu education in independent India is not up to the task of producing a readership that demand high press standards. In its turn, the generally low level of the Urdu press has largely failed to play a constructive role in shaping Muslim sensibilities in post-Independence India, in the sense of enabling the community to face up to the challenge of adjustment as a large minority group in a secular nation. This vicious circle is unlikely to be broken, since Urdu journalism has a tendency to reinforce a sectarian and emotional outlook among readers. In some north-Indian states, particularly UP, the new generation of Muslims is barely conversant with Urdu. It is therefore the educationally backward Muslims, who stayed on after Partition and could read a little Urdu, that actually constitutes the regular readership of Urdu newspapers. Urdu newspapers, often linked to Muslim politicians, evolved a political strategy of reinforcing a ghetto mentality by playing on the sensibilities of this very section of north-Indian Muslims. Moreover, in most Urdu newspapers, the staff consists of a few calligraphers and a couple of sub-editors whose general attributes are a working knowledge of Urdu and Hindi. They usually do not speak English, for they are the product of religious schools, and are paid a low salary. Fortunately, the state of Urdu journalism is better in those linguistic regions where Muslims actively share the region's cultural ethos and have a pragmatic rather than emotional attitude towards Urdu.[32]

A look at the Indian National Bibliography indicates that Urdu publications appear in large numbers. Closer scrutiny shows that these publications are mainly poetry, fiction, criticism, and history books and texts on Islamic studies (commentaries and translations, religious law, sectarian tracts, sufi literature, etc.). Current events, political and economic history, sociological issues and such, have never been big in Urdu, and that continues to be the case.[33] There are practically no scientific and technical books in Urdu. This cannot be a surprise, given the fact that in UP, Urdu education means teaching Urdu language as a subject. In the other famous centre of Urdu culture, Hyderabad, whose Osmania University has the credit of making Urdu the medium of higher education and where Urdu was the medium of education even for engineering and medical sciences before Partition, textbooks in Urdu are now hardly available. Andhra Pradesh has a provision that students can read books in other languages (regional or English) and answer question papers in Urdu at the examinations—this is the state of Urdu at the college level! The English vocabulary is abundantly in use, especially in the study of science, commerce, and technical subjects. In Bihar, where the main reason for the popularity of Urdu is the deep attachment of the poorer sections of Muslim society to Islam, and where *madrasa*s have also started technical education, the course books are difficult to get. Though the educational standard is very low, it is overlooked because only the backward and lower middle-class Muslims have opted for the Urdu medium of education. Maharashtra is a happy exception, the reason being the relentless efforts of various trusts and voluntary Muslim organizations. The Urdu-medium schools and colleges run by private bodies and leading Muslim businessmen are well managed, with a respectable faculty of Urdu teachers and regular classes. The course books are prepared by the Textbook Bureau initially in Marathi, and then translated and published in Urdu. This means that the course material in Urdu and Marathi is the same.[34] From the organization of education to other spheres of practical life, the position occupied by Urdu has neither become a hurdle to development nor come in conflict with regional identity— unlike in north India.

All these considerations strengthen the idea that the Urdu–Hindi question can be solved by adopting a pragmatic, open, and pro-integration attitude along the lines that farsighted leaders such as Zakir Husain had drawn. Urdu can, then, at least try to be a competitor of Hindi in the political game of alphabetization of the illiterate Muslim masses, and put an end to the young Indian Muslims' increasing ignorance of their culture. This can be done by applying

Article 350-A of the Constitution (Facilities for Instruction in Mother Tongue at Primary Stage), which provides: 'It shall be the endeavour of every State and of every local authority within the State to provide adequate facilities for instruction in the mother tongue at the primary stage of education to children belonging to linguistic minority groups and the President may issue such directions to any State as he considers necessary or proper for securing the provision of such facilities'. Urdu-speaking intellectuals and politicians have to prove equal to the task of demonstrating that their mother tongue has a vital role to play in Indian culture and society. Self-pity and putting the blame on others will not get them far. If Muslims can teach their children to vocalize the Quran, they can also teach them to read Urdu. Where they have to be most active is in the area of primary education, which should be made available to every child in his or her mother tongue. That, unfortunately, has not been the case— particularly in the so-called Hindi belt where, Zakir Husain's efforts notwithstanding, it proved impossible to secure for Urdu the status of a regional language. The damage caused by the official proponents of Hindi, who successfully opposed the demarcation of an Urdu-speaking region, has not been corrected yet.

To save Urdu, it is necessary to resist the prejudice of those who hold that the choice of Urdu education is tantamount to betraying the Indian national identity, which they conceive as essentially Hindu in its Brahminical and highly Sanskritized version. But it is also necessary to fight against Muslim communalism that exploits the language issue as an instrument of negotiation with the state. The debate about the social and official position of Urdu in independent India should not be treated as a subject of exclusive Muslim interest, related only to safeguarding the rights of the Muslims. If it is true that Urdu is the main language of the Muslim minority, it is also true that it has historically never been an exclusive appanage of the Muslims. And, to make Urdu accepted as an essential part of Indian civilization is a pre-condition to eventually give it the role it deserves in the composite culture of secular India.

Notes

1. R. Corsetti (a cura di), *Lingua e politica*, Roma: Officina, 1976, p. 7.
2. P. Brass, *Language, Religion and Politics in North India*, Cambridge: Cambridge University Press, 1974, pp. 119–276.

3. John J. Gumperz, 'Sociolinguistics in South Asia', in Thomas Sebeok (ed.), *Current Trends in Linguistics*, Vol. 5: *Linguistics in South Asia*, The Hague, Paris: Mouton, 1969, p. 598.

4. Ibid., pp. 601–2.

5. See David Easton, *A System Analysis of Political Life*, New York: Wiley, 1965, p. 185.

6. Jyotirindra Das Gupta, 'Official Language Problems and Policies in South Asia', in Thomas Sebeok, *Current Trends in Linguistics*, Vol. 5: *Linguistics in South Asia*, The Hague, Paris: Mouton, 1969, p. 579.

7. See the resolution quoted in M.P. Desai, *The Hindi Prachar Movement*, Ahmedabad: Navajivan Publishing House, 1957, p. 14.

8. R. Russell, 'Some Notes on Hindi and Urdu', *The Annual of Urdu Studies*, no. 11, 1996, p. 204.

9. Christopher King, *One Language, Two Scripts: The Hindi Movement in Nineteenth Century North India*, New Delhi: Oxford University Press, 1994; Rai, Alok, 'Making a Difference', *The Annual of Urdu Studies*, no. 10, 1995, p. 141.

10. N.S. Gorekar, *Glimpses of Urdu Literature*, Bombay: Jaico Publishers, 1961, p. xiv.

11. Mahmud-ur-Rahman, *Jang-i Azadi ke Urdu Shuara*, Islamabad: Qaum Idarah bara-yi Tanqiq-i Tarikh o Saqafat, 1986, p. 37; Abida Riasat Rizvi, *Auraq-il zarrin, The Leaves of Gold*, Karachi: Begam Daulat Khanam Hidayatullah: Milne ke pate, Pakistan Ridars Gild, 1976, p. 340.

12. Mushirul Hasan, *India Partitioned—The Other Face of Freedom*, New Delhi: Roli International, 1995, p. 22.

13. See Ali Jawad Zaidi, *A History of Urdu Literature*, New Delhi: South Asia Books, 1993, ch. XX, *passim*.

14. For a definition of these ideas, see the relevant chapters of Aziz Ahmad, *Islamic Modernism in India and Pakistan*, London: Oxford University Press, 1967.

15. In Z.A. Ahmad (ed.), *National Language for India*, Allahabad: Kitabistan, 1941, there is a selection of these speeches and writings.

16. Assamese, Bengali, Gujarati, Hindi, Kannada, Kashmiri, Malayalam, Marathi, Oriya, Punjabi, Sanskrit, Tamil, Telugu, Urdu, and, later, Sindhi was added.

17. S. Ehtisam Husain, 'Multilingual aspect', *Seminar*, July 1960, p. 23. For an excellent statement of the Hindi–Urdu question, see A. Ahmad, *Studies in Islamic Culture in the Indian Environment*, London: Oxford University Press, 1964, pp. 239–62.

18. Das Gupta, 'Official Language Problems and Policies in South Asia', pp. 586–9.

19. Jawaharlal Nehru, *Letters*, vol. 3, 1 August 1953, p. 350.

20. J. Das Gupta, *Language Conflict and National Development: Group Politics and National Language Politics*, Berkeley: University of California Press, 1970, pp. 131–2.

21. Mushirul Hasan, *Legacy of a Divided Nation: India's Muslims Since Independence*, Boulder: Westview Press, 1997, pp. 157–8.

22. Ibid., p. 159.

23. Quoted in B. Sheik Ali, *A Great Teacher, Life and Work of Dr Zakir Husain*, Mysore: Prasaranga, 1997, p. 9.
24. Zakir Husain, *Ta'limi Khutbat*, Delhi: Maktaba-yi Jami'ah, 1955, pp. 240–8.
25. Danial Latifi, 'Urdu in UP', *Nation and the World*, 16 August 1999, p. 44.
26. Quoted in Ali, *A Great Teacher*, pp. 96–7.
27. For a study on caste-like Indo-Muslim social groups, see Imtiaz Ahmad (ed.), *Caste and Social Stratification among Muslims*, Delhi: Manohar, 1973.
28. Muhammad Mujeeb, *Islamic Influences on Indian Society*, Meerut: Menakashi Prakashan, 1972, p. 201.
29. Syed Shahabuddin, Letter to the Editor, *The Annual of Urdu Studies*, no. 14, 1999, p. 348.
30. C.M. Naim, 'Urdu in India', in Idem., *Ambiguities of Heritage—Fictions and Polemics*, Karachi: City Press, 1999, p. 98.
31. Danial Latifi, 'Urdu in UP', *Nation and the World*, 16 August 1999, pp. 44–5.
32. Ather Farouqui, 'The Emerging Dilemma of the Urdu Press in India: A Viewpoint', *South Asia*, vol. XVIII, no. 2, 1995, pp. 91–103.
33. Naim, 'Urdu in India', p. 99.
34. Ather Farouqui, 'Urdu Education in India: Four Representative States', *Economic and Political Weekly*, vol. 29, no. 14, 2 April 1994, pp. 784–5.

8

Whither Urdu?
Language, Community, and Power in India Today[1]

KELLY PEMBERTON

The question of Urdu's status in India today is inherently tied into
its viability as a language of influence and empowerment. In its social
dimension Urdu remains, at the level of everyday communication,
as much a link among various communities—religious, class, tribal,
linguistic, cultural, and regional—as Hindi. In its political dimension,
Urdu has become increasingly identified as the language of Muslims,
despite the rule of Indian politics that discourages the association of
linguistic demands with religious identity, and despite the belief of
many of Urdu's supporters that it is a language not only of Muslims
but also of Hindus, Christians, Sikhs, and others. As a consequence,
Urdu's overwhelming identification with a single religious community has fuelled its image as the representative of narrow, sectarian
interests, while its association with Pakistan has hastened the drive
for its elimination or reduction as part of a nationalist agenda.[2] Such
attitudes towards Urdu are reflected in central and state government
policies; in the stances adopted by many of the Hindu revivalist
groups, particularly those dominated by intellectuals and élites; and
in the views of many of the Urdu-speaking élite, all of whom have,
in one way or another, effectively worked to promote and reinforce
separatist tendencies, to paint Urdu as a hapless victim of nefarious
forces, and ultimately, to undermine Urdu education in India. Despite these circumstances, Urdu's extant links to institutions and
foci of power can still work to sustain it as well as increase its profile

as a viable and valued medium of communication—nationally, regionally, and at the grassroots level.

The Politics of Urdu after Partition

To begin to assess Urdu's future potential, and the prospects for actualizing this potential, it is necessary to understand where the efforts of the past have failed. One obvious factor is the way in which the responsibility for Urdu's preservation has been placed at the feet of state and central agencies and commissions. If we accept the current political rhetoric that tacitly defines Urdu along the lines of its associations with Muslims and Muslim culture, then it is not difficult to assume that the responsibility for Urdu lies largely with the central and state governments as the parties responsible for the protection of minority interests. Such has been the attitude of many Muslim intellectuals, members of the press, voluntary associations, and religious organizations. Interested politicians and special-interest groups, such as the Gujral Committee, have also adopted this attitude. The Gujral Committee's report, submitted to Parliament in 1975, sought to advance the cause of Urdu by recommending, among other measures, the establishment of Urdu-medium primary schools where the population of Urdu speakers in any single village or urban ward exceeded 10 per cent; the compulsory inclusion of Urdu (along with Hindi and English) in the Three Language Formula for schools; and the establishment of public facilities for the use of Urdu as a language of official communication at the local level (Brass 1990: 158–9).

Unfortunately, the recommendations of the report were never put into effect. The hostility of the Janata Dal government towards Urdu, the objections of cabinet members such as Jagjivan Ram, Minister for Agriculture and Irrigation at the time of the report's submission,[3] the hostility of other Members of Parliament toward concessions for Muslims and Urdu speakers, and I.K. Gujral's own inability to implement the proposals upon his rise to the office of prime minister have been cited as overt reasons for the failure of the committee's efforts (Brass 1990: 158; Russell 1999: 44; Latifi 2001: 533). Aside from these tangible variables, the association of Urdu with Muslims, and the casting of the Hindi–Urdu conflict in communalist terms (whose antecedents lie in the efforts of nineteenth-century Hindu intellectuals to subordinate Urdu to a form of Hindi they sought to standardize through the inclusion of a greater number of Sanskrit words), remain important contingent factors as well (Das Gupta 1970: 84–5).

Far from promoting the cause of Urdu, the Gujral report merely served to foster its image as a language separate and distinct from Hindi and entitled to treatment as such. This image had been previously promoted by Muslim intellectuals such as Sir Sayyid Ahmad Khan and the early generations of the Aligarh movement, who saw in the efforts of Hindu intellectuals to promote Hindi a self-conscious attempt to undermine Muslim influence in north India (Das Gupta 1970: 85, 91). In fact, it is the dual aspect of such treatment of Urdu—its association with the Muslim minority community, in which it is both conceived and treated as a victim of anti-Urdu forces in need of saving, and its subordination to and artificial bifurcation from Hindi—that has undermined its status. This despite the ostensible efforts of government commissions, voluntary associations, a variety of intellectuals, and the Urdu press to maintain and preserve it as a language of influence and importance, recognized, and sincerely treated as such at the central and state level.[4]

Post-Partition approaches to language policy have unfolded in complicity with notions of linguistic identity that were formulated in the period of the British Raj, despite the strength of the general and widespread belief in the autonomy of the Indian nation from its former colonial rulers (Ramaswamy 1999: 356). One such notion presumes a classificatory scheme of the Indian nation in which its constituent parts exist as singular, substantive entities with determinate boundaries: the notion of majority and minority communities defined in terms of religion, tribe, or language, for example. The taxonomies of census reports, especially as they are used to fashion demands for and against political concessions, have also shaped and fuelled demands for linguistic parity in official and administrative apparatuses at the national, state, and local level.

National integration in India—defined as an endeavour beginning with the nation or state and seeking to develop loyalties to it which transcend attachments to primary groups (for example, religious, caste, class)—has unfolded against a process of forced homogenization (see Brass 1974: 4–5) that has involved the sometimes real and sometimes perceived subordination of regional languages and dialects to a single language, Hindi.[5] The concept of national integration as it has been pursued as a matter of policy (and otherwise) in India is belied by two assumptions that undermine its effectiveness. One is that it is possible to simultaneously promote an official policy of 'unity in diversity,' touted as a nationalist slogan at the level of central government, while still giving ample scope to the expression of regional linguistic identities. The other is that in practice, all Indian languages have been eclipsed by English, which according to the Constitution of India, was to remain in use 'for a period of fifteen years from the commencement' of the Constitution, with the proviso that Parliament could choose to retain English for official purposes after the fifteen-year period (Constitution of India, Part XVII, Chapter 1, Article 343). Most policies instituted by the central and state government have continued to preserve the importance of English at the level of administration and other official business.[6]

Although both regional- and national-level politicians generally champion competence in both Hindi and English, it is English, rather than Hindi, in the words of Partha Ghosh (Director of the Indian Council of Social Science Research in New Delhi), that 'opens windows to the world,' as mastery of English brings opportunities for employment in élite and élitist institutions both domestic and foreign (Ghosh 1996: 63–4). The social and economic cleavages between English and non-English speakers is thus often much greater than those among speakers of the various officially recognized Indian languages vying for prominence. This observation is not meant to de-emphasize the intensity of the conflicts among the Indian languages, but rather to point out that at least on the national stage, the conflicts over recognition of the regional languages are overshadowed by the rising prominence of English. Beyond this prominent division between English and non-English speakers, the regional languages—particularly those that have been elevated to the distinction of official state languages—have themselves become infused with associations of separate, and often mutually hostile, cultural identities. In view of both the rising prominence of English as a mark of élite status and the rivalry among the regional languages, or rather the conflicts that have ensued between the regional languages and Hindi since Partition, Urdu has fallen—at least at the levels of administration and lower-level education—into decline.

The Failures of the Three Language Policy

One of the major efforts to give scope to the regional languages involved the Three Language Formula, recommended by the Union

Education Commission and later by the Secondary Education Commission, both convened in the early 1950s; the formula was implemented in the late 1960s.[7] One of its obvious objectives was to promote national linguistic integration. However, the formula made provisions for instruction in the declared 'official language' of the Indian Union, Hindi written in the Devanagari script; in the secondary, or *de facto* associate official language of the Union, English; in the designated Hindi-speaking states of the north, a 'modern Indian language'[8] (this latter a vague category that has become the subject of much conflict and controversy); and in the non-Hindi speaking states, a regional language or a choice of languages.[9] The Uttar Pradesh (UP) and Bihar state governments made provisions for Sanskrit to serve as an alternative to the choice of a 'Modern Indian Language,' although in effect Sanskrit has come to assume the status of a compulsory subject. Moreover, it has been generally the case with the application of the Three Language Formula in the north-Indian states that Sanskrit has become one of its major components for the majority of secondary students, (Brass 1974: 210–11, 214–15) while in the non-Hindi speaking states, Urdu's position as third choice (where it is offered as such) is overshadowed by the offer of instruction in a regional language.

The fact that the Three Language Formula exists in a somewhat modified form from state to state has only added to the confusion and difficulties in its implementation. According to Ather Farouqui, in effect, the formula (and its various interpretations at the state level) has played a major role in bringing an end to provisions for Urdu education. Through it, Hindi was given a major thrust, beginning in the 1960s.[10] North India was declared a Hindi belt, Hindi was recorded as the mother tongue of the population in that region, and census records were manipulated to reflect this (Farouqui 1994: 783; Latifi 1999: 1321). Thus, the right to Urdu education at the primary level in the north was effectively obviated, while provisions were made for the inclusion of Sanskrit—a language spoken by less than one per cent of the total Indian population—in the secondary and post-secondary level school curricula. (Farouqui 1994: 783; Shahabuddin 2001: 15) Reactions to this state of affairs among supporters of the regional languages was swift, and in some cases violent. Beginning in the mid-1960s, in West Bengal and in the south (particularly Tamil Nadu), protests and riots against the imposition of Hindi as the official language (enshrined in the Constitution and reiterated in the 1963 Official Language Bill) undermined the authority of the central government. It was feared that Hindi would overshadow and subvert the regional languages. Urdu fared badly under these circumstances: in the agitations that took place in the south, Urdu was effectively squeezed out as a possible choice for medium of instruction at the primary and secondary levels (Ramaswamy 1999: 347; Farouqui 1994: 783). In both the north and south, the facilities to study Urdu at the primary and secondary levels were largely denied, or weakened to the point that even where the language received tacit recognition or financial support at the state and central levels, its vitality as a language of influence and importance on the national and regional scenes was severely undermined, except in Jammu and Kashmir, where it remained the official state language (Farouqui 1994: 783). Thus, while purporting to promote linguistic integration, the Three Language Formula in effect served to foster diversity and intense rivalry by leaving the implementation of policy in the hands of state governments.

Nevertheless, efforts to give official recognition to Urdu have continued. The installation of Urdu as a second official language in UP and Bihar in recent times would seem to prove a feather in the cap of Urdu's supporters, but such recognition has been stymied by the poor state of Urdu education in these states, as elsewhere. Much fuss has been made about the lack or inadequacy of facilities for primary and secondary education in the Urdu language. Criticisms of the state of Urdu education at these levels usually focus on the following points: one is that there is no distinction made among the study of Urdu as an obligatory subject, the study of Urdu as a non-obligatory subject, and Urdu as a medium of education, and these matters require very different approaches (Shahabuddin 2001: 12, 2002: 19).[11] A second is that even where Urdu-medium schools are offered, the calibre of teachers is inadequate, and they often do not understand the meaning of the phrase 'Urdu medium' (that is, whether or not it constitutes teaching a variety of subjects in the Urdu language or the teaching of Urdu as a subject itself) (Russell 1999: 46; Farouqui 1994: 784). Another is that Urdu is given as an optional subject but is pitted against a choice of English, prompting students to choose the latter for practical reasons. Alternatively, as is the case in UP, provisions exist for administering junior-high-school examinations in the Urdu language, but most students opt instead for Hindi.[12] A fourth is that, as in the case of UP, most of the private schools are unrecognized or, alternatively, are only partially recognized. This, according to some accounts, has encouraged two practices: in one, arrangements may be made for students at unrecognized schools to appear as private candidates in the junior-high-school examinations in recognized schools, and in the other, examination results may be purchased at recognized schools by the parents of students attending unrecognized Urdu-medium schools (Farouqui 1994: 783, 784).

Critics of central and state government policies toward Urdu cite the depressed economic status of the students attending Urdu-medium schools as an important contingent factor in the sad state of Urdu education in India. Ather Farouqui links economic factors to the high drop-out rate of Urdu-medium students in Andhra Pradesh, though in Bihar, poverty has not had the same effect on Urdu education. He attributes this situation to the 'deep attachment of the poorer section of Muslim society to Islam,' which has been a boon for the Islamic religious institutions, or *dini madaris*, which provide Urdu education in that state. However, one must also consider that the Bihar government's recognition of the degrees provided by the dini madaris, despite the corruption and lack of systematization inherent in these institutions, is one of the most important variables behind the boost in the popularity, if not the quality, of Urdu education in Bihar (Farouqui 1994: 785). One palpable effect of the Bihar government's recognition of Urdu was that job opportunities increased in the state, though the literacy level in its rural areas remains, by one estimate, as high as 98 per cent below the national average.[13]

Regional Variations

The prospects for improving the standards of Urdu education in the south seem much more favourable than is the case in north India, and there are certainly economic factors at work. Farouqui links the high economic status of the Muslims of Maharashtra (and one must note here the association between religious and linguistic identities), largely from business communities, with the favourable condition of Urdu education in that state. The *Islamic Voice*, a fifteen-year-old English-language monthly based in Bangalore, altogether disputes the notion that Urdu education as a whole is suffering from neglect. A recent editorial maintains, in fact, that Muslims in Maharashtra have widened their base of primary and secondary education through a vast network of Urdu-medium schools. While the surveys conducted by the *Islamic Voice* (which maintain that for the past three years, Muslim students coming from Urdu-medium high schools have topped the tenth standard board examinations in Maharashtra) may be called into question in consideration of the allegations of false or deceptive examination results made by Ather Farouqui, the fact that quality Urdu-medium schools exist and seem to be on the rise makes one wonder if, in fact, the accusations of discrimination against Muslim Urdu speakers is exaggerated, at least in the case of competitive examinations in the south.[14]

This circumstance may lie partly in the fact that, on the whole, the Muslims of south India tend to be more prosperous than their counterparts in the north, and in the fact that in the south, Muslims have begun to assert their relationship with Urdu (Khurshid 1998) and have made strong cases for its continued vitality and importance, not only as a language cherished and spoken by Muslims, but by a wide cross-section of the population of India. Thus, while on the whole Urdu education may have declined markedly since Partition, new avenues for its implementation and promotion have opened up. One such avenue has been the implementation of the policy objectives of the Buland Shahr branch of the Delhi Public School Society, which accommodates students from deprived and economically backward sections of society, and offers them the option of learning Urdu as a third language (Narang 1998: foreword, 1, 3).

These spots of hope are often obscured by the rhetoric of many of Urdu's supporters in the north, particularly in UP, where the Hindi–Urdu conflict has been largely concentrated.[15] This rhetoric, which highlights Urdu's differences from, rather than similarities with, Hindi and other regional languages, was precipitated in part by the agitations of Hindi revivalists and by Urdu-speaking élites. Rather than highlighting Urdu's importance as a language of common, everyday use, a language that exemplified the rich cultural heritage of not only Muslim India, but Hindu, Sikh, and Christian as well, both Urdu's supporters and detractors have emphasized Urdu's exclusivity and (in the case of Urdu's supporters) its right to be considered for special treatment by government agencies precisely because it was the language of an oppressed minority. Such a contention has given ample ammunition to Hindu revivalists who argue against the government's 'coddling' of minorities (in particular, the

Muslim minority, which tends to be the focus of such criticisms). In effect, rather than emphasizing what Urdu has to offer India as a whole, Urdu's supporters and the organizations they represent have tended to consign the language to victimhood. Rather than pinning the blame on lack of government sponsorship, Urdu speakers themselves play a decisive role in implementing the strategies that will restore the language to a place of dignity, viability, and importance in the public eye.

Some Suggestions for Improving the State of Urdu

Some strategies in this direction have been suggested by scholars who are well grounded in the history and specifics of Urdu's evolution and political currency, and here a brief mention of some of the more insightful suggestions proposed are in order. In recent articles, Ralph Russell, C.M. Naim, and Danial Latifi have proposed ways in which Urdu's proponents can work to both divest it of its associations with narrow, sectarian interests and adopt positive, pro-active, and grassroots approaches to promoting it. One suggestion is that Urdu's proponents cast off the mantle of victimization. Instead of focusing on where government policy has fallen short, all three writers favour focusing on the publication of works that exemplify the best in the tradition of Urdu literature. Part of this strategy would involve the establishment of organizations that are independent of government funding as a matter of policy, as Ralph Russell has recommended. Such is the case with the Sikandarabad-based (UP) non-governmental organization (NGO), the Maulana Abul Kalam Azad Research and Educational Foundation. Organizations like these, it has been suggested, could publish critical editions of some of the classics such as *Indar Sabha*, *Dastan-i Amir Hamza*, and *Gul-i Bakavali*, as well as poetry collections, and the works of major figures associated with the Progressive Writers' Movement. However, even those organizations that rely on the support and assistance of government institutions, such as the Maulana Azad Research and Educational Foundation, established in 1989 (in Delhi), have a role to play in preserving and opening new avenues for the study of Urdu (Russell 1999: 46). The main objective of the foundation has been to formulate and implement schemes (with the assistance of the Ministry of Social Justice and Empowerment) for the promotion of education among the 'educationally backward' sections of society. By the end of March

2001, the foundation had sanctioned grants-in-aid of over Rs 49 crore to 355 NGOs in twenty states.[16] Others, such as Ather Farouqui, have suggested that the model followed by the Delhi-based Sardar Patel Senior Secondary (Public) School for Hindi at the primary level be adopted for Urdu. Such a strategy, he argues, 'gives children an opportunity to learn fast with-out imposing a false consciousness of belonging to some English-speaking élite.'[17]

The question of the role of *madrasas* in preserving and furthering Urdu education in India continues to be a hotly debated topic in which criticisms of Islam as a religious system are often embedded. As Ather Farouqui points out, madrasas have largely been the repositories of Urdu education in the north, and it is often the case that parents who want their children to learn Urdu send them to these institutions.[18] Yet, madrasas themselves are too often characterized— even more so in the post-9/11 atmosphere of extreme paranoia about Islam and things Islamic—as bastions of fundamentalism that pro-mote religious exclusivism, backward thinking, isolationism, and chauvinism. Children who go to madrasas, it is often argued, are alienated from modern secular education, which makes them prime targets for fundamentalist mullahs and maulvis. In many cases this is true. These accusations—and they are levelled against madrasas by 'secular' Muslims as much as by non-Muslims and the Bharatiya Janata Party (BJP)—are not only one-sided, misleading, and uninformed, but they are dangerous because they exploit an already tense atmosphere over all things Islamic. No doubt in India, as in Pakistan, most efforts to reform madrasa education have been plagued with problems. The 'saffronization' of madrasas and the failure of the National Council for the Promotion of the Urdu Language (NCPUL) to bring about reform in the system of madrasa education in India have been demonstrated in several recent publications (Ara 2004: 34; De 2004: 5085). In addition, government-sponsored initiatives aimed at introducing new, secular subjects into the curricula of these institutions have been interpreted by many proponents of madrasa education as a threat to Islam and Muslims and an attempt to undermine the authority of the Muslim religious scholars (*ulema*). Such being the case, resistance to reform has acquired a kind of political currency for the ulema in both India and Pakistan.[19] On the other hand, madrasa education has never been completely static. The intellectual history of the madrasa as an institution bears witness to a general openness to changes in the Dars-e Nizami curriculum in pre-colonial India (under Mughal rule). In more recent history, so-called modern subjects have come to be tolerated by these institutions, if begrudgingly. This is particularly the case when the rhetoric used to introduce such subjects incorporates a pledge to preserve the 'religious integrity' of madrasa education.[20] For instance, at the Dar ul-'Uloom Deoband (hereafter Deoband), students may take, alongside the religious sciences, elective courses in journalism, computer technology, and English literature. At the Dar ul-'Uloom Nadwat ul-'Ulama (hereafter Nadwat), English is offered alongside the Islamic sciences from the primary stage onward, while a course in comparative religions is offered at the post-graduate stage.[21]

The accusation that madrasa education is hostile to the modern sciences is often true. Political, religious, and class interests lay behind much of this hostility (Zaman 2002: 79–81; Ara 2004). On the other hand, an examination of the positions publicly articulated by madrasas such as Deoband and Nadwat reveals that such hostility is equivocal. The stated educational policy of the Nadwat is to integrate the fundamentals of the Islamic faith with the ever-changing values of human knowledge. On the Deoband website a link titled 'The System of Education' contains a subsection titled 'The Removal of a Doubt,' which addresses this question. This subsection seeks to impart the basic principle that madrasas have a responsibility to preserve and revive the 'old' religious sciences as a means of fostering intelligence and ability (the implication here is analytical and critical thinking skills). Both of these skills, in the reasoning of the author (who remains anonymous), are presented as excellent foundations for the comprehension of the modern sciences.[22] Several studies have demonstrated that class privilege affords a wider range of options for madrasa-educated élites to study the modern sciences. That is to say, many of the élites who were educated and/or have taught within the dini madaris are able to acquire secular education, sometimes even abroad in Europe or America (Ara 2004: 36–7, Zaman 2002: 83). By contrast, poor Muslims cannot afford such options; for many among them, madrasa education is an appealing alternative. In light of circumstances such as these, it would seem a fallacy to concentrate blame upon the dini madaris system for the lack of opportunity poor Muslims have to engage the wider world. On the contrary, there are far more complex social, political, and economic factors at work that serve to isolate the Muslim poor and marginalized, making them prime targets for narrow political and religious interests.[23]

Secular education in and of itself does not guarantee the absence of religious extremism, or the isolation from the wider world that is often experienced by the marginalized, any more than madrasa education in and of itself promotes hostility to the modern world. On the contrary, the dini madaris have sought to address the concerns of Muslims not only as Muslims, but as Muslims whose needs are changing in response to the challenges they face today. The language employed by these institutions promotes the notion of the complementarity of the religious and modern sciences (and indeed, there is precedent for this in Islamic traditions of reform and renewal). Whether this is mere rhetoric or the actual policy followed by instructors at Deoband and Nadwat, the institutions' stated positions on the role of the madrasa in teaching the modern sciences reveals something important about madrasa education: its key purpose is to increase the understanding of Muslims of their own faith and to enable them to live according to the principles of the Shari'a (however precarious this may be) *in accordance with* the challenges of modernity. What secularists often overlook or dismiss is the fundamental need that human beings have for faith. Parents do not send their children to dini madaris primarily for Urdu education but to strengthen their knowledge of and faith in Islam. Whatever practical motives (that is, economic) may also lie behind such choices, this is the crux of education in dini madaris. In Islam there is no centralized religious authority, but the notion of Islamic Shari'a (law) as unifying symbol of religious faith is a very potent one that has the capacity to unite Muslims globally (if only ideologically). One cannot effectively argue for reform of education among Muslims in India without taking into account the primacy of Shari'a as symbolic capital and the dini madaris as the primary vehicle for comprehending—and living—Shari'a. It is unlikely that madrasas will disappear in any foreseeable future, and those who wish to preserve and promote Urdu in India would do well to continue seeking ways of allying themselves with the dini madaris. The goals of so-called religious and secularist camps need not be mutually exclusive.

Aside from forging alliances with dini madaris for the cause of Urdu education, the publication—whether by independent or government-sponsored groups—of non-literary works such as political speeches, technical, and scientific works (translated from English) would also do much to serve the cause of promoting Urdu, and with the advent of computer software that can produce such literature in the *Nastaliq* style of calligraphy, the task is made more feasible (Russell 1999: 45, 47–8; Latifi 1999: 1321). C.M. Naim also advocates looking at the purchasing habits of readers of Urdu works by the Tablighi Jama'at and the Jama'at-e-Islami, and conducting detailed surveys on the reading habits of the members of these organizations. More broadly, he advocates surveying the list of Urdu bestsellers and inquiring as to what they can tell us about the cultural and educational goals of their readers, presumably as an indicator of strategies that will be effective in marketing Urdu publications to these kinds of audiences (Naim 1999: 100). One important consideration in this regard would be considering ways to attract Hindi speakers as well as those who do not understand Urdu's script—by publishing Urdu works in English, in the Devanagari script, and in other scripts, with appropriate modifications to the alphabets of each. Although there is a contingent of Urdu supporters who oppose using the Devanagari script, to offer Urdu works in only the Perso-Arabic script would alienate many potential readers. The appeal of such works is already visible in the mass publication of demotic texts, pamphlets, and chapbooks that are sold at sufi shrine bazaars throughout India. While many of these texts are religion-oriented, others—letter-writing manuals, cookbooks, and translations of popular tales—are not. Versions of these Urdu works have been published in the Roman and Devanagari script, as well as in the scripts of regional languages such as Punjabi, Bengali, and Gujarati. The popularity of these kinds of texts—attested by the large numbers of their vendors and readers, in so far as I could tell from interviewing pilgrims as well as *pirs* (spiritual guides) and their families at shrines in Delhi, Ajmer, and Bihar—is quite substantial among a wide cross-section of the faithful.

Another possibility for tapping into potential non-Muslim readership of Urdu literature would involve publishing works in Urdu that will be useful for those travelling for employment in countries such as Oman and the United Arab Emirates, where Urdu has become one of the most commonly used and understood languages by South Asians and Arabs alike.[24] In fact, some non-Muslims have begun to study Arabic for the simple reason that the Gulf states offer considerable opportunities for employment to South Asians. And in the Gulf states, Urdu often functions as the medium of communication among

Muslims, Hindus, Christians, and other migrants from South Asia. Despite the validity of Syed Shahabuddin's argument that the decline or progress of Urdu must not be measured primarily in the publication of Urdu works—as this would essentially amount to confining such progress to the results that can be observed among those who can read, speak, and write the language proficiently, while ignoring the importance of those who are largely illiterate but conversant with Urdu (Shahabuddin 2001: 13)—the fact remains that the publication and promotion of works written in Urdu will be an important part of increasing its profile among both its lettered and unlettered supporters, whether in India or abroad. Improving Urdu's image is as important a task in its promotion as its practical implementation at the level of education and administration, for without the former, the latter will only be a hollow and short-lived victory.

The Importance of Ideological Fashioning in the (Re)conceptualization of Urdu[25]

One final, but perhaps the most fundamental, task in reconsidering the place of Urdu in India today is to address the problems with its conception. In other words, what exactly is meant by Urdu? One of the most perplexing questions has been the problem of definition, which would lead to some measure of standardization. While arguments against standardization sometimes point to the problems that occurred in successive efforts to sanskritize Hindi, a lack of agreement on, for instance, the form(s) of the Urdu language to be printed in textbooks promises to create more confusion than clarity, and to obfuscate already sticky points of view on Urdu's identity (for instance, whether the *lingua franca*, classical, or neo-classical forms of the language are more acceptable for school primers, whether or not all three should be taught, and at what stages in a child's education). According to one school of thought, Hindi and Urdu are different languages with many linguistic differences. Another school of thought maintains that Urdu and Hindi are essentially the same language, albeit with different scripts, some differences in grammatical construction, and the (often artificial) insertion of Arabic and Persian vocabulary on the side of Urdu, and Sanskrit on the side of Hindi. The language termed Hindustani is conceptualized as a prime example of this link; for instance, the colloquial Hindustani writings of Premchand were written in both scripts, and claimed as works of both Hindi and Urdu literature (Shapiro and Schiffman 1981: 1). This latter school of thought is linked ideologically with the notion of India as a composite culture, but it is far from being a homogenous set of ideas. In the hands of Hindu revivalists, such links between the two languages obviated the need for separate or special treatment of Urdu at the level of central and state government policy. In the hands of state governments like that of UP, Urdu is treated as the language of a state minority, but Urdu speakers themselves are not recognized as belonging to a particular community, culture, or religious group (Brass 1974: 204, 215–16). Mahatma Gandhi's views on composite culture are well known: not only did he, along with Dr Rajendra Prasad, share the view of Hindi and Urdu's basic commonality, he also sought to forge a sense of that commonality by founding the Hindustani Prachar Sabha, one of the goals of which was to promote Hindustani as a link language between Hindus and Muslims. Unfortunately, his efforts had little palpable effect. What this suggests is that early on, the bifurcation of Hindi and Urdu into Hindu and Muslim camps, despite stated objectives to the contrary, was put into effect. At the same time, the concept of Urdu itself suffered from a lack of adequate definition, as have other languages of India, with the result that languages and language families have been treated as possessing homogeneous codes, which is far from being the case.

The linguists Michael Shapiro and Harold Schiffman have suggested, to the contrary, that all South Asian languages show socially-determined (and contextually-determined) structural differences, which makes taking into account local usages and conceptions of language an important criterion in their definition (Shapiro and Schiffman 1981: 2–4, 12). The problems with census-gathering methods, as well as the larger problem of categorizing languages and language families, reflect this confusion. Take, for instance, the concept of 'mother tongue.' In both the colonial and post-Independence periods, this phrase has meant different things at different times. For the majority of Indians, the sense of mother tongue and official definitions of language diverged widely, with the result that census reports were flawed or, at worst, deliberately manipulated in favour of Hindi (Brass 1974: 193). In many places, there exist a large variety of dialects and languages, with mixture among these common. Nowhere in India (or even Pakistan, for that matter) is Urdu a continuous and systematic formulation. At the level of the local and regional, it takes on many hues: in Bihar it is coloured by Magahi, Bhojpuri, and Maithili. In Punjab it is influenced by Punjabi. In Rajasthan it is mixed with the Rajasthani dialects. Such is the case that, on the local and regional levels, Urdu is conceived not as the literary form of the language, but as an everyday, multifaceted, and flexible means of communication. While government policy operates according to rather essentialized definitions of language, manifest in the idea that there exists a 'pure' language, the distinctions among common, national, and official languages have remained obscure in practice. In effect, the implementation of such acts as the Three Language Formula or the UP Official Languages (Amendment) Act of 1989[26] has highlighted, if anything, the complexity of language in its formation, evolution, and everyday use. It is this complexity that must be taken into consideration in the construction and implementation of language policies if Urdu is to be accorded an important place in the national consciousness of India.

Such a consideration need not bring about further social or political conflict. As Jyotirindra Das Gupta has argued, social divisions need not bring about political cleavages, since the distribution of such cleavages in a political system may in fact be mutually offsetting. What this suggests is that group conflict in one area (as in the disputes over the places of Hindi, Urdu, and the regional languages in the nation) may actually produce integrative consequences in another (Das Gupta 1970: 2–3). One way to actualize the positive integration of Urdu into the national consciousness of India would involve a concerted effort to modify its image. As Robert Alter points out, the standardization of language's linguistic forms, vocabularies, and meanings is not the only variable involved in the process of its nationalization. Equally important is its ability to be ideologically refashioned[27] (cited in Ramaswamy 1999: 341). This fact was not lost on the former president, Dr Zakir Husain, who realized the importance of preserving Urdu as a link language among Indians of all creeds, religions, and ethnic groups. Assessing the impact of popular and political assumptions about Urdu upon its implementation in state, regional, and national institutions is beyond the scope of this essay, but the arguments advanced herein suggest that a reconsideration of the meaning of the language is in order if the negative connotations that have come to be associated with Urdu and its supporters are to be moderated. Perhaps most importantly in this regard, the notion that Urdu is the language of Muslims, or that it represents a 'foreign' language, must be dispelled by all means. The importance of Urdu in the development of literary and cultural traditions of India (as well as its importance to the Hindi films of Bollywood, where its role as a link language is perhaps at its most visible), must be promoted at the level of the institutional as well as the popular. And as Syed Shahabuddin has suggested, the implementation of Hindi and Urdu as a composite course may be effective in the non-Hindi-speaking states, though probably not in the Hindi-speaking states.[28] A de-emphasis on political arguments for and against Urdu and a greater focus on changing attitudes toward it must also accompany such efforts. Of course, this is only a small part of the work to be done: it is perhaps an obvious point, but pertinent nonetheless, that these efforts should not be consigned solely or primarily to central and state agencies, nor to the Muslim community, for the results stand to benefit all those who hold dear the best that Indian culture has to offer.

Notes

1. This piece was first conceived as a presentation for the seminar 'Agenda for Urdu Education in 21st Century India with Special Reference to Dr Zakir Husain', held in New Delhi in February 2002. The arguments and observations contained herein have benefited from personal communication with, and commentary by Syed Shahabuddin, Ather Farouqui, and Maggie Ronkin. I am grateful for their insights and suggestions, though the responsibility for any errors or misunderstandings is entirely mine.
2. Thanks are due to Syed Shahabuddin for pointing this out to me.
3. Jagjivan Ram, who also held the defence portfolio from 1970–4 and 1977–9, arrived on the political scene in the 1930s as a representative of the Scheduled Castes. In 1977, he broke with the Congress party to join the Janata opposition.
4. For a more detailed treatment of this aspect of the undermining of Urdu, see Mas'ud Husain Khan's work, *Urdu ka Ilmiya*, Aligarh: Maktaba Jami'a Limited, 1973.
5. This is also pointed out by Ather Farouqui, 'Urdu Language and Education', *Economic and Political Weekly* 37, no. 25, 22–8 June 2002, p. 2406.
6. A study by Tariq Rahman elucidates the impact of language policy on the decline of regional languages. As his work demonstrates, despite a divergence in stated official policies towards regional languages, the effects upon the latter were similar. In Pakistan, the regional languages were subordinated to Urdu as a matter of policy and as part of a program of national integration, without lip service being paid to the importance of the regional languages at the level of government policy and education, as was the case in India.

As in Pakistan, English in India survives as a powerful national language, in part because of the practical difficulties faced by the central government in trying to elevate minority or regional languages to the status of official language. See Tariq Rahman, *Language and Politics in Pakistan*, Karachi: Oxford University Press, 1996. These arguments are taken up again in light of more recent events in India and Pakistan in his latest work, *Language, Ideology, and Power: Language-learning among the Muslims of Pakistan and North India*, Karachi: Oxford University Press, 2002.

7. The Three Language Formula was developed as a 'compromise formula' by a conference of chief ministers of states after the opposition of non-Hindi speaking states to the policy of official language promoted by the lower house of Parliament (Lok Sabha).

8. This was the wording used for the Delhi provisions.

9. Among the non-Hindi states, Urdu is designated as one of the choices in Andhra Pradesh, Kerala, and the Andaman and Nicobar Islands. Confusion over the precise provisions of this formula are more complicated than I have stated here; they are in fact modified by, among other things, various provisions at the primary, middle, and secondary stages of education. The provisions of this formula were available on the website of the government of India, Ministry of Human Resource Development as 'Statewise Position of the Implementation of the Three Language Formula, With Particular Reference to Urdu' *http://shikshanic.nic.in/cd50years/u/47/3Y473Y0Q01.htm*, accessed on 21 October 2002, but the link is no longer available.

10. Cf. details in the Department of Education's 'National Policy on Education' (1968), under the subheading 'Teaching of Hindi', in which Hindi is declared to be compulsory in most of the non-Hindi-speaking states and union territories, excluding Tamil Nadu, Tripura, and the Karaikal region of Pondicherry. See *http://www.education.nic.in/htmlweb/natpol.htm*, accessed on 21 October 2002.

11. I would make the same criticism about there being a lack of distinction made among 'Urdu education', 'education administered in the Urdu language', and 'education about Urdu' (as a language or literary form). See also Ather Farouqui, 'Urdu Language and Education', p. 2407, on this.

12. Syed Shahabuddin suggests that the existence of provisions is obviated by the lack of their enforcement. According to him, the Board of High School and Intermediate Education in UP, which is the only board in operation in the state, does not actually permit anyone to take examinations in Urdu. Rather, students must opt for either Hindi or English. See his 'Urdu zaban, ta'lim, aur Musulman', *Urdu Duniya*, pp. 12–13, cf. 'Urdu in India,' *Mainstream* vol. 40, no. 28, 29 June 2002, p. 19.

13. Mushirul Hasan, 'Muslims in Free Fall: Myths of Appeasement', *http://www.indian-express.com/columnists.mush/20010207.html*, accessed on 11 December 2001. This article is no longer available online, but print copies are still extant.

14. Editorial, 'Karnataka Regresses, Maharashtra Excels', *Islamic Voice*, November 1999. See *http://www.islamicvoice.com/november.99/editorial.htm*, accessed on 11 December 2001, this article is no longer available online, but print copies are still extant.

15. Tariq Rahman offers additional perspectives on recent improvements in Urdu's status in north India. See his book, *Language, Ideology, and Power*, pp. 256–7.

16. Ministry of Social Justice and Empowerment, 'Schemes for Welfare of Minorities', *http://www.socialjustice.nic.in/obcs/minority.htmmaulana*, accessed on 11 December 2001.

17. Ather Farouqui, 'Urdu Education in India: Four Representative States', *Economic and Political Weekly*, vol. XXIX, no. 14, 2 April, p. 106.

18. See Ather Farouqui, 'Urdu Language and Education', p. 2407.

19. Muhammad Qasim Zaman, *The Ulama in Contemporary Islam: Custodians of Change*, Princeton and Oxford: Princeton University Press 2002, pp. 79–81.

20. Ibid., pp. 81–3.

21. This information is readily available on the following websites: *http://www.darululoom-deoband.com*, accessed on 10 April 2005; *http://www.nadwatululama.org/*, accessed on 10 April 2005. For a more comprehensive look at the changes occurring in the dini madaris system of education, changes which refute the accusations of its detractors that it is a stagnant and exclusivist system of education, see M. Shoyeb Ansari, *Education in Dini Madaris: An Opinion Survey of Curriculum, Method of Teaching, and Evaluation in Dini Madaris*, New Delhi: Institute of Objective Studies, 1997. See also the following recent articles attesting to the state of education in the dini madaris today and the backlash against madrasas: Muzaffar Alam, 'Modernization of Madrasas in India,' *The Hindu*, 23 April 2002, available online at *http://www.hinduonnet.com/thehindu/op/2002/04/23/stories/2002042300050100.htm*, and Yoginder Sikand, 'The Indian State and the Madrasa', in *Akhbar: A Window on South Asia*, no. 2, 2001.

22. See 'The System of Education: the Removal of a Doubt', *http://www.darululoom-deoband.com*, accessed on 10 April 2005 and 'Introduction: Aims and Objects,' *http://www.nadwatululama.org/*, accessed on 10 April 2005.

23. Arjumand Ara demonstrates how this is similarly the case for poor and marginalized Hindus in India. See her article 'Madrasas and the Making of Muslim Identity in India', *Economic and Political Weekly*, vol. 39, no. 1, 9 January 2004: 34, p. 37.

24. See data on 'Middle East Countries at a Glance', *http://www.mideastweb.org/countries.htm*, and the US Department of State's statistics on the United Arab Emirates, *http://www.state.gov/r/pa/ei/bgn/5444.htm*.

25. A more nuanced perspective on the implications of ideology for language acquisition in India and Pakistan is given in Tariq Rahman, *Language, Ideology, and Power*, pp. 239–43, 279–80, 529ff.

26. This act sought to accommodate Urdu for official purposes, including the entertainment of petitions and submission of replies to these, the publication of important government rules, regulations, and notifications, and the issuance of government circulars of public importance.

27. For an assessment of language ideology, see Bambi B. Schieffelin, Kathryn A. Woolard, and Paul V. Kroskrity (eds), *Language Ideologies: Practice and Theory*, New York and Oxford: Oxford University Press, 1998.

28. E-mail communication with Syed Shahabuddin, 8 April 2002.

References

BOOKS AND ARTICLES

Ansari, M. Shoyeb, *Education in Dini Madaris: An Opinion Survey of Curriculum, Method of Teaching, and Evaluation in Dini Madaris*, New Delhi: Institute of Objective Studies, 1997.

Ara, Arjumand, 'Madrasas and Making of Muslim Identity in India', *Economic and Political Weekly*, vol. 39, no. 1, 9 January 2004.

Brass, Paul R., *Language, Religion and Politics in North India*, London: Cambridge University Press, 1974.

————, *The Politics of India since Independence*, Cambridge: Cambridge University Press, 1990.

Das Gupta, Jyotindra, *Language Conflict and National Development: Group Politics and National Language Policy in India*, Berkeley, Los Angeles, and London: University of California Press, 1970.

Datta, Asis, 'Agenda for Urdu Education in the 21st Century with Special Reference to Dr Zakir Husain', lecture delivered at the Second Dr Zakir Husain Memorial Lecture, New Delhi, 3 May 1998.

De, Bikramjit, 'Abuse of Urdu', *Economic and Political Weekly*, vol. 37, nos 25 and 27, November 2004: 5085–8.

Farouqui, Ather, 'Urdu Education in India: Four Representative States', *Economic and Political Weekly*, vol. 29, no. 14, 1994, pp. 782–5.

————, 'Urdu Language and Education', *Economic and Political Weekly*, vol. 37, no. 25, 22–8 June 2002, pp. 2406–7.

Ghosh, Partha, 'Language Policy and National Integration: The Indian Experience', *Ethnic Studies Report*, vol. 14, no. 1, January 1996, pp. 49–72.

Khan, Mas'ud Husain, *Urdu ka Ilmiya*, Aligarh: Maktaba Jami'a Limited, 1973.

Khurshid, Salman, 'Urdu: Mind the Language, Please', *The Nation*, Lahore, 13 May 1998.

Latifi, Danial, 'Preserving Urdu through Self-Help', *Economic and Political Weekly*, 29 May 1999, pp. 1321–2.

————, 'Urdu in UP', *Economic and Political Weekly*, vol. 36, no. 7, 17 February 2001, pp. 533–5.

Naim, C.M., 'Urdu in India: Some Observations', in *Ambiguities of Heritage: Fictions and Polemics*, Karachi: City Press, 1999.

Narang, Harish, 'Language Policy and Planning in 21st Century India', address delivered at the First Dr Zakir Husain Memorial Lecture, 8 February 1998.

Rahman, Tariq, *Language and Politics in Pakistan*, Karachi: Oxford University Press, 1996.

Ramaswamy, Sumathi, 'Sanskrit for the Nation', *Modern Asian Studies*, no. 33, 1999, pp. 339–81.

Russell, Ralph, 'Urdu in India since Independence', *Economic and Political Weekly*, vol. 34, nos 1 and 2, 9 January 1999, pp. 44–8.

Schieffelin, Bambi B., Kathryn A. Woolard, and Paul V. Kroskrity (eds), *Language Ideologies: Practice and Theory*, New York and Oxford: Oxford University Press, 1998.

Shahabuddin, Syed, 'Urdu Zaban, ta'lim, aur Musulman: ek taslis-i be-kalisa', *Urdu Duniya*, February 2001, pp. 12–16. Reprinted as 'Urdu in India,

Education, and Muslims—a Trinity without a Church,' *Mainstream*, vol. 40, no. 28, 29 June 2002, pp. 19–23.
Shapiro, Michael C. and Harold F. Schiffman, *Language and Society in South Asia*, Dordrecht, the Netherlands: Foris Publications, 1981.
Zaman, Muhammad Qasim, *The Ulama in Contemporary Islam: Custodians of Change*, Princeton and Oxford: Princeton University Press, 2002.

ONLINE ARTICLES

Alam, Muzaffar, 'Modernisation of Madrasas in India', *The Hindu*, 23 April 2002, accessed on *http://www.hinduonnet.com/thehindu/op/2002/04/23/stories/2002042300050100.htm*, accessed on 11 April 2002.
Department of Education, Government of India, 'Teaching of Hindi', in 'National Policy on Education', *http://www.education.nic.in/htmlweb/natpol.htm*, accessed on 11 April 2005.
Dar ul-Uloom Deoband, 'The System of Education,' *http://www. darululoomdeoband. com*, accessed on 10 April 2005.
Dar ul-Uloom Nadwat ul-'Ulama, 'Introduction,' *http://www.nadwatululama.org/*, accessed on 10 April 2005.
Editorial, 'Karnataka Regresses, Maharashtra Excels', *Islamic Voice*, November 1999. *http://www.islamicvoice.com/november.99/editorial.htm*, accessed on 9 April 2005.
Government of India, Ministry of Human Resource Development with National Informatics Centre, 'Statewise Position of the Implementation of the Three Language Formula, With Particular Reference to Urdu', *http://shikshanic.nic.in/cd50years/u/47/3Y/473Y0Q01.htm*, accessed on 21 October 2002 (link no longer available).
————, 'UP' in 'Introduction', *http://shikshanic.nic.in/cd50years/u/47/3x/473x0f01.htm*, accessed on 21 October 2002 (link no longer available).
Government of India, Ministry of Social Justice and Empowerment, 'Schemes for Welfare of Minorities', *http://www.socialjustice.nic.in/obcs/minority.htm#maulana*, accessed on 11 December 2001.
Hasan, Mushirul, 'Muslims in Free Fall: Myths of Appeasement', *http://www.indian-express.com/columnists.mush/20010207.html*, accessed on 11 December 2001.
Mid East Web, 'Middle East Countries at a Glance', *http://www.mideastweb.org/countries.htm*, accessed on 9 April 2005.
Sikand, Yoginder, 'The Indian State and the Madrasa,' *Akhbar: A Window on South Asia*, no. 2, 2001, *http://www.ercwilcom.net/~indowindow/akhbar/200102/edu.htm*, accessed on 10 November 2002 (link no longer available).
US Department of State, Bureau of Near Eastern Affairs, 'Background Note: United Arab Emirates', *http://www.state.gov/r/pa/ei/bgn/5444.htm*, accessed on 1 November 2002.

PART III

Civic Space, Education, and Urdu

9

A Trinity without a Church:
Urdu Language, Urdu Education in India, and Muslim Indians

SYED SHAHABUDDIN

There is an unusually poetic, Urduesque ambiguity in the phrase 'Urdu Education'. Most writers on the state of Urdu in India lose their way in the maze of this ambiguity and are apt to confuse the issues, reach wrong conclusions, and miss the core problems. While surveying the overall status of Urdu, 'Teaching of Urdu' and 'Use of Urdu as a Medium of Education' (which are two completely different matters) are lumped together under the heading of 'Urdu Education'. Obviously, for dealing with the educational problems confronting Urdu, their correct delineation is essential for an accurate assessment of the situation and for proposing appropriate remedial measures. Even 'teaching of Urdu' has many aspects: 'the study of the Urdu language as a compulsory subject' or 'as a non-compulsory optional subject in schools, at the primary and secondary level' or 'study of Urdu literature at the university level'. All these aspects are no doubt inter-connected, but they need to be treated specifically. The inclusion of Urdu as a language in the curriculum at all levels—school, college, and university—and the position of Urdu as a medium of education at those levels merit our special attention.

The basic fact of life today is that most Urdu-speaking students do not have the choice of learning their mother tongue or receiving education through their mother tongue even at the primary level. At the higher levels, their choice of Urdu as a language for compulsory or optional study depends to a large extent upon their relative proficiency in Urdu and other languages, the availability of Urdu in the curriculum, the facilities available at the institution, and the wishes of the parents. As for the use of Urdu as the medium of post-primary school education, there are a limited number of Urdu-medium middle or high schools in Andhra Pradesh, Bihar, Delhi, and Maharashtra. As for Urdu as the principal or optional subject for a university degree, hundreds of colleges and scores of universities offer courses. Most of those universities also have post-graduate departments of Urdu that offer the MA course as well as facilities for research. It is obvious that the Urdu pyramid is upside down, and its survival depends on a highly unstable equilibrium.

Urdu in the World

In principle, as long as Urdu is alive in Pakistan or elsewhere, we have no need to worry about the future of Urdu in general. But we are concerned with its survival and progress in India, which has nothing to do with its survival and progress in Pakistan. Pakistan, the Gulf States, the United States, and the United Kingdom can in no way change the status of Urdu in India. Therefore, whatever progress Urdu makes at the international level beyond the frontiers of India will not benefit the younger generation of Urdu-speakers in India who have, since Independence, gradually become cut off from Urdu literature and scholarship and distanced from its cultural heritage.

We cannot compensate for the decline and contraction of Urdu in India with the advance and expansion of Urdu elsewhere. If we merely console ourselves with the vision of green pastures outside and do nothing, Urdu as a living language will die a natural death in due course in the land of its birth, perhaps to be preserved as a classical language or as a series of local dialects.

Urdu and its Relationship to the Muslims of India

Incidentally, when assessing the status of Urdu in India, every writer thinks of the relationship between Urdu and the Indian Muslims, even though this may not always be spelled out. Clarity again gives way to ambiguity. But there is no doubt that the identification of Urdu with Islam, inadvertent or deliberate, further complicates the problem of Urdu.

Admittedly, religion and language are not two sides of the same coin, but today it is a fact that 99 per cent of those who declare Urdu as their mother tongue are Muslims, and the Muslim identity, at least in north India, has become so intertwined with Urdu that it is impossible to separate them. However, in the 1991 census only 61.2 per cent of the Indian Muslims declared their mother tongue to be Urdu, and there were probably no non-Muslims among them. Truly, Urdu has now become the language only of the Muslims, even though it is not the language of all the Muslims. The state-wise percentage of Indian Muslims who declared Urdu as their mother tongue varies from about 90 per cent in Karnataka to about 50 per cent in Uttar Pradesh (UP), among the states with a Muslim population of, say, 10 million.

Responsibility of the Government in Education

Totally impracticable advice is often volunteered to the Urdu-speaking community that it should make its own arrangements for teaching Urdu to its children or that it should take steps to establish special institutions for the purpose, outside the mainstream of education—as if it was a community of immigrants. In our developing, but poor and deprived society, it is a primary task of the government to provide education to all. Indeed, since the recent amendment to the Constitution raising universal education from the 'Directive Principle of State Policy' to 'Fundamental Rights', the state is obliged to provide free and compulsory elementary education to every child up to the age of fourteen. The Constitution also provides for use of the mother tongue as the medium of instruction, at least at the primary level, and recognizes the right of linguistic and cultural minorities to conserve their language (Article 29). There is no reason, then, why the Urdu-speaking community should deprive itself of the right to have its children receive at least their primary education through the medium of their mother tongue under the state educational system and, in addition, the right to study their mother tongue as a compulsory subject right through school.

The same problem is faced by other minority languages in every state but, apart from Urdu and Sindhi, all 'national' languages have homelands—one or more states in which they command a majority, and enjoy the privilege of being the principal and dominant language to be employed for all government and administrative business. This gives them not only a foothold, but also a strong home base. Urdu and Sindhi have no home states of their own. They are without a homeland in their own homeland.

Muslim Educational Establishments

In the context of Urdu, the most important thing to bear in mind is that, since the inclusion of Urdu as a compulsory or optional subject in the curriculum and the use of Urdu as the medium of education are governed by state regulations, the question of Urdu should be treated separately from the question of minority educational institutions (MEIs), which, under Article 30 of the Constitution, may be established by religious or linguistic minorities. Urdu-speaking Muslims have also founded such institutions, doubly entitled as they are, being a religious as well as a linguistic minority. But even in an Urdu concentration state as is UP, not all the Muslim educational institutions in the educational mainstream necessarily offer facilities for teaching Urdu, far less of education through the medium of Urdu. This is largely because the regulations of the state prescribe the teaching of languages other than Urdu as compulsory subjects, or bracket Urdu as an optional subject with a more 'useful' subject, or bar the schools from using any language other than the principal language of the state or English as the medium. Besides, the secondary or higher secondary examination boards may not permit an examinee to take the examination through the medium of any language other than the principal language of the state (Hindi in UP) or English.

Facilities for teaching Urdu as an optional or even additional subject in the MEIs established and administered by the Urdu-speaking/Muslim community depend upon the general educational status of the area, the availability of space for Urdu in the official curriculum that is to be followed by government or non-government schools alike, and the preference of the parents. Therefore, from the point of view of Urdu, there is not much difference between Muslim educational institutions and government or other private institutions in the area. Urdu-speaking children face the same situation in both. Let us be clear: Urdu is not receiving particular support from Muslim educational institutions whose objective is promotion of education, not of Urdu, if it is not purely commercial.

We should be perfectly clear on one more point. At this time, it is virtually impossible to make Urdu the medium of education at the secondary level except in an exceptional situation.

However, that does not mean that the Urdu-speaking community should wholly discard the idea of Urdu-medium high schools. In every Urdu-concentration *zila*, either the government or the community should establish at least one or more Urdu-medium high schools, which can feed the few Urdu-medium higher secondary and degree-level institutions, at least in the social sciences and humanities where they would be joined by the students of higher *madrasas*. Those who pass out of Urdu-medium high schools and major in Urdu and other subjects at the BA/MA level would be comparatively few, but they would contribute to the progress and development of Urdu as a medium of modern knowledge and provide school teachers for Urdu as well as Urdu-medium students.

Shrinking Academic Space for Urdu

What is appalling is the lack of concern about academic space for Urdu in the curriculum at the official level. By and large, Urdu today stands expelled from the school curriculum both by design and by default. For example, through a recent decision of the government of Delhi, English will be compulsory at the primary level, while Hindi is already compulsory—hence, there will be no room at all for any minority language. In UP, both Hindi and Sanskrit are compulsory at the primary level. Where is the space for Urdu?

Academic space—for Urdu especially, and for all other minority languages in general—is slowly being eroded everywhere with the upsurge of Hindi and the state languages. While Urdu-speaking/ Muslim parents would like to send their children to school, the community is politically so impotent that it is unable even to articulate a demand for the most basic Constitutional right of its children. They reason that if the children speak Urdu at home, or become acquainted with the basic Urdu in the local *maktabs*, or with the help of private tutors, there is little point in their making a political issue of facilities for teaching Urdu at school.

In the near future, in such states as Andhra Pradesh, Bihar, Karnataka, Maharashtra, and UP (five states that together have 80 per cent of the Urdu-speaking population), the proportion of Muslim children learning Urdu as a compulsory or even as an

optional subject will sharply decline. So while Muslims will definitely progress educationally, Urdu will retreat and decline.

In assessing the future of Urdu in India, little importance should
be attached to the statistics of Urdu books published or of those
purchased by the Library of Congress in Washington DC, which
some western scholars writing about the present state of Urdu in
India emphasize. Unfortunately, increased publication of Urdu books
does not in the slightest degree help solve the problems that Urdu
faces in the field of education. In fact, the publication of books
does not reflect the real picture of Urdu but actually represents the
policy of token government patronage. This tokenism in the public
domain is itself, to a large extent, responsible for the decline of
Urdu. Publication does not represent market demand. In fact, many
volumes lie unsold and gather dust or are presented to friends and
admirers. Editions seldom exceed a hundred, even for the record,
and in some cases the actual number may be even less. We thus have
'ghost publications', just as we have Urdu newspapers with phantom
circulations.

What is more important is the fact that most of these books are
of indifferent quality and limited in the choice of subjects. A comparison between Urdu books published in India and those published in
Pakistan would show that Indian publications are largely limited to
poetry, short stories, novels, and literary criticism. Much fewer books
deal with the social sciences. Books on science and technology and
on other professions are almost non-existent. Indeed, degree-level
original textbooks are yet to be written in Urdu. The recently established Maulana Azad National Urdu University is largely dependent
on translations from English textbooks on various subjects to Urdu
published by Osmania University—seventy-five years ago, it became
the first university in the country to teach through a 'native' language.

The poor demand, limited range and indifferent quality of Urdu
books has its roots in the low proficiency in Urdu. Because of the
limited provisions for 'Urdu education' in all its dimensions, the
younger Urdu speakers are obliged to accept it as a language that
they can speak but which one they can neither read nor write.

Falling Demand for Urdu

Regrettably, far from growing, the preference of Urdu-speaking
parents for Urdu as an optional subject is decreasing. They are often

uneducated, or have received little education, and as such do not appreciate the cultural value of their children learning Urdu. They normally argue: *'Urdu padh ke kya hoga'* (Learning Urdu will yield nothing), or *'ghar par hi sikh lega'* (Urdu can be easily mastered at home), or *'Maktab mein padh liya hai, kafi hai'* (Knowledge of Urdu acquired at the part-time school of Islamic learning is sufficient and enough).

The growing indifference toward Urdu in the Urdu-speaking minority and the falling demand for Urdu teaching has socio-economic and cultural reasons, apart from those political and educational.

Urdu is declining even as a medium of religious education or of *da'wa* (propagation of Islam)—the religious organizations are publishing their reports and religious literature in the state languages. Madarsas are teaching Hindi and other state languages. The Jama'at-e-Islami Hind, which has a vast programme of publication, is shifting to Hindi and other state languages to reach the younger generation of Muslims. Indeed, the last remaining fortress of Urdu is crumbling before our very eyes.

The future of Urdu depends on the people who can speak, read, and write the language proficiently, not on those who speak it but do not know how to read and write it. A saving grace is that at least some of the former will buy Urdu books and periodicals, and express their thoughts in prose and poetry, and keep Urdu alive. The census figures only gives the number of those who declare Urdu as their household language or as their mother tongue. The majority of them are illiterate, or have dropped out of school after a certain level due to circumstances beyond their control. They have not acquired due proficiency in reading and writing Urdu. The logical scenario is that while the Muslim population increases along with the number of those who declare Urdu as their mother tongue, the coefficient of Urduization falls. The demand for Urdu and, therefore, for curricular material and extra-curricular literature in Urdu decreases proportionately.

Question of Script

The only possible course available for transmitting Urdu to the next generation is to at least make sure that Urdu-speaking children are taught Urdu at the senior-secondary level as a compulsory, first language. If they are, then by the time they complete their senior-secondary education, they would have acquired the necessary proficiency and interest, and with their life-long support, Urdu will be able to survive even in a hostile or indifferent milieu.

But the Urdu-speaking community is under constant pressure to adopt the Devanagari script. Hindi and Urdu, like many other pairs of languages that originally sprang from the same roots, have become two different languages even though they both reflect the same cultural and social milieu. Despite the protests of the Hindi diehards, Urdu words are coming back into circulation in the mass media, though with poor pronunciation and sometimes with a distorted spelling rooted in Hindi. The future of Urdu, however, will not be determined by sharing a common social space with Hindi, or worse, sharing Hindi's social space—nor through the language of films or the electronic media or even the print media. Usually those who wish, one way or another, to merge Urdu with Hindi argue that Urdu-speakers should accept the status of Urdu as a *shaili* (style) of Hindi. The reason lies in the quest of the Hindi-speaking community to enjoy a linguistic monopoly nationally, or at least in Hindi concentration states, for the simple reason that linguistic monopoly means political power. For the last 150 years, Hindi has deliberately moved along this trajectory, forcing Urdu to vacate administrative and judicial space, and occupying the vacated space. The Hindi community is, in the present phase, concentrating on assimilating Urdu and pressing Urdu to adopt its script. The Hindi lobby does not ask any other national language to change its script and to adopt Devanagari. Leaving aside the major languages of the Dravidian family—Tamil, Telugu, Malayalam, and Kannada—the Hindi community has never dared to suggest this to Bengali, Marathi, Gujarati, or Assamese. The pressure to abandon its script has been applied on Urdu alone as part of a broader strategy to exile Urdu from the shared territory. The objective is to annihilate the linguistic identity of Urdu and thus approximate the ideal of 'one nation, one culture, one language' and, in due course, one religion. To keep Urdu alive with its own identity and status, the Urdu community needs to resist this pressure. Regrettably, some Urdu writers, in order to gain advantages for themselves, have associated themselves with the movement to have Urdu written in the Devanagari script, but their numbers are not yet significant. While nobody can object if Urdu books are translated or transliterated into Hindi, there is no reason for Urdu to change its script.

It is often forgotten that the Urdu script, which is not synonymous with the Arabic or Persian scripts, as commonly claimed due to ignorance and malevolence, is much more comprehensive phonetically than Devanagari, Arabic, or Persian. Devanagari is incapable of representing the sound and rhythm of even common Urdu words. In fact, the rampant mispronunciation of Urdu words in the electronic media and in public announcements is obviously because the reader/ speaker has not learnt Urdu or is unfamiliar with its script. There is no doubt that the Roman or the Devanagari or the Arabic or the Persian scripts cannot do justice to Urdu.

Simultaneous publication of Urdu literature in Devanagari will at least expand the market for Urdu writers, whose own market is shrinking.

Role of the Urdu Élite

It is disturbing that the Urdu élite, with a view to gain political advantages, have been striving to expand Urdu teaching and research at the college and university levels, but have seldom put pressure on the government to ensure teaching of Urdu or through Urdu at the primary or secondary level. Such an anaemic approach was welcome to the central and state governments, which never had any compunctions about drying up or even cutting at the roots of Urdu and sprinkling water over the leaves and adorning the edifice of secularism with artificial creepers. The Urdu élite have been perpetually mesmerized by the verbal tributes to Urdu by politicians and governments. This explains why, far from exerting due and legitimate pressure on the government to prepare the ground for Urdu at primary and secondary levels, they have been silent and callous spectators to the apathy toward Urdu.

Successive governments have generally been responsive to demands for facilities needed to teach Urdu at the university level, and may give more concessions on further pressure. The governments, both central and state, tout these concessions or the performance of official institutions such as the National Council for Promotion of Urdu Language, and Urdu academies, and publicize official patronage reflected in *mushaira*s and seminars. The purpose, it appears, is to divert the attention of the Urdu-speaking community away from the most fundamental questions relevant to the future of Urdu. The Urdu movement is therefore reduced to agitating for the sanction of a few more posts of Urdu teachers and translators or filling up the vacancies of sanctioned posts. The Urdu élite has failed to realize that this short-sightedness would only spell the extinction of the language.

Academic Standard and Literary Creativity

Studying Urdu as a second or third language at the secondary level cannot provide students with the ability to absorb and appreciate the beauty of Urdu literature at the university level, nor can it generate any creative impulses in their mind. This explains why the standard of teaching Urdu in the universities is falling. University teachers of Urdu have been termed *Johla ki Chothi Nasl* (fourth-generation ignoramuses) by those well-versed in Urdu. The poorly-taught Urdu-speaking students go mechanically through degree courses, earn masters or doctorate degrees, and become ineffectual college/university lecturers of Urdu literature. This sets up a cycle of decay, which is the reason that university-level education by itself will not help the long-term dissemination of the Urdu language and literature as living idioms.

As the situation now stands, the revival of Urdu in India is not a question of producing rich literature, nor one of literary research in criticism and history. An increase in BA (Honours) and MA students is of no use, nor will those who take PhD degrees in Urdu be able to save the edifice of the language, which is now lying in ruins.

Measures for Revival of Urdu

The need of the hour is a strong foundation based on quality teaching and learning from the primary level upward. To reiterate, Urdu needs to be used as medium of instruction at the primary level and taught at the high school and intermediate level. It is regrettable that those who have Urdu as their mother tongue and who, according to educational principles, official policy, and constitutional mandate, ought to enjoy the right to study it as the first language, do not have the right to study it even as the second or the third language. This is especially so in UP, and is generally the case in other states of north India, where the majority of Urdu-speaking people live. This is the slow-acting poison deliberately administered by the doctor! There is no antidote.

The Urdu community will have to agitate democratically for the right to have Urdu as the medium of instruction at the primary level without any ifs and buts and to have Urdu taught at the secondary level as the first language. Almost everywhere Sanskrit and English, representing revivalism and modernism respectively, have taken the place of the second and the third language, and Urdu—first displaced from the position of the first language—has been completely eased out of the school curriculum. In theory, a student may offer it as an optional language if he forgoes his classical language or a 'useful' subject.

One feels that at the national level the linguists, the educationists, and the administrators are incapable of visualizing the real tragedy of Urdu. The Urdu community will have to agitate democratically for the right to have Urdu as the medium of instruction at the primary level without any ifs and buts and to have Urdu taught at the secondary level as the first language. In the northern region, a campaign has been going on for marginalizing all minority languages and to promote only Hindi, the principal language of the Hindi-speaking state. If there is no room in Delhi for Urdu, then neither there any for Punjabi or Tamil or Bengali or Gujarati for the children of those linguistic groups living in Delhi or UP or Bihar or MP or Rajasthan or Haryana.

In south India, the situation of the non-Hindi minorities is even more precarious. There, after the principal language, Hindi, and English have been allotted the three slots, there is no room left. Therefore, in non-Hindi states, the Urdu-speaking community should press for a composite Hindi–Urdu course as an optional substitute for Hindi, which can be introduced without much difficulty at the school level.

When the younger generation of the Urdu community is being distanced from Urdu, for no fault of theirs, who will be able to read Urdu books and newspapers or the name plates or signboards or voters' lists, or address government officers in Urdu? The principal language dominates every aspect of life—employment, economy, and government. A linguistic minority finally tends to come to terms with the situation and accept the status of its mother tongue as an 'ethnic' language, a 'household' language, or the language of social intercourse within the family and among friends. Little does it realize that future generations may undergo further cultural assimilation and cease to take any interest in their own language, even at home and among friends.

The Urdu lobby or the Urdu élite have never given thought to reviving the roots and endeavouring to change the situation at the school level. They have been content with awards, college and university lectureships, token advertisements for fictitious newspapers, jobs of translators with nothing to translate, and typists with nothing to type.

This is the beginning of a new age in which every child will enter the field of education. It cannot be overemphasized that primary education for Urdu-speaking children should be through the medium of Urdu, and at least up to the tenth class—ideally up to the twelfth— they should have the unconditional opportunity to study Urdu as a compulsory language. This is a problem common to all Indian languages wherever they form a linguistic minority at the state level. Urdu, suffers most because it is a minority everywhere, and thus becomes the largest linguistic minority in the country—100 per cent as against 3.4 per cent for Malayalam. Also, because Urdu-speakers suffer the double jeopardy of being a religious minority as well, Urdu has to lead the battle for linguistic equality and justice and, therefore, democracy and secularism. Until all minority languages in every state are recognized for education, information and administration, and for public communication, Indian democracy remains incomplete and justice to linguistic minorities at all levels shall remain the unfinished agenda of Indian democracy.

10

Urdu Education in India:
An Overview—A Case Study of
Five Representative States

ATHER FAROUQUI

This article is based on a survey conducted to ascertain the facts regarding the status of Urdu education in India.[1] It would be clear to anyone who cares to look at the general Muslim scenario in India that the Muslims have not progessed far on the education front. This is not due to religious prejudice, although it has traditionally been cited as the cause. The reasons for their stagnation are complex—socio-economic, occupational, and historical. Since a fairly comprehensive debate has evolved on this question, little is likely to be gained by reiterating it here. Suffice it to accept that the Muslims are, in general, educationally backward and depressed—a fact of Muslim social life in contemporary India.

Among the many factors that hold back Muslims in the field of education, the substantial withdrawal of official patronage and inadequate facilities for education in Urdu are significant. Many commentators on the plight of Urdu in post-Independence India have argued that the withdrawal of official patronage for Urdu has had disastrous consequences. Élite and middle-class Muslims realized that educating their children through the Urdu medium would not enable them to find a place in the job market. As a result, their children grew up knowing little Urdu or knowing it only as a spoken language. On the other hand, poorer Muslims oriented toward self-employment gave their children a traditional *madrasa* education. Thus, Urdu, which was once the language of élite and middle-class Muslims, became the language of the lower-middle-class community.

This argument will remain plausible until a comprehensive analysis of educational facilities for Urdu—and official policies regarding Urdu and their impact at the grassroots level—is undertaken. An evaluation of the state of Urdu education in contemporary India is required before definitive formulations can be derived.

Our findings have led us to believe that Urdu has been marginalized in India to such an extent that it has now become the language of Muslims alone. It is today confined to, and has become a part of, Muslim education.

During the course of research on the subject, a survey of five representative states was conducted. Months of travel through these states revealed, surprisingly, that not a single non-Muslim student had enrolled for studying Urdu even as an optional subject at the primary or secondary level, let alone choosing Urdu as the medium of education. This clearly indicates that it is only Muslim students who are studying Urdu at any level.

It is disheartening to note that, hitherto, little authentic information is available on the subject. Neither the government nor any private educational body has ever tried to conduct any research in this field. On the contrary, after Independence, every attempt was made to erase Urdu from Indian soil. Some financial assistance was given to organizations for the promotion of Urdu, but its recipients chose to align themselves to the government rather than work sincerely to promote Urdu, and one still finds Urdu writers competing with one another in an effort to associate themselves with the power-structure.

Before undertaking fieldwork for this article, a basic parameter was outlined through some statistics and information. The first survey was conducted in Uttar Pradesh (UP). An analysis of the state of Urdu education in the other states mentioned earlier is made in this article in order to draw a true picture of the condition of Urdu over a wider area. It examines the drop-out rate in five schools from each of the four states, and also presents the results of interviews with teachers, students, and parents.

The entire canvas, however, may not be complete as available material on Urdu education cannot be regarded as authentic or reliable. Most of it consists of articles written for seminars organized by Urdu academics, who often tend to merely present the policies of the government in a favourable light.

The condition of Urdu in India today is that it is taught in some schools as an optional subject either from the sixth standard onwards or, in certain schools, from the first to tenth standards. There is a provision for teaching Urdu as an optional subject from the sixth to eighth standards at a few places in UP. Besides, there are some schools where Urdu, apart from being taught as an optional subject till the tenth standard, is also the medium of instruction. In some schools, English and Hindi were made compulsory at almost every stage.

It is interesting to note that, even in Urdu-medium schools, subjects such as science and mathematics are generally taught in English or in the regional languages. The main reason for this is a lack of adequate scientific vocabulary. Thus, in these Urdu-medium schools, Urdu is the medium for only social-science subjects such as history and geography. In a few states, some private publishers have begun printing Urdu books on science and technology using technical vocabulary drawn from Pakistani publications, and some in Maharashtra have gone to the extent of re-printing Pakistani books illegally. This practice is, however, still in its initial stages.[2] In Hyderabad, before Independence, the experiment of conducting higher education through the medium of Urdu was initiated by the then Nizam. In this connection, an institution for translation, Daruttarjuma, was set up to translate technical books into Urdu. After Partition, when Urdu had already come to be accused of helping and precipitating the Partition of India, Urdu was abolished as a medium of education, and there were reports of the burning of the stock of books produced by Daruttarjuma under suspicious circumstances.

There are a few Urdu-medium degree colleges in Andhra Pradesh but in practice Urdu remains merely a medium of examinations and not of instruction, since most of the textbooks are available only in English or the regional language. Students whose mother tongue is Urdu prefer Urdu as the medium of examinations rather than the regional language.

In almost all the states in India, except Maharashtra, Urdu education is rapidly dying. Middle- or low-income or lower-middle-class people who have their children educated in the Urdu medium have to face a number of difficulties besides that of the lack of provision of Urdu as a medium of higher education. The provision of the Urdu medium can only be found up to the secondary standard. Consequently, Urdu-medium students lag behind those students who study in the regional language or in English. When Urdu-speaking students opt for the regional language as a medium, they have perforce to drop Urdu, and since they therefore lose their command over Urdu, they are also unable to pursue the study of Islamic religious literature as this is available only in Urdu. Of late, the Jama'at-e-Islami has begun publishing the Quran and Islamic literature in other languages, but this work is still insufficient. Muslims have yet to take a clear decision on whether to adopt Urdu or to abandon it completely in the regions where sentiments of regionalism are strong. However, one fact is clearly visible: the number of students getting an education in the Urdu medium is rapidly decreasing.

The Three Language Formula and Urdu

Even before the promulgation of the Constitution in January 1950, the question of making every child proficient in (1) the mother tongue; (2) the principal language of the state in the case of linguistic minorities or other Modern Indian Languages in the case of Hindi-speaking students; (3) Hindi, as the official language of the Union and the future link language of the country in non-Hindi states; and (4) English, had engaged the attention of the government as well as Indian educationists.

They faced five problems from the very beginning: a) the rejection of Hindi as the link language, particularly in the south; b) the desire to assimilate the Urdu-speaking minority gradually into the fold of Hindi in the Hindi belt; c) financial limitations of the state for providing teaching of the mother tongue as well as instruction through its medium to all school children; d) revivalist pressure to teach Sanskrit to all students; and e) the question of the medium of secondary education.

The Three Language Formula for secondary education was enunciated by the Central Advisory Board of Education (CABE) in 1949 and reshaped by the chief ministers in August 1961. This original formula was simple: mother tongue, another Modern Indian Language, and English, with Hindi as the second language for those whose mother tongue was not Hindi. This formulation was endorsed by the National Integration Council in September 1961. In 1968, it was incorporated in the National Policy on Education.

Though all major Urdu-speaking areas such as Delhi, UP, Bihar, Mumbai (now Maharashtra), Hyderabad (now Andhra Pradesh), and Mysore (now Karnataka) remained in India, identification of Urdu with the Pakistan movement had created a general environment of hostility towards Urdu in the land of its birth. The national leadership, as well as the Union Government, made efforts through all available constitutional means to safeguard linguistic minorities, but because of the historical rivalry between Urdu and Hindi in the Hindi belt—where most of the Urdu-speaking population lived— Urdu bore the brunt of attacks upon them. Lack of financial resources was given as a reason for putting 'numerical conditions' on the government opening Urdu-medium schools or on providing Urdu-teaching facilities to all students whose mother tongue was Urdu.

Administratively, these numerical conditions came to be known as 10/40 because the state was to provide an Urdu teacher only if there were ten Urdu-speaking students in a class or forty in the primary school as a whole. What is worse, the conditions were applied not only strictly but fraudulently, so that Urdu was virtually exiled from the school system, particularly in UP and Bihar. The state could have devised the alternative of horizontal aggregation of Urdu-speaking students within walking distance of a common school. Instead, it chose to deny them their basic human and constitutional rights.

The report of the committee for the promotion of Urdu—generally known as the Gujral Committee—submitted in 1975, brought out in detail the incomplete and uneven implementation of the Three Language Formula in all the states of Urdu concentration, and proposed the following formula:

In Hindi-speaking States

Present Formula (in 1975)	Proposed Formula
(i) Hindi	(i) Hindi (with Sanskrit as part of a composite course);
(ii) English	(ii) Urdu or any other Modern Indian Language excluding item (i);
(iii) Modern Indian language (preferably one of the southern languages), a category which was, absurdly, taken to include Sanskrit	(iii) English or any other modern European language.

In Non-Hindi-speaking States

Present Formula	Proposed Formula
(i) Hindi	(i) Regional language;
(ii) English	(ii) Hindi;
(iii) Regional language	(iii) Urdu or any other Modern Indian Language excluding (i) and (ii); and
	(iv) English or any other modern European language.

Non-Hindi speaking states could also adopt, as an alternative, the following formula, which is being implemented in Andhra Pradesh for the Urdu-speaking population:

(i) Urdu and Hindi (a composite course);

(ii) Regional language; and

(iii) English or any other modern European language.

The Gujral formula thus endorsed the shift of Urdu (*inter alia*, all minority languages of a state) from the status of the first to that of the second language by giving primacy to the principal language of the state rather than the mother tongue. This promoted the interest of Hindi, against all other national languages, particularly at the cost of Urdu, in the Hindi-speaking states. This hit Urdu hardest because it was not the principal language of any state. Second, as the second language, Sanskrit—a classical language—was not excluded from the optional list of Modern Indian Languages, this made it impossible for Hindi or non-Urdu students from learning Urdu as an optional language. Third, it did not include the classical languages—Arabic and Persian—from which Urdu devised most of its vocabulary, or Sanskrit, even as optional third languages. Sanskrit was accommodated in the composite course as a first language. It therefore closed the door of secondary education to Urdu-speaking students who wished to study Arabic or Persian in lieu of English. For Hindi states, it suggested a composite course of Hindi and Sanskrit, and of Hindi and Urdu in non-Hindi states—but it failed to suggest a composite course of a principal language of the state and Hindi in at least some non-Hindi states in order to reduce the burden of languages from four to three.

In this sense, the Gujral Committee struck a fatal blow against the constitutional right of the Urdu-speaking child to achieve due proficiency in his mother tongue.

Another red herring was introduced by the Narasimha Rao government in the form of preferential teaching of south-Indian languages as the second language. This idea has not taken off, but it has also reduced the opportunity of Hindi students to learn Urdu or any other minority language in the Hindi states.

After considering all these intertwined aspects, the International Conference on Minorities and their languages held from 8–11 February 2002, studied the decades of motivated and hostile implementation of national and state policies on Urdu, and placed the 'Urdu Question' within the national framework of just and equitable treatment of all languages that constitute minorities at the state level. Emphasizing the constitutional right of every child to learn his mother tongue as the first language throughout his school education, and the duty of the state to provide due facilities—both at the primary stage, where the mother tongue should be the medium of instruction and examinations for children belonging to linguistic minorities, and at the secondary stage—the conference made a valuable contribution to the national debate on language policy by evolving a universal solution in the larger context of minority languages in all states that would also solve the problem faced by the Urdu-speaking minority. In effect, it suggested:

First Language:	Mother tongue (without any condition but, if necessary, with horizontal aggregation and opening of parallel sections for linguistic minorities)
Second Language:	Any other language spoken in the state, but the principal language of the state as compulsory for linguistic minorities
Third Language:	English, Hindi, Sanskrit, Arabic, or Persian

Since Urdu and Hindi are sister languages, and since several national languages are written in the Devanagari script, the conference envisaged a composite course of Urdu and Hindi for the Urdu minority as the optional first language in non-Hindi states, as well as a Hindi–Sanskrit composite course as an optional first language in Hindi-speaking states. One could also envisage composite courses of Hindi with principal languages of the state in some non-Hindi states, such as Maharashtra and Gujarat.

There is a tendency to increase the burden of languages on children at the primary level itself by asking them to learn Hindi and

English as well as Sanskrit. This needs to be avoided, as for a child belonging to a minority linguistic group this would mean learning four languages in five years of schooling! Here, again, introducing the Hindi–Sanskrit composite course would help. The conference also emphasized the need to establish Urdu-medium primary schools, in accordance with the national norm, at the grassroots level, in the urban mohallas and the villages. Thus, the conference has made a signal contribution to the resolution of the language question in keeping with the tenets of educational psychology, the linguistic plurality of the country, and its federal polity.[3]

The Case of UP

The position of the Urdu language and Urdu education is most precarious in UP, a state that was the traditional centre of Urdu for centuries. There is not a single primary Urdu-medium school in the entire state and the only two existing Urdu-medium high schools are those run by and affiliated to the Aligarh Muslim University. Consequently, the generation born and brought up in the state after independence is quite unfamiliar with Urdu. They are neither aware of the problems faced by Urdu nor do they have any emotional attachment to it. Phrases such as 'Urdu literature' or 'Urdu culture' are alien to the new generation. Occasional references to them are found only in Urdu newspapers and, of course, in history books. Over the last decade, there has been a mushrooming of private schools all over, a phenomenon that has given rise to several technical complexities in the field of education. Around 50 to 60 per cent of such schools are unrecognized. It is, however, surprising that the middle- and lower- middle-class populace opt to send their children to these schools, although it is well known that these institutions are merely business centres. These unrecognized schools, which are nothing more than teaching shops, give admission to children up to the fifth standard, after which the students have no option but to seek admission in the civic-body schools, which can be obtained only by bribing the concerned officials. The certificates of government schools entitle them to get admission to high schools or intermediate colleges.

Interestingly, though there is no facility for teaching Urdu in UP, students can opt for an Urdu paper in junior-high-school examinations. At some places, high-school and intermediate students of science and commerce are allowed to take Urdu as an optional subject. However, this option is not available to students of agriculture, which means that this arrangement leaves no option for them other than to drop Urdu. There are two reasons for this: English, by and large, still enjoys great popularity, and the technical terms used in science and commerce have no equivalent in Urdu. It is quite clear that the curriculum scheme has been fixed in such a manner that, even if a student wants to, he cannot opt for Urdu. Besides, even the number of schools offering Urdu as an optional subject is negligible.

A majority of the privately run schools are not recognized in UP. Some of them have recognition only up to the fifth standard. It has become a common practice for unrecognized schools to arrange for their students to appear in high school examinations in recognized schools as private candidates. People who are familiar with the system of primary and high school education in the state know well that there are instances of irregularities in the examination and evaluation processes.

No less than 20 million Urdu-speaking people live in UP. There was once a provision for their wards to appear for the junior-high-school-level examinations in the Urdu medium though the number of such students was small—less than 500 in 1982, as compared to nearly 40,000 in Bihar in the corresponding year. The people in predominantly Muslim regions in UP now gladly admit their children for high-school examinations in the Hindi medium. There is only one Urdu-medium junior-high school, in district Badaun, in the state. The status of Urdu in this school can be assessed from the fact that only three girls from this school appeared in the junior-high-school examination in 1987. That, too, was reduced to two in 1988. In district Moradabad, only two girls' schools provide education through the Urdu medium. Those who run the Muslim high schools admit that Muslim students prefer the Hindi medium to Urdu, and a sizable number of Muslim parents transfer their children from Urdu- to Hindi-medium schools.

Urdu is not the medium of education in UP. Schools that prepare their students for the high-school-level examinations in Urdu have Hindi as the medium for all subjects. Urdu in these schools is taught only as a subject. Teachers capable of teaching through the Urdu medium are generally not available in the state. At a few places, Urdu-medium primary schools are run by local bodies; their teachers were appointed under the Bahuguna scheme.[4] However, in most of these schools, Urdu is taught only as an 'optional' subject, for most of these teachers, generally do not have a proper understanding of the term 'Urdu medium'.

In UP, therefore, education in Urdu actually means teaching the language as a subject. Worse, most so-called Urdu teachers there cannot even read the books in the Urdu script that are meant for the primary classes. It has also been found that the Urdu teachers in UP are basically engaged in other occupations, such as agriculture and milk dairies, and come to school only once or twice a month. It would appear that the recruitment of teachers of Urdu under the Bahuguna Scheme was intended only to appease the Muslims. H.N. Bahuguna, then chief minister of the state, was referred to as the Messiah of the Muslims. That was the time when Muslims were indiscriminately recruited as Urdu teachers. These people were given nominal training in teaching, and were later granted opportunities to appear in Oriental Urdu examinations. Ironically, it was difficult to find young matriculates who knew Urdu from among the large Muslim population. Even today, there are innumerable Urdu teachers recruited under the scheme who cannot read the Urdu script. A point with loaded implications: the weekly holiday in these Urdu-medium schools is observed on Friday, the day on which Muslims offer congregational prayers and which for them has a special importance. This clearly indicates that even the government stresses that Urdu schools are Muslim schools, and that Urdu is the language of Muslims alone. All the teachers recruited under the Bahuguna scheme are followers of Islam.

Bihar

In Bihar, the status of Urdu is more or less satisfactory, even though it enjoys no government favour or aid. The basic reason for the popularity of the language in the state is the deep attachment of the poorer sections of Muslim society to Islam. These communities prefer to send their children to *dini madaris* (religious institutions) for religious education. Besides, most religious literature is available only in Urdu because no language other than Urdu is capable of conveying Muslim religious thought adequately.

In Bihar every year, at least 50,000 students take high-school examinations in the Urdu medium. The state has twenty-three colleges and eighty high schools where Urdu is taught. Urdu-speakers are not drawn to English-medium education because the majority of the Muslim population belongs to the backward sections or to the lower-middle-class. Dini madaris have therefore played a significant role in the development of Urdu in the state. The state government also recognizes the degrees of the Bihar Madrasa Education Board as equivalent to the degrees of other recognized boards and universities. Unfortunately, this board is the most unsatisfactory of all the educational bodies in the country and is a centre of irregularities and widespread corruption. Should the state government decide to take measures to systemize its functioning, there would be a revolutionary change in the Bihar education system.

Though the curriculum in Bihar is devised by the Rajya Bhasha Vibhag (state language department; hereforth RBV), textbooks for Urdu are hard to get. As National Council of Education Research and Training (NCERT) books are almost impossible to find, students have to fall back on RBV books—even though they are released very late in the academic year.

On the whole, although the general condition of Urdu education in Bihar is not disappointing, it certainly is the worst managed, and therefore the lowest in standard. This is perhaps ignored because only the backward sections and lower-middle-class Muslims have opted for Urdu-medium education.

Maharashtra

Maharashtra is perhaps the only state where there is no apparent obstacle in the way of getting an education in the Urdu medium. This is largely due to the sustained efforts of various trusts and voluntary Muslim organizations and because the state government puts no apparent hurdles in the way of those who wish to learn Urdu. As most of the Urdu-teaching schools and colleges are run by private bodies and leading Muslim businessmen, there are less chances of mismanagement. This is reflected in the regular presence of Urdu teachers and routine classes in the Urdu-medium schools.

The Maharashtra government's attitude toward registration of Urdu schools has been sympathetic and cooperative. In Mumbai city alone, there are 124 registered Urdu-medium schools. In the whole of Maharashtra, including Mumbai, there are 230 such schools. The standard of Urdu teaching at the primary level is also satisfactory and encouraging, in comparison to the schools for other languages run by the state government.

TABLE 10.1 Indian Language Schools in Maharashtra

	Marathi	Urdu	Hindi
Primary Schools	569	230	185
Students	372,375	122,475	126,911
Teachers	9316	2727	2592

Source: Author's own.

There are only two centres for training primary-level Urdu teachers; where thirty teachers train over 300 prospects.

Interestingly, in Maharashtra even middle-class Muslims prefer an Urdu-medium education for their children, unlike in other states where people prefer to send their children to public/convent schools. In the latter states, only lower middle-class Muslims send their children to Urdu-medium schools. A possible reason is that the Muslims of Maharashtra in general, and of Mumbai in particular, tend to have a business mentality. While some public schools also offer Urdu as an optional subject, neither the students nor the teachers show much interest in Urdu.

There is another facility in Maharashtra that is not available in other states: from primary- to college-level, Urdu can be offered as an optional subject even in schools and colleges where there is no provision for teaching it owing to a dearth of the required number of students and teachers. Students are allowed to take it as an optional subject and appear in the examinations, but they have to study and prepare on their own.

In Maharashtra, the course books are prepared by the Textbook Bureau, and are initially prepared in Marathi and then translated and published in Urdu. This ensures that the course material is the same in both Urdu and Marathi. There are also some private publishers who publish Urdu textbooks.

Andhra Pradesh

Hyderabad, the capital of Andhra Pradesh, has been a historical centre of Urdu. The Osmania University of Hyderabad has the credit of having made Urdu the medium of higher education; it was here that Urdu was the medium of education for engineering and medical science before Partition. After Independence and the subsequent reorganization of states in 1956, Hyderabad became a part of Andhra Pradesh—from which point the decline started. The historic *police action*[5] in Hyderabad was, in fact, the beginning of the downfall of Urdu there. The older generation of Hyderabad, for whom Urdu was the symbol of their culture, is now dying out. In UP, policies that contributed to the decline of Urdu were implemented immediately after Independence. In other states, the process has been slow, but well organized.

It would appear that the days of Urdu in the new generation of Muslims of Hyderabad, too, are numbered. It is only the lower sections of the Urdu-speaking population who are continuing Urdu education in their homes and at the madrasas. The middle- and upper-class sections of the Urdu community are bidding adieu to the Urdu language and its literature, not to speak of Urdu as a medium of instruction.

In Andhra Pradesh, there still remains some provision, albeit not very satisfactory, for Urdu-medium education and for the teaching of Urdu as an optional subject. A fair number of students attend private Urdu-medium educational institutions run by Muslims. Some of these institutes provide teaching from the primary to the college level. In Hyderabad, there are a few convent schools too where Urdu is taught as an optional subject. However, the students learning Urdu as an optional subject up to the primary level in these schools have only a nominal knowledge of Urdu.

As in other states, more than 90 per cent of the Urdu-medium students in Andhra Pradesh come from the lower strata of the Muslim community. Most of these students are those who have studied the Quran at home. There are some children who attend Urdu-medium schools in the morning, and acquire religious knowledge in the evening in the madrasas. Apparently, not many obstacles are imposed by the government to hinder Urdu education in the state. Yet, the state of affairs is not really encouraging. The drop-out rates of Urdu-medium students in the primary to secondary level in Hyderabad are very high at 83 per cent. The drop-out percentage among Muslims from the first to seventh standards is 90 per cent, although the national drop-out percentage is 57 up to the sixth standard.

NCERT books are usually used in the state because, though books published by the Urdu Academy or by other government institutions are cheaper, they are seldom available. By the time these books do reach the market, nearly half of the academic session is often over.

Due to the economic deprivation of the Muslim people of Hyderabad, most cannot afford to continue sending their children to these schools, if they do send them to school at all. This is a major factor behind the disappointing ratio of drop-outs.

The state education system allows students to read textbooks in other languages (regional or English) but answer question papers in Urdu at the college level. English vocabulary is abundantly used, especially in the study of science, commerce, and technical subjects. Some elements of the half-a-century-old vocabulary devised by the Daruttarjuma are undoubtedly still in use, but this is gradually becoming a thing of the past. Today, Urdu books are available for only a few subjects.

Despite these difficulties, the new generation of Andhra Pradesh has a psychological and sentimental attachment to Urdu, just as it does in UP and Delhi. The downfall of Urdu in Hyderabad started much later than in the north, but the consequences have become visible now. Today, Urdu is of little value to even people of the older generation. This writer had the opportunity to attend two Urdu literary seminars in Hyderabad. None of the participants was below forty; the number of people attending at any one time did not exceed a meagre thirty.

West Bengal

West Bengal provides the greatest possibilities for education in the mother tongue. Primary education in the mother tongue is the clear policy of the state government, and the mother tongue is the medium of education in all government institutions. The minority language schools, too, are recognized on this basis.

The state is faced with the unusual problem that there are not enough schools to cope with the large number of Urdu students. There are several areas where there is only one Urdu-medium school for a population of 20,000 people. A significant flaw in government policy is that it does not make population the basis for recognition of schools; facilities for primary schools are granted on the basis of all minority communities clubbed together. This policy gives great benefits to Christians and other smaller religious and linguistic minorities, but proves disadvantageous to the Urdu-speaking minority in the sense that it widens the progress gap between them and other communities.

West Bengal provides aid for all primary students to the extent that it ensures free textbooks for all classes up to the fifth standard.

Unfortunately, the Urdu books sometimes reach the student only by the end of the academic session. As a result of this delay, students are compelled to purchase books from the market.

A dearth of adequate resources for Urdu educational institutions is a major problem for the Urdu-speaking minority. Most of them are in a shocking condition—a visit to the Sir Syed Group of Schools and a few others on Hussein Shah Road illustrates, succinctly, the state of affairs. They do not look like schools—the classrooms and family residential quarters are adjacent to each other.

Appendix: Police Action

Hyderabad was a sovereign nation for nearly 400 years before the British finally quit India. The understanding when they did leave was that the new states of India and Pakistan would give a choice to the princely states, and mutually agree on their accession or independence. The Nizam of Hyderabad was left in a quandary—should he accede to India, given his geographical position and the Hindu majority in his realm, or accede to Pakistan, as the new Muslim state? The bitterness remains, especially among the ruling élite of Hyderabad who lost power and prestige, and migrated in large numbers to Pakistan. Sardar Patel was already convinced that Hyderabad belonged to India, given its Hindu population, and his case was only weakened by the fact that, in the case of Kashmir, the argument was reversed. There, the argument for accession to India was based on the fact that its Hindu ruler had opted to accede to India.

Professor Wilfred Cantwell Smith writes that the Muslim community fell before a massive and brutal blow, the devastation of which left those who did survive reeling in bewildered fear—'Thousands upon thousands were slaughtered; many hundreds of thousands uprooted.' For the 'Police Action' in Hyderabad, the intelligentsia used the Indian army's term Operation Polo, as the armed forces were involved, not the police, and hence there was no 'police action'. It was Nehru's Goebbellian first lie told on All India Radio on 18 September 1948. The instrument of the disaster was, of course, vengeance. Particularly in the Marathwara region of the state and to a less, but still terrible, extent in most other areas, the story of the days after 'police action' is grim. The only careful report on what happened in this period was made a few months later by investigators—

including 'a Congress Muslim and a sympathetic and admired Hindu' commissioned by the Indian Government to study the situation. The report was submitted, but has not been published. It is widely held that the figures mentioned therein for the number of Muslims killed is 50,000. Most conservative estimates by pro-establishment observers hold it that the correct figure is at least 200,000, and some of the Muslims themselves put it at still higher. The lowest estimates, even those offered privately by apologists of the military government, came to at least ten times the number of murders of which previously the Razakars[6] were officially accused. Of the total Muslim community in Hyderabad, it would seem that somewhere between one in ten and one in five of the adult males may have lost their lives in those few days. In addition to killing, there was alleged rape, arson, looting, and expropriation. A large percentage of the entire Muslim population of the districts fled in destitution to the capital or other cities; later efforts to repatriate them met with scant success.[7] Cantwell Smith was referring to a report by Pandit Sundarlal (1886–1980) and Kazi Muhammad Abdul Ghaffar (1889–1956).[8]

Notes

1. When 1 started working on my MPhil dissertation in 1988, I realized that no empirical data was available on the state of Urdu or its education, and the writing on both the themes was either polemical or very superficial. So I embarked on my own fieldwork, covering Bihar, West Bengal, Andhra Pradesh, Maharashtra, and my home state of Uttar Pradesh. Various articles based on the fieldwork were published in Urdu, and 'Urdu Education in India: Four Representative States,' was published in *Economic and Political* Weekly (vol. XXIX, no. 14, April 2–14, 1994). This, as far as I know, represents the first and last fieldwork done by any scholar to collect empirical data on Urdu language and Urdu education, and it was done without any institutional support.

2. To the best of my knowledge, most people/organizations associated with the process of preparing Urdu textbooks have not dealt with school education and hardly any of them have reflected on the academic aspects of teaching Urdu at the primary, secondary, and senior-secondary level. On 28 June 2010, I spoke to Dr Khaliq Anjum, General Secretary of Anjuman Taraqqi-e Urdu (Hind), which happens to be the oldest representative body of the Urdu-speaking people having huge resources, and also claims to be their voice. He confirmed my views, with the additional information that 'Urdu language books are prepared mainly by professors of Urdu and Urdu critics, so technically they can be termed as "original books" although their standard is far below the books prepared for the teaching of other languages.' He also stated that the books in Urdu on other subjects—such as

the sciences and social sciences—are poor translations of Hindi books, which pose major problems for Urdu-medium students. 'Moreover, books in Urdu on various subjects are only made available when half the academic session is complete.'

3. 'Statement of Consensus', *The Annual of Urdu Studies*, No. 18, Part 2, Madison: University of Wisconsin, 2003, pp. 564–6.

4. When H.N. Bahuguna became the Chief Minister of UP, Urdu-language teachers were appointed for the first time after independence in government-run schools there. Since there was no provision for teaching Urdu as a subject in schools, Urdu-knowing people with the requisite qualifications were not available for teaching it. So the state government recruited all and sundry—even people with just a matriculation certificate and having no knowledge of the language. Most of them have now retired after remaining in service for twenty-five to thirty years, so, the state of Urdu instruction in UP schools is the same as it was sixty-three years back. I could not lay my hands on any official document regarding the scheme for reference.

5. See Ibrahim Jalis, 'Do Mulk, Ek Kahani', *Naya Waraq*, vol. 8, no. 21, December 2004–February 2005, pp. 149–217.

6. 'Razakar' literally means 'volunteer'. The people who volunteered for the military struggle against the Indian state after Independence were called 'Razakars' in this particular context. The idea of the struggle was actually to include Hyderabad in Pakistan, but the public statement issued by the leaders of the movement claimed that the people of Hyderabad wanted their state to be autonomous. The movement was supported by the Muslim League and the Nizam of Hyderabad. Both, of course, had their own reasons for this. The Indian state came out heavily against the move and within no time the Indian army forced the Nizam and the leader of the Razakars to surrender. The army operation was termed as 'police action', but the atrocities against the common man were so horrible that these will not fade away from the memories of Hyderabadis for centuries to come.

7. Wilfred Cantwell Smith, 'Hyderabad; A Muslim Tragedy', *Middle East Journal*, vol. 4, 1950; for a detailed study, please see Aziz Razvi, 'Betrayal; A Political Study of British with the Nizams of Hyderabad', Karachi: South Asia Publications, 1998. A detailed description is also available in 'Do Mulk, Ek Kahani' by Ibrahim Jalis, reproduced in *Naya Waraq*, Bombay Quarterly, vol. 8, no. 21, December 2004–February 2005, pp. 149–217.

8. This report is reproduced by Omar Khalidi entitled 'A Report on the Post-Operation Polo Massacres, Rape and Destruction and Seizure of Property,' in *Hyderabad: After the Fall*, Wichita, Kansas, USA: Hyderabad Historical Society, 1988, pp. 95–115. A.G. Noorani has also published further excerpts as 'A Massacre Untold,' in *Frontline*, 3–16 March 2001. Dr Yusuf Husain Khan, a nationalist intellectual and brother of Dr Zakir Husain, accompanied the Hyderabad Delegation to the United Nations (UN) in September 1948 as French interpreter to the delegation since the UN Security Council session on Hyderabad was held in Paris.

11

A Foreigner's Reflections on the Status of Urdu and Urdu Education in India

CHRISTINA OESTERHELD

Urdu education in India is a subject I had always taken interest in, but never really dealt with in depth. My main field of research is Urdu literature, especially prose literature of the earlier two centuries. Though I have been teaching Urdu at the university level to German students for twenty-five years, this experience is completely different from teaching Urdu to Indian students in primary, secondary, and high schools. Moreover, I have not systematically been following the developments in the field of Urdu education in India. Therefore, my knowledge of the ground situation, of statistical data pertaining to Urdu education, and of secondary sources is rather sketchy. All I can outline here are a few stray observations and impressions.

Much has been written about the sorry state of Urdu, and particularly Urdu education, in India. Notwithstanding all the (quite liberal) provisions for minority languages in Articles 345, 347, and 350 of the Indian Constitution, state governments in north India saw to it that Urdu speakers were not able to profit from these constitutional safeguards. The Government of India refused to enforce its policy towards Urdu. The following recommendations were formulated in the government's press note of 14 July 1958 following the Kripalani Committee Report:

In areas where the Urdu language is prevalent, the following facilities should be especially provided:

1. Facilities should be provided for instruction and examination in the Urdu language at the primary stage to all children whose mother tongue is declared by the parent or guardian to be Urdu.

2. Arrangements should be made for the training of teachers and for providing suitable textbooks in Urdu.

3. Facilities for instruction in Urdu should also be provided in the secondary stage of education.

4. Documents in Urdu should be accepted by all courts and offices without the necessity of translation or transliteration in any other language or script, and petitions and representations in Urdu should also be accepted.

5. Important laws, rules and regulations, and notifications should be issued in the Urdu language also in areas where this language is prevalent and which may be specified for this purpose.[1]

Though the Kripalani Committee's attitude toward minorities and minority cultures was judged by Paul Brass as 'contrary to Articles 29 and 30 of the Constitution of India',[2] these five points more or less reflect the demands of Urdu speakers to this day, which is ample proof of the official hostility toward Urdu.

It seems that one way to circumvent the implementation of these recommendations was to deny Urdu speakers the status of a linguistic minority, defining them instead as 'a certain percentage of persons'.[3] In 1974, Brass summed up with regard to Uttar Pradesh (UP): 'In fact, the stated policy of the UP government and the administration of that policy have been consistently marked by three features—minimization of the size and importance of the Urdu-speaking minority, deliberate deviation from the policy guidelines set by the Government of India and inter-state committees, and persistent and recurrent deficiencies in providing the facilities for Urdu-speakers which the state government itself has conceded in principle.'[4]

There is no need to add to the long list of grievances and accusations. It is well known how official neglect and discrimination finally discouraged Urdu speakers from getting their children educated in Urdu, which led to the vicious circle of diminishing opportunities for and declining interest in Urdu. Eventually, Urdu has come to be regarded as the language of Muslims in India. But who are the Muslims actually reading and writing Urdu and getting their children instructed in Urdu? We must not forget that many Muslims in India have a mother tongue other than Urdu. How many of them adopt Urdu as a second or third language? Are these figures available?[5]

What is the actual state of primary education in Urdu in UP, Bihar, and other north-Indian states, and what about the situation in south India? It would be interesting to get precise statistical data regarding these questions. Some data has been provided in Ather Farouqui's article 'Urdu Education in India: Four Representative States'.[6] The figures given in the article are not sufficient, however, to get an overall picture of the situation prevailing with regard to Urdu education. It would also be interesting to find out whether the demand for Urdu education really surpasses its availability.

During the last decades, research on Indian Muslims has broken up the monolithic picture of the community and shown its differentiation along social, ethnic, and cultural lines. Has similar research been carried out with regard to the language behaviour of different Muslim groups and their attitude toward Urdu in particular? How is the fact that Urdu education is better off in Maharashtra, which is stated by several authors, to be explained? Ather Farouqui remarks that in Maharashtra even middle-class Muslims prefer Urdu education for their children and offers as an explanation 'that the Muslims of Maharashtra in general, and of Bombay in particular, hail from business communities'.[7] What does this explain? Why does the business community take more interest in Urdu than other communities? Is it because this community is more or less self-employed and therefore does not have to rely on employment in governmental institutions, the civil service, etc.? Or does it simply reflect the better economic position of Muslims?

The Utility of Urdu

The main question in the present context seems to me whether Urdu in India will be able to maintain—or to recover—the role of a functional language in a broader, public context, or will it be reduced to a cultural symbol, a language of religious and, to some extent, literary discourse? Urdu has been declared the second state language in, as far as I know, three states of the Indian Union. In the Urdu press, it is often lamented that these declarations did not have any practical consequences. Recent information on Andhra Pradesh, where Urdu is now recognized as the second official language in thirteen districts, sounds quite encouraging.[8] I would be happy to learn about the practical effects of these measures, because unless Urdu will really be used for official purposes and business transactions in certain areas, I do not see any future for it as a functional language.

Here, some kind of a vicious circle can be perceived: After 1947, the role of Urdu has systematically been reduced by the authorities in its heartland, and at the same time most of the Urduwalas themselves have adopted other languages (Hindi, English) as functional languages in their dealing with officials, in education, trade, etc. (By the way, none of the children of the Urdu-teaching colleagues at Indian universities I happened to meet knew how to read or write Urdu!). Shamsur Rahman Faruqi put it very harshly:

However, if the existence of Muslims is tied up with Urdu[9] but they cannot exert themselves individually to preserve it, then concessions and academies and scholarships by the government are not likely to improve Urdu's affairs. The fact is that individual Muslim efforts on this count have been negligibly small. Muslim intellectuals especially have played a most disappointing role in this regard. Not only did they not have Urdu taught to their children, but also found the stupidest reasons for their inaction. Eventually, this has made the problem even worse.[10]

C.M. Naim gives one of the explanations often put forward: '...your parents would not find any Urdu-medium primary or secondary school in the city, not to say the neighbourhood, and if they did, it would be so bad they would not send you to it.'[11]

In a highly competitive society as the contemporary Indian is, parents after all have to think of their children's careers and job opportunities; there is nothing wrong with that. But if you intend to maintain a separate cultural identity symbolized by Urdu, then some extra personal effort will have to be made. And if you expect Urdu to be employed for official purposes, then there must be people sufficiently proficient in Urdu to use the language in such contexts. Does such a class exist at all, or will it have to be trained afresh? There can be no dispute about the fact that primary education in Urdu is the precondition for any further development of Urdu education, and for the use of Urdu as a functional language. Would this not also imply the need for all Urdu-speaking parents to send their children to Urdu-medium schools, or at least to schools teaching Urdu as the first Indian language once they would be available? How many parents of the middle class would be willing to do so?

I fully agree with C.N. Naim's remark,[12] that the Urdu curriculum at Indian universities is not at all helpful in this regard. It concentrates on literature (and here also not the latest authors and works), leaving aside functional aspects of the language and the contemporary discourse in the humanities. The concept of Urdu as primarily or even exclusively a literary language—a language of love poetry at that—causes much damage to the way Urdu instruction is designed. And it helps in commercializing and trivializing Urdu literature, particularly through the *ghazal* and *qawwali*. On the other hand, it seems to be exactly the entertainment value of these forms of Urdu culture that keeps at least part of it alive.

Many writers have observed that, through *madrasa* education, a new class of Urdu-knowing youth is produced. But where do Urdu language and literature figure in the madrasa syllabus? Where the medium of instruction is Urdu, students at least acquire the basic language skills. My knowledge of madrasa education is too limited to allow for any further comment, but I have often heard complaints from university professors about the lack of any knowledge of, for instance, Urdu's literary heritage and contemporary Urdu literature on the part of madrasa graduates. This fact is also admitted by Qamaruddin in his survey of religious educational institutions.[13] Apparently, some are also largely ignorant of any modern developments in science and the humanities.

There, are, however, attempts in quite a number of madrasas to include modern subjects in the curriculum. Instead of general statements condemning madrasa education, one has to take a closer look at individual schools to arrive at a more differentiated picture. Some field studies currently under way may help us to obtain concrete facts and data.[14] On the other hand, among the younger generation, at least some of the madrasa graduates are said to be the only persons possessing a proper grounding in Urdu. I think that only dialogue and building bridges across the boundaries of ideologies, power politics, clashing interests, and pride of place may help to overcome this impasse.

It would be interesting to study whether and how these two groups—madrasa graduates and graduates of 'modern' schools—ever meet to combine their skills. Together, they could perhaps bring fresh life to Urdu literature and Urdu culture. Is there any serious dialogue between modernist intellectuals and the madrasa-educated (apart from mutual attacks and emotionalized polemics)? If not, then why? Have the lower middle-class or (formerly) backward Urduwallas succeeded in creating their own press to voice their views and interests? Are not these Urduwalas regarded as second-rate by the upper strata of (Muslim) society and simply ignored, despite the fact that widening its social background and area of operation is perhaps one of the last chances left to Urdu as a living language in India? On the other hand, linking Urdu even closer to predominantly religious education, as is done in the madrasas, may limit its scope even further. Urdu is the language adopted by many Indian Muslims as a symbol and carrier of their distinct identity, but this identity may be cultural as well as—or even instead of—religious. Only providing real alternatives, that is, high-quality Urdu-medium or Urdu-teaching government schools in all localities where there is a demand for them, could challenge the appeal of madrasas—and perhaps also serve as an incentive to strive for better quality of education in the latter.

A Path Forward

It appears that simultaneous efforts in several directions would be needed to revive Urdu as a language used for practical purposes. The following suggestions have been made time and again by various renowned scholars in India and abroad, and I have just tried to combine them to include measures I deem necessary.

Possible measures for reviving Urdu as a functional language:

• use of Urdu as the medium of instruction for the children of those who regard Urdu as their mother tongue, as envisaged in Article 350-A of the Constitution, and teaching of Urdu as the first language to such pupils; preconditions: correct registration of language in census reports, etc; dropping of Sanskrit from the Three Language Formula as a compulsory 'modern' language (responsibility of the state)

• teaching of Urdu as an optional Modern Indian Language to children whose mother tongue is other than Urdu (responsibility of the state)

• use of Urdu as the language not only of education, but also of administration,[15] commerce, etc. by officials and by the population who claims to be speakers of Urdu, thus opening up job opportunities for persons educated in Urdu (responsibility of the state and of individuals, commercial units, etc.)

• private efforts of Urdu-speaking parents to have Urdu taught to their children even if they opt for other languages in their children's formal education.

It should be noted, however, that the Three Language Formula proves to be impracticable, even when Sanskrit is excluded, in states where the state language is other than Hindi. In Karnataka, for instance, a student would for all practical purposes be required to learn Urdu, Kannada, Hindi, and English. Wahab Andalib has suggested that from class VIII onwards, students could study Urdu and Hindi in combined classes.[16] It is comparatively easy for students of Urdu to learn Hindi, or vice versa, and there had been a tradition of teaching both languages side by side before 1947. For any student of Hindi or Urdu it would need only a very small extra effort to acquire both scripts and study the additional basic vocabulary, conversational patterns, etc. of the other language. The textbooks for learning Urdu on the basis of Hindi I have seen so far, seem to focus on the instruction of small children, and are totally unfit for elder children and adults. To some degree, this is true also of the new course books for distance education published by the National Council for Promotion of Urdu Language. As a whole, combining education in Hindi and Urdu (at least in the foundational stage) could be an easy way to solve many problems. Both languages share the same grammatical structure. It is comparatively easy for a student to acquire both scripts (preferably one after the other). Even our German students who are completely ignorant of any Urdu or Hindi are able to master the script within four to six weeks.

But even if Urdu education in government schools was easily available, say, in UP, would parents send their children to them? Would they not prefer English or, as the second preference, Hindi-medium schools? S.S. Desnavi named employment orientation as one of the reasons to opt for English or for the respective state language instead of Urdu.[17] Why is the situation different in Maharashtra where, according to Ather Farouqui, all subjects are taught through the Urdu medium in Urdu schools?[18] I would also like to know why there is such a vast gap between the figures of Urdu students in UP and in Bihar. One explanation for this may be the different attitude of the state government, but why is the 'attachment of poorer section of Muslim society to Islam'[19] deeper in Bihar than in UP? Or are there other reasons why less Muslim parents send their children to *dini madaris* in UP?

One argument for not using Urdu as the medium of instruction is the lack of scientific terminology. Ather Farouqui, too, states this fact though he himself in his article pointed at the glossaries and dictionaries compiled at Osmania University.[20] Some of the terms coined in Hyderabad may have become obsolete, but new glossaries have been produced in India and Pakistan, and a good number of Urdu schoolbooks for various subjects, including science, has been published by the NCERT. Another set of textbooks produced by the Bureau for Promotion of Urdu is mentioned by S.S. Desnavi in the article referred to above. Therefore, it should be possible to teach all subjects in Urdu if only the political and parental will were there. It would be interesting to learn whether at all and where these books are used. In the case of Urdu readers and history books, there may be ample scope for religious and cultural resistance to texts translated from other languages (Hindi or English), which may present a Hindu bias. Such problems should, however, be absent in books of mathematics and science.

Availability of books, too, seems to be a big problem. But this one should be able to solve if only persons of means and influence take an interest in the matter. In advanced science courses, English would perhaps be the better choice, but this is a disadvantage faced by all institutions in the non-English speaking world. In Germany, too, English as the medium of instruction in advanced science courses is currently being discussed. Scientific publications, international conferences, and seminars use English anyway. Therefore, this problematic is not restricted to Urduwalas. However, elementary instruction in the sciences would probably yield better results if conducted in the mother tongue of the pupils.[21] As a whole, the formula suggested by S.S. Desnavi (Urdu as medium of instruction up to class VII with the regional language as a subject from class III onwards, etc.; Urdu continued as the first language up to class XII; medium of instruction from classes VIII to XII: regional language)[22] looks practicable to me. And what about distance education in Urdu? Are there any figures on enrolment and results?

The English Syndrome

The main reason for advocating English as medium of instruction at all levels, of course, lies in the predominance of English in all higher spheres of education, administration, and business. In accordance with this privileged position of English, education in any medium other than English is looked upon as second-rate, and unfortunately the quality of education in other languages often is inferior to that offered in English-medium schools. But this has nothing to do with inherent weaknesses of the respective languages; it is the natural result of neglect and contempt.

Now, the question arises whether the social, political, and economic status of children from the lower strata of society would get any better if English would be introduced as the medium of instruction in all schools, right from grade one onwards. Without improving the overall situation in the respective schools, English alone will not be of any help. Furthermore, would children from a non-English-speaking background be able to follow what is talked about at school? Would it really enable them to catch up with their better-equipped class-fellows, or would they not rather be doomed to complete failure right from the start? Apart from those unable to catch up with English, will not all other students trained through the English medium tend later on to conduct all their affairs in English? Will they not be proud to be unable to speak any Indian language properly? This, at least, has been my experience with people 'having English'—with the exception of writers, journalists, etc., using Indian languages and earning their living through them.

What could be the solution to this problem? Is it possible to train Indian pupils and students in such a way that they may be equally proficient in English and in an Indian language? Could this be achieved by teaching some subjects in English and some in the respective mother tongue? Or should English be taught only as a subject in the first two or three years? The urgency of this problem for Urdu is perhaps greater than for any other Indian language because it is closely connected with the survival of Urdu as a functional language. I fear that relegating Urdu to the role of only a subject, with English as the medium of instruction, will in the not too long run deprive the language of its users/speakers. It could even accelerate the process of turning Urdu into a dead language that is only of academic interest.

But let us assume that all measures would be taken to provide high-quality Urdu education at different levels. Still, the vital question remains: Who would be the people to adopt (or re-adopt) Urdu as their primary medium of education, communication, and for all practical transactions? Would they not consist only of those who cannot afford education in any other language, or of those who adhere to Urdu as a marker of their religious identity? What really is the demand for Urdu education in India? Is it still possible to revive

Urdu as a full-fledged functional language in India, or has it not already irretrievably lost its base? How many parents from the Muslim élites get their children educated in Urdu? And what about the Muslim middle class? Campaigners for the cause of Urdu tend to come from the latter two strata, whereas it are the former who constitute whatever mass base Urdu still has. The wide gap and lack of communication between these two groups, to my mind, is one of the main hurdles in the way to any improvement in Urdu education.

Should we then quietly accept the status quo with regard to Urdu education? Certainly not! Urdu instruction at any level should be of high quality, imparted by highly motivated teachers, and with teaching materials that should be at par with material in any other language. As mentioned above, I feel that the question of the quality of Urdu instruction is closely linked with the social groups it caters to. As long as elementary instruction in Urdu is left to those looked down upon by any person endowed with a 'modern' education, the situation will not improve.

Data I received recently from three branches of Delhi Public School point to the fact that Urdu as a third language is taken up by quite a number of non-Muslims. Despite its sad fate in practical matters, Urdu still enjoys a high prestige as a language of literature and of a refined culture. This fact was recently also stressed by the Hindi poet Vishnu Khare in a talk at our institute. We may like it or not, but the future of Urdu in India perhaps lies more in the fields of literature, history, and the media than in those of administration, commerce, and modern education in general. For studies in history and literature, excellent knowledge of the language is a prerequisite. It has been stressed again and again that even for the teaching of Urdu literature at college and university levels, a solid education in the basics of the language is essential. Strategies will have to be developed to ensure that: (1) Students of Urdu at the high school level and above should get no admission unless they have qualified in an elementary and secondary/advanced course of the language and are able to read and write the Urdu script correctly and fluently. (2) Stricter selection of Urdu students for MA and PhD research projects to achieve a higher standard of the respective degrees. If Urdu in India is reduced to the status of a classical literary and a media language, then adequately educated specialists should be available in at least these two fields.

To conclude, let me briefly turn to the attitude of Urduwalas toward Hindi. The contempt or inferiority complex many Urdu speakers feel because Urdu, as a functional language, has been replaced by Hindi is often matched by a 'superiority complex' with regard to Urdu's literary heritage, and the refinement and elegance of the language. In the long run, this contempt for Hindi will do Urdu no good. Ugly, heavy-sounding neologisms, irregularities, and deviations from the rules can be found in spoken and written Urdu as well as in Hindi. And there is a lot in modern Hindi literature that can very well compare with modern Urdu literature. As long as élitist Urdu proponents will demonstrate equal arrogance with regard to lower-class Urdu-speakers and to Hindi language and literature, they are likely to cut off vital nerves guaranteeing the very existence of Urdu in India. Instead of rivalry, co-operation should govern the mutual relations between writers and scholars of Urdu and Hindi. (I am fully aware of the fact, though, that there is more rivalry than co-operation even among Urdu writers and intellectuals.) There are, of course, instances of such a fruitful co-operation, and an increasing number of translations from Hindi into Urdu. Therefore, I am very much in favour of translations or 'transcriptions' of Urdu works into Hindi/Devanagari. Personally, I would deeply regret the Urdu script being forsaken in India. This would really cut all future generations off from their cultural heritage, and would consequently turn Urdu into a dead language—at least in India.

Notes

1. Government of UP, *Kripalani Committee Report*, August 1962, p. 80.
2. Paul R. Brass, *Language, Religion and Politics in North India*, Cambridge: Cambridge University Press, 1974, p. 205.
3. Ibid., p. 206.
4. Ibid., p. 204.
5. Syed Shahabuddin, quoting the 1991 census, states that 61.2 per cent of Indian Muslims declared their mother tongue to be Urdu, *Mainstream*, vol. XL, no. 28, 29 June 2002, p. 19.
6. Ather Farouqui, 'Urdu Eucation in India: Four Representative States', *Economic and Political Weekly*, vol. XXIX, no. 14, 2 April 1994, pp. 782–5.
7. Ibid., p. 785.
8. See *Urdū Dunyā*, October 2001, p. 62.
9. Which, to my mind, is not the case! (Christina Oesterheld).
10. Quoted from an interview by Ather Farouqui in *Annual of Urdu Studies*, no. 10, 1995, p. 165.
11. Ibid., p. 123.

12. Ibid, p. 157.
13. See Qamaruddin, *Hindūstān kī dīnī darsgāheñ (Kul Hind sarve)*, New Delhi: Hamdard Educational Society, 1996, p. 123, where he quotes from a letter by Sayyid Husain Ahmad from Deoband. In the same volume, Qamaruddin has submitted interesting suggestions for modernization of Urdu education at the dini madaris (pp. 425–33).
14. The two studies I know of are conducted in UP by Mareike J. Winkelmann and by a team consisting of Patricia Roger and Craig Jeffrey. I am sure that Indian scholars, too, are engaged in research in the field, but unfortunately I do not have information on any such project.
15. Cp. the suggestions made by Syed Shahabuddin in 'Status of Urdu in India', *Mainstream*, Annual 1988, p. 160.
16. See *Urdū Dunyā*, November 2001, p. 15.
17. S.S. Desnavi, 'Prospects of Urdu Education in India', *The Nation*, Lahore, 16 September 1993, p. 15.
18. Farouqui, *Annual of Urdu Studies*, p. 785.
19. Ibid., p. 785.
20. Ibid., p. 782.
21. Cp. the article by Anis Chishti on the success of Urdu education in Maharashtra: *Mahārāshtra meñ urdū zarī'a-i ta'līm kī kāmyābī*, in *Urdu Duniya*, New Delhi: National Council for Promotion of Urdu Language, vol. 1, no. 4, October–December 1999, pp. 35–7.
22. See Dasnavi, 'Prospects of Urdu Education in India', p. 16.

12

The Wardha Scheme of Basic Education and the Urdu Medium

KERRIN GRÄFIN SCHWERIN

Education is the concern of all parents and elders wanting their children to know about the world, to advance materially, and to behave well according to the rules of their society. This was also the concern of the king who ordered those famous Indian stories called *Panchatantra*—a king who was 'distressed at the evil and stupidity of his sons. He entrusted them to a sage who reformed them in six months by telling them a series of fables.'

Traditional educational systems in any stratified society served different needs. While the merchant valued numbers and bookkeeping, the priest studied sacred texts and commentaries. The aristocrat considered book learning beyond his honour, and employed someone to do the reading and writing for him.

Today, we believe that every child should have an equal chance to go to school, to learn how to read and write, to learn how to face an increasingly complicated world: Education is the magic word of any advancement, morally, intellectually, and economically. While the British ruled India, the educational system was governed by liberal utilitarian ideas on higher education and the understanding that an educated Indian middle class would then be 'interpreters between us and the millions whom we govern.' This Indian middle class was English-educated. Only during the late period of the Indian freedom movement was the issue of education and the Indianization of education discussed—at a conference in Wardha in central India.

I have chosen the Wardha Scheme of Education (1937) as a central point in my paper, because it gives me a chance to take a closer look at the man who presided over the committee that was responsible for its content and phrasing. Dr Zakir Husain was one of the few Indian political leaders who was interested and well versed in the history of modern educational philosophy, who had a personal experience of different systems, and who initiated and organized one of the most successful Indian educational experiments: Jamia Millia Islamia (henceforth Jamia).

Zakir Husain completed his own education at the Aligarh Muslim University in 1920, in the year that saw the beginning of India's freedom struggle with a new emphasis on mass participation. He was among those who were ready to boycott the colonial educational institutions. He was one of the first students of Jamia. But only two years later, when the freedom movement had subsided, a friend of his expedited him to Germany for further studies.

The many details of his activities in Berlin, make interesting reading for someone who knows not only Berlin well, but who has also spent two years of her studies at Jamia. Of course, Zakir Husain had to learn German first, a fact he emphasized in his report home. Of course, Germans were taught in their mother tongue from elementary school up to university. He then enrolled at the Friedrich Wilhelm University (today Humboldt University, Wilhelm von Humboldt being the founder) to study economics under Werner Sombart, a then famous economist who, in order to complete the work of Karl Marx, wrote *The History of Capitalism*. Sombart's son (who is still alive) reports in his memoirs *Youth in Berlin* how his father on every workday appeared for half an hour in the children's room to read fairytales to them, *Robinson Crusoe*, the classic Greek fables, the *Nibelungen*, Homer, and Goethe's *Faust*. Reading to the family was part of bourgeois culture and educational tradition.

The Berlin of the twenties of the last century is known for its rich cultural and intellectual life, a certain decadence, and the beginning of fascist ideas. The Great War had left deep scars in German society, marked by a loss of values, by moral insecurity, and material poverty. An extreme inflation left millions unemployed and hungry, but this had also the effect that those three Indian students who met in Berlin—Mohammad Mujeeb, Abid Husain, and Zakir Husain—could afford to pay their way through a German university. Mohammad Mujeeb and Abid Husain lived in the house of the educationist and editor of a journal on elementary education, Wilhelm Schwaner. His son-in-law, Alfred Ehrentreich, and teachers and educationists like Schwaner introduced the young men to authors such as Georg Kerschensteiner and Eduard Spranger, and to experimental schools of the current reform movement. Zakir Husain even visited some of them, while Abid Husain wrote his dissertation on educational philosophy under Spranger.

Spranger and Kerschensteiner were two exponents of a German school reform movement, particularly of elementary education and vocational training. The small child and young adolescent were the centre of attention of child psychologists and teachers. Early childhood was now considered a most important stage in human moral and intellectual development. The so-called 'magical development stage' of children up to the age of ten years had to be taken into account in any curriculum and teaching method. To break it off too early was considered harmful. The traditional methods of instruction, with its concentration on discipline and intellectual studies, were to be replaced by methods more apt to develop the entire personality of the child—mind and body; school meant games, physical activity, festivities, excursions, cooking, theatrical plays, music, and handicraft, especially in elementary school. The child was to experience its own natural and cultural surroundings before venturing into the world via foreign languages and book learning. Different types of schools were necessary for the acquisition of different professional skills. Spranger also invented the 'Berufschule', that school which in Germany accompanies vocational training (ages 16–18).

It was in Berlin that Zakir Husain met Gerda Philipsborn, the daughter of a wealthy Jewish family, who introduced the three Indians to another social circle. In 1933, Gerda Philipsborn joined the staff of Jamia. For some years, she was involved in pre-school education and had, according to Mujeeb, 'a firm grip on Zakir Husain's time' (Mujeeb, 1971, p. 69). She was interned by the British in 1939 at the beginning of the war and died of cancer in 1942. (Jamia's girls' hostel is named after her.)

Those years in Berlin left a strong and lasting mark on Zakir Husain's mind. In 1925, the three friends decided to return to India, stay together, and dedicate themselves to the project of Jamia. But it was one thing to know about educational philosophy and educational systems, another to put one into practice. At the time of their return, Jamia was at the brink of extinction. It had lost its political character and had taken on the character of an experimental school. Mujeeb writes that its staff was dedicated, but had little experience, hardly any teaching skills, and very little money. Jamia had achieved something entirely new without rebelling against tradition. In Mujeeb's words, the school represented 'Muslim tradition and culture, without making concessions to the prejudices of the majority and without committing itself to the orthodox or to the political interpretation of the teachings of Islam. In fact, it had evolved its own Muslim character more by deviation from accepted traditions and attitudes than by adherence.' Zakir Husain encouraged painting and theatre performance, and introduced co-education in elementary school.

The success or lack of success of the Jamia experiment during those early years is not my topic. It is sufficient to observe that any such reform system will remain an ideal unless there is a favourable and enduring conjunction of political, economic, and social forces. Kerschensteiner's reforms in German education were neutralized, so far as the moral objectives were concerned, by the Nazi regime. An Indian educational system was hampered by many obstacles, not the least of which was lack of teachers' training and money.

'Vernacular school' was the term the British used for elementary schools—the medium of instruction was the local language. But what was the local language in north India? Hindi, Urdu, Hindustani? By the time Jamia was started, the Hindi–Urdu controversy was in full swing. The medium of instruction at Jamia was Urdu from kindergarten up to higher education. It was part of Jamia's philosophy. Urdu was part of the culture lived and taught at the school. Jamia was also a pioneer in starting a teachers' training college. Since the early twentieth century, the Muslim League and Urdu press had deplored the lack of Urdu-medium schools and religious education: 'Primary education is absolutely in the hands of a class which is dead against the Urdu language. Most of the inspecting authorities of the Education Department cannot even speak correct Urdu and the textbooks are full of grammatical and idiomatic mistakes.' The Uttar Pradesh (UP) government responded by opening *maktabs* (elementary religious schools) for Muslims which were run by the district boards. Maktab schoolbook committees were to provide them with reading material. The General Report of Public Instruction of 1930 reported that forty-two former English-medium schools had switched to teaching in the vernacular. '…the vernacular', it continued to explain, 'in most cases is not Hindi or Urdu, but Hindi and Urdu in which a large number of English words and phrases occur' (General Report, 1930, p. 15.). The reason was that the teachers were taught in English at university and were unable to speak uncorrupted Hindi or Urdu.

By the time the issue of education and medium of instruction came before the National Educational Conference in Wardha (22–3 October 1937), it was tinged with emotions. The names of Zakir Husain, Mohammad Mujeeb, and Abid Husain were put on the list of participants at the Wardha conference only as an afterthought. The conference was Gandhi's idea, and was organized by the Marwari Education Society of Gujarat. The central concept of Gandhi's education scheme was the perpetuation of the *takli* (spinning wheel) and all the professions going along with it. 'All the processes of cotton, wool, and silk…weaving, embroidery, tailoring, paper-making, cutting, etc.' (*Educational Reconstruction*, 1938). In content it meant putting village industries on a sound basis and combining skills with related subjects. (Later he called it 'Rural National Education through Village Handicraft'.)

The Advent of *Nai Talim*

Zakir Husain, the experienced educationist, rejected the idea of a self-supporting school; it would not work. It had nothing to do with the idea of Kerschensteiner's 'work-school'. He warned of the dangers of exploiting child labour. Although he appeared to be in a minority with his objections, Zakir Husain was asked to draft the resolutions of the Wardha Scheme or Nai Talim, as we know it. He was also chairman of the committee that drafted a syllabus reflecting the character of Nai Talim.

The scheme of 'Nai Talim', as it was also called, met with a storm of protest, partly due to misunderstandings or misconceptions. The Muslim League suspected discrimination of Muslim children. Basic Education was un-Islamic. Zakir Husain replied: The scheme did not intend to introduce child labour; it did not intend to decrease unemployment; co-education would not be compulsory. The Wardha Scheme applied only to elementary schools! Elementary and basic education of the small child was to be firmly rooted in the child's own culture, including religion, he said.

Religion, however was not included in the Wardha curriculum. It was deliberately omitted. Since there were so many denominations in India, it was impossible to teach any special religion in elementary schools. A state teacher could hardly be expected to teach every religion to all children equally well. He suggested that the state could provide for private denominational tuition at school. Denominational schools made sense only at the secondary school level. The child was then old enough to learn about literature, history, religion, and language, subjects that were closely linked to the country's culture (Zakir Husain, 1993).

And, again, he explained, what was meant by 'work' as distinguished from 'skill': Skill, he said, can be acquired by thieves also. Such skills cannot be the end of education. Work can be educative only if it serves values higher than mere personal ends, values beyond ourselves—initiative, creativity, responsibility, co-operation.

Ten years later he had to admit that he had not been properly understood. The 'work-school' was a failure. It did not go along with the Indian idea of education.

Another source of irritation was the question of language. The Wardha Scheme prescribed that the medium of instruction everywhere was to be the mother tongue. But what was the mother tongue of the people of north India—Hindi, Hindustani, or Urdu?

The author of *The Indo-Aryan Languages*, Colin Masica, calls the relationship of Hindi and Urdu in the 'what-is-a-language dilemma' the 'ultimate anomaly' (Masica, 1991, p. 27). In the socio-cultural sense, they would be counted as different languages, while Urdu and 'modern, standard' Hindi are not even different dialects in a linguistic sense. He concludes that 'they are different literary styles based on the same linguistically defined subdialects' (Masica, 1991, p. 29). M.K.A. Beg in his book *Sociolinguistic Perspective of Hindi and Urdu in India* (Beg, 1996) picked up Ashok Kelkar's convincing model of the two languages (Kelkar, 1968, p. 6). The model demonstrates the common linguistic origin of Hindi and Urdu in an open triangle, which branches out from the common base into separate directions, their differences increasing from the level of spoken language to highly specialized idiomatic language. Their differences are a matter of style, and style stands for culture. Masica's final verdict is that 'their identity as separate languages may now be

regarded as a cultural fact, however anomalous linguistically'
(Masica, 1991, p. 30).

Politicization of Language

The social and political forces that drew them apart have resulted
in another anomaly: When asked about their language, Hindus usually call it Hindi, and Muslims refer to it as Urdu, although both may
speak an identical language. (So how can one tell from a census how
many people actually speak Urdu?) Hindi and Urdu are not only
languages, they are also a cultural and a political programme.

During the last decade of the Indian freedom movement, the
Indian Muslims became 'a distinct body politic' (Mujeeb, 1967, p. 23)
whose national identity was said to be in danger. Concerns over
language, as in the debate on 'Nai Talim', had become part of
politics. The language Urdu became part of the demand for a separate Muslim state—a Muslim nation needed a national language.
Once the Muslim state was obtained, it took the language along
into foreign territory, thus denuding its actual speakers who stayed
behind of the right to their language. Urdu, the product of a composit
north-Indian culture, 'migrated' to Pakistan.

At the same time, influential Hindu politicians and organizations
propagated Hindi as the national language of India, a language
drawing its sophisticated vocabulary from Sanskrit. This reliance on
the 'sacred language' was to sanctify the national language of Bharat.
Its final victory was gained in the Constituent Assembly Debates
when Hindi was adopted as the official language of India. Thus, a
long, confusing debate on the name and character, first of the national,
then only the official language was ended. Not quite though, because
in Article 351 the Constitution provides that due regard must be paid
to 'Hindustani' in the future development of the official language.
Hidden within this name Hindustani, so to say, 50 per cent of it is
Urdu. What were the practical consequences?

Both 'Hindustani' as well as 'secularism' are terms symbolizing
a compromise, a truce to keep communal strife at arm's lenth, to
keep the peace. But meanwhile, the government of UP made 'Hindi'
sole official language of the state. Hindi is considered the mother
tongue of any child in the so-called 'Hindi belt'; Hindi is therefore
the medium of instruction as well as examination. This right is denied
to Urdu, which is spoken mainly in this very 'Hindi belt'. It is not

regarded as a 'regional language', but as the language of a minority. A language 'without regional belonging, it has become a soul without a body' (Salman Khurshid). The minority speakers of 'Urdu' may learn their language either at home, in the madrasa, or as an optional language in school. But the Indian Constitution in Article 350-A states that every state and every local authority within the state is to provide adequate facilities for instruction in the mother tongue at the primary stage of education to children belonging to linguistic minority groups. But this does not happen.

Internationally, the question of medium of instruction and discrimination of language minorities has been given much attention lately due to the extreme mobility of people—voluntary or by force. In the early nineties, Berlin alone gave shelter to 30,000 Bosnians escaping from the Balkan War, not to talk of many other nationalities. There are thousands of Russians, Poles, Italians, Indian, and black Africans living there. The Turkish community in Berlin is the largest outside Turkey. At home, they speak their own language, their mother tongue, and there is an increasing tendency of ghetto formation. Many children entering elementary school do not speak German. In France, these minorities are Tunesian, Moroccan, black African, etc.

The United Nations Educational, Scientific and Cultural Organization (UNESCO) decided over fifty years ago that the medium of instruction in elementary school must be the mother tongue. It is obvious that ethnic or foreign minorities are at a great disadvantage in a school where no teacher speaks their language. We talk about discrimination—this discrimination has many roots, not only language. Low social status, a different culture, a different colour of the skin, gender—all these contribute to it. On the other hand, if those migrants who usually do not intend to return to their home countries (except for vacation) are to be integrated into the economy and social structure of the host city, of the country they chose as their new home, they will have to learn the language of the country. If they do not, they cannot participate in the life around them.

The case of Urdu in India is different. Here, discrimination is not a consequence of migration, it is a matter of the diverse language map of the country, as well as of politics. David Corson, in his study on discrimination, stresses that language difference is not the cause of educational failure: 'Language itself has little power when it is divorced from powerful institutions and agents...Indeed the evidence suggests that the unjust use of power in maintaining minority stereotypes and class distance is the chief factor in educational failure, not language.' (Corson, 1993, p. 122). It is this unjust use of power that is responsible for the discrimination of Urdu speakers in north India.

Zakir Husain was aware of these forces that determined the fate of his language after India's independence. He launched a powerful movement for the incorporation of Urdu in the curriculum of those Muslims who claimed it as their language, and demanded that Urdu be recognized as a regional language. He collected more than 2 million signatures supporting his demand. But to no avail.

Since then, over fifty years have passed. The language that was born in north India and that brought forth an important literature, is now highly valued abroad; it is taught to students at American and European universities, its poetry is recited and sung on international radios, so-called Hindi (=Urdu) movies are popular everywhere. It is the *lingua franca* of Indians and Pakistanis outside India and Pakistan. Urdu, it seems, will not disappear from the language map of the world—because it is valued by people as a literature and a language.

It is important and essential to remind the Indian state and its governments, particularly those of UP and Bihar, of the duties required by the Indian Constitution. But it is not enough. Champions of Urdu must not wait for the government to do its job. They must actively look for support where they can find it—in the media, in the political parties, and in the universities and schools. Unless speakers of Urdu themselves value their literary heritage, their mother tongue, and quality education, unless they fight against stereotypes and prejudice, unless they themselves speak, read, and write Urdu, no one will be convinced that anything ought to be done for it.

> Desolation has reigned for long
> in the habitation of my heart—
> come, let us build a new temple in our land.
>
> —Mohammad Iqbal

References

Ali, B. Sheikh, *Zakir Husain: Life and Times*, New Delhi: Vikas Publishing House, 1991.

Beg, M.K.A., *Sociolinguistic Perspective of Hindi and Urdu in India*, New Delhi: Bahri Publishers, 1996.

Corson, David, *Language, Minority Education and Gender: Linking Social Justice and Power*, Clevedon: Multilingual Matters, 1993.

Educational Reconstruction, A collection of Gandhi's articles on the Wardha Scheme along with a summary of the proceedings of the All India National Educational Conference held at Wardha, 1937, Wardha: India Bulletin, August, 1938.

General Report of Public Institution, 1930.

Hasan, Mushirul, *India's Muslims since Independence*, New Delhi: Oxford University Press, 1997.

Husain, Zakir, *Education and National Development*, New Delhi, 1993.

Kelkar, Ashok, *Studies in Hindi-Urdu, I: Introduction and Word Phonology*, Poona: Deccan College, 1968.

Masica, Colin P., *The Indo-Aryan Languages*, Cambridge: Cambridge University Press, 1991.

Mathur, V.S. (ed.), *Zakir Husain: Educationist and Teacher*, New Delhi: Arya Book Depot, 1969.

Mujeeb, Mohammad, *The Indian Muslims*, London: Allen & Unwin, 1967.

————, *Dr Zakir Husain. A Biography*, New Delhi: National Book Trust, 1971.

Narang, Gopi Chand, *Urdu Language and Literature: Critical Perspectives*, New Delhi: Sterling Publishers, 1991.

Noorani, A.G., *President Zakir Husain*, New Delhi: Popular Prakashan, 1972.

Oesterheld, Joachim, *Zakir Husain: Begegnungen und Erfahrungen bei der Suche nach moderner Bildung für ein freies Indien* in P. Heidrich (ed.), *Akteure des Wandels*, Berlin, 2001, pp. 105–30.

13

Urdu in India:
Its Present State, and the Way Forward

HASAN ABDULLAH

The state and status of Urdu is different from other Indian languages; and the *causative factors* are also different.[1] Nevertheless, at the most fundamental level, the fate of different Indian languages—including the official Hindi—is tied together.[2] Only a rational language policy— a policy that does not discriminate against any language—can take all the languages and society forward.

However, in a rapidly shrinking world—where communication and interaction are exceedingly fast, lot of physical movement also takes place, and where time is of great essence—the language for advance interaction has to be an advanced global language. And, in the case of India, that role has to be played by English (detailed arguments for it follow later). At the same time, it is the mother tongue/regional language—a language in which the child interacts at home and at play—that the child can best comprehend. Therefore, the child must be imparted primary education through the mother tongue.[3] Moreover, the mother tongue and the regional language also help in developing the positive roots in culture, besides enabling better interaction with the people at large. How to make the two objectives—primary education through the mother tongue/regional language, and advance communication through English—compat-ible, and the transition from the mother tongue to English smooth, are the central questions.

This paper is divided into two parts. In the first discussion I have tried to raise some fundamental questions that would help us locate the reasons for the state of affairs with regard to the Urdu language today. From there, it would not be difficult to decide the desirable (and also possible, given the present-day realities) course of action. The first part essentially presents a viewpoint. In the second, I take the logic a step forward, and also make some firm, but flexible, suggestions with regard to language policy.

The Perspective

Before raising the fundamental questions, let me admit that the problem with regard to the approach I advocate is that it is not in the interest of the reactionary powers-that-be, and it is also not going to be easy to convince the common people about the desirability of such an approach. The challenge is that the people have to be convinced about the desirability of the approach, and the powers-that-be forced to act accordingly. The questions that are fundamental—and have direct bearing—on the issue of language are:

- What is/are the role(s) of a language?
- Is there a contradiction between the growth of different Indian languages?
- Can Urdu meet the requirements of a modern language?
- What are the important circumstances that govern the state of a language?
- What do the tentative answers to the above questions indicate?

What is the Role of a Language?

Language, obviously, is a means of communication. However, courtesy advancement of the world, and the diversity and differentiation it has brought in its wake, there are different aspects of communication.

- Visiting the past.
- Negotiating with the present, and preparing for the future.
- Interacting with different segments of society.

Visiting the Past

The human mind is complex, and needs myraid of inputs to satiate it. The question of human identity is multi-dimensional; undoubtedly, the rooting of the individual in the soil requires appreciation of history and culture.[4] This rooting—through history and culture—provides the much-needed stability, and constitutes an important component of identification for an individual. It is this linking with the past that provides the continuity that is needed; and, as the evolution of culture is a rather slow process, the linkage with the three epochs—the past, the present, and the future—is necessary.

In the absence of a rational appreciation of, and identification with, the culture and the past—through the mother tongue—the missing roots often play havoc with the psychology of the person; and, the vacuum is sought to be filled through irrationality, superficiality, meaningless symbolism or rituals. It is only through linking with the past that we are able to actually locate our origin or starting/reference point, and also come to appreciate how that origin got established. The reading of history and evolution of society helps in identification with the rest of the society; in the absence of identification with the surrounding people and culture through the mother tongue, the identification with the people-at-large becomes well nigh impossible. And, such an identification is a must for harmonious development of the society or, in other words, for optimal development of the faculties of every individual (corresponding to the developmental level of society, at any given point of time).

Thus, the importance of the mother tongue cannot be over-emphasized; and, there cannot be any dialogue with a person, who disgrees with regard to the above-argued need for the advancement of a language.

Negotiating with the Present and Preparing for the Future

There has been an explosion of knowledge, and the world has witnessed great advancements during the last couple of centuries. Especially during the last century, the productive forces' pace of development has been fast; with the consequent advancement of knowledge, the English language has kept pace through the corresponding addition of words. However, for historical reasons, most languages—and that includes Urdu—were left behind; as of now, it does not seem feasible that Urdu can make up for lost time. It is for this reason that knowledge of an advanced language—English in case of Indians—becomes necessary. To comprehend, and also to express, the complexities and intricacies of today's world, knowledge of English is essential.

Any student of science or an advance course in any discipline would testify to the need for a good command over the English language. English has also become the language of intellectual discourse, to an extent that the seminars on the issue of Urdu language are also conducted in English![5] It is this requirement of knowing English that creates, or is used to create, confusion in the minds of the people over the issue of language. The people are made to believe that teaching through English—and that too from day one—is advantageous, which is an outright falsehood.[6] In fact, it is harmful because teaching through English at the primary level prods the child towards enhancement of memory at the expense of understanding.[7] The efforts that should go towards enhancement of understanding go towards struggling with the language. As the world of the child is rather simple, it is not at the level of primary school that teaching of English is necessary—and certainly not teaching through English. The child can best comprehend in his/her mother tongue; and, therefore, primary education must be through the mother tongue.

Interacting with Different Segments of Society

For one interested in the harmonious development of society, the importance of interaction with the underdogs goes unsaid. For this, communication through the mother tongue is the only way, because even many of those who learn English are not proficient enough to communicate comfortably through that language. The communication with these people—and they constitute an overwhelming majority—needs to be through the mother tongue. Incidentally, this communication enriches the language also; because, for the development of the language, there needs to be a sizable body of people that uses the said language for discourse. Those who graduate to the higher level of discourse have to communicate in English; Urdu—or any other Indian language—can prosper only if we communicate with the people-at-large.

Given this understanding of the role of a language in today's India, a person with Urdu as the mother tongue has to be at least effectively bilingual (Urdu and English). Additionally, one must strive to learn the language of the region where one is located.

Is There a Contradiction between the Growth of Different Indian Languages?

The answer would depend on the perception of the role of language. In the above perception, there is no contradiction between the growth of different languages; in fact, these growths are complementary. Only in an environment of harmony and general development, the languages, particularly the ones that lag behind, would develop; even the developed language(s) would be enriched, as more and more people with different mother tongues use the language.[8] After all, language is not all about science and specialized subjects, but also deals with different cultures. (After all, why has the English dictionary incorporated so many Hindustani words?)[8] But those who perceive contradiction in the growth of different languages and advancement of different sections or, in other words, who are not interested in bridging the gulf between different classes, 'may' not find the advancement of different languages as complementary.

Can Urdu Meet the Requirements of a Modern Language?

The answer is both yes and no. In abstraction, the answer would be in the affirmative, because even today there is a sizable body of people whose mother tongue is Urdu. And, if enough investments are made and these people use their mother tongue for all purposes, except while communicating with the non-Urdu speaking, then—but only then—perhaps, Urdu can meet the requirements of a modern language. But, as any one can see, that is a hypothetical situation; it is also superfluous. Therefore, for all practical purposes, the answer to the question raised above is a definite no. In the above sense, Urdu cannot meet the requirements of a modern language. And, English shall remain the language for advance discourse—particularly in science and technology—because the pace of development in these areas is too fast for a less developed language such as Urdu to bridge the gap and keep pace. It is no aspersion on the language to say that it cannot become a modern language in the above sense. It only reflects that for historical reasons, particularly because Urdu was not the favoured language of the powers-that-be during the rapid development of science and technology, Urdu has lagged behind. And, given the present-day realities, it would not be practicable, and also not prudent, to spend energy to bridge this gap completely, and keep pace with a modern language such as English.

What are the Important Circumstances that Govern the State of a Language?

In addition to the above mentioned constraint of words, the following important factors also need to be understood to appreciate the state of the Urdu language today.

- The influence and role of the Urdu élite
- The base of Urdu-knowing Indian intelligentsia
- The social, economic, and educational background of Urdu-knowing people
- The geographical spread of Urdu-knowing people

The Influence and Role of Urdu-knowing Élite

There is complete intellectual domination of the élite; as a class, it has been playing a reactionary role with regard to the question of education of the people (with which the issue of language is inextricably linked). The intelligentsia, as also the élite as a whole, has not adopted a rational and progressive attitude to the question of the medium of instruction. This can be considered one of the most important factors responsible for the sorry state of the Urdu language today. If the children from the élite class were to receive education through their respective mother tongues, these languages, including Urdu, would not have been in their present state.

The influence of the élite is so widespread that the people are not able to even understand that teaching in English at the primary level is harmful; it is particularly disadvantageous for their wards. The reasons for imparting primary-level education through the mother tongue have been explained. It appears that the élite has adopted education through English at the primary level so that it becomes even more difficult for common children to compete, as their parents cannot guide them. It appears to be an additional measure to maintain the élite's privileged position.

The situation is now a catch-22—there are few, if any, good Urdu medium schools—especially in north India—and so the élite's wards go to English-medium schools which, in turn, results in further worsening of Urdu-medium schools. However, the élite's deliberate neglect of the common people's concerns, including education of their children, is reflected in their overall behaviour. (Incidentally, this behaviour is also reflected in the recent moves to make higher education more expensive, and thus beyond the reach of more people.)

The Base of Urdu-knowing Indian Intelligentsia

The Indian intelligentsia, as a class, has been adopting English as their *virtual* mother tongue, and has been largely unconcerned with their respective mother tongues. The base of the Indian intelligentsia employing Indian languages for (written) discourse has therefore been reducing (at least as a percentage) with time. I have no access to data—even if such data exists—with regard to Urdu. However, for three years, I had been associated with an Urdu monthly that regularly carries sections on societal affairs, economics, international affairs, and science, besides literature; the experience suggests that, leave alone getting original articles, even to get good translations of serious articles is a very difficult proposition.[9] Also, there are few periodicals or books (especially, those originally written in Urdu) that deal with different specialized subjects in any serious manner. Does all this not prove that an Urdu-knowing Indian intelligentsia is in extremely short supply? Unless large number of writers, who are expert in their respective disciplines and communicate in their mother tongue (like J.V. Narlikar, a front-ranking astrophysicist, who writes both on science and for children in his mother tongue, Marathi, also), the language cannot progress. At the very least, competent translators (who are at least good students of their respective subjects, having a reasonable command over the language) are needed.

The future is also not promising in this respect, as the general observation suggests that the number of Urdu-medium schools—at least as a proportion—is declining. Even in areas almost exclusively populated by people with Urdu as their mother tongue, such as Okhla or Jamia Nagar in New Delhi, all the new schools offer education through English only; at the most, Urdu is offered as a language.

Social, Economic, and Educational Background of Urdu-knowing People

The bulk of people with Urdu as the mother tongue come from less privileged sections of the society, and the élite and the middle class are not pursuing the language in any meaningful sense. Yet, there are several Urdu newspapers and periodicals that have reasonable circulations, indicating the existence of a sizable number of Urdu readers—at lest at the general level. (However, it appears that the number of Urdu-knowing people, at least as a proportion of population, is on the decline.) That means there is much scope for the spread of Urdu, provided that Urdu-knowing people can be convinced about the need to learn the mother tongue, and receive at least primary education through it.

The poor social, educational, and economic background of the majority of Urdu-knowing people is reflected in several observations. One, which we have already noted is the paucity of meaningful reading material in Urdu. Also, as of now, in Urdu, there is not much demand for serious reading material that would help comprehend the world and broaden mental horizons. In addition, for the Urdu press, it is extremely difficult to attract advertisements (a crucially important source of revenue),[10] which, in a way, reflects poorly on the social and economic background of the people. Even those magazines with circulations of over a lakh find it difficult to attract advertisements. However, notwithstanding all this, the absence of awareness regarding the importance of education in the modern world is most crucial.

Geographical Spread of Urdu-knowing People

The Urdu-knowing people in India are not confined to—or even largely concentrated in—one area. It obviously makes the task of spreading the language more challenging; and it also means that generalized statements need not hold good in each and every specific case. Only detailed data and specific studies can help us know the correct and elaborate picture.

It is here that the role of the powers-that-be becomes very crucial—especially with regard to the language policy. In most cases, it becomes necessary to introduce the Three Language Formula; and at places one may *like* to learn four languages (or scripts, if at the lower level, Urdu and Hindi are considered as one language)—wherever the regional language is different from Hindi. The bottom line is that Urdu medium schools need to be run in all those areas where there is adequate population of people with Urdu as the mother tongue. And, wherever that population is inadequate, Urdu can be taught as a language in at least some schools. But all this is very difficult as the people have internalized the ostensible logic of the élite, and consider English as the medium of instruction advantageous for their wards. It is crucial to dispel this misconception of the people regarding languages.

Should people be convinced about the need to receive education through the mother tongue at the primary level, the geographical spread of Urdu-knowing people would become a boon from the apparent bane that it is considered now. However, with the market reigning supreme, and government abdicating its responsibility of providing quality basic education to all through the mother tongue, there is little likelihood that this could be realized.

What Do the Tentative Answers to the Above Questions Indicate?

The foregoing discussion suggests that we need to give priority to the following:

- Primary-level education through the mother tongue.
- Teaching of Urdu as a language in higher classes (at least for Urdu mother-tongue students).
- Struggle for a rational language policy.
- Availability of general reading material in all Indian languages.
- A multi-pronged approach.
- A societal movement.

Primary-level Education through the Mother Tongue

If primary-level education is not imparted through the mother tongue, there is no way that Urdu can—and also perhaps there is no reason that Urdu should—prosper in India. For any Indian language to survive in any meaningful sense within our country, there has to be a sizable body of educated people. That is not possible unless primary education is imparted in the mother tongue—the importance of which is also dictated by social, psychological, and pedagogic reasons. Teaching through the mother tongue at the primary-level needs to be made compulsory.

Teaching of Urdu as a Language in Higher Classes (At Least for Urdu Mother-Tongue Students)

Though Urdu as a language needs to be taught in higher classes, teaching through Urdu at the primary level is more crucial. At the higher levels, the learner can acquire a better understanding of the language even if it is not formally taught. Nevertheless, teaching through Urdu and teaching Urdu are not unrelated, and both depend primarily on the general health and attitude of the people whose mother tongue it is.

Struggle for a Rational Language Policy

Without succeeding in making the powers-that-be adopt the right language policy, it would not be possible to achieve the above. A three—rather four—language formula needs to be adopted where the mother tongue needs to be placed at the top. The other three languages that one needs to learn are—the regional language, English, and Hindi (optional) in that order. Even the so-called public schools (in the private domain) must be made to conform to the rational language policy, as otherwise it would be well-nigh impossible to convince the people about the desirability of a rational language policy. However, as already mentioned, the élite would not easily accept the rational language policy as it is one of the several stratagems (and a very subtle one) that help it maintain the status quo.

Availability of General Reading Material in all Indian Languages

Once it is accepted that English has to be the language of higher-level discourse, the higher-level material need not be translated into Urdu or other regional languages. And, as the basic or primary-level education has to be through the mother tongue, it is natural that general reading material is made available in all Indian languages. (An additional bonus of providing the same material in all Indian languages would be that the biases—regional, religious, or any other— are likely to be eliminated. At the same time, it should not mean that encouragement is not given for local initiatives to produce general material). Even otherwise, the number of people requiring general reading material is much larger than the extremely small number that pursues higher studies. Moreover, more often than not, people pursuing higher-level studies prefer English to Indian languages—even when they know their respective mother tongue.

General reading material does not mean that it is of primary level alone. The example of the magazine that we cited above,[11] where serious issues of society, economics, international affairs, science, and literature are discussed, would also fall in the general reading material category. The specialized articles on science or other advanced discourse, as also the graduation-level course books, etc., would be excluded from our definition of general reading material. These are secondary and would be taken up—if at all—only after the first stage has been successfully implemented, and the people at large are educated enough through basic reading material.

A Multi-pronged Approach

In order to reach different segments of a highly differentiated society, different strategies would have to be adopted. We must not leave any section—including the illiterate elderly—from our scheme of things. The whole society would need to be taken along; and the requirements of the reading material would be different for different sections. For optimal results, it would be better if the approach is culture-specific, and also gender-sensitive. The larger the number of persons involved, the better it would be. The priority must be accorded to the basic reading material—as distinct from the specialized one.

A Societal Movement

We can always discuss 'what should be done'? But that would be divorced from reality if the important question 'how can that be done?' is not addressed. To answer the latter, the basic organization of society and dynamics of a movement would have to be understood because it is only then that appropriate responses can be formulated.

Society is an integrated whole, and no societal phenomenon of any import can be understood in isolation. The interconnections between different facets of society—whether apparent or not—are too real and powerful, and these should not be ignored. Societal movement is the vector product of the interaction of different societal forces. The only difference between the physical/material and societal movement is that, in case of the latter, a highly complex and unpredictable thinking being is involved; otherwise, here also, the laws of motion are equally valid. The involvement of thinking beings makes the task of grappling with any societal phenomenon challenging.

If the import of observations made in the preceding two paragraphs is realized, then the importance of a societal movement cannot be over-emphasized. Ultimately—whether explicitly or disguised—social issues are decided by the balance of forces. The pro-people forces will have to first agree on a common approach, and then launch a mass movement for achieving the objective—of course taking whatever support that can be got from different existing organizations. Such a societal movement would have to address the issues much beyond that of language and education—because language and education are extremely important, but these are no more than tools.

The societal movement would have to address the issues of peace, bread and butter, and health, in addition to that of language and education, because in the climate of violence and/or with a perpetually empty stomach one cannot be expected to participate in the process of learning. In the ultimate analysis, it is the power in the hands of the people alone that can change the state of affairs for the better.

We need to appreciate that the middle class has been co-opted by the powers-that-be, and adopts a reactionary attitude on this issue— as, in general, on other issues. However, to educate the people— including those from the middle class—would remain an important task in the struggle for a rational language policy.

At the minimal, hands would have to be joined with people of all other languages to jointly launch the struggle for education through the mother tongue at the primary level. And, efforts would have to be directed to provide meaningful general material (reading, audio, visual, audio-visual) in all Indian languages. However, to create enabling circumstances for millions of unfortunate Indians to become educated would remain the bottom-line.

The Proposals

Given the above understanding of different issues concerning language, let me now present some suggestions with regard to the 'Rational Language Policy' followed by the reasons for them.

My submission is that the Three Language Formula shall be modified. At least twelve of the eighteen languages mentioned in the Eighth Schedule of the Indian Constitution—Hindi, Urdu, Bengali, Marathi, Oriya, Punjabi, Telugu, Assamese, Tamil, Malayalam, Kannada, and Gujarati—can, and must, be the medium of instruction at the primary level. This is the defining characteristic of my perception of a 'Rational Language Policy'. There can be no compromise on this. Other aspects are matters of detail and/or logical corollaries of this prime objective.

I am not in a position to comment about the other six languages of the Eighth Schedule—Konkani, Kashmiri, Manipuri, Nepali, Sanskrit, and Sindhi. However, I feel that—except for Sanskrit—at least primary education can be imparted in all the languages of Schedule Eight. In fact, regional languages such as Rajasthani and Magadhi etc.—that are wrongly subsumed as dialects of *svarna* Hindi, and which are not included in the Eighth Schedule—shall also be included therein, and employed for imparting primary education. However, for secondary education, the less developed languages can give way to the regional language.

The language policy, including the Three Language Formula, needs to be:

- Mother tongue/regional language (medium of instruction—at least up to Class V).
- Regional language/mother tongue (at least as a language—from Class III to X).
- English (may start as a language—from any Class III to VI).
- Two-language terminology principle (from Class VI to graduation).
- No special place for Hindi, the official language.

Primary Education Through the Mother Tongue/Regional Language

The essence of the issue is that primary education has to be either in the mother tongue or the regional language as it is one or both of these languages that the child masters first—and most easily. The priority needs to be given to the mother tongue. However, the regional language should be the medium of instruction, and the mother tongue taught as a subject, wherever it is not feasible to impart education in the mother tongue. The regional language can substitute for the mother tongue because the child interacts with the neighbourhood children, whose mother tongue is the regional language.

Teaching through any other language at the primary level would create an artificial barrier in the learning process of the child, as s/he would have to struggle with the language itself, thereby wasting her/his energies that would have otherwise been utilized in understanding the world. That is why the child who is taught in English—from day one—has a tendency to develop 'memory at the expense of understanding'. And, even later in life, when s/he is comfortable with the language English, s/he is not able to cast off the old habit of trying to memorize rather than understand things.

The schools in the private sector must also follow the rational language policy, so that their students do not suffer from the disadvantages of learning at the primary stage in an alien language. And, in case the private sector continues to impart primary education in English, it would become well-nigh impossible to convince people-at-large that it is harmful to impart education in any language other than the mother tongue/regional language. Another drawback—also because of the language—would be that the advanced section of the society would be cut off from the rest of it. And, at a later date, for the English educated—even if one so wishes—it would be difficult to communicate in an Indian language.

In case the child from the disadvantaged section studies in an English-medium school, s/he suffers from an additional handicap—not living in an 'English environment'. Parents are not in a position to help their wards with their studies. Even if they can afford a tutor, that cannot substitute for English-educated parents and the environment.

Another very important argument in favour of primary education in the mother tongue is that it helps one develop progressive roots in the culture of the land. Otherwise, in general, one tends to place more emphasis on symbols and rituals—invariably reactionary—to compensate for the lack of roots in culture and identification with people in society.

Mother Tongue/Regional Language as a Subject

Depending on the language and the particular circumstances, a child should receive primary education in the mother tongue or regional language, and study the other—in addition to English—as a language. Here I wish to suggest a modification with regard to the content of the language course. Of course, the first task would be to teach the language. Today, in a language course, in general literature is taught. That needs to be changed. Given the ever-increasing pace of knowledge development, it is necessary that the children be taught what is closely related to their day-to-day life. Literature, being far removed from the hustle-bustle of daily life, can at best constitute a small portion of the language course. Naturally, those interested in literature can opt for the same—but in no way can it be allowed to dominate the language syllabus at the school-level.

The course content of the language should be such that the child develops general vocabulary pertaining to different aspects of life, so that s/he becomes multilingual in the real sense. Later, if the student comes back as a teacher or joins the media, then this knowledge of the regional language and/or the mother tongue would come in handy. The changed language syllabus would be more attractive, and would also enable one to interact with a much larger section of fellow citizens later in life.

The kind of course content suggested here would also help in clubbing the language classes in a school, if required. The bodies meant for propagation of languages can be made to play—through public pressure—a meaningful role in this respect. Even madrasas (schools primarily for education of Islam)—where a sizable population of Urdu-knowing students resides, especially in north India—can be meaningfully engaged in this exercise, and special course-books can be prepared for them.[12]

Transition to English as the Medium of Instruction

There has to be a transition—from mother tongue/regional language to English—for the simple reason that the body of advanced knowledge is not available in any Indian language, and that knowledge is developing at a very fast pace. Besides, for historical reasons—as also those of the present day—English is our best bet. Today, US imperialism holds sway; we were colonized by the British. Moreover, English has an edge over other developed languages, and it is easier for us anyway to switch over to English compared to any other developed language.

This establishes the need to receive primary education in the mother tongue and higher education in English. And, for compatibility and smooth transition from one to the other, it is essential that all the other components of the language policy be suitably dove-tailed. This is because, in general, higher education is imparted in English, and English is also the language of intellectual discourse. English should be taught—whether from the third standard, or the sixth, or any other, could vary from case to case. For late-starters (with regard to English) special English courses could be introduced to bridge the gap.

The change in the medium of instruction could vary, and may also depend upon the language and the subject of study. At one extreme, the change in medium of instruction could be from the sixth standard, whereas at the other extreme this change-over could be at the gradu-ation level. In any case, at least up to the fifth standard, the mother tongue/regional language should be the medium of instruction, and university education—especially for those who wish to go in for higher studies in a subject—needs to be in English.

Two-Language Terminology Principle

There needs to be a 'two-language terminology'—starting from the sixth standard (and up to the graduation level). By two-language terminology, I mean that the student must be familiarized with the terminology in both English and the mother tongue/regional lan-guage—irrespective of the medium of instruction. For this, the language syllabus—of English and the mother tongue/regional language—all would have to be re-designed.

And, this two-language terminology principle should be followed up to the graduation level—or at least offered as an option. There would not be much of a problem at the graduation level, because even if a teacher is unable to help the student of a particular language, s/he could take recourse to self-help. A two-language terminology would give an immense boost to the Indian languages, as essentially it is lack of familiarity with the terminology in the regional language that acts as a deterrent for people to use an Indian language for a written discourse.

Hindi, the Official Language

The official language, Hindi, could have at best served as the link language within the country because English, as the language of international discourse was, and is, unavoidable. However, a significant element of this proposal of a rational language policy pertains to the treatment of Hindi at par with at least eleven other languages of the Eighth Schedule of the Indian Constitution. It is another matter that because of fewer people who use the language or a less developed stage, an Indian language of the Eighth Schedule may not be at par with other Indian languages. Sanskrit, along with Pali, Persian, and Arabic, should be treated as a classical language; and none of these should be taught at the school level.

There is no special place for the official language Hindi—at least with regard to the language policy. If the powers-that-be so desire, they can certainly pay special attention to the development of Hindi for higher-level discourse, that is, to make Hindi an alternative to developed European languages, such as English. (However, I have my doubts with regard to both the desirability and plausibility of this.) Apart from people hailing from non-Hindi areas, even Hindi-knowing people have to converse in English, if the topic relates to an advanced/specialized area of knowledge.

Teaching of Hindi as a third language does not make a person proficient enough to indulge in higher-level discourse in Hindi without a special effort—particularly when specialized vocabulary is involved, which is invariably the case today. Moreover, because one prefers to read and write in a language one is more proficient in, Hindi—learnt as a third language—is not the natural choice. And, therefore, because of less exposure to Hindi, one is not able to develop adequate proficiency.

The experience since Independence and also the increasing tendency of the world towards globalization suggest that the 'official' Hindi need not be given any special place, and ought to be treated at par with other Indian languages. However, by virtue of Hindi being the mother tongue of a very large number of people, and additionally Urdu being similar to Hindi (notwithstanding crucial difference of script), the latter would surely not only advance but is also likely to be ahead of most other Indian languages.

Hindi could have functioned as an official language in the past—if the policies and their implementation were right. And, in that case, it might have continued to play that role—albeit partially. However, given the past experience, and the present status, there is no way that Hindi can function as an effective official language. For example, when the official (public) assets are being sold, where will the official language be used? In fact, propagating Hindi—the way it has been done—has created a sort of apartheid, where the underdogs are imparted sub-standard education in Hindi, and the children from the privileged class get the best education in English.

It is not the fault of the language but that of the policies and their implementation that Hindi did not become as advanced as Japanese or Russian or Chinese. We never followed a rational language policy; and, as a result, all our languages suffered—more, or less, is a different question. Today there is little rationale for giving any special status to Hindi. Because of the exponential growth in the world of knowledge, only an international language can be the 'official' or 'unofficial' link language of a country's educated populace.

In Short

The population of India is the second largest in the world—large enough for the propagation of at least twelve different languages of the Eighth Schedule of the Constitution to be viable; and these ought to be propagated on an equal footing. Primary education must be in the mother tongue/regional language—if we are interested in developing a progressive nation and an egalitarian society. Multilingual Indians, being well versed in their respective mother tongues, would be a great boon for society, and would inevitably help in the educational churning of Indian society. The positive multiplier effect of the rational language policy would be highly dramatic.

We are in an era of globalization. We cannot, and also need not, attempt to escape from it—even when we try to fight against the harmful effects of globalization. So far as the issue of language is concerned, almost all the people working in advanced areas of knowledge learn English—even if it is not their mother tongue—so that they can keep abreast with the latest. English has an edge, for it is not only the language of the erstwhile colonialists, but also that of the present-day imperialists. Not only is it the language of the largest international educated minority, but also the language in which the largest body of advanced knowledge is first published.

Language is a means to communicate; *per se*, it is not progressive or reactionary. (For instance, the revolutionary Karl Marx and the fascist Hitler both used the German language.) We must use English, if we are to be amongst the knowledge leaders. And if we wish to develop as a nation and appreciate our rich heritage, we also must be proficient in our respective mother tongues—which is an integral part of our cultural heritage. As far as Urdu is concerned, one must learn it, if for nothing else then to appreciate Urdu poetry, above all that of the all-time great Ghalib!

Hai kahan tamanna ka dusra qadam yarab?
Ham ne dasht-e imkan ko ek naqsh-e pa paya
(Where is the next step of longings and desires?
We found a footprint on the wild possibilities)

Notes

1. There is much truth in the assertion that…mainly because of communal hostility of the Hindu revivalists and the resultant discrimination against Urdu, particularly in north India…Urdu has (suffered), Ather Farouqui, 'The Question of Urdu's Survival', *Mainstream*, 27 December 2003, pp. 79–82.

2. Jagdish S. Gundara, 'Linguistic Diversity in Global Multicultural Civil Politics: The Case of Urdu in India', *Social Scientist*, Delhi, vol. 32, nos 5–6, May–June 2003, pp. 38–56.

3. Ather Farouqui, 'Urdu Education in India', *Economic and Political Weekly*, vol. XXXVII, no. 2, 12 January 2002, p. 106.

4. Yogendra Singh, 'The Significance of Culture in the Understanding of Social Change in Contemporary India', in *Cultural Change in India: Identity & Globalization*, Jaipur and New Delhi: Rawat Publications, 2000, pp. 25–39.

5. International Seminar on 'Minorities, Education and Language in 21st Century Indian Democracy: The Case of Urdu', New Delhi, 8 to 11 February 2002.

6. Hasan Abdullah, 'Goal of Education: Towards Better Schools', The *Statesman*, Delhi, 14 November 1991.

7. Hasan Abdullah, 'Memory Obsession is the Basic Malady', The *Hindu*, Delhi, 8 July 1997.

8. It is the task of good dictionaries to keep abreast of the rising tide of words that threaten to engulf us; grant them admission where permanence is more or less assured…Mario Pei in 'A Historical Sketch of the English Language', *New Webster's Dictionary of the English Language (College edition)*, Delhi: Surjeet Publications, 1989, pp. ix–xv.

9. My three years' association with Urdu monthly *Hayat*, New Delhi, edited by Shameem Faizee, showed that, except for the literature section, most articles had to be translated from English. Also, often, articles in different Urdu newspapers are by those who write more in English or Hindi.

10. *Pakeezah Anchal*, Delhi, an Urdu monthly, with substantial circulation, generally has only one advertisement (on the back-cover, excluding adverisements of its sister publications like *Mehakta Anchal*, etc.)

11. Shameem Faizee (ed.), Urdu monthly *Hayat*, New Delhi.

12. Arjumand Ara, 'Madrasas and Making of Muslim Identity in India', *Economic and Political Weekly*, vol. 39, no. 1, 9 January 2004, pp. 34–8.

References

Brass, Paul R., *Language, Religion and Politics in North India*, Cambridge: Cambridge University Press, 1974.
———, *The Politics of India since Independence*, Cambridge: Cambridge University Press, 2nd Indian ed., 1994.
King, Christopher R., *One language, Two Scripts: The Hindi Movement in Nineteenth-Century North India*, New Delhi: Oxford University Press, 1994.
'Learning: The Treasure Within': Report to United Nations Educational, Scientific and Cultural Organization (UNESCO) of the International Commission on Education for the Twenty-first Century, UNESCO Publishing, 1996.
Russell, Ralph, *How Not to Write the History of Urdu Literature & Other Essays*, New Delhi: Oxford University Press, 1999.

14

Living with Urdu, Living without Urdu

J.S. GANDHI

My concern with the Urdu language has been very basic to start with—it was my first medium of instruction. I want to reflect on the issue of 'topicality' of the language mainly from a biographical angle and not just plunge into vituperation against those who are politicizing the issue of the Urdu language. Nor will I go into the issue of communal divide on the use of the Urdu language or the policy of the Indian state of excluding or including Urdu from the education policy. As perhaps I would be able to demonstrate through my own experiences and perceptions, it is high time that we take a clear position on the nurturing and promotion of the Urdu language in our national life. I shall approach this issue by recalling some of my own experiences, and interpreting them in the light of some policy perspectives. All these recollections, relevant as they seem to me to the issue in hand, tumble out of my mind with the utmost of ease and without any deliberate effort.

I

My father is nearing ninety and lives in Amritsar. He still likes to visit Delhi almost twice a year to stay with me for a few days. Once the day of his arrival is fixed, I instruct the newspaper delivery boy to supply an Urdu daily along with English dailies that I already receive. The newspaper boy does not know what to do. The only papers he volunteers to supply are *Rashtriya Sahara* and *Qaumi Awaz*, but he grumbles even when he agrees to do so. It is very difficult, he says, to obtain the Urdu paper 'only for a week', the period for which I need it, since my father rarely stays in Delhi beyond a week. In the morning, however, when my father browses through the paper after breakfast, he is often not content; says that the newspaper is not very pleasant to look at, has undergone a sea-change over the years...there are too many advertisements, etc. I can appreciate only to an extent what he feels, but I do realize that the cultural ambience has changed, and I also feel it, but in my own way.

II

I am standing in a row along with other second standard students, with my *takhti* (a wooden board) with Urdu dictation written on it. The teacher—a *sardarji* (a Sikh)—passes by the row giving an approving or disapproving nod as he passes by a student. When the 'mistake' detected by him is a serious one, he looks furiously at the defaulter, who then stretches out his hand and the teacher obliges with a matter-of-fact cut with his cane; the student caves in with a 'hiss' and again picks up his 'takhti'...The image rolls on... I could never connect with one 'Sharma' boy who always wrote correct dictation and wrote it beautifully, for which he received the occasional pat from the teacher. Ahmad, on the other hand, was my close friend and wrote as wretchedly as I myself did.

III

As recently as 1996, I am listening to a speech being made by a mullah on the issue of Muslims and their status as citizens of India: '...We cast our lot with India and now we are suffering for it...we are being made to realize that we cannot hold our head high like members of other communities...we cannot learn our own language—Urdu, the language of Muslims is being slaughtered...' He goes on, but the later part of his speech falls upon my deaf ears. I feel a strange churning in my stomach '...Is Urdu the language of Muslims only?', I ask myself. 'Is it not my language?' I have learnt it as others have done. Are the *ghazal*s sung by Jagjit Singh read out to him by Muslim friends? How is Urdu the language of only Muslims? Is the holy Quran written in Urdu—no, it is not!... Then, why is Urdu the language of Muslims?'

IV

It was in 1966 that I met Ramadani (a fictitious name) in Delhi University campus. I studied in the Delhi School of Economics, and stayed on in the campus after my classes were over. I had long walks in the campus, with Ramadani, as with others. Whenever I was with him, I exchanged several ideas with him on the integral character of Indian culture, cutting across communal lines. I still remember: he spoke with a slight slur, unable to say 'k' properly and correctly, so he often uttered 't' instead. He often shared with me his dread of living in Indian society, in which he feared he would not be able to pursue a successful career. All this, he said, was very vital for him since he had so many sisters to marry off. We would take long walks and discuss several dream-projects—of promoting greater harmony and mutuality among Hindus, Muslims, and Sikhs. After I left the campus, I never heard of him... Later, a friend told me that Ramadani had settled in an Arab country as an Arabic teacher. He would surely have paid several visits to the homeland, but he has never met me since.

V

It was the time of happy juvenilia and I was living in Shimla in the early 1960s, toying with the idea of taking the Indian Administrative Service (IAS) examination, though my heart was not in it. I never missed any opportunity of developing friendship with 'literary' or *adbi* persons. Several *mushairas* (poetic symposia) were held during my four-year stay at Shimla. A characteristic feature of these functions, I recall, was that all the participants were non-Muslim. There were probably no Muslim poets around that the organizers could invite. It used to be a happy time, and the symposia were very popular. As I recollect, the language of the participants was simple Urdu, with no heavy Persianized expressions! There were women participants too, who read their poems.

VI

Sometimes in 1993, I meet an old Muslim friend and we have a long chat. We talk of various things from the past. Unmindfully, I get into the old mould and start using a few simple Urdu expressions. He feels uncomfortable and tells me to talk in simple 'Hindi'.[1] I ask him why. He says that, by using Urdu expressions, I am being ostentatious. I am shocked.

VII

I am invited by a friend to participate in the Urdu Day celebrations and to share my thoughts about the language with my colleagues and students. When called upon to speak, I narrate how I have grown up in the midst of Urdu-speaking people; how the joy of living for me implied that I could enjoy that language being spoken and appreciated. I also share with the audience how proud I feel about the fact that I had known some people who went on to become great literators.[2] I sit down after a brief speech. The gentleman who had presided over the function suddenly refers to my great love for the Urdu language. I grow red in the face, realizing fully well that I had had only a basic access to the language and could not by any standards be called an *adbi shakhsiyat*. What really shocked me was the fact that the gentleman started appreciating the fact that I could converse in Urdu. I remember clearly what went on in my mind at the time. I was thinking, '...even if I try, can I divest myself of Urdu, which already has become a part of my mental and emotional architecture? This was my first medium of instruction.... Why should I be praised for being what I am?'

VIII

I am leaving for Paris in April 2000 to do some research for a month. I have been abroad before, but this time I feel a bit nervous. Maybe, I am a bit old now, I say to myself, '...a full month of staying away from home!' But, leave I must. Everything is settled; the required formalities are all over! I decide to visit my university library. I scan through books on my own subject and find them a little too familiar, a bit too pedantic, unable to strike a different mood and to provide cheer in the lonely moments that lie ahead. Unwittingly, I find myself foraging through the works of some Urdu humorists, Krishan Chander and others. I pick up *Takalluf Bartaraf* by Mujtba Hussein. Later, while in Paris, even though the daily routine is hectic, I find time hanging heavy on my nerves after the day's work— *Takalluf Bartaraf* then provides me great relief and lifts my soul from a painful sullenness. I read a chapter or so before I fall asleep. I exercise restraint and read only a few pages at a time, fearing that the little book may finish too soon.

IX

Just when I am about to finish this brief paper, an acquaintance from my hometown visits me to deliver a letter written by a childhood friend for whom I had been scouting for several years and not seen for about forty-five. As far as I remember, when the two of us had parted company in the early fifties, his family had moved away to a nearby town. We had just completed our matriculation. I tried over all these years to establish contact with him till his letter arrived. It was written in Urdu. Through his script, I could clearly discern the profile of my friend, his face, his entire being. The past was virtually in my lap once again. My friend could not have done any different than writing in Urdu. This was the only medium he knew for writing a letter to me, the medium we had learnt together.

Comments, Deductions, and Observations

The above insertions are not meant to draw any 'flawless' *empirical deductions* from or to draw an overall trajectory of the development of the Urdu language over the last fifty years or so, nor to sentimentalize the issue by recalling several subjective situations. Also, there is no deliberate selectivity in recalling these situations. Rather, they have all tumbled in my mind involuntarily, as I addressed myself the question to 'Urdu in our lives'. I am also sure that those of my age group, who have studied and grown up with me, would not view these experiential situations as odd or atypical. Even so, I can be quite legitimately asked what was the *import* of all these recollections? Why this nostalgic recall, and what do they imply?

(a) First of all, my life-profile in conjunction with the incidents I have recollected reflect a declining use and currency of the Urdu language in our daily lives. As a matter of methodology for discerning this decline, one does not need to sift through a plethora of policy documents or interpret the public postures—sometimes strange and outlandish—taken by our leaders in the last fifty years or so. Instead, one could arrive at a completely authentic perspective by an age-old sociological technique, that is, by talking to people who were either attaining or had already attained adulthood around the time that the Partition of the country took place. In Punjab, therefore, those of my generation or that of my father's would remember with a twinge the aura and ambience of Urdu in their lives, the easy, natural, and automatic access they had both to its letter and literary products— poetry, fiction, or even the symposia that were held frequently.[3] It also needs to be emphasized that it is not ordinary Muslims but their self-styled leaders, including some self-righteous researchers and scholars, who have made and continue to make tireless claims of the cultural exclusivity of Muslims over the Urdu language.

(b) Among the most tragic occurrences of the recent times in India, therefore, has been the labelling of Urdu with Muslims and the politicization engaged in by both Muslim and non-Muslim leaders. This has happened through the conjunction of several factors, foremost of which has been the language policy of the Indian government. This has been both confusing and wilfully oblivious of the reality that only Hindustani and not Hindi could justifiability be the *lingua franca* of the masses. As well-documented by several scholars, some of the nationalist leaders, including Jawaharlal Nehru, were pressurized by Hindi-zealots to vote Hindi as the national language of the country.[4] This askewed and unrealistic decision resulted in a serious fall-out, both politically as well as in terms of communal disharmony in the years that followed. The incendiary manner in which the implementation of this decision was greeted (particularly in the south) is history now, but it was actually in keeping with the spirit of this decision that states like Uttar Pradesh (UP) laboriously and ridiculously went about denying a rightful place to Urdu as the third 'modern' language.[5] Such developments gave enough space and opportunity to the clerics and political opportunists, both among the Muslims and Hindus, to spew fiery slogans and vitiate the social and political scene.

(c) It seems absolutely logical and sensible not to lay waste the integral character of the Urdu language, and thereby let go one of the resources of national togetherness.[6] To appreciate this, it is as much desirable to understand the historical backdrop in which the language came into being—as a medium of communication among the Mughal *lashkars*—as also the fact that Urdu copiously draws from the vocabulary of such diverse languages as Turkish, Persian, Arabic, and several indigenous and local languages. Reciprocally, various linguistic traditions including those of south India—Telegu and

Kannada, for example—have been enriched by the Urdu language. Punjabi, which is associated with Punjab and Punjabis, inheres a huge stock of Urdu words. To appreciate the wider cultural context of linguistic integration, one simply needs to consider the historicity of medieval poetry (particularly devotional poetry), which employs a vast stock of vocabulary from Persian and Arabic—two of the foundational languages of modern India. Illustratively, *Jap Sahib*, one of the holy compositions of the Sikhs by their tenth guru Guru Gobind Singh, is heavily inlaid with Persian and Arabic vocabulary, besides Sanskrit, Braj, Avadhi, etc. This composition invokes the Almighty through His various attributes.

(d) I would like to afford yet another illustration of this traditional 'cultural capital' of India, that of linguistic integration, which has found rich and fervent expression in the holy book of the Sikhs—*Adi Granth*—compiled in the medieval period.[7] It would therefore be churlish, or rather suicidal, to let go the integral framework that has provided for centuries the cultural backdrop of Indian society—both for intra-and inter-community communication. As an application of this macro logic, we could say that Urdu needs to be preserved and perpetuated, so that it can serve as the fountainhead of communication across diverse communities.[8]

Solutions for Today, and Tomorrow

Let me now briefly consider some of the core issues linked with the 'appropriate' language policy being proposed by a range of scholars. I do not think it necessary to list all the minor variations on this theme. Rather, I will attempt a broader canvas of what, in my opinion, needs to be done in this regard, and why? In doing so, I dare say, I will eschew the temptation of launching a critique of state policy, finding fault with leaders, parties, and ideologies. First, the question of *why*?

As already mentioned, the integrating character of the Urdu language is a time-tested resource and, therefore, should not be ignored by anybody even dimly imbued with the sentiment of national solidarity, and also by the lovers of Urdu. That it is possible, for a variety of reasons, to bind people of diverse communities and ethnic stocks together through this common heritage and day-to-day use of Urdu cannot be doubted. *Ipso facto*, therefore, it will be foolhardy to think that the promotion of this language will promote the interests of only a specific community. Also, it needs to be kept in view by all those voicing a loud concern for national unity that ignoring or deliberately suppressing the collectivistic élan of the Urdu language would be tantamount to national suicide for more than one reason.

It is a jarring comment on the thinking of Muslim intellectuals and community leaders that, despite repeatedly acknowledging that mere state subsidy cannot create conditions for the survival of the Urdu language, what they have done mostly is either to criticize the government for neglecting the teaching of Urdu language or for not providing adequate finances to run the various institutions vested with the task of promoting the language. It has somehow escaped their attention that perhaps the most essential requirement for promoting the chances for survival of Urdu is to garner the will and support of non-Muslims. This is especially so when such a constituency[9] still exists despite discouraging circumstances for several decades. It is vital that in any struggle for the promotion of the Urdu language, individuals, scholars, and leaders from non-Muslim communities are involved.

The foremost consequence of perpetuating the over-identification of Urdu with Muslims would cause further distancing between Muslims and the majority community of Hindus. And, to think that we can have a harmonious national life without enhancing goodwill and accommodation between these two major chunks of our society is to live in an unreal world. To achieve this, one of the foremost mechanisms can be the promotion of the Urdu language with the joint effort of both Muslims and non-Muslims. It is tragic that the struggle for the promotion and protection of Urdu in the last few decades has been spearheaded mostly by the Muslim leadership— a phenomenon for which both leaderships are responsible. An expected and natural consequence of this has been a progressive withdrawal and disengagement of the non-Muslim leadership from issues concerning the Urdu language. This phenomenon is an apt illustration of 'structuration through signification.' That the repeated assertion over the years of 'Urdu as the language of the Muslims only'[10] has come to structure a false social cognition is for all to see.

The pursuit of an Urdu agenda exclusively by the Muslims and their leadership alone has brought to fore, and also perhaps inten-sified, serious fissures within the Muslim community itself. Some-times of course, it has brought out inter-personal differences among

Urdu scholars as well[11] and clashing headlong with each other on what is the best pill for the rejuvenation of the Urdu language.

A Recipe For Urdu—Its Health and Survival

I wish to conclude with some clear suggestions and guidelines that need to be followed if some headway is to be made out of this imbroglio.

First and the foremost, the efforts for the promotion of the health and perpetuation of the Urdu language have to be viewed and pursued not as a *jihad*, but as an all-embracing movement in which all those who have any love or affinity for the language must be involved. As all scholars analysing the phenomenon of neglect of the Urdu language would bear me out, certain consolidation of forces located both in the state apparatus as well as out in the broader society has been responsible for the neglect that the language has suffered so far. Any declaratory (*elaniya*) jihad, therefore, is bound to prove counterproductive, invoking all those forces to come together once again and to resolutely retain the ground (wherein Urdu has been on the run) covered already during the last fifty years or so.

It is therefore essential to involve all those forces, groups, and persons located both among Muslims and non-Muslims, in evolving steps and policies that need to be taken for the promotion of Urdu. As pointed out already, the role that non-Muslims can play in the whole process has been piteously ignored. The goodwill of those who have not yet gone off the scene but have had their essential grooming via the Urdu language and the associated culture, must be harnessed and somehow turned into a viable constituency to pressurize the state into conceding Urdu an added space in the state administration in such states as UP, Bihar, and Punjab.

Carrying this logic further, one may also say that non-Muslim scholars and policymakers must be involved in the functioning of some of the state-funded bodies set up for the promotion of the Urdu-language, to lend the 'promotion of Urdu' agenda a respectable public face, which it has lost over the years.

Apart from the efforts, that members of the Urdu-speaking community may be making in deliberately teaching Urdu to their children, the *madrasas* must also play their effective role. One way they can do so is by letting some prominent and known people with a high-profile background in secular education, play an effective role in administering these madrasas and developing useful liaison with several other institutions, including industries and education ministries, in various states.[12]

Finally, an all-out effort with an all-embracing, cross-community support base must be launched to extend Urdu-based primary education wherever justified, even according to the existing governmental norms. In order to give this demand justifiable legal backing, appropriate legalistic research is also imperative.

* * *

At the beginning of the twenty-first century I am satisfied to take note of the fact that some of the younger intellectuals of the Muslim community are stirred with fresh zeal to do what they can for the promotion and furtherance of the Urdu as a functional language. These scholars—among them Ather Farouqui—are mostly from a progressive political background and are trying to project a generalized viewpoint for a linkage between the interests of minority languages and the rights of all linguistic and religious minorities for keeping alive their linguistic traditions through a formal system of state-sponsored education especially up to the secondary level. We should not forget that all Eighth Schedule languages have a minority status outside the states where they are the principal languages, and since practically every state and district is increasingly multilingual, given the increasing social mobility in the country, there is a clear need for evolving a uniform National Policy on Minority Languages at various levels in accordance with the letter and spirit of the Constitution. The recent constitutional amendment (86th of 2002) making education a fundamental right should be supplemented by statutory provisions covering the medium of primary instruction, educational uniformity, national norms for establishment of primary and secondary schools, and location of schools on demand. The age limit for compulsory elementary education should be raised from fourteen years to fifteen years, which is the minimum age for appearing for the secondary examination. In particular, Urdu must be included in school curricula at the primary level as the medium of instruction for those who declare Urdu as their mother tongue in all government and government-aided schools and schools affiliated to recognized Boards of Education.

All this is good enough in spirit! Yet, the capacity of the majority-managed state apparatus to kill the linguistic capital of the nation in a selective manner should not be under-estimated. As has been hinted by some participants in a conference,[13] there is an endless array of silent stratagems through which such an end can be achieved.[14] But all such possibilities have to be scotched insightfully.

As discussed earlier, a broader[15] forum needs to be formalized, which will deal with the constitutional promise for equal promotion and equal protection of all languages. Such a measure would at once lift the issue and the problematic concerning Urdu from that of *a* language (associated with *a* community) to the wider issue of violation of the constitutional promise for the safeguard of all languages, including Urdu. There is no point in citing various Acts again and again without in the least suggesting that a clear case of *constitutional neglect* can be made against the government of the day, in that it is subverting the cultural capital of the minority communities. If the *legal and jurisprudential scholarship* is as good and genuine as it is understood to be, the legal and constitutional bulwark ought to surface to safeguard the Urdu language in contemporary India.

There are a few more issues that merit discussion at this juncture:

(1) The issue of Urdu cannot be considered constructively without including the formulation of an education policy and its implementation—especially at the state level. Quite importantly, it seems a logical continuation of the policy laid down by the Constitution that at the school level, a child should be provided education in her/his mother tongue as declared by her/his family or community.[16] This need not deter school authorities from introducing Hindi or English at the secondary or higher secondary levels along with Urdu—the choice should be left to the parents not the schools.

(2) It is important to see that the madrasas, the traditional centres of Urdu learning, have a role to play in reinforcing the ethos and culture of the community. But in order to save them from being sucked into the politics of state funding, the state should stop funding them altogether by scrapping the Madrasa Modernization Scheme and other initiatives.[17] It is on record that there are huge funds available from the community for running these institutions. However, to ensure that these institutions stay clear of such insinuations as 'hot-beds of terrorism', bodies constituted of intellectuals from across communities should visit them and suggest steps that will help serve better the interests of students receiving education here. But all this should be done entirely at the initiative of these institutions and their management. The government, especially when the Bharatiya Janata Party (BJP) was in power, is mainly responsible, for making

Urdu and madrasas synonymous, and quite shamefully, even for administrative purposes. The National Council for Promotion of Urdu Language under the Ministry of Human Resource Development, that had become a Rashtriya Swayamsevak Sangh (RSS) outlet when the BJP was in power, decided to monitor madrasas in the name of their modernization and introduction of a secular curriculum. This was something which had long been on the agenda of the RSS because in the madrasas, the Urdu, Arabic, and Persian languages are taught compulsorily. It is evident that neither the Muslim minorities' education nor modernization programme was, or is, officially within the jurisdiction of an Urdu organization.

(3) The leaders of the Muslim community should also spare a thought as to how the teaching at madrasas can be effectively integrated with the education of the Muslim children in secular schools without jeopardizing their careers in terms of the time spent in preparing them to take up professions.

(4) So far as the state is concerned, utmost importance should be given to provide both teaching in and through the Urdu medium on totally secular lines—at par with teaching in other languages. All this is possible only if the state can come out of its shackled mindset which views Urdu as the language of the Muslims only. It is indeed pernicious of the state—as it has been doing so far—to keep backing the madrasa system where, according to the statistics, published by the government: '...half a million madrasas are working and about fifty (50) million students are enrolled in them. Part-time and evening madrasas are not included in this list.'[18] It is important to speculate on what is likely to be the fate of these 50 million students in the years to come. What careers can they pursue? After all, how many millions of them will find jobs as religious preachers? Alternatively, how many of them have the potential for any gainful employment? It is sheer mockery to Muslims and madrasas that the government should claim to spend Rs 2 crore annually for the modernization of the madrasas programme. In the first place, funding of religious instruction at the expense of the public exchequer is unconstitutional, and one is really at a loss to evaluate the extent of modernization of half a million madrasas with 50 million students on an annual expenduture of Rs 2 crore.

(5) This leads us to the trickiest dimension of the whole problem. On the one hand, Muslims ought to enjoy autonomy in running their religious institutions, madrasas, for which the community is self-

sufficient in terms of funds. On the other hand, millions of people who train at these seminaries have no scope of finding decent employment in the market due to the lack of any useful or productive skills. The madrasa system does not contribute at all to the modernization and social change among the Muslims in India. Further, funding of these institutions by the state creates parasitism,[19] inasmuch as those who are beneficiaries of the state-issuances are willing to make all kinds of compromises with the interest of the language or of the Muslim community.

Notes

1. I wish to put it on record that I took no degree or diploma in the Urdu language as part of my education; Urdu was simply my *medium* of education—wholly till fourth standard, and partially till matriculation. Besides, I kept reading Urdu fiction and poetry—not at all out of place with my normal routine and not as something which could be recognized as denoting a distinctive trait or special cultural embellishment. Rather, it was as much a routine with friends who grew up with me as my own.

2. One such well-known person was the Urdu poet Puran Singh Hunar who authored a collection of poems—*Ahange Gazal*, which was very well received in literary circles. Hunar Sahib had been my teacher in school. After the publication of the compilation, he was often referred to as 'Ustad shaiyer'. He has since passed away.

3. The important part that events like symposia played in the yesteryears was to reinforce inter-community and inter-religion togetherness.

4. Harish Narang, *Language Policy and Planning in 21st Century India*, 'First Dr Zakir Hussain Memorial Lecture', Dr Zakir Hussain Study Circle, Jamia Nagar, New Delhi, 1998. As Professor Narang mentions, this decision, to start with, was taken by the Congress party and later incorporated in the Indian Constitution. Article 343(1) states: 'The official language of the Union shall be Hindi in Devanagari script.'

5. This was done so shabbily that it will perhaps be difficult to find another example of this administrative high-handedness; learners were given the choice of Sanskrit as the 'modern' language and not Urdu.

6. Indeed this is more pragmatic.

7. This is of special significance for the simple reason that the languages in which canonical texts of various religions—Christianity, Islam, Judaism, and Hinduism—have been written are held as a sanctity and also identified with the corresponding communities. As against all these, the *Adi Granth*—the religious text of the Sikhs—heavily draws from various languages spoken around the time of the *Granth's* compilation not only in various parts of India, but also in certain other parts of Asia and the Middle East, such as Pushto, Arabic, Persian, etc.

8. The potential for this is already present on account of the widespread popularity of several forms and literary products of the Urdu language, such as ghazals and mushairas.

9. By *constituency*, I mean that of the votaries of the Urdu language.
10. Both by the Muslim and non-Muslim leadership.
11. These differences may pertain to whether or not some of the classical works of the Urdu language be translated in the Devanagari script (Ather Farouqui vs. Ralph Russell), or whether (once again between the same authors) the madrasas could usefully play their role in the promotion of Urdu. These differences have been aired in Ralph Russell, 'Urdu in India since Independence,' *Economic and Political Weekly*, vol. 34, nos 1 and 2, 9 January 1999, and Ather Farouqui, 'Future Propspects of Urdu in India,' *Mainstream*, Annual, November 1992, pp. 99–107. Additionally, Syed Shahabuddin, 'Letters to the Editor', *Economic and Political Weekly*, 6–13 March 1999, p. 566, also pitches in with 'If Urdu is still alive, despite suffocation in the Hindi belt, it is largely due to such utilization of the muktab-madrasa system. Given the situation, I would not have Urdu expelled from the madrasa milieu, when I have no alternative to offer.'
12. Once again, the importance of inducting some well-meaning non-Muslims in the madrasa administration cannot be over-emphasized.
13. *The Conference on Minorities, Education and Language in 21st Century Indian Democracy—the Case of Urdu with Special Reference to Dr Zakir Hussain, Late President of India*, 8–11 February 2002.
14. Among the facilitating factors for this, one also needs to keep in view the 'autonomy' that the *states* enjoy in structuring—or at least interpreting the education agenda of the Indian state. All this makes it fairly easy to obviate the constitutional goal of the promotion and protection of the minority languages.
15. 'Broader' than just the forum for the protection of Urdu language.
16. As Ather Farouqui says, '...the battle for the Constitutional rights under Article 350-A of the Urdu language at the primary level along with other langues as a medium of education and at the secondary level as the First Language for those who claim Urdu as their mother tongue is not simply a question of the survival of a language. It is question of the survival of the rights of minorities including Muslims'. Ather Farouqui, 'The Question of Urdu's Survival', *Mainstream*, 27 December 2003, p. 27.
17. Such a point of view also emerged as a part of the *Statement of Consensus*, at the Conference on Minorities, Education and Language in 21st Century Indian Democracy:
    > Funding of religious instruction at the expense of public exchequer is undersirable and unconstitutional. Hence, the Madarsa system which serves the limited purpose of instructing Muslim children in the basic tenets of Islam and producing religious functionaries needed by the community and of maintaining the continuity of religious scholarship should be left entirely to the community to evolve in accordance with demand. (As reported in *Social Scientist*, vol. 31, nos 5–6, May–June 2003, p. 81.)
18. Cited by Arjumand Ara in 'Madrasas and Making of Muslim Identity in India', in *Economic and Political Weekly*, vol. 39, no. 1, 9 January 2003, p. 34.
19. Bikramjit De, 'Abuse of Urdu', *Economic and Political Weekly*, vol. XXXIX, no. 48, pp. 5085–8.

PART IV

Minority Language and Community—Legal Concerns

15

Education for Linguistic Minorities:
The Legal Framework

FALI S. NARIMAN

When the British came, saw, and conquered India in 1774, Warren Hastings, the first governor-general of Bengal, decreed that the English in India should acquaint themselves to the fullest extent with Indian languages and culture in order to better associate themselves with what were called the 'Orientals' and Oriental surroundings.

It was this policy that led to the establishment of the famous college of Fort William in Calcutta where Arabic, Persian, and Sanskrit were taught, and students could avail themselves of courses in Hindu and Muslim law as well as English law.

This policy continued for the next fifty years till the 1830s, when it was reversed. Macaulay's now infamous Minute on Education—compiled in the spring of 1835—changed the entire course of British educational policy. Macaulay favoured English and the curriculum was adapted accordingly—all of which had fateful consequences. For both the Indians and the British.

For the Indians, the educational policy tended to produce, in the end, not a learned class imbued with the best that the English language and literature could offer but, rather, a large English-speaking secretarial and professional class, without a tradition of responsibility and power.[1]

'Education for clerks'—that is how Nehru[2] summed up British educational policy in India during the nineteenth century. As for the British, looking back in 1964, Malcolm Muggeridge, editor of *Punch* magazine, said in a BBC broadcast that 'education was about the worst thing the British did to India and appropriately enough this contributed to our departure.'[3] Muggeridge then embellished his assertion with a rhetorical query: 'Was it not enraged and unemployed graduates who chased us out, hurling after us curses and copies of the *Oxford Book of English Verse*?'

C.F. Andrews, a vigorous supporter of Indian Independence, had phrased the same sentiment earlier but very differently—and more eloquently. In a letter addressed in 1898 to the private secretary to the viceroy (Lord Minto), C.F. Andrews had written:

English as the language of education has justified itself, in spite of great drawbacks. It has had a supreme political justification. It has made India no longer only a geographical expression but a political unity. *It has created the hope and the possibility of an Indian Nation.* English history and literature have fashioned the political thought of modern India and fashioned it inevitably on national lines.[4]

The Constitution, Religion, and Language

The 'hope and possibility' of becoming an Indian nation was achieved almost fortuitously, when the British suddenly left India in 1947—somewhat in pique—leaving Indians to come up with a written Constitution of their own. It is in this background that our document of governance came to be drafted by members of existing elected assemblies who formed themselves into a Constituent Assembly—most of whom were fluent in English.

The 1950 Constitution is one of the longest in the world—'too long, too detailed and too rigid', was the laconic comment of Sir Ivor Jennings, the constitutional historian of the Commonwealth. Its length was due not merely to the size of the country but also to the problems of accommodating, in a federal parliamentary Constitution, the divergent points of view of representatives of peoples speaking different languages and observing varied faiths, all striving at the same time to transform a rigid, hierarchical social order into an egalitarian society.

India is a pluralistic society—linguistically and religiously. Next to the several cults of Hinduism, the main religion is Islam—which has been on Indian soil since AD 650, a few years after the Prophet's death, when Arab traders settled on the western seacoast of Malabar (now part of Kerala). Their descendants are so Indianized that they speak the same language as their Hindu brethren and read the Quran—but only in Malayalam. Forced conversion in Europe and Central Asia in the Middle Ages effectively destroyed the identity of religious minorities. But not so in India (at least not till very recently).

Religion in India not only means the profession of faith but also encompasses places—temples, gurudwaras, mosques, churches, and synagogues. It includes idols and deities and offerings to them, bathing places, graves, tombs, and properties attached to and owned by religious institutions. All this—faith, worship, ritual, and the secular activities of religious groups—had to be provided for in the Constitution, in the Chapter on Fundamental Rights, beyond the reach of legislative or executive interference.

The Objectives Resolution, moved by Jawaharlal Nehru at the first sitting of the Constituent Assembly on 13 December 1946, contained a pledge that in the Constitution 'adequate safeguards shall be provided for minorities, backward and tribal areas and other backward classes.' This pledge was made good by our Founding Fathers.

Article 30(1) of the Constitution guaranteed to all minorities, whether based on religion or on language, the right to establish and administer educational institutions; the state was prohibited from discriminating against any educational institution on the ground that it was under the management of a religious or linguistic minority (Article 30[2]). When the right to acquire and hold property was deleted from the chapter on Fundamental Rights by a Constitutional Amendment in 1978, an exception was carved out for minority educational institutions: their property could be compulsorily acquired for public purposes *only* if the state ensured that the amount fixed or determined by law for the acquisition was such as would not restrict or abrogate the right guaranteed under Article 30(1).

Despite declarations of constitutional rights, minorities in society cannot find adequate protection in the normal political process; they definitely need the protection of courts. The courts in India, when dealing with minority rights, have in the past tended to conceptualize their role as that of a political party in opposition.

Ever since the inception of our Constitution (and till 1997) on almost every occasion that the minorities had approached the Supreme Court complaining of infraction of their rights (mainly educational and linguistic), the challenge was upheld. The reason for this was explained in a footnote contained in a famous judgement (footnote 4 in the Caroline Products Case; a decision of the US Supreme Court— 303 US 144 at 152).

Footnotes go unread in the works of many authors. But footnotes in judgements of the US Supreme Court receive more attention. The most famous footnote in American constitutional history is Footnote 4 in the *Caroline Products* case—a decision of 1938 in which a judge of the US Supreme Court[5] spoke of *'discrete and insular minorities'* within a nation-state and how deserving they were of special judicial protection: that is, he meant those groups who were prevented by prejudice of majorities from protecting themselves through the democratic political processes upon which people ordinarily rely.

The Supreme Court Role

The minorities in India had been consistently protected by pronouncements of our Supreme Court. In a celebrated decision rendered in 1974, the great Justice Khanna (himself a member of the majority community in India) gave the reason why minority interests are so zealously protected by the highest court:

The Constitution and the laws made by civilized nations, generally contain provisions for the protection of minority interests. It can, indeed, be said to be an index of the level of civilisation and catholicity of a nation as to how far their minorities feel secure and are not subject to any discrimination or suppression.

He spoke these stirring words in the *St. Xavier's College* case more than twenty-five years ago.

But alas, times have changed, and so have the judges. Regrettably, the political winds of change have blown through courtrooms as well. I find that the judges are now somewhat less enthusiastic than before to protect the minorities—which to me is deeply disturbing. The reason for this reluctance has been frankly stated—both in and outside court by the judges themselves. It is said that many minority educational institutions have abused the privilege given to them under Article 30 of our Constitution. This is true in many cases, but the remedy for this was stated way back in 1959 in the first landmark decision on minority rights in the *Kerala Education* case (1959) in which Chief Justice S.R. Das (himself a staunch Hindu, but also a staunch liberal nationalist) proclaimed that the safeguard against abuse was built into the framework of Article 30 itself.

That Article says that minorities have a right to *establish* and *administer* educational institutions *of their choice*. The right is given to minorities to administer such institutions—not to *mal-administer* them. When they do mal-administer, they can be dealt with under ordinary laws. In the name of preventing mal-administration, the fundamental right of minorities (religious and linguistic) is now being fast eroded—particularly by state legislatures and state administrators, without much check from the courts. The emphatic view of the Supreme Court in 1959 in the *Kerala Education* case was expressed by Chief Justice S.R. Das in words that keep echoing over the years:

The right to establish educational institutions of their choice must, therefore, mean the right to establish real institutions which will effectively serve the needs of their community and the scholars who resort to their educational institutions. There is, no doubt, no such thing as a fundamental right to recognition by the State but to deny recognition to the educational institutions except upon terms tantamount to the surrender to their constitutional right of administration of the educational institutions of their choice is in truth and in effect to deprive them of their rights under Art. 30(1).

But somehow, this eloquent exposition—in a landmark decision—is now less and less remembered.

What were believed to be authoritative, time-honoured pronouncements of larger benches of the Supreme Court—benches of seven and nine judges had been referred recently (in 1997) for reconsideration by a Full Bench of eleven judges: The eleven-judge Bench later sat to determine what was left of the protection of educational rights of religious and linguistic minorities. But the Court spoke in different voices. The very fact that a reference had to be made to a Bench of eleven judges had a most chilling effect on both minorities, and on minority educational institutions. Even unaided schools and colleges are now being increasingly regulated (even in matters of pure administration) in many states, and the existing managements of such institutions are able to continue only on periodic doses of oxygen administered by the court in the form of limited interim orders. This is by no means a healthy trend.

The minorities in India feel threatened by the majority community: The periodic assaults on Christians have not in any way lessened the sense of danger that we all face in this great pluralistic society that we proudly call 'Our India'.

At the time of Partition it was believed by many Muslims that only a separate homeland, carved out of united India, would free them from what was then described by Jinnah as 'Hindu domination'.

Unfortunately, as an article in the *Hindustan Times* by Rafiq Zakaria shows,[6] the Muslims in India are made to feel they are under permanent Hindu domination.

In undivided India, the Muslims were in political power in five out of the eleven provinces; being one-third of the population, they were also a decisive factor at the centre. After Partition, they have been divided into three parts: *Pakistani* Muslims, *Indian* Muslims, and *Bangladeshi* Muslims, with little contact with one another. Far from being freed of 'Hindu domination', two-thirds of them have been now put under 'permanent Hindu domination' (to adapt Jinnah's unfortunate turn of phrase). In Bangladesh, politics is highly contentious and has occasionally exploded into domination by the military, and in Pakistan they have neither democracy or basic human rights.

Lack of education is at the root of all our problems—there are the problems of poverty, of over-population and, above all, intolerance; and the latter is tearing at the fabric of our civilized society. If post-World War II, democracies have gone to seed—replaced either by dictatorships or anarchy—the reason has been that while giving themselves freedom, they did not remember to give themselves adequate education.

The international community has woken up to the need and importance of the right to education—emphasized in Article 13 of the Covenant on Economic, Social, and Cultural Rights (to which covenant India is a party state). The general comments of the Committee on Economic, Social and Cultural Rights at its meeting in November/December 1999 on this important article—the very first paragraph of general comment No. 13—reads as follows:

Education is both a human right in itself and an indispensable means of realizing other human rights. As an empowerment right, education is the primary vehicle by which economically and socially marginalized adults and children can lift themselves out of poverty and obtain the means to participate fully in their communities. Education has a vital role in empowering women, safeguarding children from exploitative and hazardous labour and sexual exploitation, promoting human rights and democracy, protecting the environment, and controlling population growth. Increasingly, education is recognized as one of the best financial investments the state can make. But the importance of education is not just practical: a well-educated, enlightened and active mind, able to wander freely and widely, is one of the joys and rewards of human existence.

In other words it helps in the pursuit of happiness. And, if we invest in meaningful education, problems of governance will get resolved almost without, or at least despite, elected governments.

The Right to Education

An eminent educationist like the great Dr Radhakrishnan, affirmed that 'providing public schools ranks at the very apex of function of a state.' That is why the Supreme Court said in the Mohini Jain case (1992) that 'the right to education is implicit in the right to life' and a five-judge Bench later explained in Unnikrishnan (1993) that this right must be construed in the light of the Directive Principles in Part-IV of the Constitution—that is, the right to primary education is part of the right to life, and so has become a Fundamental Right though it does not encompass higher education.

Primary education to any group can only be given in the language they speak at home—recognition of a regional language in areas where Urdu is generally spoken leads to a great hindrance to educational development.

In northern India, for instance—where Hindi is the medium of education and Sanskrit is taught in Class III as a Modern Indian Language (with English introduced from Class VI)—there is little scope in areas where Urdu is spoken (particularly in Uttar Pradesh [UP]) for Muslims, most of whom are under-privileged and unable to afford education in English-medium schools, to broaden the mind and develop the aptitudes of their children. It is essential that, in government schools located in Urdu-speaking areas, Urdu the medium of education, at least up to Class V. Hindi could be introduced from Class III so that children would conversant in the national language as well: and English can be taught in the higher classes. Without this, most Muslims would remain under-privileged and backward—which is not good for the national integrity that our Constitution enjoins.

Having said this, I must also sound a note of warning: *madrasas* all around the subcontinent, which were greatly encouraged by Lord Hastings and Wellesley in the eighteenth century, have now earned a bad name because of what is taught in many of them. What is imparted in some religious schools of the Muslims are not only the inspiring teachings of the Quran but also incitement to hatred and violence.

Hatred has never cured anything, and the distrust that has increased over the years is because it is believed I think wrongly believed by many of our Hindu brethren—that many of the Muslims in this country are no longer nationalist. This is a wild canard. But we have to prove that those who say this are wrong: The Muslims, too, have to improve their image in the eyes of those who are not fanatical but right-thinking liberals.

What I would call the small-letter factor is the only way to get rid of this barrier of distrust between the two main communities. In an article I read a couple of years ago in the *Times of India*—it was an interview with Sulak Sivaraksa from Thailand, who was on his way to the Millennium World Peace Summit in New York. He is a prominent activist and had been persecuted by many Thai military dictatorships, and is now forced into exile. He was asked whether he felt that the major world religions need to reinvent themselves in order to be more effective. He answered with an emphatic *yes*.

He was then asked why there were great disparities in the way Buddhism was being practised.

His answer was significant, and for all of us, crucial:

I make a distinction between Buddhism with a capital 'B' and buddhism with a small 'b'. Sri Lanka has the former, in which the state uses Buddhism as an instrument of power, so there are even Buddhists monks who say the Tamils should be eliminated. Thai Buddhists are not perfect either. Some Thai Buddhist monks have compromised with the kind and possess cars and other luxuries. In many Buddhist countries, the emphasis is on being goody-goody, which is not good enough. I am for buddhism with a small 'b' which is non-violent, practical and aims to eliminate the cause of suffering...

If I were to project myself into the mind of the Founding Fathers to review what they thought were the rights of the minorities in the context of freedom of religion, I would lay great emphasis on the fact that while most of them started the business of constitution-making in 1947, defining minorities with a big *M*, within a couple of years they began to accept the fact that in the vast Indian Union, the minorities had a great future if their sights were lowered—if they chose to accept minorities with a small *m*.

When you discuss the political scenario today, never forget its historical context: Minority with a small *m* should be the watchword. Minority with a small *m* helps to carry the majority with it. And I would say to their Hindu brethren: majority with a small *m* also helps to carry the minority along. The possibility of conflict arises when one or the other of these groups stresses the big *M* factor.

In 1984, at a conference in New Zealand, its then Human Rights Commissioner (Justice John Wallace) said: 'The minority view is generally right, *provided the minority can carry the majority with it'*. His was the voice of experience, not of mere human rights rhetoric.

Reason and tolerance, on one side, begets reason—and tolerance on the other.

Pluralism has been India's greatest weakness—it is also its greatest strength.

Let us then not forget—let not the people forget—that great concepts, and important words like Religion, Majorities and Minorities can assimilate and get on very well if we all—the public, press, and media included other—eschew capital letters and stick to small letters: religion with a small *r*, majority with a small *m*, and minority also with a small *m*. This is how we can all live together and survive in the country we all live in and love—India.

There is an Indianess about Urdu

That many Muslims from the largest single minority in UP have not been successful in establishing Urdu as their second language speaks volumes on the intolerance in our society.

Urdu has become embroiled in a litigious process ever since 1982, when the UP Official Language Ordinance provided that, in the interest of Urdu-speaking people, the Urdu language shall be used as the second official language in UP. In the more than twenty years that have elapsed since then, there has been no implementation of this law simply because the judges have dragged their feet, then differed and, despite the brave decision of Justice Brijesh Kumar (later a Judge of the Supreme Court) which held that the Urdu-speaking population of UP does fulfil the requirements of Article 347 of the Constitution, the inordinate delay in the disposal of the Hindi Sammelan's appeal against the decision now pending in the Supreme Court has led to much heartburning. As a consequence, despite there being no stay order, Urdu which next to Hindi is the main language spoken over by 12 million people in UP—has not been cleared and adopted as the second language in the state.

All of which only exemplifies not merely the law's interminable delays, but the regrettable lack of tolerance on the part of the majority community in the state. The lesson of history, both in this country and abroad is that intolerance in one group fosters intolerance in another.

The longer Urdu takes to achieve second-language status, the less number of Muslims will speak the language—thus destroying by sheer neglect one of our great Indian languages, as the census statistics show.

What needs to be repeated and stressed is what most people know, yet do not care to be reminded of—that Urdu is and remains essentially an Indian language. The word is derived from *Zaban-E-Urdu-Muala*, the language of the 'exalted camp', which was the camp or court of the ruling sultan of Delhi.[7]

Urdu and Hindi have proceeded from the same source, that is, from the Khariboli speech of Delhi and surrounding areas. Khariboli was a spoken language that prevailed around Delhi since the thirteenth century. When the Delhi Sultanate disappeared and the British became the rulers, Sir Sayyid Ahmad Khan (1817–98) started a revival of Urdu as the language of the Muslims in India, and modern Urdu was born.

Language must never be confused with religion: Languages, as Dr Samuel Johnson once said, are the pedigree of a nation. Hindi, Urdu, and the languages in the Eighth Schedule (and yes, even Indian English as we all speak and write it) are the pedigree of the people of Hindustan.

It is to this rich unifying culture of India (which Pandit Nehru wrote about in *Discovery of India*) that we owe the development of the so-called Indian style of Persian poetry that was partly inspired by the tradition of classical Sanskrit poetry with which Muslim poets were familiar through extensive translations done during the reign of the Mughals. For most part, the history of Urdu poets in India is the story of the Urdu *ghazal*, the favourite not only of poets but of vast audiences of different faiths throughout the northern part of the subcontinent—including Pakistan. As an anonymous wit said, the Urdu ghazal was the Muslims' greatest gift to India after the Taj Mahal!

Recently, a friend of mine from Bombay sent on to me an anthology of Urdu ghazals which I found fascinating: They express thoughts that are wise and almost untranslatable. One such couplet was by that great master of social satire, Akbar Allahabadi, who with his inimitable wit and humour has exposed the hypocrisy of the priestly class and castigated our contemporary craze for the western way of life. He says:

Hoo-ay Iss Qadar Māhāzzab
Kabhi Ghar ka Moo-n naa Dekhaa
Kāti Umr Hotlō meiñ

Mürray Haspataal Jā Kar
(So civilized have we grown, never do we see our home,
In hotels we spend our lives, in hospitals we die)

Notes

1. Percival 'Bentinck' Spear, *Cambridge Historical Journal*, vol. 6, no. 40, 1938, p. 78.
2. Jawaharlal Nehru, *Glimpses of World History*, London: Oxford University Press, 1942, p. 434. Reissue edition, *Glimpses of World History*, Centenary Edition, New York: Oxford University Press, 1 December 1989.
3. Malcolm Muggeridge, 'Twilight of Empire,' The *Listener*, LXXII, 1964, p. 966.
4. Andrews to Dunlop-Smith, 1 March 1908, 'Martin Gilbert, Servant of India: A Study of Imperial Rule from 1905 to 1910' as Told Through the Correspondence and Diaries of Sir James Dunlop-Smith, London, 1966, p. 132.
5. Justice Harlan Stone, Re: *Carolene Products case*, 1938–304 US 144 at 152.
6. Rafiq Zakaria, *Hindustan Times*, Sunday, 13 January 2002.
7. Urdu is only spoken in three countries around the world—India (51,338,000), Pakistan (11,570,000), and Mauritius (7,000).

16

Minorities in the Twenty-first Century*

SOLI J. SORABJEE

Protection of minorities is the hallmark of a civilized nation. President Woodrow Wilson's perceptive remark way back in 1919 that, 'Nothing is more likely to disturb the peace of the world than the treatment which might in certain circumstances be meted out to minorities' has been fully substantiated by recent events. According to Mahatma Gandhi, the claim of a country to civilization depends upon the treatment it extends to the minorities. Lord Acton added another dimension: 'The most certain test by which we judge whether a country is really free is the amount of security enjoyed by minorities'.

May I add to that another dimension—namely, the degree and extent of cultural autonomy that is in fact enjoyed by minority communities.

What matters most to the minorities is their religion, their educational institutions, their language, and their culture. These concerns were recognized by the Founding Fathers and are reflected in the constitutional guarantees of Articles 25 and 26, Articles 29 and 30 enshrined in Part III of our Constitution, which guarantees fundamental rights.

At the outset, I must refer to the rationale, the basic principle underlying guarantee of minority rights and safeguards for minorities.

---

* The references for this chapter are no longer available.

Albania, subsequent to her admission to the League of Nations, signed a declaration relating to the position of minorities in Albania. The first paragraph of Article 4 of that declaration ran as follows: 'All Albanian nationals shall be equal before the law, and shall enjoy the same civil and political rights without distinction as to race, language or religion'. Sometime thereafter, all private schools were closed by the Albanian government and provision was made for compulsory primary education for all Albanian nationals in state schools.

The plea of the Albanian government before the International Court of Justice was that the abolition of private schools in Albania constituted a general measure applicable to the majority as well as to the minority, and there was therefore no violation of the rights of the minorities. The court rejected the plea and held that there would be no true equality between a majority and a minority if the latter were deprived of its own institutions, and were consequently compelled to renounce that which constitutes the very essence of its being a minority. The court emphasized, that in addition to equality in law, there must be equality in fact, which may involve the necessity of different treatment in order to attain a result that establishes equilibrium. The equality must be an effective, genuine equality.

Our Supreme Court, in its celebrated decision in the *St. Xavier's College* case has approved of the judgement of the International Court and affirmed this principle.

The same approach is adopted by the United Nations Human Rights Committee functioning under Article 40 of the International Covenant on Civil and Political Rights (ICCPR) 1966. In its general comment on minority rights that are guaranteed under Article 27 of the ICCPR, the committee emphasized that, for effective protection of minority rights, positive measures of protection are required not only against the acts of the state party itself, but also against the acts of other persons within the state party, namely non-state actors. Mere abstention from discriminatory acts is not enough. What is required are positive measures by states to protect the identity of a minority, and the rights of its members to enjoy and develop their culture and language, and to practise their religion, in community with the other members of the group.

Unfortunately, in public discussions and also in the course of forensic debates, this vital principle is overlooked. An impression is sought to be created that minorities are a selfish, pampered lot, whereas all they are seeking is the faithful fulfilment of the solemn pledge given to them and enshrined in the Constitution.

Religion and Language

Freedom of religion guaranteed by Article 25 is not confined to citizens but extends to every person. It includes the right not merely to profess and preach one's religion, but also the right to propagate it. The exercise of this freedom is subject to public order, morality, and health. The expression 'propagate' received an unduly restrictive interpretation by the Supreme Court in *Rev. Stainislaus* v. *State of Madhya Pradesh*. It held that the propagation of religion does not include the right to convert another person to one's own religion. The most amazing part is that no reference whatsoever is made in the judgement to the debates in the Constituent Assembly that were cited before the court and on which strong reliance was placed during arguments.

Article 18 of the ICCPR recognizes freedom of religion in these terms: 'Everyone shall have the right to freedom of thought, conscience and religion. This right shall include freedom to have or to adopt a religion or belief of his choice, and freedom, either individually or in community with others and in public or private, to manifest his religion or belief in worship, observance, practice and teaching'.

The Human Rights Committee, in its general comment relating to freedom of religion observed:

The freedom to manifest religion or belief in worship, observance, practice and teaching encompasses a broad range of acts. The concept of worship extends to ritual and ceremonial acts giving direct expression to belief, as well as various practices integral to such acts, including the building of places of worship, the use of ritual formulae and objects, the display of symbols, and the observance of holidays and days of rest. The observance and practice of religion or belief may include not only ceremonial acts but also such customs as the observance of dietary regulations, the wearing of distinctive clothing or head coverings, participation in rituals associated with certain stages of life, and the use of a particular language customarily spoken by a group. In addition, the practice and teaching of religion or belief includes acts integral to the conduct by religious groups of their basic affairs, such as, inter alia, the freedom to choose their religious leaders, priests and teachers, the freedom to establish seminaries or religious schools and the freedom to prepare and distribute religious texts or publications.

The committee further observed that 'the freedom to "have or to adopt" a religion or belief necessarily entails the freedom to choose a religion or belief, including, *inter alia*, the right to replace one's current religion or belief with another'. The right of conversion is thus clearly recognized. Of course, the exercise of this right must be subject to public order, morality, and health. There should be no fraud or farce involved in conversion of a person from one religion to another one.

A few words about culture and cultural autonomy are relevant here. Article 29 of the Constitution guarantees that any section of the citizens residing in the territory of India, or any part thereof, having a distinct language, script or culture of its own shall have the right to conserve the same. Culture is not defined. However, it is not confined to particular practices or customs such as preference for certain foods or manner of dress. It is generally understood in a broad and comprehensive sense to include language, religion, beliefs, histories, traditions, customs, rituals, and ceremonies. Each culture has a dignity and value that must be protected and preserved.

In my view, implicit in the right to conserve culture is the right to cultural autonomy. What is meant by autonomy? It means and implies the right of an individual to make informed choices about what is valuable and worth pursuing in life. Accordingly, some aspects of cultural autonomy would be participation by members of different groups in the cultural life of the community, the right to protect their cultural heritage and traditions. It also includes the right to set up educational institutions and vocational centres of their choice and the right to receive education in their own language, which is often a vital component of the identity of minorities by furnishing an interactive context.

Education and Language

Cultural autonomy in essence means the freedom to develop and preserve, in condition of full equality, cultural identity without forcible assimilation. In principle, the right to maintain and develop a cultural identity is a universal moral right. Cultural autonomy is necessary for harmonious inter-group relations and helps to subside threats to language and religion that are potent sources of conflicts. Cultural autonomy properly understood and practised can civilize and harmonize rival demands and aspirations. Cultural autonomy comprehends the right of the members of the minority community to own their own media and other means of communication, and to have access on the basis of equality to state-owned or publicly-controlled media. It also includes the right to set up educational institutions and vocational centres of their choice and the right to receive education in their own language, which is often a vital component of the identity of minorities by furnishing an interactive context.

While the need is recognized for one or more official languages for state-wide communication, states should allow for, and take special measures to ensure, education in and the use of regional and minority language, as appropriate. Minorities should receive education about their own culture and also about the culture of other groups in society, majority or minority.

International Law and Language

The historic United Nations Declaration on the Rights of Persons belonging to National or Ethnic, Religious, and Linguistic Minorities, which was unanimously accepted by the General Assembly on 18 December 1992, also recognizes that to afford full equality, states are obliged to 'take measures to create favourable conditions to enable persons belonging to minorities to express their characteristics and to develop their culture, language, religion, traditions and customs'. Another significant provision of the declaration is Article 4.4, which requires the states to 'take measures in the field of education, in order to encourage knowledge of the history, traditions, language and culture of the minorities existing within their territory. Persons belonging to minorities should have adequate opportunities to gain knowledge of the society as a whole'. This Article reflects the concern that in many states, the culture, history, traditions, and customs of minority groups may be subject to distorted and biased representations, generating low self-esteem in the groups and negative stereotypes in the wider community.

It cannot be over-emphasized that diversity and unity are not necessarily opposites leading to inevitable conflict and chaos. Many people have multiple loyalties, which can be harmonized. Majority communities should be aware of and be sensitive to the cultural rights of the minority communities. In their turn, the minority communities should also respect national legislation and the cultural customs and traditions of the majority community in the state in which they reside. Cultural autonomy does not confer a licence to the minorities to flout the laws of the state.

Constitutional provision, and regional and international declarations of minority rights are no doubt necessary for the recognition, protection, and promotion of minority rights. However, the real protection of minorities will lie in the attitudes and the mind-set of the members of both the majority and minority communities. It must be accepted by the majority that special provisions and measures for minorities are not invidious privileges offered on a platter to minorities, but are actually rooted in the principle of equality whose purpose is the creation of conditions which, to the degree possible, are equivalent to those enjoyed by the majority. At the same time, the criteria for according differential treatment to the minority should be rational, and must not sanction invidious or hostile discrimination against the majority.

In the ultimate analysis, the solution of the problem of minorities lies in the hearts and minds of our people, in our tradition of tolerance and catholicity of outlook, regarding as our own all the inhabitants of our great land from whose shore none has been or shall be turned away.

17

Legal Aspects of Minority Languages

YOGESH TYAGI

The recognition of cultural diversity is a necessity in international society, especially after the beginning of liberation from Eurocentrism. Starting with the Statute of the Permanent Court of International Justice (PCIJ) in the early twentieth century to the Rome Statute of the International Criminal Court (ICC) in the late twentieth century, most international legal instruments reflect the inter-civilizational approach.[1] One may rely on this approach to underline the importance of respect for the dignity of each group of persons. It is difficult to promote respect for the dignity of a people having a specific linguistic identity without promoting the use of their language. Language rights are therefore human rights. Besides, the development of human beings and their collectivities is not possible without promoting their ways and means of expression and communication. The exercise of the right to development is linked to the enjoyment of language rights.

In the present context, at least four aspects merit attention: the concept of minority languages; the domestic law basis of obligations in respect of minority languages; the international legal framework with regard to minority languages; and an international approach toward the promotion of regional minority languages in general, and Urdu in particular.

The Concept of Minority Languages

The existence of a minority community in a given state does not depend upon a decision by that state but requires to be established by objective criteria.[2] In case a community is identified in terms of both language and culture, there are ninety-one in India. The Constitution does not specifically define the term 'linguistic minority'. However, Articles 29 and 30 treat linguistic minorities to be collectivities of individuals residing in the territory of India or any part thereof having a distinct language or script of their own. The language of a minority group need not be one of the twenty-two languages included in the Eighth Schedule to the Constitution.[3] In fact, a linguistic minority at the state/union territory (UT) level means any group of people whose mother tongue is different from the principal language of the state/UT. Accordingly, even Hindi is a minority language in the majority of states/UTs (for example, Andaman and Nicobar Islands, Andhra Pradesh, Arunachal Pradesh, Assam, Dadra and Nagar Haveli, Daman and Diu, Goa, Gujarat, Jammu and Kashmir, Karnataka, Kerala, Lakshadweep, Maharashtra, Manipur, Meghalya, Mizoram, Nagaland, Orissa, Pondicherry, Punjab, Sikkim, Tripura, Tamil Nadu, and West Bengal).

According to the Supreme Court, the expression 'linguistic minority' refers to a linguistic group that is in a numerical minority in the state/UT, not in the country as a whole.[4] Also, the expression refers the state/UT as a whole, as distinguished from any particular area or region therein.[5] The complexity of this formula may be illustrated by the fact that while Punjabi is the majority language in Punjab as a whole, Hindi is the majority language in Punjab's capital, Chandigarh, and the Hindi-speaking people in Punjab can speak Punjabi as well. This is the reason why the Supreme Court held in *D.A.V. College, Jullunder* v. *State of Punjab* that Arya Samajis in Punjab were a linguistic minority. In the court's view, a minority could be a minority on account of a distinct language or distinct script of the language of the majority.[6] This understanding echoes the views of B.R. Ambedkar, who 'intends to give protection in the matter of culture, language and script not only to a minority technically, but also to a minority in the wider sense of the term.'[7]

In spite of its dominance in the working of the state system, English is not a majority language in any state/UT, thus implying its minority status along with its privileged position in society. In a sense, therefore, all the languages in India are minority languages. Among these are 114 identifiable languages, and many unidentifiable. The most important factor that distinguishes a minority language such as English from another minority language like Urdu is the factor of dominance. It does not carry much weight under the domestic law of India, but its importance under international law is well recognized.[8] Thus, the concept of minority languages must take into consideration both numerical and dominance factors.

At the international level, the United Nations Human Rights Committee (HRC) holds the view that the expression 'linguistic minority' refers to a linguistic group that is in a numerical minority in the country as a whole, not merely in a province or part thereof.[9] There are five official languages of the United Nations: Arabic, Chinese, English, French, Spanish, and Russian. Even so, Chinese is not a working language of all the bodies and organs of the United Nations (UN). Among all international languages, English is the most widely used. English is the language of the greatest colonial power of yesterday; it is the language of the only Super Power of today; and it is the main language of the Internet. Most important, English is the most preferred language of modern generations who have catalyzed the process of globalization. In effect, all other languages are minority languages. Since English is itself a minority language in the majority of countries, ranging from Afghanistan to Uruguay, all languages in the world are minority languages in one sense or another. Obviously, Urdu is a minority language within the large family of minority languages. The factor of dominance should be taken into account in distinguishing the real minority languages from the notional.

Some of the minority languages are endangered languages. There are many methods of defining language endangerment. The United Nations Educational, Scientific and Cultural Organizations (UNESCO) refers to six categories:

1. Potentially endangered language: children begin increasingly not to learn the language.

2. Endangered language: the youngest speakers are young adults.

3. Seriously endangered language: the youngest speakers are middle-aged or past middle age.

4. Moribund language: only a few aged speakers are left.

5. Probably extinct language.

6. Extinct language: no speakers are left.

According to UNESCO:

Basically, any language of a community which is not learned any more by children, or at least by a large part of the children of that community (say at least 30 per cent) should be regarded as 'endangered' or at least 'potentially endangered'. If a large portion of the children switch to another language, it will mean that more and more children will do this until there are no children speakers left, and the language will therefore eventually disappear with the death of its last speakers.[10]

Further, according to UNESCO, relatively few languages are in danger of disappearing in the Indian subcontinent and the main reason for their active maintenance is the presence of very widespread egalitarian bilingualism and multilingualism.[11] The languages in danger of disappearing are tribal and other relatively 'small' languages, and its uncertain how many people are aware of the growing endangerment to them. What is the role of law, policymakers, educational institutions, and other entities in respect of minority languages? The focus here is on the role of law, for the body of law governs the role of others as well.

Domestic Law Obligations

Cultural diversity, including linguistic heterogeneity, is a fascinating feature of Indian society. Despite dangers to a majority of minority languages, there is an increasingly healthy trend of bilingualism or multilingualism.[12] Education, migration, urbanization, and globalization have contributed considerably to this trend. As the citizens of India are extremely conscious of the linguistic dimension of their personality as a significant aspect of their independent entity and identity, legal safeguards for linguistic minorities are instrumental in removing the fear of cultural or linguistic assimilation from the citizens' minds. Since linguistic minorities are a natural corollary to the enormous linguistic heterogeneity in India, it is imperative that their rights are clearly defined and safeguarded through the rule of law.

The legal safeguards for the linguistic minorities in India derive their authority from three sources: the Constitution; the scheme of safeguards agreed to from time to time; and judicial decisions.[13] All are worthy of elaboration.

The debates of the Constituent Assembly reveal that the consti-
tution-makers gave serious thought to the protection of the rights of
linguistic minorities, though they had different viewpoints on the
subject. Some members of the Assembly wanted a strong regime for
the rights of linguistic minorities. Representing their viewpoint, Z.H.
Lari suggested, among other things, that 'minorities in every unit
shall be protected in respect of their language, script and culture, and
no laws or regulations may be enacted that may operate oppres-
sively or prejudicially in this respect.'[14] In contrast, some other
members wanted to subject the rights of linguistic minorities to the
broader interests of society. Loknath Misra gave expression to this
view and moved an amendment: 'Without detriment to the spiritual
heritage and the cultural unity of the country, which the state shall
recognize, protect and nourish, any section of the citizens residing
in the territory of India or any part thereof, claiming to have a distinct
language, script and culture shall be free to conserve the same.'[15] In
order to expand the scope of the rights of linguistic minorities, K.T.
Shah suggested: 'Any section of the citizens residing in the territory
of India or any part thereof having a distinct language, script or
culture of its own shall have the right to conserve and develop the
same.'[16] Damodar Swarup Seth suggested that since minority based
on religion or community should not be recognized in a secular state,
only minorities based on languages should be recognized. All these
motions were rejected. Finally, Ambedkar succeeded in drafting the
rights of linguistic minorities in the broadest sense and gave them
the status of fundamental rights. As a result, the Constitution seeks
to protect the rights of linguistic minorities with built-in institutional
arrangements under Articles 29, 30, 347, 350, 350-A and 350-B, along
with Articles 32 and 226.

Article 29 grants the linguistic minorities the right to conserve
their language, script, and culture, and Article 30 confers upon them
the right to establish and administer educational institutions of their
choice. The two Articles create two separate rights, although it is
possible that they may meet in a given case. Also, the width of Article
30(1) cannot be cut down by introducing in it considerations on which
Article 29(1) is based.[17] Articles 29 and 30 therefore create mutually
supportive rights for minorities and minority institutions. In *The
Ahmedabad St Xaviers College Society* v. *State of Gujarat*,[18] the Supreme
Court defined the scope of Articles 29 and 30 and observed that these
two confer four distinct rights: the right of any section of the resident

citizens to conserve its own language, script, or culture; the right of all religious or linguistic minorities to establish and administer educational institutions of their choice; the right of an educational institution not to be discriminated against in the matter of state aid on the ground that it is under management of a religious or linguistic minority; and the right of a citizen not to be denied admissions into state-maintained or state-aided educational institutions on grounds only of religion, caste, race, or language. In *Rev. Sidhajbhai Sabhai* v. *State of Bombay*,[19] the Supreme Court held that, unlike the fundamental freedoms guaranteed by Article 19 of the Constitution, the right established by Article 30(1) is a fundamental right declared in absolute terms and is not subject to reasonable restrictions. The importance of the rights enshrined in Articles 29 and 30 may be understood from Justice Khanna's opinion that 'no tampering with those rights can be countenanced'.[20] This opinion of the proponent of the doctrine of the basic features of the Indian Constitution carries considerable weight. In the same vein, it is important to note the Supreme Court's observation that a minority community can effectively conserve its language, script, or culture by and through educational institutions.[21] This observation underlines the importance of those institutions which promote the use of minority languages. Obviously, states ought to help such institutions.

Article 347 of the Constitution provides for a Presidential direction for official recognition of a language. According to Article 350, every person is entitled to submit a representation for redress of any grievance to any officer or authority of the Union or a state in any of the languages used in the Union or in the state. Article 350-A provides for facilities for instruction through the mother tongue at the primary stage of education.[22] There is a violation of Article 29(1), read with Article 350-A, if a state compels a linguistic minority, at a primary stage, to study a regional language, that is, a language other than their own, but not so if they are given an option in this respect.[23] Similar safeguards are available at the college stage as well. In *D.A.V. College, Bhatinda* v. *State of Punjab*,[24] the Supreme Court held that while the Punjabi University of Patiala can prescribe Punjabi as a medium of instruction, it can neither prescribe it as the exclusive medium nor compel affiliated colleges established and administered by linguistic or religious minorities or by a section of the citizens who wish to conserve their language, script, and culture, to teach in Punjabi or take examinations in that language with Gurumukhi script.

In *English Medium S.P.A.* v. *State of Karnataka*,[25] the Supreme Court held that the object of Article 350-A is to safeguard the interests of the linguistic minorities that have particularly come into existence as a result of reorganization of states.

Article 350-B lays down the foundation for the institution of the Commissioner for Linguistic Minorities in India (CLM).[26] The office of the CLM exists since 30 July 1957. In accordance with Article 350-B, it is the duty of the CLM to investigate all matters relating to the safeguards provided for linguistic minorities under the Constitution, and to report to the President upon those matters at such intervals as the President may direct, and the President shall cause all such reports to be laid before each House of Parliament and sent to the governments of the states concerned.[27]

Since the states have primary responsibility for the implementation of safeguards for linguistic minorities, they may devise schemes to promote minority languages. At the same time, their language policies must be compatible with fundamental rights. In *Hindi Hitrakshak Samiti* v. *Union of India*,[28] the Supreme Court made it clear that, subject to constitutional restraints, it would not interfere with the government's formulation of its language policy and implementation thereof. The policy would, however, be unconstitutional if it prescribes that at the primary level, Hindi or any other regional language shall be the sole medium of instruction.

The National Commission for Minorities Act 1992, along with the 1995 amendment thereto, may be interpreted to extend the commission's umbrella to the victims of violation of language rights of minorities. The Protection of Human Rights Act 1993 may also be interpreted to the same effect. According to the 1993 Act, the National Human Rights Commission (NHRC) has the responsibility to monitor the implementation of the international covenants on human rights in India. Since the International Covenant on Civil and Political Rights guarantees the rights of minorities under its Article 27, the NHRC has a mandate to monitor the implementation of that article within the territory/jurisdiction of India. So far, it has not received any complaints regarding violation of minority language rights. The main reason is not the lack of violations, but the victims' lack of familiarity with their language rights safeguards under the auspices of the NHRC.

Most important, as the Supreme Court held in *Jagdev Singh Sidhanti* v. *Pratap Singh Daulta*,[29] the right to conserve the language of the citizens includes the right to agitate for protection of the language. This is a populist version of the right to a remedy under Article 32 of the Constitution. Unhappily, the agitational approach has not strengthened the constitutional approach to the protection and promotion of minority language rights.

International Legal Obligations

The history of international law relating to minority language rights began with the end of the World War I. President Woodrow Wilson's Fourteen Points advocated the self-determination of nations, much to the dismay of the colonial powers. Implementation of this principle at the Paris Conference of 1919–20 demanded recognition and protection of the rights of all minorities, including those linguistic. The recognition of language as a basis of discrimination was one of the major achievements of the Paris Conference, and it was reaffirmed at the San Francisco Conference more than twenty years later. The delegates at the Paris Conference agreed that the protection of minorities would be dealt with not in the Covenant of the League of Nations but rather by minority treaties and declarations. The Paris Conference required sixteen central and eastern European countries to guarantee minorities' rights, and the League of Nations admitted five European and Middle East countries, including Albania and Iraq, with the condition that they make declarations on the protection of minorities. Most of the minority treaties/declarations included both the minimal negative right of non-discrimination and the special positive right of promotion of minority languages. Some of the minority treaties/declarations obligated the public educational systems of the nations concerned to provide adequate facilities for ensuring that, in the primary schools, the instruction would be given to the children of such nationals through the medium of their own language.

According to a commentator, 'These treaty obligations and declarations included some of the most extensive and expansive guarantees of linguistic rights ever to have been drafted in the international context.'[30] As another commentator observed, 'The resulting network of obligations constituted the first full-blooded effort on the political and legal level to provide for the protection of minorities.'[31] The international machinery for protection of minorities was provided by the most powerful political institution—the Council of the League of Nations—and also by the most respected judicial institution (the

PCIJ) that time. For example, the PCIJ tried to redress the grievances of linguistic minorities in Albania by responding to the Council's request for an advisory opinion in the *Minority Schools in Albania* case,[32] where the Court underlined two principles: the principle of perfect equality for members of minorities with other nationals, and the principle of preservation of the special traditions and characteristics of the minorities. Although the international machinery for protection of minorities was effective to some extent, it did not survive political division between the wartime Allies.[33] As a result, people have more or less forgotten the first success story in the field of international minority language law.

The contemporary incarnation of that law may be gleaned from the following: the Charter of the UN; the International Bill of Rights; the UN Declaration on the Rights of Persons Belonging to National or Ethnic, Religious and Linguistic Minorities; the UNESCO Convention against Discrimination in Education; the International Labour Organization (ILO) Conventions concerning indigenous and tribal populations; certain other international and regional instruments; and practices developed by those international institutions that are devoted to the promotion and protection of the rights of minorities.

Article 1(3) of the UN Charter states that the UN shall promote international cooperation in various fields without any discrimination. Language is one of the four bases upon which discrimination is prohibited. Articles 13(1)(*b*), 55(*c*) and 76(*c*) of the Charter also refer to language as a basis of non-discrimination. Apart from the negative right of nondiscrimination, however, the Charter does not impose any obligation upon states to recognize or protect positive linguistic rights at the national level. The drafters of the Charter left this task to the drafters of human rights instruments.

Like Article 1 of the UN Charter, Article 2 of the Universal Declaration of Human Rights (UDHR) contains a non-discrimination clause, but its ramifications are wider in the context of language protection. This is the only reference to language in the UDHR, and one may wonder why the UDHR is economical in its expression of linguistic rights. The inclusion of these rights was rejected only after careful consideration of the implications of protecting such collective minority rights in the international context. The Secretariat of the United Nations and the governments of several countries (for example, Denmark, France, the Soviet Union, the United Kingdom, and Yugoslavia) argued for the inclusion of a provision for the protection of the rights of a 'minority to use its own language and to maintain schools and other cultural institutions.'[34] Other countries, especially the United States, favoured a more moderate policy of assimilation with regard to language groups. Some stressed that, in view of the comprehen-sive non-discrimination clause, there was no longer any need for a distinct system of protection for minorities. Others thought an article on minorities was not only unnecessary but also undesirable, while a few felt it might result in alienating minorities from the mainstream of national life, frustrating their emancipation and full development, and denying them equal oppor-tunity. African nations felt that the protection of linguistic rights would interfere with their general goals of political unification and economic centralization. Giving effect to these views, China, India, and the United Kingdom proposed the deletion of the entire article on minorities. Eleanor Roosevelt (United States), the then Chairperson of the UN Commission on Human Rights, supported this proposal.[35] As a result, absolute recognition and protection of linguistic rights were excluded from the UDHR.[36] However, several provisions of the UDHR, such as Articles 10 (the right to a fair trial), 18 (the right to freedom of thought, conscience, and religion), 19 (the right to freedom of opinion and expression), and 26 (the right to education), may implicitly protect linguistic rights.

Article 2(2) of the International Covenant on Economic, Social and Cultural Rights (ICESCR) enshrines the general non-discrimination clause of the UN Charter and of the UDHR, thus prohibiting discrimi-nation on grounds of language. However, it deals with individual rights, contains no positive guarantees to use one's own language, and adds little to the substantive law of language rights.

Besides the linguistic-rights guarantees incorporated in the UDHR, the ICESCR, and the International Covenant on Civil and Political Rights (ICCPR) stipulates several additional guarantees, amongst which is Article 27: 'In those States in which ethnic, religious or linguistic minorities exist, persons belonging to such minorities shall not be denied the right, in community with the other members of their group, to enjoy their own culture, to profess and practice their own religion, or to use their own language.'

Giving the most progressive interpretation of Article 27 of the ICCPR, the HRC observed: 'The right of individuals belonging to a linguistic minority to use their language among themselves, in private or in public, is distinct from other language rights protected under the Covenant [ICCPR]. In particular, it should be distinguished from the general right to freedom of expression protected under Article 19. The latter right is available to all persons, irrespective of whether they belong to minorities or not.[37]

The HRC also made it clear that,

Although Article 27 is expressed in negative terms, that article, nevertheless, does recognize the existence of a 'right' and requires that it shall not be denied. Consequently, a State party is under an obligation to ensure that the existence and the exercise of this right are protected against their denial or violation. Positive measures of protection are, therefore, required not only against the acts of the state party itself, whether through its legislative, judicialor administrative authorities, but also against the acts of other persons within the state party.[38]

Accordingly, the government of India and also the governments of states/UTs have an obligation to adopt all necessary measures not only for the promotion and protection of minority languages but also against all possible governmental and non-governmental violations of minority language rights.[39] The HRC has the capacity, willingness, and opportunities to assess whether the government has done that or not. In case of the government's failure to discharge its obligations in respect of minority languages, India may be subject to comments and criticisms. It is preferable to be a focus of attention at the international level by virtue of an impressive record of compliance with ICCPR obligations, implying respect for minority language rights. In July 1997, the HRC considered India's third periodic report and 'appreciated' the establishment of the Minorities Commission of India.[40] However, the fact that the HRC did not find any wrong with India's compliance with Article 27 obligations cannot be considered conclusive evidence of compliance. In any case, the continuity of obligations implies the compulsion of continuing compliance.

Article 27 of the ICCPR has inspired the UN to create several information-seeking bodies to investigate the nature of minority rights and to set more definitive standards. The efforts of these United Nations institutions to define and evaluate linguistic minorities have served to focus international attention on the significance of language rights as fundamental human rights.

Drawing inspiration from Article 27 of the ICCPR and joining the process of elaborating minority rights, Article 1(1) of the UN Declaration on the Rights of Persons Belonging to National or Ethnic,

Religious and Linguistic Minorities declares:[41]

States shall protect the existence and the national or ethnic, cultural, religious and linguistic identity of minorities within their respective territories and shall encourage conditions for the promotion of that identity.

Article 2 of the Declaration enumerates a number of minority rights, including:

Persons belonging to national or ethnic, religious and linguistic minorities...have the right to enjoy their own culture, to profess and practise their own religion, and to use their own language, in private and in public, freely and without interference or any form of discrimination.

In order to implement these rights, states are expected to adopt appropriate legislative and other measures, including those pre-scribed in Article 4 of the Declaration:

2. States shall take measures to create favourable conditions to enable persons belonging to minorities to express their characteristics and to develop their culture, language, religion, traditions, and customs, except where specific practices are in violation of national law and contrary to international standards.
3. States should take appropriate measures so that, wherever possible, persons belonging to minorities may have adequate opportunities to learn their mother tongue or to have instruction in their mother tongue.
4. States should, where appropriate, take measures in the field of education, in order to encourage knowledge of the history, traditions, language, and culture of the minorities existing within their territory. Persons belonging to minorities should have adequate opportunities to gain knowledge of the society as a whole.

Article 5 of the Declaration provides, among others, the following guideline:

National policies and programmes shall be planned and implemented with due regard for the legitimate interests of persons belonging to minorities.

By its Article 23, the ILO Convention concerning the Protection and Integration of Indigenous and Other Tribal and Semi-Tribal Populations in Independent Countries (Convention No. 107 of 1957) establishes that measures be taken for the preservation of the mother tongue or language most commonly used by the group, especially in schools.[42] Since India ratified the Convention on 29 September 1958, it is bound to respect its provisions. Article 23 has considerable significance for a large number of persons speaking tribal languages in India, some of which are unidentifiable and endangered languages. In the wake of the stronger movement for the protection of the rights of indigenous peoples in the 1980s, the ILO adopted the Convention concerning Indigenous and Tribal Peoples in Independent Countries (Convention No. 169 of 1989), which includes the language rights of indigenous and tribal peoples.[43] India has not yet ratified Convention No. 169, but it remains bound by Convention No. 107. The ILO has a well-established procedure to monitor the implementation of its Conventions.

At the regional level, the most conspicuous institution in the field of minority rights is the Office of the High Commissioner for National Minorities of the Organization for Security and Cooperation in Europe (OSCE). The Office of the High Commissioner was established in 1992 to identify and seek early resolution of ethnic tensions that might endanger peace, stability, or friendly relations between OSCE participating states. One of the tools used by the High Commissioner are recommendations made to governments of OSCE participating states regarding the treatment of their national minorities.[44] In respect of linguistic minorities, however, the European Charter for Regional or Minority Languages (henceforth the European Charter) enshrines the most systematic law and procedure.[45] It seeks to protect and promote regional and minority languages as a threatened aspect of Europe's cultural heritage. Its overriding purpose is cultural. It covers regional and minority languages,[46] non-territorial languages,[47] and less widely used official languages. Within its scope are the languages traditionally used within a state's territory, but it does not cover those connected with recent migratory movements or dialects of the official language. It is intended to ensure, as far as is reasonably possible, that regional or minority languages are used in education and in the media, to make possible and encourage their use in legal and administrative contexts, in economic and social life, for cultural activities and in trans-frontier exchanges.

The European Charter is based on an approach that abides by the principles of national sovereignty and territorial integrity. It does not conceive the relationship between official languages and regional or minority languages in terms of competition or antagonism. Development of the latter must not obstruct knowledge and promotion of the former. A deliberate decision was taken to adopt an intercultural and multilingual approach of language taking its rightful place. In each state, the cultural and social reality must be taken into account. The European Charter does not establish a list of European languages corresponding to the concept of regional or minority languages, but defines (in Article 1) the terms used. The languages covered by the European Charter exist in a very wide range of contexts—social, political, and economic. By providing for 'a la carte' commitments, it makes it possible to adapt the scope of the protection afforded to suit the particular context of each language, and also to take account of the costs of application.

The European Charter makes provision for a committee of independent experts, comprising one member for each contracting party, appointed by the Committee of Ministers of the Council of Europe from a list of individuals of the highest integrity. The Committee of Experts is made up of people from a variety of backgrounds: jurists, linguists, historians, and experts on minority and language issues. It is responsible for examining states' periodic reports, as well as any other information from associations and other bodies legally established in the state concerned and with an interest in the field of languages.

Although the European Charter is not applicable to non-European states, its principles (Article 7) are relevant to all those countries that have minority languages:

1. Recognition of regional or minority languages as an expression of cultural wealth.

2. Respect for the geographical area of each regional or minority language.

3. The need for resolute action to promote such languages.

4. The facilitation and/or encouragement of the use of such languages, in speech and writing, in public and private life.

5. The provision of appropriate forms and means for the teaching and study of such languages at all appropriate stages.

6. The promotion of relevant transnational exchanges.

7. The prohibition of all forms of unjustified distinction, exclusion, restriction or preference relating to the use of a regional or minority language and intended to discourage or endanger its maintenance or development.

8. The promotion by states of mutual understanding between all the country's linguistic groups.

An International Approach

It makes sense to think of both domestic and international approaches to the promotion and protection of those languages that are spoken in more than one country and are still vulnerable because of their minority status. There are millions of Urdu-speaking people in the world, especially in Bangladesh, India, Mauritius, Pakistan, and South Africa.

For the promotion and protection of Urdu in those areas where this language is in an endangered or potentially endangered situation, one can explore the language protection schemes of UNESCO. India and Pakistan are not yet in the intangible heritage network of UNESCO, but some linguists like Karl Gadelii regard both the countries highly interesting and relevant for such a network. Linguistic projects could also be considered within the UNESCO Participation Programmme, to which one can apply via the Indian National Commission for UNESCO. Also, India could take some initiatives to create a dynamic minority language promotion regime. The South Asian Association for Regional Cooperation (SAARC) could be the hub of the Urdu promotion programme in the region. Besides promoting regional minority languages, such initiatives (even nongovernmental) will renew and strengthen cultural, emotional, and intellectual bonds with those who are on the other side of the hedge. There is a suggestion that 'if durable peace is to prevail in SAARC countries… language should be brought to centre stage'.[48] Urdu could be an indigenous, inexpensive, and effective tool of Track II diplomacy in the nuclear-powered Indian subcontinent.

Summation

It is unwise to ignore UNESCO's warning that close to half of the 6,000 languages spoken in the world are doomed or likely to disappear in the foreseeable future. Some of them are Indian. The concept of minority languages exposes the vulnerability of every linguistic minority. The linguistic majority at one place must remember its minority status at another. Both Indian and international law are based on the premise that majority languages can prosper along with minority languages. The development of minority languages can contribute to the development of majority languages as well. This is borne out by the fact that several Asian languages have enriched the English language. It is therefore in everybody's interest to promote and protect minority languages. This is not only a matter of common sense, but also an issue of legal obligation. The constitutional scheme of promotion and protection of minority languages in India is apparently reasonable. However, a few critics consider it inadequate;[49] a few fear 'linguistic fascism';[50] and many feel frustrated from the unresolved controversy arising out of *Uttar Pradesh Hindi Sahitya Sammelan v. State of Uttar Pradesh*.[51] The critics of the constitutional scheme ignore the complexity of Indian society. In fact, they can take pride in claiming that, while some countries such as France and Kuwait do not even recognize the existence of minorities, linguistic minorities have constitutional safeguards in India in the form of fundamental rights. The Supreme Court has strengthened those safeguards. Its recent decision in a Kerala case, holding that even a single person can establish and administer a minority educational institution,[52] reaffirms the judicial security of minority rights. Given this framework of liberal policy, every linguistic controversy ought to be resolved in the spirit of mutual respect and understanding. There is a need to develop alternative dispute settlement mechanisms to resolve linguistic issues.

Although Urdu is a minority language, it is not the language of only a minority community. It is also the language of a large number of people belonging to the majority. It is not just an Indian language— it is an international language, with speakers and admirers across the border as well. It represents India's intellectual creativity, constitutes an integral part of our secular polity, and possesses the potential to reduce the enmity with our western neighbour. It is true that Urdu's current status does not match its historical significance, but not only governments are responsible for this situation. The painful Partition of the country, the strikingly low rate of literacy, the powerful market forces, and the increasing western influence have inflicted blows on a great many languages, and Urdu is no exception. However, the contributory negligence of governments cannot be easily condoned. This is true with regard to many other minority languages as well.

In order to enhance the effectiveness of efforts to promote and protect minority languages, it is appropriate to explore the possibility of establishing a nationwide database on linguistic minorities. This kind of database is feasible, in view of the latest census in the country. The database on linguistic minorities would enable various national and international bodies, including the CLM and the Working Group on Minorities, to increase their access to accurate and reliable information, thereby enhancing their capacity to make fruitful suggestions and outline programmes of action. The database would benefit international, national, and regional organizations addressing issues pertaining to linguistic minorities. It would also help policymakers, the media, the public, as well as linguistic minorities themselves. There would be similar advantages from the establishment of a database on Urdu in South Asia.

A number of bodies and organs of the United Nations system have addressed the problems of minorities. However, a bird's-eye view of their work suggests that they have been primarily concerned with the problems of ethnic or religious minorities, not those of linguistic minorities. The Declaration on the Rights of Persons Belonging to National or Ethnic, Religious and Linguistic Minorities inspires states to take separate and joint action to promote and protect minority languages. The General Assembly appeals to states to make bilateral and multilateral efforts, as appropriate, in order to protect the rights of persons belonging to linguistic minorities in their countries, in accordance with the declaration. The supporters of Urdu should build upon this provision in the South Asian context, and explore the possibility of formulating a SAARC convention on the promotion and protection of minority languages.

Notes

1. For an elaboration of the inter-civilizational approach, see Onuma Yasuaki, 'Toward an Intercivilisational Approach to Human Rights', in Joanne R. Bauer and Daniel A. Bell (eds), *The East Asian Challenge for Human Rights*, Cambridge: Cambridge University Press, 1999, pp. 103–23.
2. HRC General Comment No. 23, which deals with the rights of minorities under Article 27 of the International Covenant on Civil and Political Rights. See UN Doc. HRI/GEN/1/Rev.5, 26 April 2001, para. 5.2.
3. Following the Constitution (21st Amendment) Act of 1967, the Constitution (71st Amendment) Act of 1992, and the Constitution (92nd Amendment) Act of 2003, Schedule VIII identifies twenty-two languages: Assamese, Bengali, Bodo, Dogri, Gujarati, Hindi, Kannada, Kashmiri, Konkani, Maithili, Malayalam, Manipuri, Marathi, Nepali, Oriya, Punjabi, Sanskrit, Santhali, Sindhi, Tamil, Telugu, and Urdu. There is a demand to include the Bhoti language in Schedule VIII on the grounds, inter alia, that while some of the Schedule languages are only 150 years old, Bhoti has been the mother tongue of Himalayan people for the last 1,300 years. In support of this demand, the Himalayan Buddhist Cultural Association, a Delhi-based non-governmental organization (NGO), organized a conference on 27 January 2001.
4. *D.A.V. College, Jullunder* v. *State of Punjab*, AIR 1971 SC 1737, p. 1742.
5. *Reference on the Education Bill*, AIR 1958 SC 956.
6. AIR 1971 SC 1737.
7. *Constituent Assembly Debates*, vol. VII, no. 22, p. 922.

8. See Francesco Capotorti, *Study on the Rights of Persons Belonging to Ethnic, Religious and Linguistic Minorities,* UN Doc. E/CN.4/Sub.2/384, 1978.

9. See *John Ballantyne and Elizabeth Davidson, and Gordon McIntyre* v. *Canada,* Communication Nos. 359/1989 and 385/1989, *Report of the Human Rights Committee,* General Assembly Official Records, forty-eighth session (1993), suppl. 40, UN Doc. A/48/40, vol. II, Annex XII P, pp. 91–103.

10. Stephen A. Wurm (ed.), *Atlas of the World's Languages in Danger of Disappearing,* Paris: UNESCO, 1996, pp. 1–2.

11. Ibid., p. 2.

12. According to the 1991 census, as many as 19.44 per cent of India's population is bilingual. This compares very favourably with the national average of 13.34 per cent recorded in 1981, 13.04 per cent recorded in 1971, and 9.7 per cent recorded in the 1961 census. The national average for trilingualism is 7.26 per cent of India's population (excluding Jammu & Kashmir, where no census could be conducted) in the 1991 census.

13. For a background, see Ram Singh, 'Problems of Linguistic Minorities: Constitutional Safeguards and Legal Solutions', in Tahir Mahmood (ed.), *Minorities and State at the Indian Law: An Anthology,* New Delhi: Institute of Objective Studies, 1991, pp. 121–33.

14. *Constituent Assembly Debates,* vol. VII, no. 21, p. 893.

15. Ibid., p. 892.

16. Ibid., vol. VII, no. 22, p. 896.

17. *Rev. Father W. Proost and Others* v. *State of Bihar,* AIR 1969 SC 465, at pp. 468–9.

18. AIR 1974 SC 1389, at p. 1394.

19. 1963 (3) SCR 837.

20. *The Ahmedabad St. Xaviers College Society,* at p. 1414.

21. *Reference on the Education Bill,* AIR 1958 SC 956.

22. Article 350-A reads as follows: 'It shall be the endeavour of every local authority within the State to provide adequate facilities for instruction in the mother tongue at the primary stage of education to children belonging to linguistic minority groups; and the President may issue such directions to any State as he considers necessary or proper for securing the provision of such facilities.'

23. *English Medium S.P.A.* v. *State of Karnataka,* AIR 1994 SC 1702.

24. AIR 1971 SC 1731.

25. AIR 1994 SC 1702.

26. The protection of the rights of linguistic minorities became a prime concern in the early 1950s, when the states were being reorganized, primarily on the basis of language. The States Reorganization Commission (SRC), appointed in 1953 to examine the question of reorganization of states, recommended reorganization of states, *inter alia,* on a linguistic basis. The SRC suggested a number of safeguards for linguistic minorities, most important of which was the recommendation for an agency to enforce these safeguards. This resulted in the enactment of the Constitution (Seventh Amendment) Act, 1956, which, inter alia, inserted Article 350-B in the Constitution, providing for appointment of a Special Officer for Linguistic Minorities, formally designated as the Commissioner for Linguistic Minorities in India.

27. For details of the CLM's mandate, its implementation and its related aspects, see *The Thirty-fifth Report of the Commissioner for Linguistic Minorities in India* (*For the period July, 1994, to June, 1995*), New Delhi: Government of India, 1999.

28. AIR 1990 SC 851.

29. *Jagdev Singh Sidhanti* v. *Pratap Singh Daulta*, 1964 (6) SCR 750.

30. Joseph P. Gromacki, 'The Protection of Language Rights in International Human Rights Law: A Proposed Draft Declaration of Linguistic Rights', *Virginia Journal of International Law*, vol. 32, 1992, p. 521.

31. Ian Brownlie, *Principles of Public International Law*, Oxford: Oxford University Press, 1973, p. 549.

32. In accordance with its conditional admission to the League of Nations, Albania made a Declaration on 2 October 1921. The Declaration provided for the protection of minorities in Albania, including their right to establish, maintain, manage and control schools and other educational institutions, along with the right to use their own language. In 1931, religious instruction in Albanian schools was abolished. Two years later, private schools were abolished. This led to various petitions to the Council of the League, which in turn sought an advisory opinion of the PCIJ. The PCIJ had two important issues: first, whether the Declaration had any legally binding effect; and second, whether the abolition of all private schools, including those of minorities, violated the letter and spirit of the Declaration. The PCIJ answered both in the positive and also specified the general principles of the treaties for the protection of minorities. As a result, the government of Albania felt obliged to modify its domestic law on private schools for minorities. See *PCIJ, series A/B, no. 64*; and *series C, no. 76*.

33. Brownlie, *Principles of Public International Law*, p. 550.

34. Cf. Louis B. Sohn, 'The Rights of Minorities', in Louis Henkin (ed.), *The International Bill of Rights*, New York: Columbia University Press, 1981, p. 272.

35. Ibid., p. 471.

36. Gromacki, 'The Protection of Language Rights in International Human Right Law,' p. 549, n. 30.

37. UN Doc. A/2929, 1 July 1955, para. 185.

38. General Comment No. 23, para. 6.1.

39. Asbjørn Eide (UN Doc. E/CN.4/Sub.2/AC.5/2001/2, 2 April 2001, paras. 28 and 69) and Soli J. Sorabjee (UN Doc. E/CN.4/Sub.2/2001/22, 22 June 2001, para. 18) point out the possibility of violation of minority rights by non-state actors.

40. See UN Doc. CCPR/C/79/Add.81, 4 August 1997.

41. For details of Article 1 and also those of other provisions of the Declaration, see Asbjørn Eide, *Commentary to the Declaration on the Rights of Persons Belonging to National or Ethnic, Religious and Linguistic Minorities*, UN Doc. E/CN.4/Sub.2/AC.5/2001/2, 2 April 2001.

42. Article 23 of Convention No. 107 reads as follows:

    1. Children belonging to the populations concerned shall be taught to read and write in their mother tongue or, where this is not practicable, in the language most commonly used by the group to which they belong.

    2. Provision shall be made for a progressive transition from the mother tongue or the vernacular language to the national language or to one of the official languages of the country.

3. Appropriate measures shall, as far as possible, be taken to preserve the mother tongue or the vernacular language.

43. Article 28 of Convention No. 169 reads as follows:

1. Children belonging to the peoples concerned shall, wherever practicable, be taught to read and write in their own indigenous language or in the language most commonly used by the group to which they belong. When this is not practicable, the competent authorities shall undertake consultations with these peoples with a view to the adoption of measures to achieve this objective.

2. Adequate measures shall be taken to ensure that these peoples have the opportunity to attain fluency in the national language or in one of the official languages of the country.

3. Measures shall be taken to preserve and promote the development and practice of the indigenous languages of the peoples concerned.

44. For details, visit *http://www.osce.org/hcnm*.

45. The European Charter was drawn up on the basis of a text put forward by the Standing Conference of Local and Regional Authorities of Europe, was adopted as a convention on 25 June 1992 by the Committee of Ministers of the Council of Europe, and was opened for signature in Strasbourg on 5 November 1992. It entered into force on 1 March 1998. As at 17 February 2005, it had been ratified by 17 states (Armenia, Austria, Croatia, Cyprus, Denmark, Finland, Germany, Hungary, Liechtenstein, Netherlands, Norway, Slovakia, Slovenia, Spain, Sweden, Switzerland, and the United Kingdom). Another 13 states have signed it.

46. As defined by the European Charter, 'regional or minority languages' are languages traditionally used within a given territory of a state by nationals of that state who form a group numerically smaller than the rest of the state's populations; they are different from the official language(s) of that state, and they include neither dialects of the official language(s) of the state, nor the languages of migrants.

47. The expression 'non-territorial languages' means languages used by nationals of the state that differ from the language(s) used by the rest of the state's population by which, although traditionally used within the state's territory, cannot be identified with a particular area thereof. For details, visit *http://conventions.coe.int/treaty/EN/cadreprincipal.htm*.

48. T.K. Oommen, 'New Directions for South Asia', *The Hindu*, 4 February 2002, p. 8.

49. Iqbal A. Ansari, 'Inadequacy of Constitutional Protection of Minority Languages in India', in Sanghasen Singh (ed.), *Language Problem in India*, New Delhi: Institute of Objective Studies, 1997, pp. 149–59.

50. Syed Abdul Bari, 'Urdu: A Victim of Linguistic Fascism', in Sanghasen Singh (ed.), *Language Problem in India*, New Delhi: Institute of Objective Studies, 1997, pp. 134–48.

51. This case originated from the opposition to the Uttar Pradesh government's decision to grant Urdu the status of the second official language of that state. For some reflections, see Danial Latifi, 'The Struggle for Urdu in UP', *The Indian Advocate*, vol. XXIX (1999–2000), pp. 44–50.

52. *Times of India*, 1 February 2002, p. 4.

Appendix 1

꙳Ꙭ꙳

Delhi Urdu Conference*

[*Editor's Note*: An 'International Conference on Minorities, Education and Language in Twenty-First Century Indian Democracy—the Case of Urdu with Special Reference to Dr Zakir Husain, Late President of India,' sponsored by the Dr Zakir Husain Study Circle (ZHSC) and the Modern Education Foundation, was held in New Delhi, 8–11 February 2002. Soon thereafter, Mr Salman Khurshid, President, Dr Zakir Husain Study Circle, New Delhi, got in touch with me and expressed his desire to publish the entire proceedings of the Conference in the *Annual of Urdu Studies (AUS)*. Readers will recall that the *AUS* has published in several of its back issues quite a bit of material along these lines generated by sundry conferences of a similar nature held in New Delhi in the preceding years. Publishing the entire proceedings of the recent Conference would have seriously strained the resources of the *AUS*; additionally, the situation of Urdu in India, although grave and certainly the concern of all those individuals who are interested in its fate and continued well-being, can only occupy a proportionate share of the attention of the *AUS*. I offered instead to point a few representative items, and particularly the Program of the Conference for its obvious usefulness. Mr Khurshid agreed and, later, also informed me that the entire proceedings would be published by Oxford University Press, India. *Alḥamdu li 'Lāh*.

Regrettably, I could not obtain the Program which reflected the actual papers delivered. The one I did get was printed well before the Conference. I might also mention that the versions of papers presented here have been revised and edited both by their authors and the *AUS* and thus differ, in some cases substantially, from the papers presented at the Conference.]

* From *The Annual of Urdu Studies*, No. 18, Part 2, 2003, ed. Muhammad Umar Memon, Dept. of Languages and Cultures of Asia, University of Wisconsin-Madison, p. 545.

STATEMENT OF CONSENSUS*

The Conference on Minorities, Education and Language in Twenty-First Century Indian Democracy—the Case of Urdu with Special Reference to Dr Zakir Husain, Late President of India, after due deliberation, arrived at the following consensus:

1. Since all Schedule 8 languages, including Hindi, have a minority status outside the states where they are the principal languages of the state and since practically every state and district is increasingly multilingual, given the increasing social mobility in the country, there is a clear need for evolving a uniform national policy on minority languages at various levels in accordance with the letter and spirit of the Constitution.

2. Urdu (along with Sindhi) is unique in that while it is spoken all over the country, it is not the language of the majority in any state. But while Urdu demands special attention at the national level, at the state level the problems it faces are the same as those faced by other minority languages and can be resolved only within the framework of a uniform national policy accepted by all states, which should crystallize into a national code for linguistic minorities.

3. In this context, several languages which are claimed as a mother tongue by millions of people in the Hindi region and which are striving to come into their own but have so far remained submerged, should be recognized, placed in Schedule 8 and given due place in the educational system.

4. Evaluation of public policies and monitoring the status of Urdu, including an assessment of the facilities available for instruction through Urdu and the teaching of Urdu from the primary to the senior-secondary level, should be a continuous exercise for the development of a suitable strategy for finding Urdu its due place in the curriculum of secular education.

5. The educational backwardness of any region or community can only be remedied by maximizing its access to modern education which is, in the Indian context, almost wholly, the responsibility of the state. The state governments should provide due place and adequate facilities within the educational system to every language that is claimed to be the language of inhabitants of any region of India.

6. In particular, Urdu must be included in the school curriculum at the primary level as the medium of instruction in all government and government-aided schools and in the schools affiliated to the recognized Board of Education, for those who declare Urdu as their mother tongue.

* From *The Annual of Urdu Studies (AUS)*, No. 18, Part 2, 2003, pp. 564–6.

To promote universalization of elementary education, Urdu-medium primary schools must be opened in Urdu-concentration localities in both rural and urban areas in accordance with the national norm of one school for every 300 Urdu-speaking families. Children from scattered Urdu-speaking families should be horizontally aggregated in Urdu-medium primary schools within a reasonable distance.

The regional or principal language of the state should be introduced in Urdu-medium schools from Standard III.

While the common medium of secondary education from Standard VI onwards should be the regional language or the principal language of the state. Urdu must be taught to Urdu-speaking children, from Standard VI to X under the Three Language Formula, as a compulsory first language, along with Hindi or the principal language of the state as compulsory second language. But Urdu may also be included as an optional second language for non-Urdu students from Class VI.

Also in non-Hindi states, Urdu as first language should have an alternative Urdu–Hindi composite course.

The secondary students should have the option of learning English or a classical language as third language.

The Conference recognizes the role of Sanskrit as a rich heritage of India, but it should not displace any mother tongue from the primary level in the educational framework.

7. Funding of religious instruction at the expense of the public exchequer is undesirable and unconstitutional. Hence, the *madrasa* system, which serves the limited purposes of instructing Muslim children in the basic tenets of Islam, producing religious functionaries needed by the community, and maintaining the continuity of religious scholarship should be left entirely to the community to evolve in accordance with demand. In any case, the madrasa system contributes only marginally to the development of education among Muslims.

8. The age limit for compulsory elementary education should be raised from fourteen to fifteen years, which is the minimum age limit for appearing at the secondary examination.

The recent Constitutional amendment making education a Fundamental Right should be supplemented by a statutory provision covering the medium of primary instruction, educational uniformity, national norms for the establishment of primary and secondary schools and the location of schools on demand.

Also, Article 350-A, pertaining to primary instruction through the mother tongue, should be amended to make it mandatory.

The term 'substantial population' in Article 347 on special provisions for a linguistic minority of a state should be clarified by an explanation that 'substantial' means 'not negligible' and, in any case, due facilities should be provided at every administrative level for any language spoken by at least 5 per cent of the population at that level.

The Commissioner for Linguistic Minorities (CLM), despite his status as a constitutional authority, enjoys no authority and state governments do not even supply the required information to him. The reports of the CLM, though tabled in the Parliament, are not discussed and do not receive attention as they hardly contain up-to-date information. The Conference proposes that the post be abolished and replaced by a National Commission for Linguistic Minorities with quasi-judicial authority.

9. The survival of democracy in a plural society indeed lies in the survival of minority languages and cultures. Urdu is par excellence a symbol of our composite culture and a vehicle of secular values and deserves special attention.

In order to protect Urdu from extinction in its land of birth, while it flourishes abroad, a national movement for the revival of Urdu commanding strong political will is the need of the hour. Such a movement should struggle for the educational and cultural rights of all linguistic and cultural minorities in all states of the country and for the elaboration and implementation of the national code as mentioned above.

The Conference appeals to the people, irrespective of political affiliation and linguistic loyalties to extend their support to this movement.

ATHER FAROUQUI
Secretary, ZHSC

Appendix 2

Valedictory Address*

Ladies and Gentlemen:

It is indeed a great pleasure to be associated with the 105th birth anniversary celebrations of the late Dr Zakir Husain. The holding of this conference on Urdu education is an apt and imaginative way of paying tribute to this great educationist and humanist, to a man who added unusual luster to public life and who epitomized Indian civilization and culture at its glorious best.

I am also privileged to be with such a galaxy of distinguished scholars and intellectuals from different parts of the world who have, through their scholastic pursuits of Urdu language and literature, closely observed the growth and development of Indian nationalism. You are here to participate in what may be described as the most unique gathering on Urdu in Delhi since Independence. Through this conference, the organizers have appropriately highlighted the need for Urdu education to be made an important component of the National Policy on Education. This will prove to be a milestone in the arduous journey to attain nation-building itself.

Over the past century and more, Urdu and the Indian National Congress have been synonymous. Urdu has contributed to the shaping of the linguistic and cultural life with other major Indian languages much in the same way as Congress has helped in building the national character of India. Progressing very rapidly from its birth and becoming the *lingua franca* of most of India in the seventeenth century, Urdu also became the repository of a very large and valuable treasure of literature. By pursuing similar goals and traversing the path that Urdu had taken earlier, in the post-independence era, Hindi expanded its base in various states and regions of the nation.

* This address was given by Congress President Mrs Sonia Gandhi on the occasion of the International Conference on Minorities, Education and Language in Twenty-First Century Indian Democracy—the Case of Urdu with Special Reference to Dr Zakir Husain, Late President of India, on Monday, 11 February 2002, at Vigyan Bhawan, New Delhi.

As a literary language Urdu had seeped into and strengthened social structures and impacted various local and regional languages in a decisive manner that shaped the composite cultural character of Indian polity. When Hindi, with a linguistic structure similar to Urdu, endeavoured to extend its roots to the south, the existing literary traditions of Urdu helped in a significant way.

Historically, Urdu and Hindi are sisters, allies in cultural and political renaissance, and not adversaries. The rich works of Ameer Khusrou and, in our times, of the great Premchand himself, are a permanent proof of this. It was the rich amalgamated form of Urdu–Hindi—what we call Hindustani—which the Indian National Congress recognized from the very beginning of our freedom struggle as our national language.

It was the Hindustani slogan of *Inquilab Zindabad* that reverberated in our national consciousness and united us all in our struggle for national independence. It was Gandhiji who proposed Hindustani as the national language of India. Today, Hindustani lives on in the homes and streets of India despite not having official recognition.

After Independence, the Indian National Congress included Urdu, along with other major Indian languages, in the Eighth Schedule of the Constitution of India. Urdu is the mother tongue of millions of Indians living in almost all parts of the country. Its warmth, beauty, and elegance continue to attract many people who are not natural-born speakers of Urdu. It is important that friends or foes of Urdu do not confine it to one community or religion. Urdu is the language of brotherhood and camaraderie. It is the language of amity and harmony.

It is not the language of any one region or any one community. It is part of India's composite heritage. It is said that certain forces, playing politics of language, tried to label Urdu as a foreign language while it is a well-known historical fact that Urdu was born and developed in the same region of Delhi where we are meeting today. Having failed in their designs to slot Urdu as a foreign language, they tried to undermine the independent existence of Urdu by declaring it to be a stylistic variant of Hindi. The intention behind such a move was also to deny Urdu the status of a second official language in Hindi-speaking states of the north, particularly Uttar Pradesh where the speakers of Urdu are most numerous. Unfortunately, the very forces that are inimical to Urdu are also sowing the seeds of hatred among various communities. They have extended their stranglehold over political power and are promoting social and religious stereotypes unbecoming of our nation. The cause of Urdu is common with the concepts of humanism and peaceful coexistence that are at the heart of all religions. The future of Urdu and of our secular, liberal traditions are intrinsically linked.

The most significant and practical necessity is the need for promoting Urdu as a school subject of study. This would be possible only when, in the Three Language Formula evolved and accepted under the National Education

Policy, Urdu, as the mother tongue of millions, is assigned the same status as its sister Indian languages. For this, continuous efforts need to be made at the level of curriculum development and curriculum introduction so that the teaching and learning of Urdu are made interesting and meaningful.

At the level of curriculum, there is considerable concern about the National Council for Education Research and Training (NCERT) and its dangerous attempts to rewrite history. Rajivji [Rajiv Gandhi] had purposely given the Ministry of Education the nomenclature of the Ministry of Human Resource Development. Now this very Ministry is being converted into a workshop for fabricating and putting into practice an agenda that will undermine the secular and composite cultural character of India.

Urdu is uppermost in the list of features to be vanquished. Among the other similar targets are the *madrasas* for imparting religious education. Under the pretext of modernizing them, and of internal security concern, there will be an attempt to subvert their noble traditions and heritage.

Of course many farsighted persons involved in madrasa education recognize that religious madrasas need to be modernized and given a solid scientific and technological foundation. Rajivji had initiated a scheme for this. While the madrasas are recognizing the necessity to move with the times, the self-styled cultural police refuse to recognize the fact that the relegation of the teaching and learning of Urdu only to the madrasas is actually due to the fact that it is not being made available as an integral part of school curricula.

To promote the teaching/learning of Urdu at the primary and secondary levels of education is the responsibility of the state and Urdu speakers in every state must demand this. After the 93rd Amendment to the Constitution of India, the right of Urdu speakers to obtain education in the medium of their mother tongue has to be recognized as a fundamental right. The situation must be addressed with a sense of urgency. While the minorities have a valuable right to set up religious institutions for religious education, it would be unfair to equate Urdu with Islam alone.

I hope that your deliberations have been useful and fruitful. As I said, Delhi is the birthplace of this beautiful language, a language that has verily defined India—*kārvāṅ bastē ga'ē, Hindōstāṅ bantā gayā*. Your stay in the city I hope has convinced you that the cradle of the Urdu language shares its beauty and large-heartedness.

Glossary

Aligarh Movement (Tehrik): The movement launched by Sir Sayyid Ahmad Khan (1817–98) and named for the Muhammadan Anglo-Oriental School, founded in the town of Aligarh in 1875, which later emerged as a College and University. In its early years, the movement sought to train members of the Muslim élite in the English language and cultivate a place for Muslims in the British government, after they had been singled out as opponents in the uprising against the British in 1857. The movement also represented the interpretation of Islam as it was associated with modernism.

Aligarh Muslim University: Influential centre of Indian Muslims' intellectual and political life, established with the object of imparting to the Muslim youth a modern, scientific education.

Anjuman: An organization, an association, and a poetic term.

Arya Samaj: A movement of modern Hindu social and religious reform founded by Swami Dayanand Saraswati (1824–83) in 1875, on the ostensible basis of Vedic teachings. It favoured an end to image worship and was associated with the movement in favour of Hindi as a language of government and instruction.

Ashkenazim: East European Jews.

Avadhi, Brajbhasha, Maithili, Magadhi: Regional Languages of India

Berufschule: German vocational school accompanying vocational training (age 16–18) with theoretical subjects such as mathematics, accounting, physics, etc.

CE (common era): This dating system (beginning with the years 1, 2, 3, etc.) has come into use as a more inclusive alternative to the Christian-centred BC (before Christ) and AD (*Anno Domini*, 'in the year of our Lord').

Dalit: The oppressed; militant self-designation for Scheduled Castes.

Devanagari/Nagari: the Nagari (lit. 'belonging to the city') or Devanagari (lit. divine nagari') alphabet was developed around the eleventh century CE. Originally used to write Sanskrit, it has been adapted for the use of other languages, including Urdu. There are some currents of opinion that hold, however, that Urdu written in the Nagari script is no more than a modified form of Hindi.

Dini madaris: Islamic institutions of learning. These include the *maktab*, part-time institutions, and the *madrasa*, an institution which may teach from the primary to the post-graduate level. The madrasas primarily teach the Islamic religious subjects associated with reading and exegesis of the foundational scriptural texts of Islam.

Gujral Committee: the committee for the promotion of Urdu, appointed by Indira Gandhi to look into the grievances of Urdu speakers.

Hindavi: term indicating 'the language spoken in Hindi', proto-Urdu and Hindi.

Hindi belt: A political connotation for the regions of north and central India where modern Hindi is the primary language.

Hindustani: often thought of a form of Hindi as included in the Constitution of India, Article 351. It is a blend of vernacular Hindi and Urdu. Hindustani exists somewhere in the middle of a long linguistic chain whose extremes may be thought of as heavily Sanskritized Hindi and heavily Arabicized and Persianized Urdu.

Hindutva: movement as expression of 'cultural nationalism'.

Jagirdar/zamindar: landholder/estate owners in a feudal system.

Jamia Millia Islamia: founded in 1920 by Dr Mukhtar Ahmad Ansari, Hakim Ajmal Khan, etc. in response to on appeal by Mahatma Gandhi to set up vernacular schools.

Kayastha: third of the four castes in Hindu society. They rose to prominence and held important positions in administration in the medieval period and also under British rule.

Khilafat Movement: Muslim movement in favour of preservation of the Ottoman Caliphate in the aftermath of the First World War. Mohammad Ali Jinnah opposed the movement terming Khilafat as an exploitative institution.

Madrasa Modernization Scheme: The Government of India's scheme for modernization of madrasa education under which the study of mathematics and science was introduced. The government provided monetary assistance for the scheme's implementation. Madrasas did not welcome the scheme.

Madrasa: see dini madaris above; madrasa is the singular form of madaris.

Magadhi, Bhojpuri and Maithili: languages commonly spoken in many districts of Bihar. Bhojpuri and Maithili are also spoken in other parts of eastern India and in Nepal, while Magadhi is spoken in some parts of West Bengal as well. All three are officially referred to as dialects of Hindi, although this classification is hotly disputed by speakers of these languages.

Maktab: Elementary school for religious education.

Mehfil: A place for gathering, or the gathering; a council, society, or literary party.

Mohajir: Indian Muslim who settled down in Pakistan after Partition.

Moharram: month of Shi'i celebration of Imam Husain's martyrdom at Karbala.

Mullah, maulvi: local Islamic religious leader (S. 'aalim; pl. 'ulema).

Nastaliq: a style for writing in the Arabic script. Its name is derived from two other styles—Naskh and Ta'aleeq.

Panchayat: village council.

Rajput: warrior caste of Kshatriya varna.

Samajwadi Party: political party founded by Other Backward Castes in Uttar Pradesh.

Tehrik: movement.

'Ulema: religious scholars, those who have been educated in the Islamic sciences and are qualified in some degree to interpret the sources of Islamic Shari'a law.

Varna-jati: caste and subcaste in Hinduism.

Wardha Scheme: a national scheme of basic education, launched by the Indian National Congress, following the establishment of provincial ministries in seven provinces in 1937. It entailed a work-oriented approach to education, experiential learning, and education in the mother tongue. Work school emphasized the teaching of handicrafts (next to theoretical subjects) such as gardening, cooking, or wood carving in order to develop the diverse aspects of the child's character and abilities.

Contributors

HASAN ABDULLAH is an engineering researcher by profession who has been writing on societal issues, for almost three decades. For the last five years, he has studied the evolution of Ghalib's thought, mainly through the poet's Urdu *ghazals*.

ARJUMAND ARA is Assistant Professor of Urdu, University of Delhi. She writes on various aspects related to Urdu literature and has translated Ralph Russell's autobiography, *Findings, Keepings: Life Communism and Everything*, into Urdu.

DANIELA BREDI is Associate Professor of History and Institutions of Islam in South Asia, Department of Oriental Studies, and Coordinator, Doctorate in Civilizations, Cultures, and Societies of Asia and Africa, University Sapienza of Rome, where she also teaches Urdu.

ATHER FAROUQUI has studied the socio-political aspects of the Urdu language in post-Partition India, for which he was awarded a PhD from Jawaharlal Nehru University. He has written extensively about the theoretical framework for making Urdu a functional language in India. He has also edited *Muslims and Media Images: News versus Views*.

J.S. GANDHI retired from Jawaharlal Nehru University as a professor of Sociology, and is currently appointed as distinguished scholar at the same university.

SALMAN KHURSHID is the Minister of State (Independent Charge) for the Ministry of Corporate Affairs and the Ministry of Minority Affairs. Besides being an active politician, he is a practising Senior Advocate in the Supreme Court of India.

PRATAP BHANU MEHTA is President, Centre for Policy Research, New Delhi.

BARBARA D. METCALF is Professor Emerita of History, University of California, Davis. Her writings include *Islamic Contestations: Essays on Muslims in India and Pakistan, Islamic Revival in British India: Deoband, 1860–1900*, and *A Concise History of Modern India* (co-authored).

FALI S. NARIMAN is the President of the Bar Association of India. He is a Senior Advocate of the Supreme Court of India.

CHRISTINA OESTERHELD teaches Urdu at the South Asia Institute, University of Heidelberg. She wrote her PhD dissertation on the Urdu novelist Qurratulain Hyder. Her main research interest is Urdu fiction from the nineteenth century to the present. She has also translated Urdu short stories und poetry into German.

KELLY PEMBERTON is Assistant Professor of Religion and Women's Studies, George Washington University. Her work covers Sufism, religious activism, development, and Islamic reform in South Asia and the Middle East, especially as these relate to gender. Her co-edited volumes include *Women Mystics and Sufi Shrines in India*. She is currently working on a book about Islamic medicine in today's South Asia and the Middle East.

KERRIN GRÄFIN VON SCHWERIN received her PhD in Modern South Asian History from Heidelberg South Asia Institute. She wrote her dissertation on the Hindi–Urdu controversy in Uttar Pradesh. Her writings include *Indirekte Herrschaft und Reformpolitik im indischen Furstenstaat Hyderabad* and articles on Muslim grave cults.

SYED SHAHABUDDIN as a Member of the Indian Foreign Service served as Ambassador to Algeria and Joint Secretary in the Ministry of External Affairs. He resigned to enter public life in 1978 and was a Member of Parliament for three terms between 1978 and 1996. He edited *Muslim India* from 1983 to 2002 and 2006 to 2010. Since 2000, he is the President of All India Muslim Majlis-e-Mushawarat.

YOGENDRA SINGH is a sociologist and Professor Emeritus at the Center for Study of Social Systems, School of Social Sciences, Jawaharlal Nehru University, New Delhi.

SOLI J. SORABJEE is a former Attorney General for India.

YOGESH TYAGI is a professor of International Law at School of International Studies, Jawaharlal Nehru University, New Delhi.

THEODORE P. WRIGHT, Jr, is Professor Emeritus of Political Science, State University of New York in Albany, USA. He has done research on the politics of Indian Muslims and Muhajirin in Hyderabad, Bombay, Karachi, and Lahore for fifty years.

AMINA YAQIN teaches Urdu at the School of Oriental and African Studies (SOAS), University of London.

Index